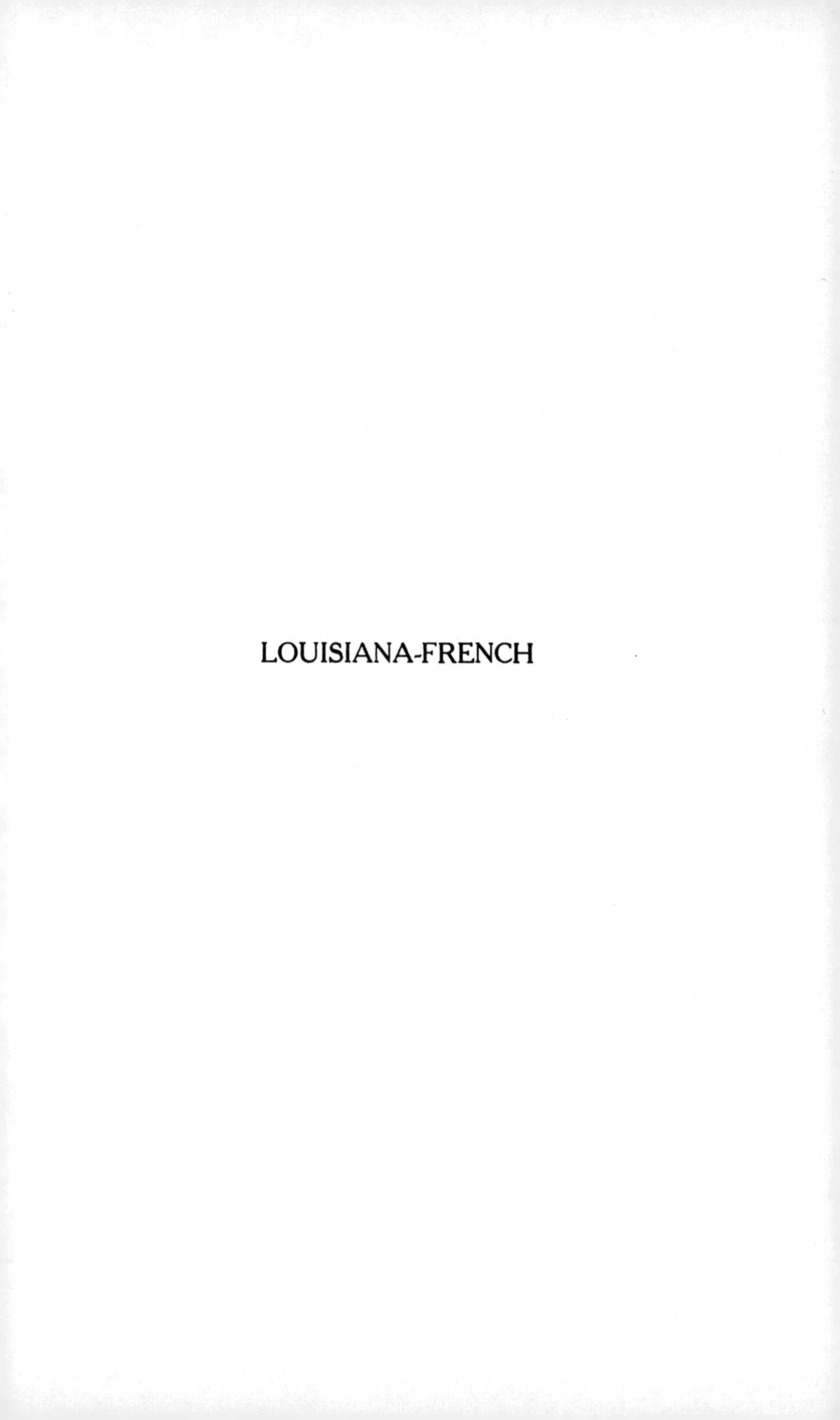

LOUISIANA-FRENCH

LOUISIANA-FRENCH

William A. Read

Revised Edition

LOUISIANA STATE UNIVERSITY PRESS · 1963

Library of Congress Catalog Card Number 63-13241

TO

JOHANNES HOOPS

PROFESSOR OF THE ENGLISH LANGUAGE
AND LITERATURE

IN THE

UNIVERSITY OF HEIDELBERG

FOREWORD

This edition of *Louisiana-French* again makes available one of the classics in the field of American linguistic scholarship. It is also a volume of much interest to students of Louisiana history and of the culture of the region generally, and its republication serves as a fitting memorial to its author, William Alexander Read, who died in Miami, Florida, on July 31, 1962, at the age of ninety-two. Dr. Read became Professor Emeritus of English Language and Literature at Louisiana State University in 1940 and spent most of the time following his retirement in Florida. That these were not idle years is attested by the list of his writings that is included in the present volume. *Studies for William A. Read* (published by Louisiana State University Press in 1940) contains his bibliography complete up to that time. Some seventeen items appearing after that date have now been added to the list, which, extending as it does from 1897 to 1955, serves as his own best monument.

The text of this volume is a photographic reproduction of the book as originally published in 1931 with, however, such corrections and additions of the author's as could be included. Two of the illustrations (on pages xvi and 108) are new because the originals could not be reproduced satisfactorily. Some supplementary material, too extensive to be incorporated in the body of the work, has been added in an appendix. Special thanks are due to Mr. Hoguet A. Major, Professor Emeritus of French at Louisiana State University, without whose assistance this appendix would not have been nearly so accurate or complete. Dr. Read possessed six copies of *Louisiana-French* and annotated all of them. Professor Major cumulated and edited this material as only a person of his unique learning could. A word of special appreciation is due to Mr. Wyeth A. Read (who inherited his father's library) for having made available to the LSU Press the six copies of *Louisiana-French* referred to above and to his wife, Mrs. Mary Gray Read, who went through Dr. Read's papers and located most of the items that have been added to the author's bibliography.

THOMAS A. KIRBY

February 22, 1963

PREFACE

SOME time ago I studied the place-names of Louisiana, and published two papers on those of Indian origin.[1] While at work on the Romance place-names, I became aware of the numerous words of novel form or meaning in the vocabulary of the French inhabitants of the State. Confining my attention, therefore, to the more unusual or difficult French and Spanish place-names, I began at the same time to collect material for a glossary of the French language of Louisiana. During the course of my investigations I visited almost every part of the State where French is spoken, and I received aid from many people. Though considerations of space unfortunately forbid my naming all those who answered my questions, I cannot refrain from expressing my gratitude to the following persons. Their names and addresses are:

	Post Office	*Parish*
ALLEMAN, PROFESSOR L. J.	Natchitoches	Natchitoches
ARSEMANT, MR. BERNARD	Myrtle Grove	Plaquemines
BARBIN, MISS VELMA	Marksville	Avoyelles
BIRD, MR. CECIL	Baton Rouge	East Baton Rouge
BLANCHARD, MR. E. L.	Labadieville	Assumption
BONIN, MRS. MARIE	Loreauville	Iberia
BREAUX, MISS CANDIDE	Loreauville	Iberia
BROWNRIGG, MISS AUDREY	New Roads	Pointe Coupée
BUCHANAN, MISS ANN SPOTSWOOD	Lafayette	Lafayette
COBB, MISS CARLETA	Baton Rouge	East Baton Rouge
DICHARRY, MISS YOLANDE	Gramercy	St. James
DORNIER, MR. J. B.	Convent	St. James
DUMEZ, MR. EUGENE	Houma	Terrebonne
DUPONT, MR. JULIUS	Houma	Terrebonne
DURAND, PROFESSOR SIDNEY	Youngsville	Lafayette
FALGOUT, MR. LEONARD	Raceland	Lafourche
FAVROT, MR. J. ST. CLAIR	Baton Rouge	East Baton Rouge
FLETCHER, MR. L.	Ponchatoula	Tangipahoa
FONTENELLE, MR. L. T.	Pointe à la Hache	Plaquemines
FRANCIONI, PROFESSOR J. B.	Baton Rouge	East Baton Rouge
GASPARD, MR. OSCAR	Cut-Off	Lafourche
GUILBEAU, PROFESSOR F. T.	Baton Rouge	East Baton Rouge
JARREAU, MR. L.	Oscar, (*mail*, Livonia)	Pointe Coupée
JUNOD, MRS. A.	Baton Rouge	East Baton Rouge

[1] *Louisiana State University Bulletin*, XIX, No. 2 (February, 1927); *The Louisiana Historical Quarterly*, XI, No. 3 (July, 1928), 445-462.

	Post Office	*Parish*
KLIEBERT, MR. M.	Vacherie	St. James
KNOBLOCH, MR. F. L.	Thibodaux	Lafourche
LANDRY, MR. J. P.	French Settlement	Livingston
LACROIX, MR. E. A.	Baton Rouge	East Baton Rouge
LEJEUNE, MR. J. F.	Baton Rouge	East Baton Rouge
LOVELL, MR. A.	Theriot	Terrebonne
MALBROUGH, MR. SIDNEY	Colyell Bay, (*mail,* Port Vincent)	Livingston
PERRAULT, MR. L. L.	Opelousas	St. Landry
PICOU, MR. EMILE	Houma	Lafourche
PORTERIE, MR. G. L.	Marksville	Avoyelles
RHODES, MR. T.		Terrebonne
SIMON, MR. L. P.	St. Martinville	St. Martin
THIBODEAUX, MR. C. B.	Breaux Bridge	St. Martin
TRAHAN, DR. E. O.	Baton Rouge	East Baton Rouge
WADDILL, MR. FRANK H.	New Orleans	Orleans
WHIPPLE, MR. CHARLES	Bourg	Terrebonne
WHIPPLE, MR. GEORGE	Bourg	Terrebonne
WHIPPLE, MR. THOMAS	Bourg	Terrebonne
WOGAN, MR. D. S.	New Orleans	Orleans

Numerous as these names are, they fail to show the full extent of my obligations; for he who tries to collect a general vocabulary of a dialect must soon realize how inadequate his training has been in many departments of knowledge. It is not sufficient to say, for instance, that the Acadians speak of a certain kind of fish as *une truite verte,* "a green trout," and that some of them apply the term *loulou* to a larva known in Virginia as a "camel," and in Louisiana as a "doodle-bug." For such designations as these science demands an accurate nomenclature; and in order to obtain the correct terms in various fields of research, I have relied less on text-books than on the guidance of my colleagues, Professor Warren N. Christopher, Dr. William H. Gates, Professor Charles F. Moreland, Dr. Oscar W. Rosewall, Dr. J. R. Fowler, and Dr. C. A. Brown.

My cordial thanks are due, in the next place, to Professor James F. Broussard, Professor Hoguet A. Major, and Mrs. Judith Major, all colleagues of mine in the Department of Romance Languages. The information given me by these three friends has been simply invaluable. Timely suggestions, too, have been received from other members of this department, particularly from Dr. Charles E. Mathews, Professor Wyatt A. Pickens, and Professor E. O. Bourgeois. I am indebted to Miss Mary E. Graham and Mr. Carl Campbell, both of the State Land Office, for assistance in the examination of surveys. For many courtesies my thanks are likewise expressed to the officials of the Hill Memorial Library at the Louisiana State University, the Howard Memorial Library in New Orleans, the Cleveland Public Library, the University of Texas Library, and the Library of Congress. My colleague, Professor W. J. Olive, kindly verified a few of my quotations when he was studying at the University of Chicago. I am under special obligations to Mr. James A. McMillen, librarian of the Louisiana State University, for such assistance as could have come only from one who is at once a versatile librarian and a gifted scholar.

Though my preface has already become very long, it fails as yet to indicate the scope of the present study. This study aims to give appropriate illustrations both of the native and of the foreign element in the French dialects of Louisiana. It includes comments on a few Indian place-names, on a number of difficult or novel Romance place-names, and on the etymology of some Louisiana-French surnames. It does not exhaust any phase of its subject, but seeks to show the nature rather than the extent of the influences that have moulded Louisiana-French.

WILLIAM A. READ

LOUISIANA STATE UNIVERSITY
AUGUST 15, 1931

CONTENTS

ABBREVIATIONS, SIGNS, AND SYMBOLS

Among the abbreviations, signs, and symbols used in this study, the following alone seem to require explanation:

ASP.........*American State Papers*
Beih. ....*Beiheft*
Can.-Fr. .....Canadian-French
Dial. ....Dialect(s) or dialectal
Fr. ....French
La.-Fr. ......Louisiana-French
NED.........*New English Dictionary*
Norm. ......Norman
OF ....Old French
OHG ....Old High German
Pic. ....Picard
Prov. ....Provençal
REW........ Meyer-Lübke, *Romanisches Etymologisches Wörterbuch*
Rom. ....*Romania*
So. ....French dialect of South Louisiana
Sp. ....Spanish
St.-Fr. ......Standard French
Sw. ....French dialect of Southwest Louisiana
Wb. ....*Wörterbuch*
ZRPH....... *Zeitschrift für Romanische Philologie*
á or *à*........Choctaw h*á*cha
æ ....English h*a*t
ẽ ....English h*a*t nasalized; Acadian *un* (*ẽ; ẽn* plus vowel); *une* (*ẽn*)
j ....English *j*oy or French *j*oie
* ....hypothetical
+ ....indicates material is to be found in the supplement

LIST OF ILLUSTRATIONS

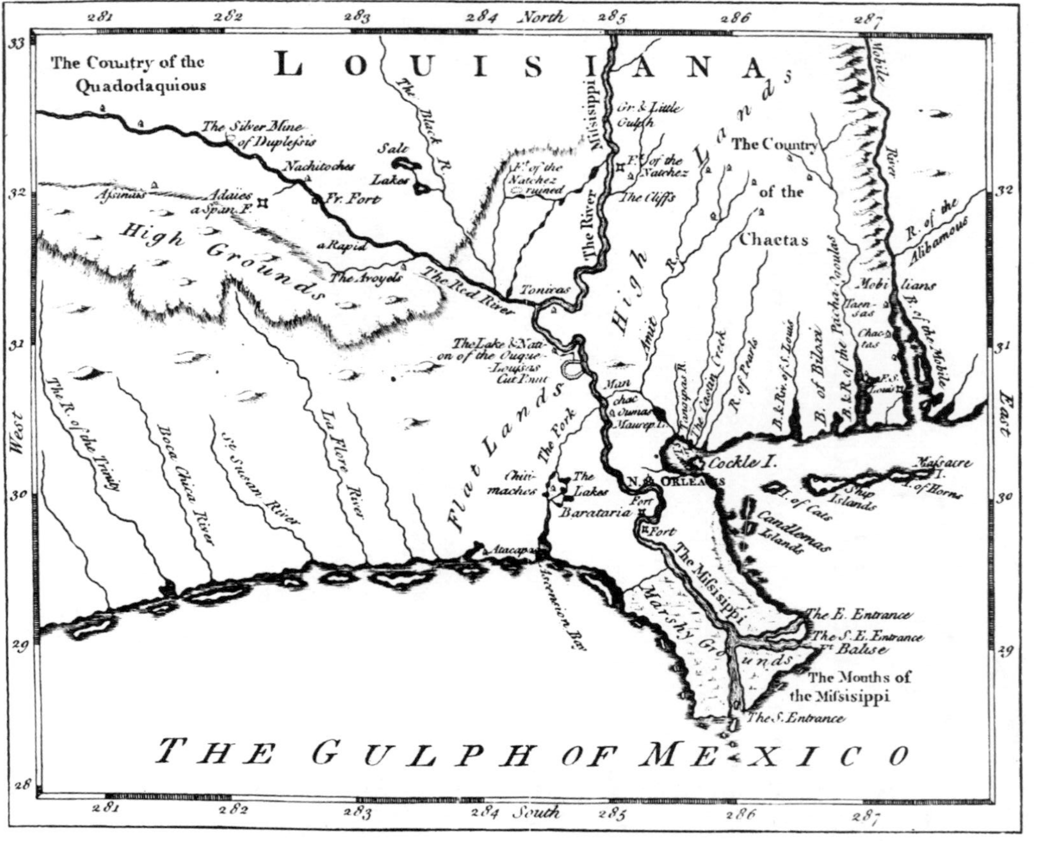

Map from Du Pratz's *Histoire de la Louisiane*

INTRODUCTION

THE FRENCH LANGUAGE IN LOUISIANA

1. Dialect of the Creoles

Two varieties of French, different yet closely related, are spoken in Louisiana. The first variety is represented by a dialect which is not far removed from Standard French in syntax, vocabulary, and pronunciation. This is the speech of most Creoles and of many cultivated Acadians. Naturally some new words are used, and various old words have acquired senses unknown in Standard French.

The Latin element that came to Louisiana during the Colonial Period and shortly thereafter included Frenchmen from the Old World, French-Canadians, colonists from the French and Spanish West Indies, and the Canary Islands; French refugees from Acadia between 1765 and 1785; other refugees from Santo Domingo near the end of the eighteenth century; and still others from Cuba in 1809.

The Creoles of Louisiana are generally defined as the white descendants of the French and Spanish settlers of the Colonial Period. During the Colonial Period most Creoles lived in New Orleans; some had homes on plantations that faced the Mississippi in an unbroken chain as far up as the present site of Donaldsonville, and even farther. Many descendants of the Creoles have remained in New Orleans; others are scattered here and there throughout Louisiana. It is the Creoles who as a class speak good French; for many of them were reared in circles where pure French was almost invariably the rule; some of them—not a few, indeed—were educated in France; and consequently the Creoles of the present generation have inherited much of the culture of France as well as an excellent knowledge of their mother tongue.

2. The Acadians and Their Dialect

The second variety of French speech in Louisiana is the Acadian, which is the language not only of most Acadians, but also of many other persons who have been brought up in Acadian communities.

The Acadians of Louisiana are the descendants of the French who were formally expelled by the English from Acadie, or Nova Scotia, on Friday, September 5, 1755. More than six thousand Acadians were deported and scattered among the British colonies; but none of the exiles seem to have reached Louisiana before 1764 or 1765, and some, who had found their way to France, are said to have been sent to Louisiana as late as 1785. The Acadians settled along Bayou Teche and Bayou Lafourche; in parts of the old Attakapas and Opelousas districts of the Southwest; on the banks of the Mississippi, northward from what is now St. John the Baptist Parish into Pointe Coupée and Baton Rouge; in New Orleans and farther south along the Mississippi River; and on Bayou Terre aux Boeufs.[1]

As the Acadians have to a great extent retained their peculiar dialect, which shows kinship especially with the patois of Normandy, Picardy, Saintonge, and the region about Paris, they are still commonly distinguished from the Creoles of Louisiana by the term *Acadians* or the less dignified *Cajuns.* It is the Acadians themselves, however, who have corrupted *Acadien* into the familiar or derisive *Cadien,* pronounced *Kajẽ.* Nevertheless, many educated Acadians speak excellent French and excellent English as well.

A satisfactory survey of the Acadian dialect cannot be made without a preliminary study of the sources of French immigration to Canada during the seventeenth and eighteenth centuries. The Norman, the Picard, and the French of the Île de France form nine tenths of the Canadian-French language; the dialect of the old province of

[1] Alcée Fortier, *History of Louisiana,* I, 152-3; II, 110; Howard M. Jones, *America and French Culture,* pp. 108 ff.

Burgundy accounts for the remaining tenth, according to Benjamin Sulte.[2] Between 1608, the year that saw the founding of Quebec, and 1700, there arrived in Canada 4,894 emigrants from France, of whom 958 were born in Normandy, 621 in the Île-de-France (Paris and the neighboring region), 569 in Poitou, 524 in Aunis, Île de Ré, and Île d'Oleron, 274 in Saintonge, 238 in Perche, 175 in Bretagne, 139 in Anjou, 129 in Champagne, 124 in Guyenne, 113 in Maine, and 105 in Beauce. Though some other provinces contributed to the colonization of Canada during this period, no one seems to have been represented by as many as a hundred settlers. Provence sent, for example, but 22.

Again, between 1700 and 1780 there embarked for Canada 5,878 immigrants whose origin it is possible to trace. Among these nearly 1,782 came from Angoumois, Aunis, Saintonge, and Poitou; 1,045 from Normandy; and 789 from Bretagne, Perche, Maine, and Anjou.

It is chiefly, then, the patois of the North, the West, and the Centre of France that have formed the Canadian-French language. To this fusion of the native patois one must add certain French archaisms and a number of loans from English and Indian dialects.[3]

The speech of the Louisiana Acadians varies considerably in different localities, the dialect of Pointe Coupée containing, for instance, some words and expressions not heard at French Settlement or in Houma. The difference between Acadian and Standard French may be very slight, as when *balsamine* becomes *belsamine,* "touch-me-not" (flower), and *espadon* is changed to *espadron,* "sword-fish"; or, on the

---

[2] *La Langue Française en Canada* (1898), p. 9.

[3] See Benj. Sulte, *ibid.,* pp. 53 ff.; S. A. Lortie, *De L'Origine des Canadiens Français* (1903), pp. 11-12; A. Rivard, *Le Parler Franco-Canadien* (1903), p. 13. For further references on Canadian-French, consult J. Geddes, Jr., *Canadian-French* (1902); and especially the same writer's papers on "American-French Dialect Comparison," *Modern Language Notes* for December, 1893, January and February, 1894, December, 1897, January, February, April, and May, 1898; Kr. Nyrop, *Grammaire Historique de la Langue Française,*[2] I, (1904), 491-492; *Glossaire du Parler Français au Canada* (1930), p. XIX.

other hand, very marked, as when *j'allions* replaces *je suis allé,* and *diable* is pronounced approximately like English *job.*

It may be well to note here some conspicuous features of Louisiana Acadian.[4] Such are the following:

The nasal vowels in words like *bon, en,* and *tante* are frequently leveled under a low-back-tense-round vowel—not raised, however, like the vowel in St.-Fr. *bon;* the tense vowel in St.-Fr. *faire,* etc., becomes lax; the St.-Fr. open vowel becomes close when final in words like *français, gilet, lait, prêt,* etc.; the vowel in *femme,* etc., is usually not distinguished in quality from that in *gras,* etc., an intermediate vowel being substituted for the two St.-Fr. extremes; the vowel of *pauvre, chose,* etc., is open; "e" may at times replace "a" as in *serbacane,* "blowgun," for *sarbacane*; "a" may replace "e" as in *alle* for *elle*; *un* and *une* are pronounced respectively *ẽ* and *ẽn* (before a vowel sound). *Di,* when followed by a vowel, has approximately the value of English *j,* as in *dieu, diable*; "gn" is sometimes pronounced like English "y," as regularly in *tignon,* "kerchief," *maquignon,* "clothes pin"; *ti* before a vowel often has the value of English *"chi,"* as in *quantier,* "moccasin" (shoe); final *-re* and *-le* regularly disappear—cf. the popular pronunciation of St.-Fr. *livre, quatre,* etc. *R,* when final or followed by another consonant, is sometimes weak and tends to disappear as in *pou(r), fou(r)che*; final *r* may be vocalized, so that Fr. *faire* and English *fair* sound alike in the pronunciation of some Acadians. Metathesis is very common: note *cocodrie* for archaic *cocodrille,* though some Acadians use St.-Fr. *crocodile*; *plarine* for *praline, chesseresse* (cf. Can.-Fr.) for *sécheresse*; assimilation is far-reaching, as in *gigier* (Can.-Fr.) for *gésier,* "gizzard," *crêque-de-coq* for *crête de coq,* "cockscomb"; insertion of a consonant sometimes takes place, as in *croquecignole,* "doughnut," of Can.-Fr. origin, for St.-Fr. *croquignole,* "cracknel." The consonants after a nasal vowel are often retained, as in *attendre,* "await," *nombre,* "number."

---

[4] Cf. Alcée Fortier, "The Acadians of Louisiana and Their Dialect," *Louisiana Studies* (1894), pp. 148-197; reprinted from *Publications of the Modern Language Association of America,* VI (1891), 1-33.

Archaic forms occur: cf. *Il fait frette* or *frète* (*froid*) and *goilan* for *goéland,* "sea-gull."[5] Norman influence is evident, as in *charrer,* "to chatter," and *tondre, infra*; nautical terms abound, as in *amarrer,* "fasten," for *attacher, au large,* "out in the open," *virer de bord,* "turn around," and *haler,* "pull," instead of the less usual *tirer*; leveling of forms is frequent, as in *cardinau,* "cardinal" (bird), after the plural *cardinaux,* and *ils étions* for *ils étaient. Chardon,* "thistle" is regularly replaced by *chardron,* as in Canadian-French.[6] Agglutination of the definite article is observed, as in *lenvers,* m., for *envers,* "back."

It is obviously impossible to erect an insurmountable barrier between the language of the Creoles and that of the Acadians. Both dialects have to a great extent the same native vocabulary, and both have borrowed from the same foreign sources—English, German, Spanish, African, and Indian. Manifestly, then, each has exerted some influence on the other. Nevertheless, the Creoles of New Orleans are less likely to be conspicuous for peculiarities of diction than the inhabitants of the country or the small towns and villages. Thus the French native of New Orleans calls the flounder a *sole,* whereas the French fishermen of Lower Louisiana speak of it as a *plie*—the equivalent of English *plaice.*[7] The patrons of the French restaurants become familiar, therefore, not with *plie,* but with *sole* through the names of such dishes as *sole au gratin, sole à la Normande,* and *filets de sole à l'Orly.*

In New Orleans, too, the word for "mosquito bar" is the St.-Fr. *moustiquaire* rather than *berre* or *baire,* m., though the latter term is not unknown in the city. In many other localities the mosquito bar is designated by *baire* or by either term. Moreover, it is not unusual to hear the *r-grasseyé* in New Orleans, whereas the tongue-point *r* prevails in the country districts and small towns. The uvular

[5] Cf. Chas. Thurot, *De la Prononciation Française,* I (1881), 375.

[6] Cf. W. Meyer-Lübke, *Historische Grammatik der Französischen Sprache,* I (1908), 171.

[7] Cf. A. Thomas, *Mélanges d'Étymologie Française,* p. 155.

r, however, is used by some natives of the Teche country, and more especially by residents of St. Martinville.

Some dialectal words, however, are the common property of the city and the country: *soco,* "muscadine grape," for example, and *ravet,* "cockroach"—for the latter St.-Fr. *blatte* seems never to be used in Louisiana.

I have ventured, in spite of many misgivings, to group the dialect of the Creoles and that of the Acadians under the term *Louisiana-French.* I am debarred, unfortunately, from speaking of the former as the "Creole dialect," because this term is applied in Louisiana to the negro-French patois. I refer to the cultivated speech of France as "Standard French," without intending to specify the language of any particular locality.

A complete list of the striking words and forms, native and foreign, which are found in Louisiana-French would make an interesting glossary. In the present study I will present merely some typical examples of the vocabulary that I have collected in various parts of the State, giving, first, certain words of native origin, and secondly, those that have been derived from foreign sources.

3. French Zones in Louisiana

Southern Louisiana, according to the War Department's map of 1925, embraces that part of Louisiana which lies below a straight line drawn from near Columbus in Sabine Parish to a point a few miles north of Fairview in Concordia Parish—a line running thence southward to Torras in the northern part of Pointe Coupée, and then again eastward, along the northern boundary of West Feliciana, East Feliciana, St. Helena, and Washington parishes, as far as the state of Mississippi. It is customary to apply the term *Southwest Louisiana* to that part of this area which is comprised within the parishes of St. Landry, St. Martin, Iberia, Calcasieu, Cameron, Lafayette, St. Mary, Acadia, Vermilion, Allen, Beauregard, Jefferson Davis, and Evangeline.

French is still spoken by many residents of South Louisiana, and more especially by those who live in the Southwest. We have already noted the names of those parishes that constitute Southwest Louisiana; with these we may group some other parishes that adjoin the Mississippi and possess a large number of inhabitants of French descent—namely, Pointe Coupée, West Baton Rouge, Iberville, Ascension, Assumption, St. James, St. John the Baptist, St. Charles, Jefferson, Orleans—which includes the city of New Orleans—St. Bernard, and Plaquemines. The parishes of Lafourche and Terrebonne, which border the Gulf of Mexico, are predominantly French; farther north, and west of the Mississippi, the parishes of Avoyelles and Rapides have a fairly large French population.

East of the Mississippi the parishes of West Feliciana, East Feliciana, Saint Helena, Tangipahoa, and Washington are almost completely Anglicized. So, too, is East Baton Rouge, though the city of Baton Rouge has numerous citizens of French descent, and has naturally drawn to it French-speaking people from other parts of Louisiana. But the French language is still firmly entrenched in the southern part of Livingston Parish, notably at French Settlement (population in 1930: 202); French, too, is spoken by some natives of the southern part of St. Tammany as well as of the southern part of Tangipahoa.

In North Louisiana French is used by some citizens of Natchitoches, both in the town and in the parish of that name; and French is heard at the village of Rambin, in De Soto Parish. Those French speakers that are encountered here and there in other parts of North Louisiana are not numerous enough to warrant a serious study of their speech.

I have generally tried to indicate where this or that word may be heard in Louisiana; but I have no doubt that many a word is not restricted to those areas to which it has been assigned. Moreover, it is obvious that the names of wild fowl which inhabit the Gulf Coast are better known in Lower Louisiana than anywhere else in the State; and that, on the other hand, most every-day words or expressions are too widely scattered to be considered typical of any particular locality.

France, in Provinces, before 1789. From *The Century Atlas of the World*, by kind permission of The Century Company, New York

I

THE NATIVE ELEMENT

FRENCH WORDS

ÂGE, *f.* Age, time of life: *être de la même âge*, "to be of the same age." Dial.—Sw.; Can.-Fr.; Norm.-Picard, etc. St.-Fr. *âge* is masculine.

AIGLE À TÊTE BLANCHE, *m.* "White-headed eagle." Both Continental and Louisiana-French for the American eagle, commonly known as the Bald Eagle (*Haliaeetus leucocephalus leucocephalus* L.). This is the eagle that is emblematic of the United States. It breeds in Louisiana.

The eagles of this species were called *aigles nonnes*, "nun eagles," by Joutel,† because of the birds' white collars and the white feathers on the head. This term is no longer used in Louisiana.

AIGLON *m.* Cooper's Hawk (*Accipiter cooperi* Bonap.), called also *Chicken Hawk* or *Blue Darter*. Cf. *Aile Ronde, infra.*

AIGRETTE BLEUE, *f.* "Blue Egret." The Little Blue Heron (*Florida caerulea caerulea* L.). During the change of its white plumage to blue this bird becomes so tame that it is called *Aigrette Folle*, "Foolish Egret," or "Crazy Heron." *Calico* and *Spotted Crane* are English names for this heron.[1]

AIGRETTE CÂILLE, *f.* Louisiana Heron (*Hydranassa tricolor ruficollis* Gosse), generally called *Blue Crane*, and sometimes *Lady of the Waters*. See *câille, infra.* Another name for this bird is *Héron Dos-blanc, infra.*

AILE POINTUE, *f.* Duck Hawk (*Falcoperegrinus anatum* Bonap.); known in English also as the "Eagle Hawk."

AILE RONDE, *f.* Cooper's Hawk. See *aiglon, supra.*

AILE ROUGE, *f.* The Red-winged Blackbird and the Florida Red-winged Blackbird. Cf. *caporal, infra.*

---

† Joutel (January, 1686), in Pierre Margry, *Mémoires et Documents Originaux*, III, 215.

[1] Cf. J. J. Audubon, *Birds of America*, VI, 153.

AIR, *f.* Air, atmosphere; time. Dial.—Sw.; Can-Fr.; Norm. St.-Fr. *air* is masculine.

ALENTOURS, *m. pl.* About; for St.-Fr. *environ. Il a dans les alentours de trente ans,* "He is about thirty." Dial.—Sw.; Can.-Fr.

ALISIER, *m.* Blackhaw (*Viburnum rufidulum* Raf.).

In Europe, St.-Fr. *alisier* or *alizier* is the name of the wild service tree commonly called *sorbier des bois* (*Sorbus torminalis* Crantz) and of another variety known as *Sorbier domestique* or *S. cormier.*

AMARRER, *vb. tr.* "To fasten." A nautical term common among the Acadians in the sense of St.-Fr. *attacher,* "fasten," "fix," *lier,* "tie." Dial.—Can.-Fr.; Norm., Bret., Saintonge, etc.

AMICABLEMENT, *adv.* Amiably: for St.-Fr. *amicalement, amiablement.* Dial.—Sw.; Can.-Fr.

AMOLLIR, *vb. refl.* To grow milder (of the weather): *Le temps s'amollit.* Dial.—Sw.; Can.-Fr.

AMOUR, *m. Être en amour,* "to be in love," St.-Fr. *être amoreux*; *tomber en amour,* "to fall in love," St.-Fr. *devenir, tomber amoureux.* Dial.—Sw.; Can.-Fr.

ANIMAUX, *m. pl.* Domestic animals; St.-Fr. *bestiaux.* Dial.—Sw.; Can.-Fr.

ARBRE VOLAILLE, *f.* A variety of Manioc or Cassava (*Manihot carthaginensis* Muell.), which the French of Louisiana call *arbre volaille,* because chickens are fond of the seeds of this small tree. Dial.—Baton Rouge; Ascension Parish.

I am indebted to Mr. C. V. Morton, of the Smithsonian Institution, for the identification of the tree.

ARGENTÉ, -ÉE, *adj.* Rich. Dial.—Sw.; Can.-Fr.; Norm., Anjou, Berry, etc.

ARMOIRE, *f.* Wardrobe for wearing apparel. Those who do not speak French pronounce the word like English *armor.* Cf. St.-Fr. *armoire à glace,* "wardrobe."

Helen Pitkin has given an admirable description of an old-fashioned *armoire*: "It was an *armoire,* or wardrobe, of great height and width squared just before her, a pathetic and inapposite feature in the dismal room. The wood was mahogany, its texture grimed with a damp soil, and reared upon four large globes of brass. A broad rod ran the length of the doors, and massive ornamentation of the metal, describing embossed roses and foliage, clamped either side."[2]

ARPENT, *m.* An old French measure of land, less than an acre, 605 arpents being equivalent to 512 acres. The arpent is also a lineal measure, roughly equal to 192 feet. *Arpent* is still in common use among the French of South Louisiana. Dial.—Can.-Fr.

AVOCAT, *m.* Black-necked Stilt (*Himantopus mexicanus* Müll.). This bird has other names: *bécassine de marais,* "marsh snipe," *religieuse,* "nun," and *soldat,* "soldier."

+BAIRE, *m.* Mosquito net; mosquito bar. Dumont has the form *berre* (1719);[3] and Du Poisson describes a *baire* in a letter written to Father Patouillet on October 3, 1727.[4] An inventory taken in 1738 of effects belonging to the Chaouachas plantation, in Louisiana, includes *un Ber de toile.*[5] Berquin-Duvallon uses the term *Moutiquère ou Berre.*[6]

Baire is connected with Fr. *barre,* "cross-bar," from Low Latin **barra*; whence have come dialectal *baire,* "hedge" (Belfort), *bairro,* "enclosure" (Doubs), and *baire,* "cart-rack" (Pas-de-Calais).[7]

English *bar* is a derivative of Fr. *barre.*

BALAN, *m.* Balancing, poising; equivalent in meaning to St.-Fr. *balancement.* Dial.—Sw.; Can.-Fr.

BALIER, *vb. tr.* To sweep; St.-Fr. *balayer.* Dial.—So.; Can.-Fr.; Picard, Saintonge, etc.

+BANQUETTE, *f.* Sidewalk. The Spanish Judicial Records contain the plural *banquettes* in an ordinance issued by Governor Luis de Unzaga on December 12, 1769.[8]

Banquette has made its way into English, where it is pronounced as if written *banket,* with the stress on the first syllable.

A *banquette* was originally made of long, heavy planks.

---

[2] *An Angel by Brevet* (1904), p. 184.

[3] B. F. French, *Historical Collections of Louisiana* (1853), p. 17.

[4] *Jesuit Relations,* LXVII, 287-289.

[5] Henry P. Dart, in *The Louisiana Historical Quarterly,* VIII, No. 4 (October, 1925), 632.

[6] *Vue de la Colonie Espagnole* (1803), p. 107.

[7] W. von Wartburg, *Französisches Etymologisches Wörterbuch,* pp. 255, 258.

[8] See *The Louisiana Historical Quarterly,* VI, No. 1 (January, 1923), 160.

As Standard-French *Banquette* is a diminutive formation from *banc*, "bench," the word *banquettes* was applied to benches which the Creoles of New Orleans placed on the sidewalks and occupied in the evenings. From this custom is said to have sprung the use of *banquette* in the sense of "sidewalk."

A preferable explanation is to be found in another meaning of Standard-French *banquette*—namely, "a path by the side of a canal, railway, etc."

BARBE ESPAGNOLE, *f.* Spanish moss (*Tillandsia usneoides* L.); also called simply *mousse*, "moss." The Choctaw name of this moss is *iti shumo*, literally "tree thistle down"; but a more poetic designation seems to have been *pãsh ittula*, "falling hair." Cf. my comments on *Ponchatoula.*[9]

Pénicaut, writing in 1699 of the Pascagoula Indians and their village, says:

"As it was near the end of August, and the weather very warm, all the Indians there were as naked as when born—that is, the men and boys; but the women and girls had a little moss fastened to their thighs, which covered their nakedness, the rest of their body being entirely naked. This moss is an herb of a long, fine fibre, growing upon the trees, which the French of this part of the country called *Spanish-beard*, by way of derision, and which the Spaniards, in retort, called the *French-wig*."[10]

Barbe à l'Espagnole and *Perruque à la Françoise* are the exact terms that Pénicaut uses for "Spanish moss";[11] and his account of the origin of the name seems to be entirely worthy of credence. Du Pratz, on the other hand, incorrectly attributes the source of the name *Barbe Espagnole* to the Indians, who likened the moss, he says, to the pointed beards of the early Spanish explorers of Louisiana.[12]

The value of the moss gathered in Louisiana in 1928 was estimated at more than a million dollars.

BARBUE, *f.* Catfish; designated by the term *barbue*, "bearded," because of the barbels resembling whiskers that grow about its head.[13] If the French wish, however, to distinguish the mud cat (*Leptops olivaris* Raf.)

---

[9] *Louisiana Place-Names of Indian Origin*, pp. 52-54.

[10] B. F. French, *Hist. Coll.*, N. S., (1869), p. 48.

[11] Cf. Margry, *Mémoires*, V, 389.

[12] *Histoire de la Louisiane*, II, 51.

[13] Cf. Du Pratz's description of "la Barbue," *Histoire*, II, 152-153.

from the blue (*Ictalurus furcatus* Le Sueur), they call the former a *goujon.* The European *goujon* is a small fresh-water fish (*Gobio fluviatilis* Cuvier) that belongs to the carp family. From the St.-Fr. *goujon* has been derived the English *gudgeon. Barbue* is pronounced as in French.

The blue cat of the Louisiana rivers sometimes attains a weight of eighty or even a hundred pounds, and the annual catch of the various species of catfish in Louisiana is said to be approximately 11,000,000 pounds.[14]

The *barbue* of the European Coasts is the brill, a kind of flat fish resembling the turbot, but inferior in quality.

BARNACHE, *f.* See *oie canadienne, infra.*

BAROUETTE, *f.* Wheelbarrow. Dial.—Natchitoches, La.; Can.-Fr.; Ardenne, Aunis. St.-Fr. *Brouette.*

BARRER, *vb. tr.* To lock (a trunk, a gate, etc.) Dial.—So.; Can.-Fr.

BATISTAIRE, BATISTÈRE, *f.* An excerpt from the baptismal rolls, establishing the date of baptism, the names of the witnesses, etc. *Produire son batistaire,* "to produce his registry of baptism." Dial.—Sw.; Can.-Fr.

BATTURE, *f.* That part of the inner shore of a stream which has been thrown up by the action of the current, and which, at certain seasons of the year, may be covered as a whole or in part by the water. *Batture* is derived from *battre,* "to beat," and is used by Joutel in 1685.[15]

The word has been adopted into English. Dial.—So.; Can.-Fr.

BEBELLE, *f.* Toy, plaything. Dial.—Sw.; Can.-Fr.; Orléanais.

BEC À LANCETTE, *m.* American Snakebird (*Plotus anhinga* L.); in English commonly known as the "water turkey"—sometimes as the "negro goose" or "water crow." Cf. *Bayou Beaklance, infra.*

BÉCASSINE, *f.* Snipe; less common than *cache-cache, infra.*

Bécassine is a Southern French diminutive in *-ine* from French *bécasse,* "woodcock." *Bécasse* is from Prov. *becasa. REW* 1013.

---

[14] Harry D. Wilson, *Louisiana* (1927-1928), p. 20.
[15] See Margry, III, 153.

BÉCASSINE DE MARAIS, *f.* Black-necked Stilt. Cf. *avocat, supra.*

BÉCASSINE DE MER, *f.* Du Pratz seems to apply the term *Bécassine de Mer,* "sea snipe," to the Red-breasted Snipe (*Macrorhampus griseus griseus* Gmel.), which never leaves the sea and does not taste too strongly of oil to be eaten, he says.[16] Audubon gives the La.-Fr. names of this bird as *Bécassine de Mer* and *Carouk*; Arthur cites the Louisiana term as *Dormeur,* "sleeper." All three words are still used.

The book name of this species of snipe is now *Dowitcher,* a word of Iroquois origin—compare Cayuga and Mohawk *tawis,* Onondaga *tawish,* "snipe"; but it has been modified in form by confusion with *Deutscher,* "a German," *German* or *Dutch snipe* being the name that the natives of Long Island conferred on this bird in order to distinguish it from the English Snipe (*Gallinago wilsoni* Ord).

Carouk is probably imitative of the guttural rolling cry that this species of snipe makes when it is on the ground.[17] Or is it a corruption of *carouge,* which Larousse gives as the popular name of birds of the species *Xanthornis*? In Canadian-French *carouge commandeur* signifies "étourneau à ailes rouges."[18]

Bécassine de mer is also the name of the Avocet (*Recurvirostra americana* Gmel.).

Audubon's comments on the red-breasted snipe make clear the significance of the name *Dormeur.* "It is not at all uncommon to shoot twenty or thirty of them at once. I have been present when 127 were killed by discharging three barrels, and have heard of many dozens having been procured at a shot . . . Those which have escaped unhurt often remain looking upon their dead companions, sometimes waiting until shot at a second time."[19]

BÉCASSINE GROSSE-TÊTE, *f.* "Big-headed snipe." Solitary Sandpiper, or Bull Head (*Helodramas solitarius solitarius* Wils.).

---

[16] *Histoire,* II, 118.

[17] Cf. Audubon, *Birds,* VI, 12.

[18] N. E. Dionne, *Le Parler Populaire des Canadiens Français* (1909), p. 122.

[19] Audubon, *Birds,* VI, 12.

BEC-CROCHE, *m.* The *Bec-croche* has indeed a crooked bill: with it the bird catches crawfish, on which it subsists; its flesh tastes like crawfish, and is red; its plumage is whitish-gray, and it is as large as a capon.[20]

The *bec-croche,* "crooked bill," commonly known as the "Spanish curlew," is pure white in plumage except for the ends of some of its outer primaries, which are tipped with deep black. Its skin and flesh are of an orange color. Its food consists chiefly of crawfish, but the bird will also eat aquatic insects, snails, slugs, and fiddler crabs. The manner in which it catches crawfish, of which it is extremely fond, is very interesting. It carefully breaks up the upper part of a crawfish mound, and throws some lumps of dirt down into the crawfish hole. The crawfish, unaware of danger, pushes the dirt out, and on emerging from its hole is instantly seized by the bird.[21] The *bec-croche,* for which the technical name is "white ibis" (*Guara alba* L.), inhabits the swampy regions of lower Louisiana.

BEC DE HACHE, *m.* This bird takes its name from the fact that its red bill is shaped like the blade of a hatchet, or an ax, according to Du Pratz. The same authority asserts that it is sometimes called *pied rouge,* "Red Foot," because its feet, too, are red; that it lives on shell-fish (*coquillage*), and therefore inhabits the seashore; that it is not seen in the interior except when it foresees some great storm which its retreat from the sea announces.[22]

By *bec-de-hache* Du Pratz designates the American Oyster-Catcher (*Haematopus palliatus* Temm.), whose long red bill is compressed towards the end into a thin wedge-shaped point. The *bec-de-hache* seizes the bodies of gaping oysters, and picks up snails, small crabs, shrimp, and other crustacea. Its feet are of a pale flesh color.[23]

The term "Black Bec-croche" is given to the Glossy Ibis (*Plegadis autumnalis* Hasselq.), as well as to the White-faced Glossy Ibis (*Plegadis guarauna* L.), two species that inhabit principally the thick woods along the swamps and rivers in the southwestern parishes of Cameron and Calcasieu.[24]

---

[20] Du Pratz's description of the *Bec-croche, Histoire,* II, 117.
[21] Audubon, *Birds,* VI, 57.
[22] *Histoire,* II, 117.
[23] Audubon, *Birds,* V, 237.
[24] Stanley C. Arthur, *The Birds of Louisiana* (1918), p. 30.

The name *bec-de-hache,* pronounced approximately as if written *Beg-dosh,* is still found in Louisiana-French. The *bec-de-hache* (Littré) is likewise a species of oyster catcher (*Haematopus ostralegus* L.), in France, where it goes by the name *Huîtrier,* a derivative of *huître,* "oyster" or *Pie de Mer,* "Sea Pie," or *Bécasse de Mer,* "Sea Woodcock."

BEC-EN-CISEAUX, *m.* Literally "scissors-bill": Black Skimmer (*Rynchops nigra* L.), a permanent resident in the state. In this bird's beak the upper mandible is shorter than the lower. In searching for food the *bec-en-ciseaux* skims the surface of the water with its lower mandible.

BEC-SCIE, *m.* American Merganser (*Mergus americanus* Cass.), found in Louisiana during the winter. This duck owes its name to the fact that the teeth in its bill resemble the edge of a saw. Du Pratz was under the erroneous impression that it lives exclusively on shrimp.[25]

Bec-scie de Mer, "sea saw-bill," is the name of the Red-breasted Merganser (*Mergus serrator* L.), a winter resident in Louisiana. It is known in English as the "Spanish drake" or "fish duck."

Bec-scie du Lac, "lake saw-bill," or *Bec-scie de Cyprière,* "Cypress-swamp saw-bill," distinguishes the Hooded Merganser (*Lophodytes cucullatus* L.), from the other two species of saw-bill. In the United States a common local name for this small duck is *Hairy-Head* or *Hairy-Crown.* This duck breeds in the State.

BELLE-ÂGE, *f.* A long time; equivalent to St.-Fr. *longtemps.* Dial.—Sw.; Can.-Fr. *Belle-heure* has the same signification.

+ BELLE DE NUIT, *f.* Common Evening Primrose (*Oenothera biennis* L. and *Oenothera grandiflora* Ait.).

BÈNARI, *m.* Carolina Wren (*Thryothorus ludovicianus ludovicianus* Lath.); cf. *roitelet, infra.* I have heard *Bènari* pronounced at Charenton, Louisiana, like a French word of the form *bennari.* This name represents an attempt to imitate the song of the wren. In the department of Périgord, France, *bènari* is one of the names of a bunting (*Emberiza miliaria* L.), which is usually designated by *le proyer.* In other parts of France the ortolan (*Emberiza hortulana* L.), bears a

---

[25] *Histoire,* II. 115-116.

similar name—*benouri(t)* in the Cévennes mountains, *benari* in Languedoc, *benarric* in Toulouse, *benerit* in Rouergue. In Alais the wryneck (*Torcol*) is called *bénouri*. Cf. *roitelet, infra*.[26]

BERSE, *f.* Rocking-chair. This word is a descendant of Old and Middle French *bers,* "cradle," which points to Low Latin **bertium* or **bersium.* Dialectal forms abound, such as Pas-de-Calais *ber(s),* Norman *ber*; Vendôme, Blois *ber,* Angevin *ber,* Poitevin *ber(s).* It occurs as a feminine in Walloon *bers,* Lille and Mons *berche,* Neuchâtel *berce,* "grand berceau de bois."[27] Modern Fr. *berceau,* "cradle," is a derivative formation from *bers.*

Canadian-French uses the masculine *bers* (=*ber*) in the sense of "cradle," and also in that of "the part of a hay wagon enclosed by racks."[28]

+BÊTASSE, *f.* Dolt, blockhead. Dial.—Sw.; common in the popular speech of France and Canada as the feminine of *bêta,* "blockhead," a dialectal form of *bétail,* "cattle."

BÊTE, *adj.* *Rester bête*=remain coy, silent. Dial.—Sw.; Can.-Fr.

BÊTE À CHANDELLE, *f.* May beetle; in the northern United States called "June beetle" or "June bug" (species *calceata,* genus *Lachnosterna*). This brownish beetle is often seen flying about lights; hence the term *bête à chandelle,* "candle beast." It should not be confused with the green beetle known to scientists as *Allorhina nitida* L. and called "June bug" in a part of the South, but commonly "Fig-eater" in the far Southern States.

+BÊTE ROUGE, *f.* The Red Bug (*Leptus irritans Riley*) that burrows under the skin; erroneously called *chigger* or *jigger* in some parts of America.

BEURDASSER, *vb. intr.* To waste time; to busy oneself with trifles; to work noisily without a well-defined aim; to make a great deal of noise. This verb is used in some parishes of the Southwest—for example, in Iberia and St. Landry—in Canadian-French, and in the dialects of Berry, Maine, Poitou, Anjou, and Nivernais.

Beurdasser is a derivative formation from the stem of Low Latin *brittus,* a Breton. The verb describes actions that were sometimes attributed to a native of Bretagne, or Brittany.[29]

---

[26] Cf. Eugène Rolland, *Faune Populaire de la France,* II, 68, 197, 202.
[27] Wartburg, *Wörterbuch,* p. 337.
[28] *Glossaire du Parler Français au Canada* (1930), p. 114.
[29] Wartburg, *Wb.,* pp. 538-542.

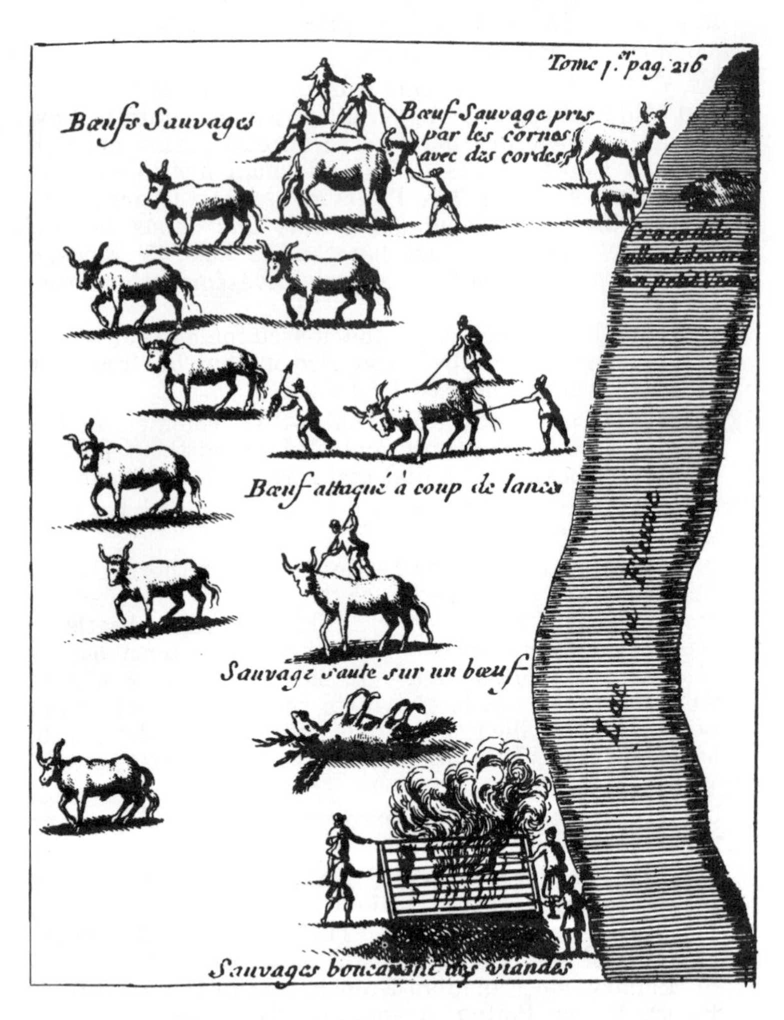

Sketches of the Buffalo. From Lahontan's *Voyages*,[2] I, 216.

BIÈRE CRÉOLE, *f.* Beer made of ripe pineapple, pineapple rind, raw rice, brown sugar, and cold water. Dial.—Sw.[80]

BIORQUE, *m.* American Bittern (*Botaurus lentiginosus* Montag). This novel word seems to be connected with dialectal French *bior, bihor,* "bittern," whence has come French *bihoreau,* a species of night heron. *Bihoreau* is derived by Gamillscheg from Gallo-Roman **buti-taurus,* in which the first element is the Latin *butio,* "bittern," and the second Latin *taurus,* "bull"; but through dissimilatory loss of the first *t* the Gallo-Roman source of *bihoreau* perhaps became **bui-taurus.* The result of the regular development of **buti-taurus,* says Gamillscheg, is French *butor,* "bittern," which is likewise used in Louisiana in the same sense. On the etymology of the difficult *butor,* one should also consult Wartburg, *Wörterbuch,* under *butio.*

The application of the name **buti-taurus* to the bittern is explained by the fact that the bird often makes a hollow noise not unlike the bellowing of a bull.

Canadian-French *biorque* signifies a sea bird whose flesh is scarcely edible.[31]

BIROUETTE, *f.* Wheelbarrow: not so common as *bourouette.* Dial.—Sw.

BISQUE D'ÉCREVISSES, *f.* Crawfish bisque. The recipe for this delicious bisque is given in *The Picayune Creole Cook Book,* pp. 13-14.

Bisque is probably taken from Norman *bisque,* "a bad drink," and the latter seems to be derived from Dutch **bîsken,* "to be excited" (Gamillscheg).

BLACK BEC-CROCHE, *m.* See *bec-croche, supra.*

BLOUSE VOLANTE, *f.* A loose dress widely known as a "Mother Hubbard." Dial.—New Orleans.

BOEUF SAUVAGE, *m.* Buffalo or American Bison (*Bison bison* L. and var. *Bison bison athabaskae* Rhoads). The early French explorers called the buffalo *boeuf sauvage* or sometimes simply *boeuf.* Joutel's reference, in September, 1685, to a river named *aux Boeufs* is clearly proved by the context to be the equivalent of "Buffalo River."[32] An early reference to *boeufs sau-*

---

[30] See Harris Dickson, "Creole Gossip," in *Good Housekeeping,* February, 1931, p. 138.

[31] Cf. Dionne, *Le Parler Populaire,* p. 76.

[32] Henry R. Stiles, *Joutel's Journal of La Salle's Last Voyage,* p. 97.

vages is found in Margry's *Mémoires,* I, 265. Du Pratz speaks of the buffalo as a *boeuf sauvage* or a *boeuf.*[33]

Stanley C. Arthur ascribes the name of the Bayou Terre aux Boeufs region in St. Bernard and Plaquemines parishes to the fact that a great number of buffaloes once spent the winters in this part of Louisiana.[34]

BOIS BLANC, *m.* Adelia or Swamp Privet (*Forestiera acuminata* Poir.). *Bois blanc* is the South-Louisiana term for this small tree.

BOIS BOUTON, *m.* Dogwood (*Cornus florida* L.). In the fall the buds of the dogwood form small buttons, which unfold in spring into lovely white blossoms. See also *bois de flèche, infra.*

+BOIS CONNU, *m.* Hackberry (*Celtis laevigata* Wild.). The present Louisiana-French *bois connu* is a syncopated form of *bois inconnu,* "the unknown tree," a term applied by the early French colonists to the hackberry, which flourishes in Louisiana. The earliest reference that I have found to what is presumably the hackberry is in the observations of A. DeBatz. He writes in 1732 partly as follows:

"Arbre incoñu. Cet arbe est actuellement sur pied aux Natchez. Les Sauvages le conservoient et le tenoient en grande Veneration, en prenoient quelque [s] Branches ou Rameaux, pour mettre dans le feu Sacré, qu'ils entretenoient perpetuelement dans leur Temple, qui étoit construit proche ledit Arbre, les Francois Brulerent et detruirent ce Temple en Fevrier 1730."

DeBatz sketches the tree and gives further details of its appearance, saying that it is always green and bears a pale white flower.[35] His statement that the tree is an evergreen does not apply to the hackberry, which drops its leaves in winter; nor, on the other hand, to the osage orange, which Bushnell, DeBatz's editor, believes to have been the tree described by the early French traveler. DeBatz was wrong, I am convinced, in taking the tree to be an evergreen. But this tree can hardly have been the Osage Orange (*Toxylon pomiferum* Raf.), which the French have long known as *bois d'arc.* DeBatz probably had in mind the hackberry, a view that is strengthened by the assertions of other

---

[33] *Histoire,* I, 312 ff.; *ibid.,* II, 66.

[34] *The Fur Animals of Louisiana,* p. 35.

[35] See David I. Bushnell, Jr., "Drawings by A. DeBatz in Louisiana, 1773-1735," *Smithsonian Miscellaneous Collections,* LXXX, No. 5 (1927), 8.

writers on Louisiana. Thus C. C. Robin gives an accurate description of a tree which he calls *Inconnu*, and which can be none other than the hackberry.[36] Amos Stoddard, too, comments on a certain tree as the "unknown wood, because it has no name, nor is it known to what tribe it belongs; it is of considerable size, and bears a small berry, with a stone something like a cherry; grafts of peaches and plums take on it."[37]

BOIS D'ARC, *m.* Osage Orange (*Toxylon pomiferum* Raf.), a tree found throughout the state of Louisiana. The Osage Indians and other Western tribes made bows of the wood of this tree.

Bodoc, the name of a hamlet in Avoyelles Parish, is corrupted from *bois d'arc*, "bow wood."

BOIS-DEBOUT, *m.* Land that has not been cleared of its timber is said to be *en bois debout*, "in standing timber." Dial.—Sw.; Can.-Fr.

BOIS DE FLÈCHE, *m.* Dogwood (*Cornus florida* L.). The Indians of the Gulf states made the foreshafts of their arrows of dogwood or of some other hard wood. The dogwood is occasionally called *bois bouton*, "buttonwood."[38]

In some parishes, especially those west of the Mississippi, the same name is applied to the stiff Cornel or Dogwood (*cornus stricta* Lam.), and to the Rough-leaved Dogwood (*Cornus asperi folia* Michx.).

BOIS DE MARAIS, *m.* Button-Bush; also called *Button-Tree*, *Globe-Flower*, and *Honey-Balls* (*Cephalantus occidentalis* L.). This shrub or small tree has a four-toothed calyx, a four-cleft corolla, four stamens, and sometimes three leaves in a whorl.

BOIS DE RAMEAUX, *m.* Magnolia (*Magnolia grandiflora* L.). This term is used in the parish of Pointe Coupée. Here, too, the magnolia leaves are called *"des feuilles rameaux,"* Cf. *rameau, infra.*

BOIS-JAUNE, *m.* Tulip Tree or Yellow Poplar (*Lirodendron tulipifera* L.); applied by some Acadians to the Osage orange—cf. *bois d'arc, supra*—and at least eight other trees.

BOISURE, *f.* Wainscoting, with change of suffix from St.-Fr. *boiserie*. Dial.—Sw.; Can.-Fr.

---

[36] *Voyages dans l'Intérieur de la Louisiane*, III, 359.
[37] *Sketches of Louisiana* (1812), p. 169.
[38] Cf. C. S. Rafinesque, *Flora of Louisiana*, pp. 77, 119.

BOSCOILLOT or BOSCOYO, *m.* Cypress Knee, one of the conical outgrowths from the roots of the Bald Cypress (*Taxodium distichum* Rich.). As cypress knees are semi-porous at the top, they serve to aerate the roots of the cypress trees, which usually grow in swampy ground or in the waters of swamps. Figuratively *un boscoyo* is "a rough or tough fellow."

Dr. E. L. Stephens, president of Southwestern Louisiana Institute, has sent me a stanza that illustrates the popularity of *boscoyo* in the Southwestern part of the State. This is the stanza as it was recited by Mr. Robert Mouton, mayor of Lafayette:

Les giraumonts qui fleurissent au printemps,
Tra, la,
Ont rien à faire avec le cas.
Voilà qu'on me dit que je dois épouser
Tra, la,
Une vieille ferzé, une poule mouillée
Tra, la,
Avec une figure de boscoyo de cypre—
Et voilà pourquoi je vous dit en mots et en chants
Je m'en fiche si les giraumonts fleurissent au printemps.

Boscoyo, or preferably, *boscoillot,* is a double diminutive—for instance, like French *Morillot,* "brown of skin like a moor"—and is connected with the Germanic stem **bosk-*, "bush," whence have come Italian *bosco,* English *bush,* and French *bois.* Compare Middle and Modern French *bosquet,* "thicket," "grove," whence are formed, with change of suffix, dialectal French *bosquiau* and *bosco.* Note, too, Provençal *bosquilho,* "petit bois," Modern Provençal *bouscalhou,* "bosquet," dialectal (Aveyron) *bouscoillou,* "bosquet," and Montbéliard *bocoillot,* "petit morceau de bois."[39]

One might be disposed at first glance to associate *boscoillot* with *bosco,* colloquial and popular French for *bossu,* "hunchback(ed)."[40] *Bosco* is found in the Louisiana-French proverb, *Le bon temps n'est pas bosco,* "Good fortune is not hunchbacked."[41] The derivation, however, from **bosk-*, I believe to be correct.

Besides *boscoyo* there are in the stanza just quoted two other words that may require explanation—*ferzé* and *cypre.* For the former, see *feusaie, infra*; for the latter, *cyprès, infra. Giraumon*(*t*)*s* signifies "pumpkins."

[39] See Wartburg, *Wörterbuch,* pp. 447-454.
[40] Wartburg, *ibid.,* p. 468.
[41] Lafcadio Hearn, *Gombo Zhèbes* (1885), p. 10.

+BOUGON, *m.* A small ear of corn with few grains. In Normandy *bougon* is the term for a short, heavy piece of wood; the upright part of a broken tree; the end of a dead tree. Canadian-French has *bougon* in various senses, as a "piece of wood," "a pipe with a short stem," "a heavy-set little man." In the popular speech of France *bougon* signifies "grumbler."[42]

BOULE D'OLIVIER, *f.* See *olivier, infra.*

BOUILLABAISSE, *f.* A stew of red snapper and redfish (*poisson rouge*), with various kinds of vegetables, all highly seasoned with pepper and spices. In France the sturgeon and perch are used in the preparation of this dish.

The name of this fish stew is derived from Modern Provençal *boulh-abaisso,* literally "boils and settles," from Modern Provençal *bouli,* "to boil," and *abaissa,* "to subside." A weekly paper entitled *lou Boui-abaisso* appeared in Marseilles, France, from 1841 to 1848 (Gamillscheg).

BOUQUET, *f.* A flower, with the meaning of Fr. *fleur.* Dial.—Sw.; Can.-Fr.; Norm.-Pic.; Saintonge, etc.

BOURDON DE LA MAISON, *m.* The Carpenter-Bee (*Xylocopa virginica* Drury), which bores tunnels in wood for its nest. This insect looks like a bumblebee; hence the aptness of the La.-Fr. term, which signifies "house bumblebee." Dial.—Pointe Coupée.

BOURDON DE TERRE, *m.* A green beetle (*Allorhina nitida* L.). Cf. *béte à chandelle, supra.* Dial.—Pointe Coupée.

BOUROUETTE, *f.* Wheelbarrow, with *r*-metathesis from St.-Fr. *brouette.* Dial.—Sw.

BOURRELET, *m.* St.-Fr. *bourrelet,* "pad," "cushion," "swelling," etc., is used by the Creoles in the additional sense of a "roll" (of bread). Note also *bourrelet aux mûres,* "blackberry roll."

BRAGUETTE, *f.* The opening in the front of a pair of trousers. The original signification of this word, formerly masculine and written *braguet, braye, brayer,* is "breech-cloth," worn by the Indians.[43] Dial.—So.

BRALINER, *vb. tr.* To bleach clothes in the sun; corrupted from St.-Fr. *praliner,* "to brown with sugar," etc., partly under the influence of St.-Fr. *brûler,* "to burn." Dial.—Lafayette Parish.

---

[42] Cf. L. Sainéan, *Les Sources de l'Argot Ancien,* I, 323, who associates *bougonner,* "to grumble," with dialectal *mougonner,* "to bellow."

[43] See *Jesuit Relations,* VII, II; XXI, 196; Margry, V, 380, 446; Dumont, *Mémoires Historiques,* I (1753), 137.

Can.-Fr. *braguette* is often used in the sense of a bathing costume. In Normandy and Saintonge the word signifies "trousers."

BUTIN, *m.* Merchandise of every description; provisions; household goods. Dial.—So.; Can.-Fr.; Lorraine. *Butin* is a collective noun, used in the singular only.

BUTOR, *m.* American Bittern (*Botaurus lentiginosus* Montag.); in Pointe Coupée, sometimes *bitor.* For notes on *butor,* see *biorque, supra.*

BUTTE DE RAT MUSQUÉ, *f.* A muskrat's house. Dial.—So.

CABANE SAUVAGE, *f.* Wigwam. The Acadians of Louisiana do not use *wigwam,* which entered Canadian-French from some Algonquian dialect. The Micmac form is *wigwom,* a variant of Algonquian *wikiwam,* properly "their house." The source of English *wigwam* (1628) is the Ojibway *wigiwâm.*[44]

CABINET, *m.* A little clothes closet. Dial.—So.; Can-Fr.; Norm., Pic., Saintonge.

CABOCHE, *f.* Head, noddle, pate. Heard at Colyell Bay in Livingston Parish; common in the popular speech of France; cf. Picard *caboche* for St.-Fr. *cabosse,* "cocoanut" (*Dict. Gén.*). The ultimate source is Latin *caput,* "head."

CACHE-CACHE, *m.* 1. Wilson's Snipe (*Gallinago delicata* Ord); almost always called *cache-cache,* "hide and seek," because it will often squat and lie still, especially when wounded or when apprehensive of danger.[45] The French name *bécassine,* "snipe," is also used. *Jack snipe* and *English snipe* are two well-known English terms for this bird, which frequents the marshes along the coast. 2. The Yellow Nut Grass, Chufa, or Earth Almond (*Cyperus esculentus* L.). The tubers of this plant are eaten by many waterfowl. English *chufa* is a loan from Spanish.

CAFÉ BRÛLOT, *m.* Brandy coffee; black coffee flavored with sugar and burning cognac or whisky.

CAILLE, *f.* Standard French *caille,* "quail," accompanied as a rule by a qualifying word or phrase, is used in Louisiana for various songbirds, such as the catbird, the meadowlark, the thrush, and the tanager.

---

[44] See J. A. Cuoq, *Lexique de la Langue Algonquine* (1886), pp. 221, 438; S. T. Rand, *English-Micmac Dictionary* (1888), pp. 134, 262; *New English Dictionary,* under *wigwam.*

[45] Audubon, *Birds,* V, 340-342.

Exactly when *caille* acquired the signification now assigned to it in Louisiana, I do not know. Du Pratz declared in 1758 that *la Caille* was very rare in Louisiana—so rare, indeed, that he had never seen the bird.[46] The fact that he was here referring to the quail becomes clear when one recalls his use of *Perdrix* in the sense of "pheasant," a term that the Acadians now apply to the quail, *infra*. Joliet, on the other hand, observed as early as 1673 that *les cailles* rose every moment in the prairies,[47] an assertion in which *les cailles* is apparently to be taken as the equivalent of "the meadowlarks." Such an interpretation, however, may be erroneous. Deceived by the flight of numerous brownish birds across the prairies, Joliet may have taken the meadowlarks to be quail. His *les cailles*, in other words, may signify "the quail."

+CAILLE DE BOIS, *f.* See *oiseau de cannes, infra.*

+CAILLE, *adj.* Marked with white and black spots, or with white and yellow (or red); spotted: *une vache caille*, "a spotted cow." Dial.—So.; Can.-Fr.; Anjou, Maine, Normandy, Orléanais.

In Poitou *caille* signifies "marked with white and red spots."

CAILLE PIVELÉE, *f.* "Speckled thrush." The Wood Thrush (*Hylocichla mustelina* Gmel.). See *pivelé, -ée, infra.*

CAILLETTE, *f.* The name given to a cow with a spotted skin (*caille*). Dial.—So.; Can.-Fr.

+CALENAS, *m.* Padlock. This word, a corruption of St.-Fr. *cadenas*, is also found in Canadian-French.

CALIMAÇON, *m.* Snail. A Canadian and Norman form for *colimaçon*. Dial.—Livingston Parish.

CANARD BRANCHU, *m.* Wood duck (*Aix sponsa* L.). This beautiful duck deserves the praise that it received from the early explorers of the New World. Charlevoix, after commenting on its lovely plumage and delicate flavor, says correctly that it owes its name to its habit of perching on the branches of trees.[48] Du Pratz describes its red eye as well as its brilliant crest, and observes that the Indians adorn their calumets, or pipes of peace, with the feathers from its neck.[49]

---

[46] *Histoire*, II, 127.
[47] Margry, I, 265.
[48] *Histoire*, II, 156.
[49] *Histoire*, II, 115; also Lahontan, *Mémoires*,[2] II (1728), 51; N. Bossu, *Nouveaux Voyages Aux Indes Occidentales*, II, 177.

The *canard branchu,* as it is called in Louisiana-French, nests in the hollows of trees and inhabits the heavily wooded regions of the State, especially those of the Southwest and extreme Northeast. With her bill the mother bird carries the young to the water as soon as they are vigorous enough to swim. *Canard des bois,* "wood duck," is another name for this duck; in English it is also called "Squealer" or "Summer Duck."

CANARD CHEVAL, *m.* Canvas-Back Duck (*Marila valisineria* Wils.). This famous species visits Louisiana in the winter. It is known to the French as *canard cheval,* "horse duck," because the shape of its head is thought to resemble that of a horse. This duck owes its English name to the color of the feathers on its back.

CANARD DES BOIS, *m.* See *canard branchu, supra.*

CANARD DES ÎLES, *m.* See *canard noir d'été, infra.*

CANARD D'INDE, *m.* Muscovy Duck (*Cairina moschata* L.).

Du Pratz divides the ducks of the Province of Louisiana into three species: *Canards d'Inde,* "Indian ducks," *Canards sauvages,* "Wild ducks," and *Canards-branchus,* "Wood ducks." The *Canards d'Inde,* he says, owe their name to the fact that they are peculiar to this province. From other details of his description—notably from his accurate reference to the musky smell of the drake—one can readily identify his *Canards d'Inde* with the Muscovy duck, a species, now widely distributed, whose habitat originally extended from Mexico to Brazil. The term *muscovy duck* is actually a corruption of *musk duck.*[50]

CANARD FRANÇAIS, *m.* The well-known Greenhead Mallard (*Anas platyrhynchos* L.), a winter resident of Louisiana.

CANARD MULET, *m.* "Mule duck." This team designates a duck bred from a muscovy drake and a mallard, Pekin, or Indian runner duck. The mule duck is sterile.

CANARD NOIR, *m.* Ring-necked Duck (*Marila collaris* Donov.), often called also "Black Duck" or "Black Jack." In the male of this species the back is black; hence the Louisiana-French name. The black duck is seen in Louisiana during the winter.

CANARD NOIR D'ÉTÉ, *m.* The Florida Duck (*Anas fulvigula* Ridgw.). This game bird, which inhabits Florida, the Gulf Coast, and the islands of Louisiana, is called either

---

[50] Cf. Du Pratz's *Histoire,* II, 114.

canard noir d'été, "summer black duck," or *Canard des îles*, "island duck." The same names are given to the Texas Mottled Duck (*Anas fulvigula maculosa* Senn.), a species extremely common in Southwest Louisiana.

CANARD NOIR DU NORD, *m.* Northern Black Mallard or Black Duck (*Anas rubripes* Brewst.), which visits Louisiana in the winter. Lahontan observes that the "*canards noirs*" of the New World resemble those of Europe.[51]

CANEÇON, *m.* Drawers (underwear); a seventeenth-century form for *caleçon*; cf. Buffet, 1668, "D'autres disent *un canesson* pour *un calson*" (Thurot, II, 261); heard, too, in Canada as well as in the popular speech of France.

CANICHE, *f.* Switch-Grass (*Panicum virgatum* L.), one of the plants on which the muskrat feeds.[52]

Whether *caniche* was coined by the French of Louisiana from *canne*, "cane," or was changed in meaning from *caniche*, which Breton lists as the Carib name of sugar cane, I cannot say. See *Dictionnaire Caraïbe Français*, p. 250.

Breton's *caniche*, at any rate, is not a genuine Carib word, but was formed by the Caribs from French *canne*.[53]

Another name for switch-grass is *paille jaune*, *f.*, literally "yellow straw."

CAP-CAP, *m.* 1. The Little Green Heron (*Butorides virescens virescens* L.); called thus because of the bird's hollow croak. In the department of Deux-Sèvres, France, the small owl that goes by the name of *Le Petit Duc*, "the little duke," is also called *cop* because of its cry.[54]

2. An illiterate Acadian, especially one of low social standing. Of such a person the Acadians say, "*Il vient du poulailler*," "He comes from (the) hen-house."

3. The perverted speech of an illiterate Acadian. *Il parle cap-cap* is as a rule more highly derogatory than *il parle Cadien* (*Kajẽ*), "He speaks Cajun."

CAP-CAP DORÉ, *m.* Least Bittern (*Ixobrychus exilis* Gmel.), called also *Cap-Cap* and *Les Yeux Clairs*. The glossy black crown of the male bird is doubtless responsible for

---

[51] *Mémoires*,[2] II, 47.

[52] See Stanley C. Arthur, *The Fur Animals of Louisiana* (1928), p. 338.

[53] Leo Wiener, "Pseudo-*Karaïbisches*," *Zeitschrift für Romanische Philologie*, XXXIII, 514.

[54] Cf. L. Sainéan, *ZRPh., Beih.*, I (1905), 99.

the use of the epithet *doré*. *Fly-up-the-creek* is a popular English name of this bird. Another La.-Fr. name is *Jean Charlot,* "John Little Charles." The personal name *Charlot,* according to the *Dictionnaire Général,* has been given jestingly to several birds, particularly to the European Curlew and a species of snipe. In Normandy the jay is called *Charlot.*

But Gamillscheg, *Wörterbuch,* p. 208, regards Languedoc *Charlot,* "curlew," rather as a modification of Languedoc *corli* (Fr. *Courlis*) under the influence of Modern Provençal *charra,* "to chatter."

CAPORAL, *m.* Red-winged Blackbird (*Agelaius phoeniceus phoeniceus* L.), and Florida Red-winged Blackbird (*Agelaius phoeniceus floridanus* Mayn.). The red feathers on the wings of the male bird reminded the French of Louisiana of the epaulettes of a corporal's uniform. Cf. *aile rouge* and *choc aile rouge.*

CARABINÉ, -ÉE, *adj.* Excellent, perfect; *un diner carabiné* is a dinner complete in every detail. *Carabiné* is formed from *carabine,* "carbine," "rifle."[55] In France and Canada the word signifies "violent," "intense," "excessive."

CARCAN, *m.* A wooden collar, usually shaped like a triangle, which prevents an animal from breaking through a fence. Dial.—Livingston Parish; Sw.; Can.-Fr. St.-Fr. *carcan* signifies iron collar; pillory; necklace.

CARCUL, *m.* Calculation. *Carcul* is derived by dissimilation from St.-Fr. *calcul.* Dial.—So.; Can.-Fr.; Norm., Pic., and other dialects.

CARCULER, *vb. tr.* and *intr.* To calculate. Dial.—So.; Can.-Fr.; Anjou; Norm.; Pic.; Saintonge, etc. From St.-Fr. *calculer.*

CARDINAU, *m.* Under the influence of the plural *cardinaux,* many Acadians have changed the regular French singular *cardinal* to *cardinau,* the designation of the Cardinal or Redbird (*Cardinalis cardinalis cardinalis* L.) This bird is found throughout the State.

CARENCRO, *m.* 1. Turkey Buzzard (*Cathartes aura septentrionalis* Wied.). 2. Black Vulture (*Catharista urubu urubu* Vieill.). These are both plentiful in Louisiana, and are designated indiscriminately as "buzzards" by those who do not speak French. In Louisiana-French

[55] D. Behrens, *Beiträge zur Französichen Wortgeschichte und Grammatik* (1910), pp. 344-345.

the turkey buzzard is specifically the *carencro tête rouge,* "red-headed buzzard," whereas the black vulture is the carencro *tête noire,* "black-headed buzzard"; but these terms are employed only when a nice distinction between the two species is desired. The head of the "carancro" is ornamented with red flesh, says du Pratz *Histoire,* II, 111. Bossu, in his comments on the "Karancro," calls attention to the soft, downy feathers under the wings of the bird, which are effective, he asserts, in stopping a flow of blood.[56]

On the Southern Pacific Railway, in the northern part of Lafayette Parish, there is a town by the name of *Carencro,* which in 1930 had a population estimated at 684. A bayou of the same name enters the Vermilion River on the southern boundary of the parish of St. Landry. Two obsolete spellings of the name of this bayou are *Caron Crow* and *Carrion Crow.*[57] Tradition has it that many years ago a mastodon died near the present site of the village of Carencro; that thousands of buzzards came to feed on its carcass; and that consequently the name *Carencro,* corrupted either from English *carrion crow* or from Spanish *carnero,* "charnel house," was bestowed on the bayou and the entire settlement.[58] This tradition apparently has no historical basis, though bones of the mastodon, it is true, have been found in Louisiana.[59] The Carencro settlement doubtless owes its name to the simple fact that vast numbers of buzzards often gathered, for some reason or other, in that vicinity. The word *carencro,* at any rate, is certainly derived from English *carrion crow,* which as a designation of the red-headed vulture occurs as early as 1699. *Carencro* is pronounced either as in French, or in English as *carrion crow* would be if its *i*-sound were omitted.[60] The Carencro settlement, I must not forget, is mentioned by Robin, an author who also pays tribute to the character of one Desclouettes, with the observation that this officer had endeared himself

---

[56] *Travels Through That Part of North America Formerly Called Louisiana.* Translated by J. R. Forster. I (1771), 369.

[57] For the former see *American State Papers,* Public Lands, III, (1816), 222, ed. Gales and Seaton; for the latter, William Darby, *Emigrant's Guide* (1818), p. 71.

[58] Cf. William H. Perrin, *Southwest Louisiana* (1891), p. 193; H. L. Griffin, *The Attakapas Trail,* p. 13.

[59] R. C. Moore, *Geology of the Salt Dome Oil Fields* (1926), p. 373.

[60] See *New English Dictionary,* under *carrion crow.*

to the Acadians by his simple, affectionate manners rather than by virtue of being at that time commandant of militia for this territory.[61]

CARENCRO DE MER, *m.* Man-o'-War Bird; Frigate Bird (*Fregata aquila* L.). Another name for this bird, which visits Louisiana during the summer, is St.-Fr. *la frégate.*

CAROUGE, *m.* See *bécassine der mer, supra.*

CAROUK, *m.* See *bécassine de mer, supra.*

CARPE, *f.* Various species of buffalo fish. *Le buffle,* "buffalo," is sometimes used in the same sense. Du Pratz remarks that the *carpe* grows to monstrous size in the river St. Louis—that is to say, in the Mississippi.[62] The annual catch of buffalo fish in Louisiana is said to amount to 10,000,000 pounds. Three species of buffalo are found in the fresh waters of Louisiana: the Common or Big-mouthed Buffalo (*Ictiobus cyprinella* Cuvier and Valenciennes), the White or Small-mouthed Buffalo (*Ictiobus bubalus* Raf.), and the Black Buffalo (*Ictiobus urus* Agassiz).[63]

The name *buffalo,* by which the American bison is generally known, is thought to have been given to the fish most probably because of the shape of its back, which rises in a slight hump near the front of the dorsal fin. The Choctaw Indians perceived, like the white man, the resemblance between this fish and the buffalo, and consequently designated the former by the significant term *náni lukfápa,* "buffalo-lick fish."

CARPICHE, *f.* Somersault; heard at Colyell Bay, Livingston Parish; cf. Can.-Fr. *prendre une carpiche* (or *capuche*), "take a header," "turn a somersault." Fr. *capuche* signifies "woman's head-dress." But note also Fr. *saut de carpe,* "somersault."

+CASBURGOT or CASSEBURGAU, *m.* 1. Fresh-Water Drum (*Aplodinotus grunniens* Raf.). 2. Common Sheepshead (*Archosargus probatocephalus* Walbaum), found in the waters of the Mexican Gulf and the Atlantic Coast. *Casburgot* is sometimes pronounced as if it were written *cassebrigau;* the aphetic forms *un gou, les gous* also occur. But those who are not familiar with French corrupt *casburgot* into *gaspergou.* The source of this name is given by Du Pratz, whose description of the fish is, freely translated, as follows:

---

[61] *Voyages,* III (1807), 67-68.

[62] *Histoire,* II, 153.

[63] Harry D. Wilson, *Louisiana Today* (1924), pp. 77-78.

"The Casse-Burgo is an excellent fish; it is usually 12 to 18 inches long; its body is round, with gilded scales; in its mouth it has two bones shaped like a file, with which it crushes the shells called *Burgo,* a fact that has given rise to its name. Its flesh, though delicate, is very firm; it is best when eaten with red wine."[64]

The Creole *casburgot au gratin* of the New Orleans restaurants is rendered into English by "baked sheepshead."

The Indian women of the Natchez tribe bedecked their ears with pendants made of the mother-of-pearl shell that the French call *burgau.*[65] The origin of *burgau* is unknown.

The Choctaw for *casburgot* is *náni háta,* "white fish."

CASSE-TÊTE, *m.* Hatchet. Cf. *tomahawk, infra.*

CASTOR, *m.* 1. Beaver (*Castor canadensis carolinensis* Rhoads). A few beaver colonies are still found in Louisiana, along the Amite and Comite rivers.[66]

The fact that beavers were formerly plentiful is proved by the popularity of *castor* as a geographical place-name. The parishes of Rapides, Caldwell, De Soto, and Vernon have each a bayou named *castor;* and the same designation is met with elsewhere in the State.

In 1813 G. W. Lovelace, a resident of Catahoula Parish, is known to have shipped on a flatboat the following articles:

Bear skins, 243
Deer skins, 450
Beaver skins, 28[67]

Audubon and Bachman, strange to say, declare in their work published in 1856: "We have heard that the beaver was formerly found near New Orleans, but we never saw one in Louisiana."[68]

2. Whirligig Beetle (family *Gyrinidae*). This small black beetle swims in circles on the surface of still water.

CATAPLÂME, *m.* Poultice. The form *cataplâme,* instead of St.-Fr. *cataplasme,* is extensively used in Louisiana, Canada, and the French dialects.

---

[64] *Histoire,* II, 153 ff.
[65] Cf. Du Pratz, *Histoire,* II, 156.
[66] Stanley C. Arthur, *The Fur Animals of Louisiana* (1928), p. 161.
[67] A. S. Kilpatrick, in *De Bow's Review,* XII (1852), 274.
[68] *The Quadrupeds of North America,* I, 357.

CATÉCHISSE, *m.* *Catechism;* St.-Fr. *catechisme.* Dial.—So. Can.-Fr.; Anjou, Bas Maine, Normandy, etc.

CATIN, *f.* Doll: St.-Fr. *poupée.* Cf. Gamillscheg, *Wb.*, p. 194. Dial.—So.; Can.-Fr.; Anjou, Saintonge, etc.

CENELLIER, *m.* 1. Two varieties of haw (*Crataegus* L.), the one bearing an edible red berry called *cenelle chevreuil, f.*, "*deer cenelle*"; the other, a slightly different red berry, *la cenelle,* which the Acadians are careful not to eat. 2. The Winterberry (*Ilex decidua* Walt.)

St.-Fr. *cenelle* is of obscure origin.

Cenellier is found in Canadian-French and some of the French dialects—for example, in those of Normandy and Maine.

CHABEC, *m.* A boat; St.-Fr. *chébec.* Cf. *canot.* Dial.—Bayou Lafourche region.

+ CHANGEUR DE CHEVAUX, *m.* A person who engages in the practice of exchanging one horse for another; a horse "swapper." Cf. the equivalent Can.-Fr. *changeux de chevaux.*

CHAR, *m.* Train, railway coach, auto. So.; Can.-Fr.

CHAR A BAGAGE, *m.* Baggage car; also Can.-Fr. Standard-French has *fourgon.*

CHARBON, *m.* *Huile de Charbon, f.*, "petroleum," "coal-oil." Dial.—So.; Can.-Fr.

CHARDRON, *m.* Thistle, (*Cirsium horridulum* Michx.), the equivalent of French *chardon*; the intrusive *r* is due to the influence of the consonant-group *rd.* Cf. Norman *cardron* and Canadian *chardron.*[69]

CHARLOTTE, *f.* The larva of a tiger beetle. Cf. *loulou, infra.* In Normandy the jay goes by the name of *Charlot,* the masculine diminutive of *Charles,*[70] as has already been noted.

CHARMILLE, *f.* Planer-Tree or Water Elm (*Planera aquatica* Gmel.). The fruit of the water elm is a valuable food for wild ducks. In South Louisiana this tree is also called *châtaigner,* literally "chestnut tree."

CHARRER, *vb. intr.* Chatter, converse. This is a Norman word, cognate with Modern Provençal *charra* and Spanish *charlar.*

---

[69] See W. Meyer-Lübke, *Historische Grammatik der Französischen Sprache,* I, 171.

[70] Rolland, *Faune,* II, 144; but cf. Gamillscheg, *Wörterbuch,* p. 208.

CHASSEPAREILLE, *f.* Sarsaparilla; corrupted from St.-Fr. *salsepareille,* which is in turn a sixteenth-century adaptation of Italian *salsapariglia.* The Italian form is due to folk etymology; *salsapariglia* is a corruption of Italian *senza* or *sènza,* "without," and *pariglia,* "like"—that is, "without a peer." *Salsepareille* has been derived erroneously from Spanish *zarzaparilla.*[71] Dial.—Livingston Parish; Sw.; Can.-Fr.

CHÂSSIS, *m.* Window; of the same meaning as St.-Fr. *fenêtre.* Dial.—Sw.; Can.-Fr.

CHAT, *m.* 1. Cat. 2. Raccoon. Cf. *chaoui, infra.*

CHAT-HUANT, *m.* Screech owl: cf. *chouette, infra.* Old French *cahuan,* from Gallo-Roman *cauannus,* a name bestowed on the owl because of its cry, was misunderstood and analyzed in the sixteenth century as "the cat that hoots"—*chat-huant.*[72]

CHAT TIGRE, *m.* Puma (*Felis concolor* L.). See *pichou, infra.*

CHAUD, *adv.* Dear: *coûter chaud* = St.-Fr. *coûter très cher.* Dial.—So.; Can.-Fr.; Anjou.

CHÊNE VERT, *m.* Live Oak (*Quercus virginiana* Mill.). Du Pratz mentions this beautiful tree.[73]

CHÊNIÈRE, *f.* Live oak forest or grove.

CHÉRANT, -ANTE, *adj.* and *n., m.* and *f.* One who asks high prices for his (her) merchandise: *ce marchand est* (*un*) *chérant*; *cette marchande est* (*une*) *chérante.* Dial.—Sw.; Can.-Fr.; Anjou, Saintonge, etc.

CHERSER, *vb. tr.* Seek, look for; changed by dissimilation from St.-Fr. *chercher.* Dial.—Livingston Parish and doubtless elsewhere.

CHÉTIT, -ITE, *adj.* Weak, delicate, frail: *un bébé chétit,* "a delicate baby"; corrupted from St.-Fr. *chetif.* Dial.—Sw.; Can.-Fr.; Anjou, Saintonge, etc.

CHEVAL DIABLE, *m.* Praying Mantid (*Stagmomantis carolina* Johannson); other English names for this insect are "Soothsayer," "Mule Killer," "Devil Horse," and "Devil's Rear Horse." Many Acadians pronounce *cheval diable* like *shfal job* (*j* as in English *job*).

CHEVALIER DE BATTURE, *m.* Spotted Sandpiper (*Actitis macularia* L.), literally "gentleman of the shore." See *batture, supra.*

---

[71] See *The Literary Digest,* CX, No. 4 (July 25, 1931), 47.

[72] See L. Sainéan in *ZRPh., Beiheft* I (1905), 97, 99; Du Cange, *Glossarium,* II (1883), 233.

[73] *Histoire,* II, 41.

CHEVELURE DE VÉNUS, *f.* Indian Pink or Cypress Vine (*Ipomoea Quamoclit* L.).

CHÈVREFEUILLE DE FRANCE, *f.* A species of Bush Honeysuckle (*Lonicera fragrantissima* Lindl.).

CHEVRETTE, *f.* Shrimp. As the shrimp makes little leaps, it is not improperly called *chevrette,* "kid," "little goat." St.-Fr. *crevette,* "shrimp," is not used in Louisiana.

Two species of shrimp are found in Louisiana: the large "lake" shrimp (*Panaeus setiferus Say*) and the small "river" shrimp (*Bithynis ohionis* Smith).

CHICOTER, *vb. tr.* and *intr.* To whittle: *chicoter un morceau de bois,* "to whittle a piece of wood"; *il chicote toujours,* "He's always whittling." Cf. Can.-Fr. *chicoter,* "to wrangle over trifles." La.-Fr. *chicoter* results from a blend of Fr. *chicoter,* "to wrangle over trifles," and *chiqueter,* "to whittle."

CHIEN, *m.* Black-necked Stilt (*Himantopus mexicanus* Müll.). This bird cries continually *cleek-cleek-cleek* on its nesting grounds; hence the fitness of the term *chien,* "dog." The stilt is also called *avocat, bécassine de marais, religieuse,* and *soldat.*[74]

CHIEN-DENT, *m.* Tall Paspalum (*paspalum dilatatum* Poir.). Can.-Fr. *chien-dent* is Couch-Grass or Switch-Grass (*Agropyron repens* L.).[75]

CHIMÈRES, *f. pl.* Foolish ideas: *bien des chimères,* "many foolish ideas." Dial.—So.; Can.-Fr.

CHOC, *m.* Blackbird. This word probably arose in imitation of the cries of the various species of Grackles or Crow Blackbirds. *Choc* is pronounced like *chock* in English *chock-ful, infra.*

CHOC AILE ROUGE, *m.* Red-winged Blackbird of the two species named under *caporal, supra.* Choc is imitative of the notes of the blackbird.

+CHOU, *interj.* One cries *chou! chou!* to call or drive away pigs. Dial.—So.; Can.-Fr. In Normandy pigs are called with the same cry.

CHOUETTE, *f.* The most common name for the Florida Screech Owl (*Otus asio floridanus Ridgw.*), which is found throughout the State.

It is also called *chat-huant,* "hooting cat," *supra.*

---

[74] Audubon, *Birds,* VI (1859), 31; Arthur, *Birds,* (1918), p. 38.

[75] Cf. George H. Clark et James Fletcher, *Les Mauvaises Herbes du Canada* (1909), p. 34.

CHOU GRAS, *m.* Pokeberry; Pokeweed (*Phytolacca decandra* L.).

CHOU VERT, *m.* Borecole or Curled Kale; a variety of cabbage with curled leaves (*Brassica oleracea* var. *acephala* D. C.).

CIGALE (ANGLAISE), *f.* A species of cicada or locust (family *Cicadidae*) that makes a rasping sound. In Lafayette, La., the usual term is *la cigale zi-zi. Zi-zi* is obviously echoic.

CIMITIÈRE, *f.* Cemetery. A Norman and Can.-Fr. form for St.-Fr. *cimetière*; used at Loreauville, in Iberia Parish, and also in Livingston Parish, and no doubt elsewhere.

CIRE, *f.* Inflammation on the edge of the eyelids. From St.-Fr. *cire,* "wax." Dial.—So.; Can.-Fr.

CIRIER, *m.* The Cedar Bird, Cherry-Bird, or Cedar Wax-Wing (*Bombycilla cedrorum* Vieill.). It has three names in Louisiana-French: *cirier, mûrier,* and *ortolan.* This bird's inner primaries, and sometimes its tail feathers, are tipped with horny red bits that look like drops of sealing wax. Hence the name *cirier,* "waxmaker." As the waxwing is fond of berries, it also bears the name *mûrier,* properly "mulberry tree." Finally, it is called *ortolan* because it is thought to resemble the European bird of the same name.[76]

In Canadian-French the cedar bird is known as *récollet,* its conspicuous crest suggesting the hood of the Franciscan order of that name.

Cirier also signifies the Candleberry or Wax Myrtle (*Myrica cerifica* L.) and the Bayberry or Small Wax-berry (*Myrica carolinensis* Mill.), the fruit of which was gathered as a source of wax by the early French settlers.[77]

CLAIR, *adv. Tout-à-clair,* "clearly," "distinctly." Dial.—So.; Can-Fr.; Bas-Maine, Berry, Nivernais, Normandy.

CLAJEUX, *m.* Poison- or Water-Flag (*Iris versicolor* L.); corrupted from St.-Fr. *glaïeul.* The Norman dialect has *glajeux* in the same sense. Dialect of Pointe Coupée.[78]

CLEEK-CLEEK, or CLI-CLIQUE, *m.* Sparrow Hawk; a name given to the bird because of its cries. Cf. *émerillon* and *mangeur poulets, infra.*

---

[76] Arthur, *Birds,* p. 66.
[77] Cf. *Robin,* III, 522.
[78] *Glossaire du Parler Français au Canada* (1930), p. 208.

CLOU-CLOU, *m;* CLOUK-CLOUK, *m.* The syllables *clou-clou* or *clouk-clouk* are thought to resemble the notes of the Greater Yellow-Legs (*Totanus melanoleucus* Gmel.), and of the related species, the Lesser Yellow-Legs (*Totanus flavipes* Gmel.). Another descriptive term is *Patte Jaune,* "yellow foot."[79]

COCHON, *m.* 1. Pig. 2. The fish called "Southern Porgy" (*Stenotomus aculeatus* Cuvier and Valenciennes).

COCOMBE, *m.* Cucumber. Dial.—Sw.; Livingston Parish; Can.-Fr.; Anjou and Berry; St.-Fr. *concombre.*

COCOTTE, *f.* Hen. Dial.—Livingston Parish; popular in the colloquial speech of France; also Can.-Fr.

COISSARDE, COSSARDE, *f.* Marsh Hawk, or Prairie Hawk (*Circus hudsonius* L.). Another designation of this bird is *chocolatière,* "chocolate pot," which has reference to the reddish brown color of the female.[80] French *cossard,* according to Littré, is one of the names of the French *buse,* a species of hawk which lives chiefly on mice, rats, frogs, and reptiles. In Lower Chartres, however, the word *cossard* is the dialectal name of the *chouette,* a species of small owl.[81]

The origin of *co(i)ssarde,* feminine as used in Louisiana, is obscure. Is *co(i)ssarde* connected with a dialectal form of *cochon,* "pig," such as northern *cosson,* or Walloon *cosset, coissot,* "little pig," or Morvan *coisson,* "little pig"? If so, then *co(i)ssarde* signifies "big pig." In this connection one may note that in Rumania the water-ouzel (*Cinclus aquaticus* Bechstein)—French *merle d'eau*—goes by the name of *purcàrus,* "little pig," because this bird inhabits marshy places;[82] and that the American marsh hawk, too, builds its nest on low ground, generally in a swampy region.

COLLE, *f.* Praline cake made of brown sugar or black molasses with pecans or peanuts. Dialect of New Orleans. Cf. St.-Fr. *colle,* "paste," "mucilage."

COLLIER, *m.* "Necklace," a name given to the Wilson Plover (*Ochthodromus wilsonius wilsonius* Ord), which has a black band across the lower part of the neck. This bird breeds on the Gulf and South Atlantic coasts.

CORBEAU, *m.* See *corneille, infra.* Also, a Negro.

[79] Cf. Audubon, *Birds,* V, p. 318; Arthur, *Birds,* p. 40.
[80] Arthur, *Birds,* p. 47.
[81] L. Sainéan, in *ZRPh., Beiheft,* I, 105.
[82] L. Sainéan, *ibid., Beiheft,* X, 87, 98.

CORBIGEAU, *m.* In a lengthy comparison of the *Corbijeau* with the woodcock (*Bécasse*) Du Pratz notes especially the size, curved bill, and blended plumage of the former bird. The flesh of the *Corbijeau* is firmer than the woodcock's and at least as delicate, he adds.[83] Audubon, on the contrary, finds the flesh of the Long-Billed Curlew (*Numenius americanus* Wils.)—which is Du Pratz's *Corbijeau*—fishy and rarely tender.[84] The curlew, furthermore, is not so small as Du Pratz's words—"as large as the woodcock"—would lead one to believe, nor is its bill, which is six to eight inches long, "reddish yellow," but black. In English this species of curlew is also called *Sickle-Bill, Sabre-Bill,* and *Buzzard-Curlew.* The name *curlew* is itself imitative of the bird's cry.

The origin of *corbigeau* is not clear. Gamillscheg, *Wörterbuch,* p. 254, suggests that it may be a hybrid descendant of OF *corbel,* "raven," and OF *jau,* "cock." Wartburg, *Wörterbuch,* II, p. 1239, considers it a blend of Fr. *courlis,* "curlew," and a derivative of *bugium,* an obscure word glossed in Old English as *haefenblaete,* "sea-gull."[85] Some dialectal forms are Norman *corbejeon,* Upper Breton *corbejeau,* Angevin and Poitevin *courbejau.* The form *corbigeau* is used in Louisiana-French.

CORDEAU, *m.* A large, heavy rope. Dial.—Sw. Can.-Fr. *cordeaux* signifies the reins attached to a bridle.

CORNEILLE, *f.* Crow (*Corvus brachyrhynchos brachyrhynchos* Brehm.) *Corneille* is far more common than *corbeau* as a designation of this bird.

CORNEILLE FOUETTEUR, *f.* "Crow beater"; that is, the Bee Martin or Kingbird. Cf. *gros grasset, infra.*

CORNARD, *m.* Jamestown or Jimson-Weed (*Datura stramonium* L.). Persons afflicted with asthma used to inhale the fumes from the burning of this plant.

The reason for the choice of the term is clear: French *cornard, adj.,* is applied to horses that are wheezy.

COSSARDE, *f.* See *coissarde, supra.*

CÔTES, *f. pl.* *Avoir les côtes en long,* "to be lazy"; literally, "to have the ribs lengthwise," a condition that would prevent one from stooping to pick up anything. See

[83] *Histoire,* II, 128.
[84] *Birds,* VI, 38.
[85] Wartburg cites *Anglia,* XLI, 113.

Kastner and Marks, *Glossary*, p. 111. Dial.—Sw.; Can.-Fr. *avoir les côtes sur le long* is used with the same signification.

COTONNIER, *m.* Sycamore Tree (*Platanus occidentalis* L.).[86] Some Creoles and Acadians apply this name to the Southern Cottonwood (*Populus deltoides virginiana* Sudw.); but the latter tree is generally called *le liard.* The sycamore owes its French name to the cottony interior of the sycamore balls, or to the fine cottony hair thrown off from the young leaves of the tree.[87]

COUAC, *m.* A name given to the American Bittern (*Botaurus lentiginosus* Montag.) by reason of its squawk of alarm. *Couac* has the same meaning in Canadian-French. This word is an echoic formation of the sixteenth century. Cf. *garde-soleil, infra.*

COU BLANC, *m.* Semipalmated Plover (*Aegialitis semipalmata* Bonap.), which spends its winters on the Gulf shore and farther southward. The lower part of this bird's white throat is encircled by a broad ring of black.

COU COLLIER, *m.* Killdeer (*Oxyechus vociferus vociferus* L.), commonly known in the United States as "killdee" on account of its plaintiff cry, owes its name *cou collier,* "neck band," to the fact that the lower part of the bird's neck is encircled by a broad brownish-black collar. Just below this collar, on its breast, is a narrower band of the same color. Another name is *pluvier doré,* which is more accurately bestowed on the golden plover,[88] *infra.* Far more usual, however, than *Cou collier* or *pluvier doré* is *piaillard,* "squaller," a name given to the bird obviously on account of its incessant cries.[89] *Ring-neck* is another English name. For *pivier,* see below.

COUCOU, *m.* Several species of the cuckoo or the raincrow—family (*Cuculidae*)—the Yellow-billed, the Black-billed, and the Mangrove Cuckoo. The author of *Le Champ d'Asile* speaks of the *Coucou* as the *messager des beaux jours*—"the harbinger of beautiful days."[90] Other La.-Fr. terms for the cuckoo are *la grânde queue,* "Big Tail," and *la longue queue,* "Long Tail." Of the three species the mangrove cuckoo is rarely seen in Louisiana.

---

[86] Cf. Du Pratz, *Histoire,* II, 40.
[87] See Joutel (1687), in Margry, III, 466; Charlevoix, *Histoire,* III, 206.
[88] Audubon, *Birds,* V, 208.
[89] Audubon, *Birds,* V, 208.
[90] *Le Champ d'Asile,* p. 91.

COUETTE, *f.* 1. A braided tuft of hair; a ringlet such as was formerly twisted with the aid of curling irons or tongs; a negress's kinky lock of hair, rolled and tied. Dial.—Widely used in Louisiana.

Can.-Fr. *couette* signifies a tress or braid of hair; a tuft of hair; a little pigtail (of hair).[91]

Behrens regards Picard *couette,* "nape," as a recent diminutive of *cou,* "neck" (from Low Latin *collum*).[92] But A. Tilander connects Picard *queuette,* "nape," "back of the neck," "little pigtail," with *kueu,* the primitive form of dialectal *kief,* which is equivalent in turn to OF. *chief,* "head," "end."[93] (Latin *caput*).

It is manifestly impossible to separate *queuette* from *couette,* "little pigtail." Sylvius 1531 gives "coue et cueue" as variants; Bovelles 1533 notes "*queue* chez les Picards (apud Belgas), *coue* à Paris"; Robert Estienne 1549 observes of *queue,* "Aucuns dient *coue,* les autres *queue.*"[94]

COUETTE, *f.* 2. Ticking, the cover or case of a pillow, mattress, etc.; used at Lafayette, and doubtless elsewhere in South Louisiana.

Couette (2) is a diminutive formation from OF *coutre, coitre,* the latter descending from Low Latin *culcita,* "pillow." St.-Fr. *couette* or *coite* signifies "feather-bed," "cushion," "socket," etc.

COUP, *m.* *Prendre un coup,* "to take a drink of wine or other spirituous liquor." Dial.—So.; Pointe Coupée; Can.-Fr.

COUPE-PAILLE, *m.* Lawn-mower. Cf. St.-Fr. *coupe-paille,* "straw-cutter." Dial.—Pointe Coupée.

COURONNE DE CHÊNE, *f.* A bunch of mistletoe (*Phoradendron flavescens* Nutt.). But the mistletoe itself is designated by *gui, m.,* the St.-Fr. term. Dial.—Lafayette Parish.

COURPION, *m.* Rump. This Acadian form is current, too, in Canadian-French, with *r*-metathesis from St.-Fr. *croupion.*

---

[91] See Sylva Clapin, *Dictionnaire Canadien-Français,* p. 95; N. E. Dionne, *Le Parler Populaire des Canadiens-Français,* p. 189; *Glossaire du Parler Français au Canada,* p. 234.

[92] *Frz. Wortgeschichte,* pp. 56-57.

[93] "Notes d'Étymologie Française," *Romania,* LII, 476 ff. Cf. A. Stimming, *ZRPh.,* XXXIX, 130 ff.

[94] Thurot, I, 460.

COURTBOUILLON, *m.* A fish stew, generally made of redfish—less often of red snapper—with tomatoes, onions, and spices. For the recipe, see *The Picayune Cook Book,* p. 34.

Courtbouillon is corrupted apparently from dialectal **ca-*, **co-bouillon,* in which the first element is a collective prefix. See Gamillscheg, *Wb.*, under *courtbouillon.*

COUTEAU DE CANNES, *m.* Sugar-cane knife.

COÛTER, *vb. intr. Coûter les yeux de la tête,* "to cost excessively." Dial.—So.; Can.-Fr.

COUVERTE, *f.* Counterpane. St.-Fr. *couverture de lit.* Dial.—Sw.; Can.-Fr.; Norm.

CRAPAUD VOLANT, *m.* "Flying toad," a name bestowed on the night-hawk, because its mouth resembles that of a toad. Compare Provençal *grapaud volant* and Meuse *bo volant;*[95] see *engoulevent, infra.*

CRÉOLE, *m. f.* 1. A white descendant of the French or Spanish settlers in Louisiana during the Colonial Period (1699-1803).[96]

Many favorite dishes are prepared *à la Créole,* as, for instance, *courtbouillon à la Créole,* "a stew of redfish," *casburgot à la Créole,* "sheepshead in Creole style," *crabes à la Créole,* "broiled soft-shell crabs," *écrevisses gratinées à la Créole,* "crawfish baked *à la Créole,*" and *perdrix sautées à la Créole,* "quail stewed in Creole style."

2. The Negro-French patois. *Il parle Créole,* "He speaks Negro-French," is synonymous with *il parle nègre* and *il parle Gombo, infra.*

II. *adj. Créole* designates anything manufactured or produced by the Creoles and considered therefore of peculiar excellence. Thus *des oeufs créoles* are presumably fresh eggs. *Mêlée créole* is a fine fish chowder, and *des poules créoles* are hardy chickens that have proved to be well adapted to the Louisiana climate. *Un nègre créole,* however, is a negro who speaks Negro-French, and who was born in the New World.

---

[95] L. Sainéan, in *ZRPh., Beiheft* X (1907), 126.

[96] But cf. J. Hanno Deiler, *The Settlement of the German Coast of Louisiana* (1909), p. 114, for a different definition.

Créole is a seventeenth-century loan from Spanish *criollo,* a person of European descent born in some other part of the world than Europe.[97]

CRIQUETTE, *f.* Any of the insects comprising the family *Grillidae,* especially the house-cricket (*Gryllus domesticus* L.) or the common field cricket (*Gryllus neglectus* Scudder).

St.-Fr. *criquet, m.,* designates any insect belonging to the family *Acrididae,* whereas Can.-Fr. *criquet* is the name of the house-cricket. St.-Fr. *grillon,* "cricket," and *grillon domestique,* "house-cricket," are used by the Louisiana Creoles, but are unknown to most descendants of the Acadians.

The meanings assigned to *criquette, cigale,* and *sauterelle*—respectively, "cricket," "locust," (family *Cicadidae*) and "grasshopper" (family *Acrididae*)—seem to be fairly uniform throughout Louisiana. At Thibodaux, La., however, one may hear the cricket called indifferently *cigale, crichet,* and *diable sauterelle,* "devil grasshopper," according to my friend, Mr. Cecil Bird, of Baton Rouge. In the same town the term *cigale* is sometimes applied to the humming bird.

The Gascons are fond of the saying *Oun y-ha gritz, Diu habite*—that is, "Where there are crickets, God dwells."[98]

CROCRO, *m.* A clumsy, badly fitting shoe; apparently a hybrid formation from *coco,* "shoe" (child's speech), and the colloquial French *croquenot,* "shoe." *Croquenot* is formed from *croquer,* a variant of *craquer,* "to crack."[99]

CROISON, *m.* Partition. Standard French has *cloison.* The same corruption is heard in Canada. A change of *l* to *r* is characteristic of the dialect in the French Dauphiné region.

CROQUECIGNOLE, *m.* Doughnut. Dial.—Pointe Coupée; Livingston Parish; Can.-Fr. Cf. St.-Fr. *croquignole,* a hard brittle cake; a cracknel.

CUITE, *f.* Thick syrup, the last drawn in the sugar house before the syrup turns to sugar. *Cuite,* the past participle of *cuire,* "cook," is shortened from *la masse cuite.*

ÇU-LÀ, *pron. m.* That one; corrupted from St.-Fr. *celui-là.* Dial.—Loreauville, Iberia Parish; Pointe Coupée. Canadian-French has both *çu-là* and *çui-là.*

---

[97] *REW* 2305.

[98] Lespy et Raymond, *Dictionnaire Béarnais,* I, 347.

[99] Cf. Sainéan, *Langage Parisien,* p. 356.

Cypress Tree and Knees. From De Cubières *Mémoire sur le Cyprès de la Louisiane*

CULOTTE, *f.* Cf. *plongeur, infra.*

CURAGE, *m.* Water Pepper. Dotted or Water Smart-Weed. (*Persicaria punctata* Small).

CUVE, *f.* Cistern; *une cuve de la terre,* "an underground cistern." Dialect of Colyell Bay, in Livingston Parish; but St.-Fr. *citerne* is very common in South Louisiana. St.-Fr. *cuve* signifies tub, vat, tank.

CYGNE, *f.* The Whistling Swan (*Olor columbianus* Ord), formerly common in Louisiana, is rarely seen there now. *Le cygne sauvage,* "the wild swan," is said to have attained a weight of twenty-six pounds, and to have furnished diadems for the Indian chiefs with its beautiful plumes.[100] Swan Lake, situated in the southeastern part of Bossier Parish, was evidently a favorite resort of these wild birds in the opening years of the nineteenth century.[101]

CYPRÈS, *m.* Red Cedar (*Juniperus virginiana* L.). Though St.-Fr. *cèdre* is not unknown, *cyprès* is the ordinary Acadian word for the red cedar, which is found in many parts of Louisiana. The Acadians generally use *cypre, m.,* for St.-Fr. *cyprès,* "cypress." Du Pratz's form for the "cypress" (*Taxodium distichum* Rich.) is *cipre*;[102] Pénicaut's, too, is *cypre.*[103]

CYPRIÈRE, *f.* Cypress forest or swamp: formed from La.-Fr. *cypre,* "cypress," with the aid of the suffix *-ière.* Cf. *chênière,* "oak forest," *pacanière,* "pecan grove," *pinière,* "pine forest."[104]

DAME, *f.* Wife. *La dame du maire,* "the mayor's wife." Dial.—Sw.; Can.-Fr.; Pic.

DÉGRÉYER, *vb. tr.* To strip a dwelling of ornaments or furniture; to clear (a table). Dial.—Sw.; Can.-Fr. Corrupted from St.-Fr. *dégréer,* "to unrig."

DÉMARRER, *vb. tr.* Untie, unfasten. Dial.—So.; Can.-Fr.; equivalent in meaning to St.-Fr. *détacher.*

DEMOISELLE, *f.* Daughter. Dial.—Sw.; Can.-Fr.; Norm.

DENTISSE, *m.* Dentist. Dial.—Sw.; Can.-Fr.; Anjou, Norm., etc. St.-Fr. *dentiste.*

---

[100] *Le Champ d'Asile* (1819), pp. 92-93.

[101] Cf. John Sibley's letter (1805), in *Annals of Congress* (Washington, (1852), column 1101.

[102] *Histoire,* II, 30, 31.

[103] Margry, V, 385, and *errata.*

[104] Cf. Charlevoix, III, 435; Robin, II, 283.

DÉPEIGNER, *vb. tr.* To disarrange the exact symmetry of hair that has been combed; formed from *de* and *peigner,* "to comb." Dial.—Iberia Parish; Can.-Fr.

DÉPENDRE (*sur*), *vb. intr.* To count, or reckon confidently on. Example: *On peut dépendre sur lui,* "one can count on him." St.-Fr. *compter sur* has this meaning. Dial.—Sw.; Can.-Fr.

DÉPENSE, *f.* Buffet; pantry where provisions are stored. Dial.—Sw.; Can.-Fr.

DIABLE, *m.* Devil-Fish (*Manta birostris* Walbaum); pronounced like English *job* by the fishermen of Lower Louisiana. Naturally, *diable* also signifies "devil."

DORMEUR, *m.* See *bécassine de mer, supra.*

DORMIR, *vb. intr. Dormir sur un rôti,* "to sleep on a roast"; that is, "to sleep on the job," "to neglect one's work or task." Dialect of Breaux Bridge.

DOUTANCE, *f.* Doubt. Dial.—Sw.; Can.-Fr.

DRAGUE, *f.* A trot-line. Cf. St.-Fr. *drague,* "dredge-net." Dialect of Livingston Parish.

DRIGAIL, *m.* Effects, belongings, furniture; everything that one owns. *Avec tout son drigail* signifies "with all his bag and baggage." Dial.—So.; Can.-Fr. Cf. *drigail,* in Anjou, Poitou; *trigal,* in Saintonge. The word is pronounced as if written *drigaille.*

ÉBOURIFFLÉ, -ÉE, *adj.* With disheveled hair. Dial.—Sw.; So.; Can.-Fr.; from St.-Fr. *ébouriffé, -ée.*

ÉCALE, *f.* Fish scale, in the sense of St.-Fr. *écaille.* Cf. St.-Fr. *écale, "shell"* (of peas), "hull" (of nuts). Dial.—Sw. Can.-Fr. *écale* = "oyster shell."

ÉCHAPE, *f.* A small splinter. Dial.—Sw.; Can.-Fr. Equivalent in meaning to St.-Fr. *écharde.*

ÉCLAIRCIE, *f.* Clear space in a forest. Dial.—Sw.; Can-Fr. Cf. St.-Fr. *clairière.*

ÉCOPEAU, *m.* Chip, shaving. Dial.—Sw.; Can.-Fr. Aunis, *écoupeau.* St.-Fr. *copeau:* sixteenth-century *escoupau.* See Gamillscheg, *Wb.*, p. 252.

ÉCREVISSES GRATINÉES À LA CRÉOLE, *f. pl.* See *Créole, supra.*

ÉGRAFIGNER, *vb. tr.* Scratch. Dial.—Sw.; Can.-Fr. St.-Fr. *égratigner.*

ÉMERILLON, *m.* Sparrow Hawk. Cf. *épervier*; *mangeur poulets, infra.*

ENGOULEVENT, *m.* Nighthawk (*Chordeiles virginianus virginianus* Gmel.) and Florida Nighthawk (*Chordeiles virginianus chapmani* Coues). These birds are commonly called "bullbats" in English.

Engoulevent was corrupted through folk etymology from Breton *golvan,* "sparrow," *engoule* being the imperative of Fr. *engouler,* "to swallow," with *vent,* "wind," as its object. In France *engoulevent* is the name of the European Nightjar or Goatsucker (*Caprimulgus europaeus* L.).

+ ÉPERVIER, ÉPREVIER (with *r*-metathesis), m. 1. Sparrow Hawk (*Falco sparverius sparverius* L.). Other names of the sparrow hawk are *cli-clique* (echoic), *émerillon,* and *mangeur poulets.*[105] 2. Small cast net.

ÉPINGLE À LINGE, *f.* Clothes-pin. Cf. *maquillon, infra.*

ÉPLURE, *f.* Peel, rind, paring. Dial.—Sw.; Can.-Fr. From St.-Fr. *pelure.*

ÉRONCE, *f.* Blackberry-bush; from St.-Fr. *ronce,* which is also heard. Dial.—Sw.; Can.-Fr., Anjou, Norm., Poitou, etc.

ESPÉRER, *vb. tr.* Wait for, await. Dial.—Sw.; Can.-Fr.; Norm.-Pic., Saintonge, etc.; Standard French uses *attendre.*

ESTOMAC MULÂTRE, *m.* The ginger bread called "stage planks"; known everywhere in French-speaking areas.

+ ÉVÊQUE, *m.* Indigo Bunting (*Passerina cyanea* L.). The indigo blue of the male bird's plumage reminded the early French settlers of the violet robes of a Roman Catholic bishop.[106] A less common term is *pape bleu,* literally "blue pope." Cf. *pape, infra.*

The *Évêque* feeds on several kinds of little grains, among which are two called by the Indians *Widlogouil* and *Choupichoul,* says Du Pratz.[107]

Elsewhere the same authority identifies *le Choupichoul* with the plant known in France as *belle-dame sauvage,* "wild goosefoot," the name of a member of the goose-foot family (*Chenopodiacae*); and he classifies *Widlogouil* as a species of millet which grows without cultivation in Louisiana.[108]

---

[105] Cf. Arthur, *Birds,* p. 49.
[106] Cf. Bossu-Forster, I, 372; Du Pratz, II, 140.
[107] *Histoire,* II, 140.
[108] *Ibid.,* I, 316-317; III, 9.

FAILLOT or FAYOT, *m.* Bean of a white variety. Cf. *fayot,* "white kidney-bean," in the dialect of Breton sailors.[109] Dial.—Livingston Parish; Can.-Fr.

+FAIS-DODO, *m.* A country dance; from the *fais dodo,* "go to sleep," of children's speech.

Catherine Carbine has described a Louisiana *Fais-dodo.*[110] *Dodo* is formed from the initial syllable of *dormir,* "to sleep."[111]

FALE, *f.* Craw of a fowl. Canadian-French has this word in various senses: (1) breast; (2) part of the clothing that covers the breast; (3) front part of the neck of birds and animals.[112]

FANFERLUCHE, *f.* Frills, gewgaws; with *r*-metathesis from St.-Fr. *fanfreluche.* Dial.—Sw.; Can-Fr.; Norm.

FEUILLES RAMEAUX, *f. pl.* See *rameau, infra.*

FEURSAIE, FEUSAIE, *f.* Nighthawk and Florida Nighthawk. This term, which I have heard along Bayou Teche, particularly at Cecilia and Arnaudville, is corrupted through *r*-metathesis from French *fresaie,* a species of owl (*Strix flamma* L.). In some pronunciations of *feursaie* the *r* is weak or disappears; the *s* always sounds like *z.* Cf. *engoulevent, supra. Fersaie* is an Angevin name of the barn owl.[113] In Normandy *fresaie* is identical in meaning with *engoulevent,* "goatsucker," "nighthawk."[114]

FÉVIER, *m.* Locust; False Acacia (*Robina pseudoacacia* L.). The yellow wood of this species of locust is extremely hard, and is therefore often used for fence posts.

FÉVI, FÉVIS, *m.* The okra pod; as in *gombo févis,* "okra gumbo," *un canne de févis,* "a can of okra," *potage de févis,* "okra soup."[115] *Févis* is formed from Fr. *fève,* "bean," apparently by analogy of such words as *radis,* "radish," *salsifis,* "salsify." The final *s* of *févis* is always silent.

FICHER, *vb. tr. Ficher le camp.* To leave, to escape; equivalent to St.-Fr. *se sauver, déserter: fichez le camp,* "get away from here!" This is a Canadian-French idiom.

---

[109] L. Sainéan, *Langage Parisien,* p. 280.

[110] The New Orleans *Times-Picayune,* Sunday, August 15, 1926, Magazine section, page 2.

[111] W. Foerster, in *ZRPh.,* XXII, 271.

[112] *Glossaire du Parler Français au Canada* (1930), p. 339.

[113] Rolland, *Faune,* II (1879), 45.

[114] L. Sainéan, in *ZRPh., Beiheft* I, 110.

[115] Cf. Célestine Eustis, *Cooking in Old Creole Days* (1928), p. 91.

FIFOLET, *m.* Will-o'-the-Wisp. Corrupted from St.-Fr. *feufolet.* Widely used by the Acadians. Dial.—Can.-Fr.; Norman.

FILÉ, *part. adj.* See *gombo, infra.*

FILLEU, *m.* Godson; St.-Fr. *filleul.* Dial.—Sw.; Can.-Fr.; Bretagne, Norm., Saintonge, etc. In the seventeenth century the final *l* of *filleul* was silent (Littré).

FILLEUSE, *f.* God-daughter. Dial.—Sw. Cf. St.-Fr. *filleule.*

FORDOCHES, *f. pl.* Trash, rubbish, brushwood, in Pointe Coupée; but *dans les fordoches,* in the parish of St. Martin, signifies *dans la misère, dans l'embarras.*[116]

Can.-Fr. *ferdoches* signifies "brushwood," "young trees in a forest"; *dans les fredoches* or *fardoches,* "in trouble," "in difficulties," with the meaning assigned to *dans les fordoches* in Southwest Louisiana.

Fridoches, "brushwood," occurs in Parisian French as early as 1667.[117]

FOSSE, *f.* Grave (underground). Dial.—Sw.

FOUETTEUR, *m.* The Coach-Whip Snake (*Zamenis flagelliformis* B. and G.), a long, slender snake, which is erroneously believed to be able to lash its foe with its tail.[118]

FOUINE, *f.* Louisiana Weasel (*Mustela noveboracensis arthuri* Hall). St.-Fr. *fouine,* "beech marten," is a derivative of Low Latin **fāguīna,* "beech marten," which is connected in turn with Latin *fagus,* "beech tree," according to Gamillscheg, *Wb.*, pp. 434-435.

In Louisiana-French the Louisiana Mink (*Putorius vision vulgivagus* Bangs) goes by the name of *belette,* which is the St.-Fr. term for the Weasel (*Mustela* L.; *Putorius* Cuvier).

FOURCHE, *f.* Pitchfork. Dial.—Sw.

+FRAPPE D'ABORD, *m.* Deer Fly (family *Tabanidae,* genus *Chrysops*); literally "strike first," *frappe* being the imperative of *frapper.* This term was brought to Louisiana by the Acadians.

FRÉGATE, *f.* Cf. *carencro de mer, supra.*

FRÊNE PIQUANT, *m.* Prickly Ash (*Zanthoxylum clavaherculis* L.).

FRÉQUENTER, *vb. tr.* To court, pay assiduous attention to a girl or a woman. Dial.—Sw.; Can.-Fr.

---

116 See Alcée Fortier, *Louisiana Studies* (1894), pp. 183, 184.

117 *Glossaire du Parler Français au Canada,* p. 341.

118 Cf. Bossu-Forster, I, 364.

Frète, *adj.* and *n. m.* Cold; St.-Fr. *froid.* Dial.—Sw.; Can.-Fr.; Anjou, Saintonge; cf. Thurot, I, 375, 409.

+Gambier, *m.* A book of cigarette papers. A single paper is *une feuille de gambier.* Dial.—Pointe Coupée.

Gambier is apparently the same word as St.-Fr. *gambier,* "gambier," a yellowish extract prepared from a Malayan plant (*Uncaria gambir* Rab.), and extensively used in dyeing and tanning. Cigarette papers were formerly dyed yellowish or brown.

Malayan *gambīr,* the source of the French word, is the name of the plant from which the extract is made.

Garaufier or Garaupier, *m.* Water or Swamp Locust (*Gleditsia aquatica Marsh*); corrupted from Standard-French *caroubier,* "locust tree." The long, heavy spines of this species of locust are dangerous; hence *garaupier* is commonly thought to be formed from *gare au pied,* "look out for your foot." The same term is also given to the Honey Locust; cf. *piquant amourette, infra.*

+Garde-Soleil, *m.* Sun-Gazer or American Bittern (*Botaurus lentiginosus* Montag.); it has the habit of standing on one leg and gazing by the hour at the sun. Hence the French have named this bird *garde-soleil,* which is an aphetic form of *regarde-soleil,* "Look at the sun." A similar term is *vise en l'air,* "aim in the air." In these phrases *garde* and *vise* are imperatives, presumably addressed to the bird.[119] *Garde-soleil* is pronounced as if written *gar-soleil.* Other names for this bittern are *biorque, butor,* and *couac, supra.*

Gargoton, *m.* Throat, Adam's Apple. Dial.—Sw.; Can.-Fr.; Anjou. Cf. OF *gargotte, gargate,* "throat," and *gargoter,* "to make a noise in swallowing."

Garocher, *vb. tr.* To pelt with stones or other missiles. Ex.: *Garocher un ouaouaron,* "to throw (stones) at a bullfrog." *Garocher,* "to throw," is found in West and Northwest France as a hybrid formation from *arocher,* literally "to throw stones at," and *garoter,* "to throw." Cf. OF *garrot,* "arrow of a cross-bow," and Angevin *arocher une pierre* for St.-Fr. *ruer une pierre,* "to throw a stone," (Sainte-Palaye, *Dict. Historique,* II, 163). See K. Jaberg, in *Archiv,* CXX (1908), 96-98. Dial.—Bayou Lafourche region and Canadian-French.

Along Bayou Lafourche the variant *galocher* is also found in the sense of *garocher.*

---

[119] Cf. Audubon, *Birds,* VI, 95.

GASTRONIA, *m.* Crape Myrtle. This designation of the crape myrtle is corrupted from *Lagerstroemia*, the scientific name of this small tree. *Gastronia* is sometimes used in Lafayette Parish. Cf. *myrte rose, infra.*

GIRAUMON(T), *m.*, GIRAUMON(T) À COU, etc. See *chouquechi, infra.*

GOILAN, *m.* Sea Gull. The sole pronunciation that I have heard points to the spelling *goïlan* instead of to Standard-French *goéland*. Du Pratz has *goïlan,*[120] and Littré cites the plural *goïlants* as a sixteenth-century form.

The laughing gull (*Larus atricilla* L.) is called *goïlan charogne* (carrion), because it feeds on garbage of almost every description.

GOU, *m.* See *casburgot, supra.*

GOUJON, *m.* See *barbue, supra.*

+GOURDE, *f.* In South Louisiana *gourde*, "gourd," is used with the value of "dollar."

The use of *gourde* for a coin began in Haiti, whence this meaning of the word was brought to Louisiana by French refugees. Henri Christophe, the negro who succeeded Dessalines as president of the black republic of Northern Haiti on December 7, 1806, rescued his country from bankruptcy by confiscating all the green gourds in Northern Haiti. His soldiers brought 227,000 gourds to Cap Haitien, and Christophe valued each gourd at twenty sous. Exchanging the precious gourds for coffee berries, he sold the latter to European traders for gold. Thus the *gourde* became a symbol of standard currency in Haiti[121]

Fr. *gourde* is from Low Latin *cucurbita.*

GRAINES À VOLÉE, *f. pl.* See *volée.*

GRAND GOSIER, *m.* The pelican is named *Grand Gosier*, "great throat," because of the large pouch that hangs from its lower mandible.[122] The gular pouch of a brown pelican measures from 6 to 10 inches in depth according to the age of the bird after the first moult, says Audubon.[123] The same authority found the length of an old male white pelican's bill to be 13¾ inches along the ridge and 15 inches along the lower mandible.[124]

[120] *Histoire*, II, 118.
[121] John W. Vandercook, *Black Majesty*, pp. 108-109.
[122] Joutel, Jan., 1686, in Margry, III, 214.
[123] *Birds of America*, VII (1859), 36.
[124] *Ibid.*, VII, 27.

Sailors used to kill the pelican and convert its pouch into a sack for their tobacco.[125] Even muffs were made of the skin of its pouch.[126]

The pelican, contrary to popular belief, does not store fish in its pouch, but uses it simply as a scoop-net in pursuit of its prey. After catching a fish, the pelican swallows it at once, to disgorge it later, if necessary, as food for its young. These vary in number from two to five.[127] Nor is it true that this bird wounds its breast, as shown on the seal of Louisiana, for the purpose of feeding its little ones with its blood. This is an old fable; hence the pelican has been depicted in art and heraldry as the symbol of redemption through Christ or of charity.

The brown pelican (*Pelecanus occidentalis* L.) inhabits the shores of the Gulf States and the Caribbean Sea throughout the year. In June, 1915, Mr. Stanley C. Arthur estimated a colony of these birds on East Timbalier Island, Louisiana, at 13,000. The North American White Pelican (*Pelecanus erythrorhyncus* Gmel.), is seen in Louisiana from October till March; some of this species also remain through the summer, though they do not breed in the State.[128]

Most reputable maps of Louisiana, from Tanner's in 1820 to Lockett's in 1882, show an island by the name of *Grand Gosier,* often corrupted to *Grand Grozier,* slightly north and east of Breton Isle, off the coast of Plaquemines Parish.

GRAND HÉRON BLEU, *m.* Great Blue Heron (*Ardea herodias herodias* L.), often erroneously called *Blue Crane.* The same French term is also bestowed on the slightly darker Ward Heron (*Ardea herodias wardi* Ridgw.). These two birds are dubbed *Sans-Joie,* "joyless"; compare the English designation *Poor Joe.*

GRAND MOQUEUR, *m.* Mocking Bird. Cf. *moqueur, infra.*

GRAND PLONGEON, *m.* "Great diver"; the Loon (*Gavia immer* Brunn.), which visits Louisiana during the winter. The name *hurleur,* "howler," is also given to this bird because of its strange cry.[129]

---

[125] Du Pratz, *Histoire,* II, 113-114.

[126] Bossu-Forster, I (1771), 374.

[127] Audubon, *Birds of America,* VII, 23, 351; Stanley C. Arthur, "The Emblematic Bird of Louisiana," *The Louisiana Historical Quarterly,* II, (July, 1919), 248-257.

[128] See Stanley C. Arthur, *The Birds of Louisiana* (January, 1918), pp. 18-20.

[129] Cf. Cooper's remarks on the note of the loon, in *The Deerslayer,* Chap. VI.

GRAND ÉCAILLE, *m.* Tarpon (*Megalops atlanticus* Cuvier and Valenciennes). The large scales of this noted game fish are responsible for the La.-Fr. name. A lake in Plaquemines Parish is called *Grande Écaille.*

GRASSEL, *m.*, or its synonym *Grasset, m.*, "fatty." The Towhee or Chewink (*Pipilo erythrophthalmus erythrophthalmus* L.), which in winter becomes so fat that it was formerly shot for the table.[130] This bird has other names, such as *Jorée, f.*, and *Joritte, f.*, both imitative of the bird's notes, *Grive* (robin) *Chéroki, f.*, Ground Robin, Swamp Robin, and Cherokee Robin, the last three names being of course English, not French. *Jorée* is apparently, too, one of the names of the Wood Thrush. (*Hylocichla mustelina* Gmel.)[131]

GRATONS, *m. pl.* The famous crackling bread of the Southern States is made of cornmeal with the addition of "cracklings," the name applied to small bits of fat pork cooked until they are quite brown. *Gratons,* "cracklings," is a corruption of St.-Fr. *cretons, m. pl.*, "tallow scraps," which is in turn a derivative of Fr. *crotte,* "dirt," "mud," etc.[132] The term for crackling bread is *du pain maïs aux gratons.*

GRENADE, *f.* The fruit of the Maypop or Passion Flower (*Passiflora incarnata* L.) A more popular form is *garnade,* with *r*-metathesis. The maypop vine is called *liane de garnade* (*grenade*). St.-Fr. *grenade* signifies a grenade and also the pomegranate fruit, whereas St.-Fr. *grenadille* is the name of the passion flower.

GRENADINE, *f.* The fruit of the pomegranate tree (*Prunica granatum* L.). The tree is called *grenadier,* just as in Standard French; but St.-Fr. *grenadine* designates the juice of the pomegranate, a kind of silk, etc.

GRENOUILLE, *f.* Any small green frog—not the bullfrog, which the Acadians call *ouaouaron, infra.* Many Acadians pronounce *grenouille* as if it were written *grounouille.* In New Orleans and in the homes of the Creoles *des grenouilles* may signify small rolls of bread baked in long rows.

GRÉYER, *vb. tr.* To equip, furnish, provide. Ex.: *Il va gréyer sa maison,* "He is going to furnish his home"; *un homme bien gréyé,* "a well-to-do man." *Gréyer* is used in Iberia Parish and in the dialects of Anjou and Canada.

---

[130] Cf. Audubon, *Birds,* III, 168-169.

[131] Cf. A. R. Kilpatrick, in *De Bow's Review,* XI, (1851), 54.

[132] Gamillscheg, *Wörterbuch,* under *creton* and *crotte.*

Gréyer is formed from St.-Fr. *gréer,* "to rig," which is in turn a back-formation from *agréer,* "to rig a ship." The ultimate source is the Old Norse substantive *greithi,* "tackle." Further details are given by Gamillscheg, *Wb.,* under *agréer.*

GRIFFE, *f.* The offspring of a negro and a mulatress;[133] of obscure origin; perhaps a back-formation from Fr. *griffon,* "griffin."

GRIVE, *f.* Robin (*Planesticus migratorius migratorius* L.).

GRIVE BATARDE, *f.* Bluebird. See *oiseau bleu, infra.*

GROGNARD, *m.* Common Croaker (*Micropogon undulatus* L.), an important food-fish known from Cape Cod to Texas. The Louisiana-French name, like the English, was bestowed on this fish because of the croaking sound that it makes when drawn out of the water.

+GROS GRASSET, *m.,* "big fatty." Kingbird (*Tyrannus tyrannus* L.), generally called *bee martin. Grasset* is a common name for most flycatchers and warblers.[134] Another significant designation of the bee martin is *corneille fouetteur,* "crow beater," a term that is based on the bee martin's hatred of crows, which the smaller bird invariably pursues and drives far from its nest.

GROS YEUX, *m. pl.* See *pluvier doré, infra.*

GROUP, *m.* Croup (disease). Dial.— Livingston Parish; Can.-Fr. St.-Fr. *croup.*

GRUE BLANCHE, *f.* Whooping Crane (*Grus americana* L.), a bird now become uncommon in Louisiana. As late, however, as the middle of the nineteenth century immense numbers of the whooping crane and the sandhill crane congregated in winter on Catahoula Lake and other bodies of water in the State.[135]

GUIGUI, *m.* An old *habitant* of New Orleans, according to Mr. D. S. Wogan. *Guigui* is perhaps the same word as Parisian *quiqui,* "chicken," a variant *of coco,* itself a derivative of *coquard,* "old sport" (slang), etc.[136]

---

[133] See Helen Pitkin, *An Angel by Brevet* (1904), p. 126 and footnote; the *New English Dictionary,* under griff.

[134] Audubon, *Birds,* III, 96.

[135] Cf. *De Bow's Review,* XI, (1850), 55.

[136] Cf. L. Sainéan, *Langage Parisien,* p. 350.

HALER, *vb. tr.* To pull. A nautical Acadian term instead of *tirer,* which is less usual; common in South Louisiana and Canada.

HARICOTS DE RAME, *m. pl.* Pole beans.

HARICOTS NAINS, *m. pl.* Bush beans of various kinds.

HERBE À COQUIN, *f.* Cockle-Bur (*Xanthium americanum* Walt.); literally "rogue-plant."

HERBE À LA PUCE, *f.* Poison, Climbing, or Three-leaved Ivy (*Toxicodendron radicans* L.). In Canada the same term is used for Poison Oak (*Rhus Toxicodendron* L.).

Some French natives of Louisiana apply this name to the Trumpet-Flower, which is also called Trumpet-Creeper, Cow-Itch, or Fox-Glove (*Tecoma radicans* Juss.). This vine grows in moist woods and thickets.[137]

HERBE À SERPENT, *f.* Probably Indian or False Mallow (*Sida spinosa* L.).

HERBE À TROIS QUARTS, *f.* Small White or Virginia Crown-Beard (*Verbesina virginica* L.). This plant or flower has a three-winged stem, and three to four oval white rays. It is found in dry open woods from Florida northward.

HÉRON DOS-BLANC, *m.* Louisiana Heron. Cf. *aigrette câille, supra.*

HÊTRE, *m.* Beech (*Fagus grandifolia* Ehrh.). I have never heard *fouteau,* a dialectal French name for this tree.

HEURE, *f.* *À belle heure,* "late," "after the appointed time." Dial.— Sw.; Can.-Fr.

HIBOU À CORNES, *m.* Great Horned Owl (*Bubo virginianus virginianus* Gmel.), distinguished by its ear tufts from other large owls. It is the most destructive owl in Louisiana.

In Savoie, France, the Great Horned Owl (*Strix bubo* L.), is called *le grande duc à cornes* (Roll.—*Faune,* II, 53).

HIBOU GROSSE TÊTE, *m.* The Florida Barred Owl (*Strix varia alleni* Ridgw.), as well as the Barred Owl (*Strix varia varia* Barton). The "hoot owls," as these species are called, are abundant in the State; but the barred owl comes to Louisiana during the winter only.

French *hibou* probably arose in imitation of the cry of the owl. The Norman and Picard dialects have *hou-hou.*

---

[137] Rafinesque, *Flora,* p. 49; Robin, III, 406.

HIBOU PAILLE, *m.* Barn Owl (*Aluco pratincola* Bonap.); known also as the Church Owl, Grass Owl, Monkey-faced Owl, and Straw Owl.

HONTE, *f.* *Avoir honte,* "to be fearful, afraid, faint-hearted, embarrassed." Dialect of Loreauville, Iberia Parish; Can.-Fr.

HONTEUX, EUSE, *adj.* Timid, diffident, embarrassed. Dial.—Sw.; Can.-Fr.

HURLEUR, *m.* See *grand plongeon, supra.*

ÎLET, *m.* A city square; a square of ground. The squares in the city of New Orleans were formerly surrounded by drainage ditches, which became filled with water and created "little islands." *Îlet* is still used in this sense by the Creoles of New Orleans.

INCOMPRENABLE, *adj.* Incomprehensible. Dial.—Sw.; Can.-Fr.

INGÉNIEUR, *m.* Engine driver; one who runs a locomotive or steamboat engine, or manages a stationary engine. Dial.—Sw.; Can.-Fr. St.-Fr. *mécanicien* has this sense.

JABOT, *m.* 1. An old-fashioned necktie with ruffles, such as was worn in colonial times. 2. A shirt front. 3. A fowl's wattles.

JARDINAGES, *m. pl.* Collection of vegetables in a garden. Dial.—Sw.; Can.-Fr.

JEAN CHARLOT, *m.* Least Bittern. Cf. *cap-cap doré, supra.*

JONC AU BARIL, *m.* Cattail (plant). See *queue de rat, infra.*

JONC PLAT, *m.* Cattail (plant). See *queue de rat, infra.*

JONGLER, *vb. intr.* To dream; to indulge in reveries; to think seriously. The same usage of *jongler* is found in Canadian-French.

JORÉE, *f.* See *grassel, supra.*

JORITTE, *f.* See *grassel, supra.*

JOUR, *m.* *Sur le haut du jour,* "very early." Dial.—Sw.; Can.-Fr.; sixteenth-century French. Standard French has *de grand matin* in the same sense.

JUSQU' À TANT QUE, *conj.* Until. Dial.—Sw.; Can.-Fr.; Anjou, Norm., Saintonge, etc. Equivalent in meaning to St.-Fr. *jusqu' à ce que.*

KORUSSE, *m.* Rooster. The word represents an effort to imitate the crowing of the rooster. Cf. Middle French *corasse* or *coresse*, "tree-frog," and French *croasser*, "to caw."[138] Dial.—Lafayette, La., Pointe Coupée, and Bayou Lafourche region.

LA GRANDE QUEUE, *f.* See *coucou, supra.*

LA LONGUE QUEUE, *f.* See *coucou, supra.*

LABOUREUX, *m.* *Laborer.* Dial.—Sw.; Can.Fr.; Angevin, Norm., etc. From St.-Fr. *laboureur.*

LAISSER, *vb. tr.* Leave. Dial.—Sw.; Can.-Fr. St.-Fr. *quitter* has the same meaning.

+

LAURIER AMANDE, *m.*, or LAURIER 'MANDE, *m.* Cherry Laurel (*Prunus caroliniana* Ait.). *'Mande* is an aphetic form of Fr. *amande*, "milk of almonds." The leaves of this tree have the flavor of almonds.

LAURIER DOUX, *m.* Sweet Bay (*Magnolia glauca* L.; *Magnolia virginiana australis* Sarg.). This tree is also called *le magnolia.*

LAURIER ROSE, *m.* See *myrte rose, infra.*

LE GROS MAGNOLIA, *m.* See *magnolia, infra.*

LES YEUX CLAIRS, *m. pl.* Least Bittern. Cf. *cap-cap doré, supra.*

LÈVE-QUEUE, *m.* Wiggletail, the larva of a mosquito (family *Culicidae*). Compare *tourne-queue, infra.* Dial.—French Settlement, Livingston Parish.

LIANE DE MIRLITON, *f.* Cf. *mirliton, infra.*

LIANE NOIRE, *f.* Trelease, Supple-Jack, or Rattan-Vine (*Berchemia scandens* Hill.)

LIARD, *m.* Southern Cottonwood (*Populus deltoides virginiana* Sudw.), of which the Indians sometimes made their dugouts[139] Some of the Acadians give the name *liard* to the sycamore; cf. *cotonnier, supra.*

Liard, found in the dialects of Anjou and Maine as the name of the poplar, is probably related to old French *liart*, "gray," which Gamillscheg thinks may be in turn a loan from Middle Irish *liath*, "gray."[140]

LICHER, *vb. tr.* Lick, lick up. Dial.—Sw.; Can.-Fr.; Anjou, Berry, Picardy, Saintonge, etc.

---

[138] H. Schuchardt, in *ZRPh.*, XXVII, 613.
[139] Cf. Du Pratz, II, 43; *Le Champ d'Asile*, p. 67; Robin, III, 521.
[140] *Wörterbuch*, pp. 558-559.

LILAS, *m.* The China-Berry or China-Ball Tree (*Melia azedarach* L.), and a variety called the *Umbrella China* (*Melia azedarach umbraculifera* Sarg.). The word was probably brought to Louisiana from Haiti, where it has the same signification as in Louisiana. The tree owes its name to the fact that its flowers resemble the blossoms of the lilac. This umbrella china is also called *Lilas Parasol.*[141]

LOTRET. See *roitelet, infra.*

MACREUSE, *f.* Pied-billed Grebe (*Podilymbus podiceps* L.). The Norman *macroule,* in the sense of *poule d'eau,* "water hen," was borrowed from Dutch *meerkol,* and at the same time was modified by analogy perhaps of French *maigre,* "any food except meat." The ending of *macroule* was so unfamiliar that it was displaced by *-euse* in *macreuse,* dialectal *macrouse.* In the parish of Pointe Coupée *macreuse* is the regular word not for the poule d'eau—the coot (*Fulica americana* Gmel.)—but for the pied-billed grebe, or as it is commonly known in America, the *didapper.* Instead of *didapper* the form *didipper* is generally used in Louisiana.[142] Compare *plongeur, infra.*

MADEMOISELLE, *f.* Yellowtail, a salt-water fish (*Bairdiella chrysura Lacépède*).

MAGNOLIA, *m.* Magnolia (*Magnolia grandiflora* L.), also called *le gros magnolia. Cf. rameau, infra.*

MALCHANCE, *f.* Misfortune; equivalent in meaning to St.-Fr. *malheur.* Dial.—Iberia Parish; Can-Fr.

MALCHANCEUX, -EUSE, *adj.* One who is a victim of bad luck, who is continually unfortunate. Dial.—Iberia Parish; Can.-Fr.

MAMOU, *m.* Coral Tree; a shrub known to botanists as *Erythrina herbacea* (L.); found at Mamou, Evangeline Parish, and in the vicinity of that village. Mamou tea—*thé de Mamou*—is made of the leaves, the roots, or the seeds of this shrub and is given to persons ill of pneumonia. The seeds, which are coral-red, are worn as necklaces by little girls. A seed is called *graine de Mamou.* (Information given by Miss Ann Spotswood Buchanan).

---

[141] Cf. *Identification du Plantes d' Haiti par Leurs Noms Créoles,* Bul. XVIII (Avril, 1930), 17.

[142] For further details of the history of *macreuse,* see Gamillscheg, *Wörterbuch,* p. 578.

Mamou is a corruption of St.-Fr. *Mammouth*, "Mammoth." Bones of the mammoth have been discovered in Lower Louisiana.

MAMSELLE, *f*. The popular name of a dragon fly (*order Odonata*), an insect generally known in Louisiana-English as the "mosquito hawk."[143]

In cultivated speech Standard-French *demoiselle* is preferred. Cf. *mastoc, infra*.

MANGEUR MOQUEUR, *m*. See *moqueur d'hiver, infra*.

MANGEUR POULETS, *m*. Sparrow Hawk. Cf. *émerillon, supra*.

MAQUERILLOT, *m*. Yellow Mackerel (*Caranx crysos* Mitchill). *Maquerillot* is of course a diminutive formation from *maquereau*, "mackerel."

MAQUILLON, *m*. Clothes-pin. Corrupted from French *maquignon*, "horse-dealer," and widely used. *Maquillon* is both Norman and Canadian-French. With the pronunciation of *maquillon* one should compare *tiyon* for *tignon*, the name of a handkerchief still worn sometimes by colored women about their heads. *Épingle à linge* is also used for "clothes-pin."

MARIER, *vb. tr*. Marry. *Il a marié une fille pauvre*, "He has married a poor girl." For the meaning, cf. St.-Fr. *épouser*. Dial.—Sw.; Can.-Fr.

MARIONETTE, *f*. The Buffle-Head (*Charitonetta albeola* L.), a name conferred on this duck because of its small size. The head of the male looks large because of its thick, soft plumage; hence the English name *buffle-head*. It is also called *butterball* in English. This sea duck comes to the State in the winter.

MARTINET, *m*. Purple Martin (*Progne subis subis* L.). Other names for this bird are *oiseau de pluie*, "rainbird," and *martinet maison*, "house martin." *Oiseau de pluie* also designates the barn swallow.

MARTINET À VENTRE BRONZÉ, *m*. Barn Swallow (*Hirundo erythrogastra* Bodd.), cf. *martinet, supra*.

MARTINET MAISON, *m*. *martinet, supra*.

MARTIN PÊCHEUR, *m*., or MARTIN PLONGEUR. Belted Kingfisher (*Ceryle alcyon* L.).

MASSICOT, *m*. Ragweed (*Ambrosia artemisiaefolia* L.)

---

[143] Cf. Rolland, *Faune*, XIII, 79.

MASTOC, *m.* A large dragon fly (order *Odonata*). This word is used at French Settlement, Livingston Parish. *Mastoc* is Standard French for a stocky man. Cf. *mamselle, supra.*

MÊLÉE CRÉOLE, *f.* Fish chowder.

MELON FRANÇAIS, *m.* Cantaloupe or Rockmelon (*Cucumis melo* var. *cantalupensis* Naud.)) The true cantaloupe generally has a hard, scaly rind and deep ribs. Some well-known varieties are the Hackensack, nutmeg, Carmes, and long yellow.

MELON MUSQUÉ, *m.* Netted Melon or Muskmelon (*Cucumis melo var. reticulatus* Naud.). The muskmelon has a netted rind, shallow ribs, and flesh of a salmon or slightly greenish color. The rind is often nearly smooth. Here belongs the variety known as the Pineapple Melon (*Cucumis melo* var. *saccharinus* Naud.), which is oblong and remarkable for its sweet, tender flesh. The famous Rocky Ford cantaloupes are muskmelons (var. *reticulatus*).[144]

Meuille, *f.* Mullet (*Mugil cephalus* L.). Standard French has *mulet* as the name of this fish.

MICMAC, *m.* Foul play, intrigue. *Il y a du micmac dans cette affaire,* "There's some underhand work in this business." Dial.—Sw.; Can.-Fr.; popular speech of France. *Micmac* is a derivative of Low German *muitmaken,* "to collect booty." *REW* 5721.

MIETTE, *f.* *Pas une miette,* "Not at all," equivalent in meaning to St.-Fr. *pas du tout.* Dial.—Sw.; Can.-Fr.; Norm.-Pic., and many other dialects. St.-Fr. *miette*=bit, morsel, particle.

MINOU, *m.* A cat; a kitten. Dial.—Sw.; Can.-Fr. Cf. St.-Fr. *minet,* "kitten."

MIRLITON, *m.* Vegetable pear, the fruit of a West-Indian vine (*Sechium edule* Sw.). The plant itself is called *pied de mirliton, m.;* but if considered primarily a vine, it is *liane de mirliton, f.* St.-Fr. *mirliton* seems to have been an old refrain (*Dictionnaire Général.*)

Mirliton is the name of the vegetable pear in *Haitian-French.* In Spain, where it is also cultivated, it goes by the name of *chayote,* a derivative of Mexican *chaiotl.*

MOLÈNE, *f.* Great Mullein; Velvet or Mullein Dock (*Verbascum thapsus* L.).

---

[144] See W. W. Robbins, *The Botany of Crop Plants,* p. 618.

MOQUEUR, *m.* The Mocking Bird (*Minus polyglottos polyglottos* L.), the most famous songbird in Louisiana—called also *le grand moqueur, supra.*

MOQUEUR DE BOIS, *m.* See *oiseau de cannes, infra.*

MOQUEUR DE CANNES, *m.* See *oiseau de cannes, infra.*

MOQUEUR DE FRANCE, *m. moqueur d'hiver.*

MOQUEUR D'HIVER, *m.* Loggerhead Shrike or Butcher Bird (*Lanius ludovicianus ludovicianus* L.). It is also called *moqueur muet, moqueur sauvage, and mangeur moqueur*; in Pointe Coupée, *moqueur de France.*

MOQUEUR MUET, *m.* See *moqueur d'hiver, supra.*

MOQUEUR ROUGE, *m.*, See *oiseau de cannes, infra.*

MOQUEUR SAUVAGE, *m.* See *moqueur d'hiver, supra.*

MOUCHE À FEU, *f.* Firefly; a luminous beetle of the subfamily *Lampyrinae.* The same term is found in the French dialects of Canada and Santo Domingo.

MOUILLASSER, *vb. intr.* To rain a little. *Ça mouillasse,* "a light rain is falling"; diminutive of *mouiller,* "to rain," a substitute for St.-Fr. *pleuvoir;* found in Canadian-French, Aunis, and Saintonge.

MOUILLER, *vb. impers.* Rain. This is decidedly Acadian for *pleuvoir;* the verb is common in Canadian-French and the French dialects of Anjou, Aunis, Lyon, Poitou, and Saintonge.[145]

+

MÛRE, *f.* Blackberry, fruit of *Rubus cuneifolius* (Pursh.).

MÛRE D'ARBRE, *f.* Fruit of the Red Mulberry Tree (*Morus rubra* L.).

MÛRE TRAÎNANTE. Dewberry fruit and plant (*Rubus trivialis* Michx.).

MÛRIER. 1. Mulberry Tree (*Morus rubra* L.); 2. Cedar bird, cf. *cirier, supra.*

Some of the Southern Indians made cloth of mulberry bark. "I was surprised," says Tonti, in his description of the Tensas, "to find their cabins made of mud and covered with cane mats. The cabin of the chief was 40 feet square, the wall 10 feet high, a foot thick, and the roof, which was of a dome shape, about 15 feet high. I was not less surprised when, on entering, I saw the chief seated on a camp bed, with three of his wives at his side, surrounded by more than 60 old men, clothed in large white cloaks, which are made by the women

---

[145] *Glossaire du Parler Français au Canada,* p. 466.

out of the bark of the mulberry tree and are tolerably well worked. The women were clothed in the same manner."[146]

MYRTE ROSE, *m.* Crape Myrtle (*Lagerstroemia indica* L.), a large shrub or small tree with flowers pink or rose-colored—sometimes white, lavender, or purple. A native of the East Indies, this beautiful tree is extensively cultivated in Louisiana. Other names that I have heard for the crape myrtle are *laurier rose, m.*, and *myrtier, m.* The latter is obviously formed by analogy of other tree-names ending in *-ier*. Cf. *gastronia, infra.*

NANANE, *m.* Candy, bonbon; corrupted from St.-Fr. *nanan;* used both in the singular—*du nanane*—and in the plural—*des nananes.* Dial.—Sw.; Can.-Fr.

NÈGRE, *m.* 1. Negro. 2. The negro-French patois of Louisiana.

NIC, *m.* Nest. Dial.—Pointe Coupée and the Southwest; Can.-Fr.; found in Old French and many dialects, including those of Normandy, Bretagne, Aunis, and Saintonge.

St.-Fr. *nid* is also used everywhere in Louisiana-French.

NIOQUE, *m.* Nest-egg. Dial.—Pointe Coupée, Lafayette Parish, and Breaux Bridge. *Nioque* is apparently a dialectal variant corresponding to Burgundian and Canadian-French *nioche,* "foolish." For the remarkable change of meaning, compare OF *niais,* "foolish" as a bird that is taken from its nest, and secondly, "nest-egg."[147]

Provençal has *ni(z)aic,* "silly," "taken in the nest."[148]

NOYER, *m.* See *pacanier, infra.*

NUIT, *f.* *À la nuit,* "at nightfall." Dial.—Sw.; Can.-Fr.; French-Swiss.

OIE AIGLE, *f.* "Eagle Goose"; the Blue Goose (*Chen caerulensis* L.); in English called also *Blue Brant, Skillet Head,* and *Eagle-headed Brant.*

---

[146] French, *Hist. Coll.* (1846), p. 61.
[147] De Sainte-Palaye, *Dictionnaire Historique de L'Ancien Language François,* VIII, 27.
[148] Diez, p. 222; *REW* 5909.

OIE CÂILLE, *f.* White-fronted Goose (*Anser albifrons gambali* Hartl.), called also *l'oie nonnette*, "the young nun goose." Other English names of this wild goose are *Speckle-Belly, Pied Brant*, and *Gray Brant*. See *câille, supra.*

OIE CANADIENNE, *f.* Canada Goose (*Branta canadensis canadensis* L.); also known as *l'outarde*, "the bustard," or *la barnache*, "the barnacle" goose; in English as *French Goose, Honker*, or *Ring-Neck.*

The name *barnache* was originally bestowed on the Brant Goose (*Branta bernicla* L.), a species of wild goose which was popularly thought to be born of certain marine shellfish called *barnacles.*[149]

OIE NONNETTE, *f.* White-fronted Goose, cf. *oie câille, supra.*

OISEAU BLEU, *m.* The Bluebird (*Sialia sialis sialis* L.), or *oiseau bleu* as it is known in Louisiana-French, spends the summer in Louisiana. Another name for this bird is *grive bâtarde*, "bastard robin."

OISEAU DE CANNES, *m.* Brown Thrasher (*Toxostoma rufum* L.). A popular term in Pointe Coupée. Other names for this bird are *moqueur de bois, moqueur de cannes, moqueur rouge*, and *caille de bois.*

OISEAU DE FLEURS, *m.* Ruby-Throated Humming Bird (*Archilocus colubris* L.). Dialect of Pointe Coupée. Cf. *colibri* and *oiseau-mouche, infra.*

OISEAU DE PLUIE, m. 1. Barn Swallow (*Hirundo erythrogastra* Bodd.). 2. The Purple Martin, cf. *martinet, supra.*

OISEAU-MOUCHE, *m.* Humming bird. This name was given to the humming bird partly because of its small size and partly because of the buzzing sound made by its wings.[150] The ruby-throated humming bird alone is seen in Louisiana.[151] *Oiseau-mouche* is also Standard French.

Colibri, another name for the humming bird, is said to have found its way into Continental French from the Carib Indian *colibri*. This name is also used in Louisiana. But cf. *colibri*,[152] *infra.*

---

[149] For details of the etymology of French *Barnache*, see Gamillscheg, *Wörterbuch*, p. 83.
[150] Thus Charlevoix, III, 157. Cf. Joutel (Jan., 1686), in Margry, III, 215.
[151] Cf. Charlevoix, I, 29.
[152] Cf. Charlevoix, III, 157.

OISEAU PAPILLON, *m.* "Butterfly bird" is the Scissor-tailed Flycatcher (*Mulvilus forficatus* Gmel.).

OLIVIER, *m.* The Large Tupelo, also called Cotton or Tupelo Gum (*Nyssa aquatica* L.). This large tree, which grows in the water of cypress swamps, bears an oval fruit, dark-blue when ripe, about an inch long, and not unlike an olive. This fruit is responsible for the La.-Fr. *olivier,* a name which in France signifies the olive tree.[153] Dial.—Livingston Parish. The fruit is called *la boule d'olivier.*

In Evangeline Parish, and doubtless other parts of Southwest Louisiana, *olivier* is the name of the Chinese Tallow Tree (*Sapium sebiferum* Roxb.). Its seeds are covered with a greasy white substance, from which candles are made; its leaves yield a black dye.

OLIVIER DE LA CHINE, *m.* Fragrant, Sweet, or Sweet-scented Olive (*Osmanthus fragrans* Lour.), an ornamental shrub, with small white flowers, imported from China and Japan.

ORME GRAS, *m.* Slippery Elm (*Ulmus fulva* Michx.).[154]

ORTOLAN, *m.* Bobolink. By *ortolan* Charlevoix designates a bird the beauty of whose song he compares to that of the French nightingale.[155] This is evidently the Bobolink (*Dolichonyz oryzivorus* L.), or Reed-Bird, which is called *ortolan* by the French and rice-bird by other natives of Louisiana.[156] In Canadian-French *ortolan* is the name of the Meadow-Lark (*Sturnella magna magna* L.).

OUSQUE, *adv.* Where. Ex.: *Ousque vous allez maintenant?* "Where are you going now?" Contracted from *où est-ce que.* Dial.—So.; Can-Fr.

OUTARDE, *f.* See *oie canadienne, supra.*

OUTI, *m.* Tool, implement; for St.-Fr. *outil.* Dial.—So.; Can.-Fr.

PAILLE CHAT TIGRE, *f.* Roemer's Rush (*Juncus roemerianus* Scheele). A species of rush that grows in brackish marshes and furnishes food and building material for the muskrat. The French term signifies literally "puma straw." Cf. *Chat tigre, supra.*

---

[153] Cf. Du Pratz, *Histoire,* II, 24; and Charlevoix, "Plantes de l'Amerique," in *Histoire,* II, 24.

[154] Cf. Robin, III, 521.

[155] *Histoire,* III, (1721), 156-157; cf. Du Pratz, *Histoire,* II, 128-129.

[156] Cf. Audubon, *Birds,* III, 96.

PAILLE-EN-QUEUE, *m.* Pintail Duck. (*Dafila acuta* L.), known locally in the United States as *Sprig* or *Sprigtail.* In the male of this species the two central tail feathers are very long. This duck winters in Louisiana.

In France *paille-en-queue, literally* "straw in its tail," is the name that is given to a tropic bird (family *Phaëthontidae*).

PAILLE JAUNE, *f.* Switch-grass, cf. *caniche, supra.*

PAIN PERDU, *m.* Lost bread or egg toast. Dial.—New Orleans and the Southwest.

PAIN TRESSE, *m.* Twist-loaf. See *The Picayune Creole Cook Book,* p. 344.

PALANQUE *f.* Trot-line. Cf. *drague, supra.* St.-Fr. *palanque* signifies "a stockade," "a blind." Dialect of Livingston Parish.

PAPABOT(T)E, *m.* Upland Plover or Bartramian Sandpiper (*Bartramia longicauda* Bechst.). The name is imitative of the cries of the bird. As a table bird the upland plover is much prized; it was formerly served in the New Orleans restaurants, appearing on the menu as *Papabotte à la Créole* (*Français-Créole*), *Papabotte Grillé,* "broiled papabotte," and *Papabotte Rôti,* "roast papabotte."

In France it is the Hoopoe (*Upupa Epops* L.), whose cries have caused it to receive a large number of dialectal names resembling La.-Fr. *papabot*(*t*)*e*—for instance, *puputt, bouboutt, poupote,* and *boubotte.*[157]

PAPE, *m.* Painted Bunting. The early French settlers of Louisiana gave the name *Pape,* "Pope," to the smaller species of thick-billed birds—the finches, buntings, and orioles—making an exception of the rice-bird alone, which they called *ortolan.*[158] *Pape,* generally used by itself, but sometimes followed by the adjective *rouge, doux, doré,* or *vert,* has become the common word in Louisiana for the Nonpareil or Painted Bunting (*Passerina ciris* L.), which with his blue crown, red underparts, and greenish back, is reputed to be the most gaudily-colored bird in the United States. The reason for the bestowal of the name *pape* is not clear. Du Pratz suggests that the painted bunting was honored with this name because of its sweet, rare voice or remarkably brilliant plumage, or because of the fact that the State

---

[157] Rolland, *Faune,* II, 99-100.

[158] Audubon, *Birds,* III, 96.

already had two birds with ecclesiastical titles, the one called *évêque*, "bishop," (Indigo Bunting) and the other *cardinal*.[159] Before the passage of the conservation laws thousands of *papes* were trapped alive every spring, to be sold as cage-birds in the markets of New Orleans.[160]

PAPE DE BOIS, *m.* See *'tit pape, infra.*

PAPE CHOC, *m.* See *choc, infra.*

PARÉ, -ÉE, *adj.* Ready, prepared; Standard French uses *prêt, -e.* Dial.—So.; Can.-Fr.; Brittany, Norm.-Pic.

PAREIL, -EILLE, *adj.* Like. *Pareil comme* = St.-Fr. *pareil à* "like," *autant que,* "as much as," *tout comme,* "quite as." Dial.—Sw.; Can.-Fr.; Anjou, Berry, Nivernais.

PATEGAU, *m.* *Pategau* is the designation of a wooden target about a foot long, constructed in the shape of a bird, at which one fires with a rifle in an effort to win a prize. This prize is a portion of a beef or a sum of money. A hit in the body of the bird wins for the marksman the head, skin, and entrails of the beef; in the head, a front quarter; in the tail, the other front quarter, and in each wing, a hind quarter. *Tirer au pategau* is the French for "to fire at the *pategau.*"

Pategau, which is used in the parish of Pointe Coupée, owes its *t* to popular substitution of Fr. *patte,* "paw," "foot" (of a bird), for *pape.* Cf. Fr. *patte-d' oie,* "goosefoot." See *papegai and papegau, supra.*

PATTE JAUNE, *f.* See *clou-clou, supra.*

PENDRIOCHE, *f.* Ear-drop, pendant; often used in the plural *pendrioches.* Dial.—Sw.; Can.-Fr.; Orléanais. Standard French has *pendeloque* and *pendeloques* (pl).

PERDREAU, *m.;* PERDRIX, *f.* The French of Louisiana give the names *perdrix* and *perdreau* to the popular game-bird known in the Northeastern and Central States as the *quail,* in the South as the *partridge,* designating the old birds by the form *perdrix* singular and plural, and the young birds by the diminutive *perdreau,* with the plural *perdreaux.* A similar distinction is observed in France between *perdrix,* "partridge," and *perdreau,* "young partridge," though the European partridge is a different bird from the American quail or Bob-White (*Colinus virginianus virginianus* L.).

---

[159] *Histoire,* II, 139; cf. Bossu-Forster, I, 371.
[160] Audubon, *Birds,* III, 94.

Among the Creole recipes for preparing the quail a few may be mentioned here, such as *Perdrix Sautées à la Chasseur,* "Quail, hunter's style," *Suprêmes de Perdreaux, Sauce Périgueux,* "Breasts of quail, truffle sauce," and *Perdreaux aux Bigarades,* "Quail with sour orange sauce."[161]

In the last-named recipe the word *bigarades,* "bitter oranges," is a derivative of Modern Provençal *bigarrado,* a participal noun from Modern Provençal *bigarra,* "to checker, to streak"; cf. French *bigarrer* in a similar sense.[162] In the second recipt *Périgueux* is the name of a city situated in a part of France which has long been famous for its truffles.

PERDRIX, *f.* See *perdreau, supra.*

PÉRIQUE, *m.* A unique kind of tobacco grown only in the parish of St. James. *Périque* is said to have been the popular pseudonym of Pierre Chenet, an Acadian who first produced this variety of tobacco.

PETIT POURPIER, *m.* Milk Purslane; Spotted or Blotched Spurge; Milkweed (*Chamaesyce maculata* L.—Small).

PETITES PÂQUES, *f. pl.* Palm-Sunday. Here Standard French has *pâques fleuries.*

PIAILLARD, *m.* "Squaller," a designation of the Killdeer, a bird usually called *killdee* in English (*Oxyechus vociferus vociferus* L.). Other names for this bird are *cou collier, m.,* "ringneck," *pluvier doré, m.,* "golden plover," and *pivier, m. Pivier,* which is extremely common, seems to be a hybrid formation from *pluvier* and *piaillard,* or what is more plausible, a dialectal form of *pluvier;* cf. A. Dauzat, *Les Patois,* p. 41. *Pluvier doré* is generally applied to the golden plover (*Charadrius dominicus dominicus* Müll).[163]

PICOTE, *f.* Smallpox; in Standard-French, *petite vérole.* Dial.—Iberia Parish; Can.-Fr. For the etymology, see Gamillscheg, *Wb.,* under *pic.*

PIED DE MIRLITON, *m.* See *mirliton, supra.*

PIÈGEUR, *m.* Trapper; formed from *piège,* "trap." St.-Fr. *trappe* and *trappeur* are also used in Louisiana-French.

---

[161] For other recipes one may consult the *Picayune Creole Cook Book,*[*] pp. 129 ff.

[162] See Gamillscheg for further details, under *bigarade.*

[163] See Arthur, *Birds,* p. 41.

PIGEON DE MER, *m.* Cabot's Tern (*Sterna sandivencis acuflavida* Cabot). The same name, which signifies "sea pigeon," is given to Forster's Tern (*Sterna forsteri* Nutt.). But the latter is also called *queue à ciseaux*, "forked tail," or "scissors tail," on account of the deep cleft in its tail feathers. In English the *queue à ciseaux* is known as the *high diver* or the *sea swallow*. Cf. *pluvier doré, infra.*

PIGEON RAMIER, *m.* The Wild or Passenger Pigeon (*Ectopistes migratorius* L.). It is now extinct, but was formerly encountered in vast numbers in the United States.[164] As late as 1850 flocks of these birds were still coming to Louisiana during the winter.[165]

PILE, *f.* A mortar hollowed out of a section of a black gum or cypress log, nearly three feet long. In this kind of mortar the Acadians, like the Indians, pounded corn with a pestle (*pilon*) for the purpose of making hominy.[166]

St.-Fr. *pile*, "a stone trough," is a loan from Provençal *pila*, which has come from Latin *pīla*, "mortar." French *ramier* is literally a "branch-dweller."

PIMENT DOUX, *m.* Several types of mild pepper—Sweet Spanish, Bell, and Ruby King (*Capsicum annuum grossum* Sendt.).

PIMENT ENRAGÉ, *m.* Several types of Red or Cayenne Pepper (*capsicum annuum cerasiforme* Miller)—(1) Little Gem, Creole, or Bird's eye; (2) Cherry; and (3) Oxheart (*Capsicum cordiforme* Miller). The terms *Cherry* and *Oxheart* are often used as synonyms.[167]

PIMENT FORT or PIMENT ROUGE, *m.* Red pepper—Chili or Long Cayenne (*Capsicum annuum acuminatum* Fingerh.).

PINIÈRE, *f.* Pine forest.

PIQUANT AMOURETTE, *m.* Honey or Sweet Locust; Three-Thorned Acacia; Black or Thorn Locust (*Gleditsia triacanthos* L.). This tree is aptly described by the term "Thorn of transient love." But *piquant amourette* is

---

[164] Cf. Lahontan, II, 47; William Bartram, *Travels* (1792), p. 467.

[165] *De Bow's Review*, XI (1851), 54.

[166] Cf. John R. Swanton, *Indian Tribes of the Lower Mississippi Valley . . . Bureau of American Ethnology*, Bul. 43, p. 67, and plate 21, preceding p. 347; David I. Bushnell, Jr., *The Choctaw of Bayou Lacomb, Bureau of American Ethnology*, Bul. 48, plate 8.

[167] See H. C. Irish, *A Revision of the Genus Capsicum with Especial Reference to Garden Varieties*, pp. 93, 94, 96.

sometimes pronounced and interpreted as if it were *piquant mort raide,* "a thorn that causes tetanus or 'rigid death.'" By some Acadians and Creoles the name *garaufied* or *garaupied* is given to this species of locust. Cf. *garaufied, supra.*

PIQUE-BOIS, *m.* Woodpecker (family *Picidae*). Charlevoix, writing in April, 1721, mentions the great beauty of birds that he calls *Picverts* or *Picque-bois.*[168] The local name for a woodpecker is now almost always *pique-bois,* though the alternative French term *le picvert* or *pivert* must formerly have been common, as witness the form *picvers,* which was used by André Le Blanc in 1850.[169]

Specific names are given to certain kinds of woodpeckers. Thus the Red-headed Woodpecker (*Melanerpes erythrocephalus* L.) is *Le Pique-bois à Tête Rouge;* the large Ivory-billed Woodpecker (*Campephilus principalis* L.), which is not yet extinct in Louisiana, is either *Le Grand Pique-bois* or *La Poule de Bois,* "the wood hen."

Pique-bois is composed of the imperative of *piquer,* "to pierce," "to stick," and the object-noun *bois,* "wood"; whereas *picvert* or *pivert* is French *pic,* "woodpecker" —a derivative of Latin *picus,* "woodpecker"—modified by the French adjective *vert,* "green."

PIQUE-BOIS DORÉ, *m.* "Golden Woodpecker." This is the name of the two species of Yellow-Hammer, or Flicker (*Colaptes auratus auratus* L.), and Northern Flicker (*Colaptes auratus luteus* Bangs). *Le Pique-bois Jaune,* "the yellow woodpecker," is another name for this bird.[170]

PIRE, *adv. Tant pire* = St.-Fr. *tant pis,* "so much the worse." Dial.-So.; Can.-Fr.; Angevin, Norm.-Pic., French-Swiss.

PIS, *adv.* Then; corrupted from St.-Fr. *puis.* Dial.—So.; Can.-Fr.; Norm.-Pic., etc.

PISTACHE, *f.* Peanut, the fruit or seed of the vine *Arachis hypogaea* (L.), widely cultivated in the Southern States. Note *des pistaches salées,* "salted peanuts," *des pistaches pralinées,* "sugared peanuts," *des pistaches à la crème,* "cream peanuts." In Haitian-French St.-Fr. *pistache* "pistachio," has the signification of "peanut vine."

---

[168] *Histoire,* III, 156.
[169] Cf. *De Bow's Review,* IX (1850), 289.
[170] Audubon, *Birds,* IV, 282.

PITE, *m.* Spanish Bayonet or Dagger, a plant (*Yucca aloifolia* L.), of the Southern States, with sharp-pointed leaves and a cluster of white flowers on a tall stalk. Cf. St.-Fr. *pite, m.,* "aloe-fibre," etc. In Haiti *pite* is the French name of the *Agave rigida* L., variant *Sisalana,* Engelm. From Span. *pita,* "century plant."

PIVELÉ, -ÉE, *adj.* Speckled, spotted. Cf. *un mulet pivelé,* "a spotted mule," *une caille pivelée,* "a wood thrush (*Hylocichla mustelina* Gmel.). The skin (*peau*) of a child who has measles is said to be *pivelée. Pivelé,* which is found in Canadian-French, is related to French *piolé, piaulé,* "black and white like a magpie" (Fr. *pie*), just as *grivelé,* "speckled," is related to thirteenth-century *griolé, "speckled,"* a derivative of *grive,* "thrush."[171]

PIVIER, *m.* Cf. *piaillard.*

PLIE, *f.* The name given by the fishermen of Lower Louisiana to the Southern Flounder (*Paralichthys lethostigmus* Jordan & Gilbert), which is found in the Atlantic from Charleston southward as well as in the Gulf of Mexico; and to the Gulf Flounder (*Paralichthys albiguttus* Jordan & Gilbert), which frequents the waters of the South Atlantic and Gulf coasts.

PLONGEUR, *m. Les Plongeons,* "the divers," disappear so quickly, under the water, on seeing the flash of the flintlock, that the bullet cannot strike them; consequently they are called *Mangeurs de plomb,* "lead eaters," says Du Pratz.[172] The name *plongeur,* "diver," is applied to several species of diving birds—the Horned *Grebe* (*Colymbus auritus* L.), the Pied-billed Grebe (*Podilymbus podiceps* L.), and a duck known as the American goldeneye (*Clangula clangula americana* Bonap.). The pied-billed grebe, generally known in English as a *didapper,* or *hell-diver,* goes in Louisiana-French by the specific name of *sac à plomb,* "bag of lead," because it can dive as swiftly as a bag of lead can sink.[173] Other La.-Fr. terms for this bird are *macreuse, supra,* and *culotte,* "breeches."

PLUVIER DORÉ, *m.* The Golden Plover (*Charadrius dominicus dominicus* L.). It frequents the coast of Louisiana during the fall and spring, and many of this species spend the winter in the State. Other names are *gros yeux,* "Big Eyes," and *pigeon de mer, "sea pigeon."*

---

[171] Cf. Rolland, *Faune,* II, 133, 134.

[172] *Histoire,* II, 115.

[173] Arthur, *The Birds of Louisiana,* p. 13.

Bossu mentions the *Pluviers dorés.*[174]

The name *pluvier doré* is less aptly given to the killdeer. Cf. *cou collier, piaillard, pivier, supra.*

POISON, *f.* Poison. St.-Fr. *poison* is masculine. Dial.—Sw.; Can.-Fr., and many French dialects, including the Norman, Picard, and Saintonge.

POISSON ARMÉ, *m.* "Armed fish." This is the appropriate name for those species of gar that infest the waters of Louisiana. The gar has long, narrow jaws full of sharp teeth, and its body is protected by hard rhombic scales. It is highly destructive of other kinds of fish, and its flesh is rank and tough. The Alligator Gar (*Lepisosteus tristoechus* Bloch and Schneider) attains a length of eight to ten feet. Two other fresh-water species are the Long-nosed Gar (*Lepisosteus osseus* L.), and the Short-nosed Gar (*Lepisosteus platystomus* Raf.).

The Choctaw Indians knew the gar as the "strong fish"—*náni kállo* or *náni kamássa.* The Indians make use of the gar's sharp teeth to scratch or bleed themselves with, and their pointed scales to arm their arrows, says William Bartram.[175]

+POISSON ROUGE, *m.* Redfish or Red Drum (*Sciaenops ocellata* L.). This important food fish of the Atlantic coast may be recognized by the black spot at the base of its tail.

POMMETTE BLEUE, *f.* A species of haw (*Crataegus brachyacantha* Sarg. and Engelm.), thus named in South Louisiana because of the bluish color of its large fruit.

POMMIER, *m.* The Mayhaw (*Crataegus opaca* Hook.). Its fruit is called *pommette, f. Pommier* may of course signify "apple-tree," and *pommette,* "little apple," "knob," etc.

POU D'BOIS, *m.* The Cattle Tick (*Maragaropus annulatus* Say), the carrier of the parasite that causes Texas fever.

POULE D'EAU, *f.* The Coot (*Fulica americana* Gmel.). Both the English and French natives of Louisiana use *poule d'eau* as the name of this bird, some of the former pronouncing it like English *pull doo.*

POUSSAILLER, *vb. tr.* Push, urge on. Cf. St.-Fr. *pousser.* Dial.—Sw.; Can.-Fr.

---

[174] *Nouveaux Voyages,* I, 110.

[175] *Travels,* p. 174.

Barbue

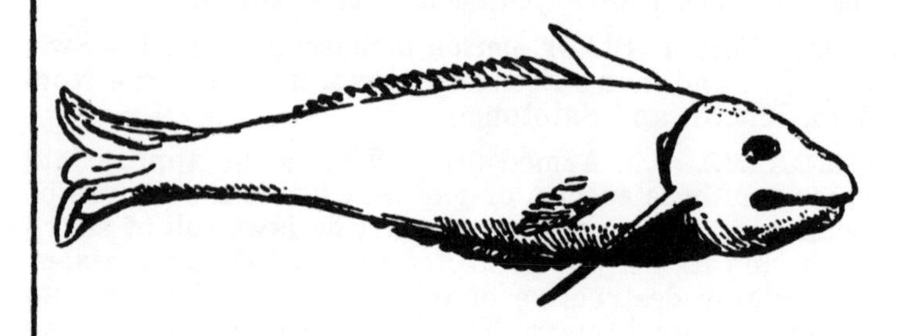

Poisson Armé.

Spatule.

Catfish, Gar, and Paddlefish. From Du Pratz's *Histoire de la Louisiane,* II, 252.

+PRALINE DE BENNÉS, *f.* Candy prepared with syrup or sugar and the seeds of the sesame plant (*Sesamum indicum* L.). *Benné, m.*, has come either from a French dialect or from English *benne;* the ultimate source is Malay *bijen,* the name of the sesame plant; but the French and the English forms are apparently due to confusion of Malay *bijen* with Malay *beneh,* "seed."

The term *pralines de bennés* is well known at Lafayette, Breaux Bridge, and the vicinity of these towns.

Benné is a different word from St.-Fr. *ben;* the latter is from Arabic *ban,* the name of the horse-radish tree (family *Moringaceae*), the seeds of which furnish an oil used in the extraction of perfumes and the lubrication of delicate machinery. In French these seeds are called *noix de ben.*

The species *Moringa oleifera* (Lam.) is sometimes cultivated in the far Southern States.

PRIE-DIEU, *m.* The Carolina wren. *Prie-dieu,* which I have heard at Charenton, Louisiana, is composed of the imperative of *prier,* "to pray," and its object *dieu.* Cf. *bènari* and *roitelet.* St.-Fr. *prie-dieu,* "praying-stool," is, of course, used also in Louisiana. Cf. *roitelet, infra.*

PU, *adv.* More. Ex.: *Pu de vingt ans,* "more than twenty years"; *pu tôt,* "sooner." It is also employed negatively, as in *je peux pu attendre,* "I cannot wait any longer." Heard in Iberia Parish; Can.-Fr.; extensively used in French dialects.

Pu is dialectal for Fr. *plus.*

QUANTIER, *m.* Moccasin or shoe made of rawhide or formerly of deerskin; hence also "old shoes"; generally used as a plural.[176] The French of Louisiana do not use St.-Fr. *mocassin,* a word derived, most probably through English *moccasin,* from Powhatan *mockasin* and Ojibway *makisin,* but designate the Indian moccasins by *quantiers* or occasionally by *souliers sauvages.*

A clue to the origin of *quantiers* is clearly indicated, I am convinced, in Du Pratz's description of Indian moccasins. "These are of deerskin," he says; "they enclose the foot like an oversock with the seam above; the skin is cut three fingers longer than the foot; the shoe is sewn only at the same distance from the end of the foot, and all the rest is folded over the foot. The rear

[176] Cf. Grace King, *New Orleans: The Place and the People,* p. 335.

part is sewn like an oversock; but the flaps (*quartiers*) are eight to nine inches high, and they are tied in front with a thong made of deerskin and extending from the ankle. Thus they form the oversock. These shoes have neither sole nor heel; those of the men and of the women are alike."[177]

Many Acadians pronounce *quantiers* as if it were spelled *quantchiers,* a form in which "tch" is equivalent to "ch" in English *chin. Quantiers* is a corruption of *quartiers,* "flaps."

QUE, REL., *pron.* "Of which," with the value of St.-Fr. *dont. Il y a bien des choses que j'ai besoin,* "There are many things that I need." Dial.—So.; Can.-Fr.; Anjou, French-Switzerland, etc.

QUÈQUEFOIS, *adv.* Sometimes; St.-Fr. *quelquefois.* Dial.—So.; Can.-Fr.; Anjou, Norm.

QUÈQU'UN, -UNE, *pron.* Some one; St.-Fr. *quelqu'un, -une.* Dial.—So.; Can.-Fr.; Anjou, Norm., Saintonge.

QUEUE À CISEAUX, *f.* Forster Tern (*Sterna forsteri* Nutt.). Cf. *pigeon de mer, supra.*

QUEUE DE RAT, *f.* The plant called "Cattail" (*Typha latifolia* L. and *Typha angustifolia* L.). The trappers of South Louisiana call the cattail *jonc au baril,* "barrel rush," and *jonc plat,* "flat rush." The muskrat eats both species of cattail.

RABOUTER, *vb. tr.* Piece, join end to end; St.-Fr. *raboutir.* The La.-Fr. form owes its ending to St.-Fr. *abouter,* "to join end to end." Dial.—Sw.; Can.-Fr.

RACCOURCI, *m.* A route shorter than the one usually pursued; a cut-off. Dial.—So.; Can.-Fr.; Anjou, Berry, Norm., etc.

RACMODAGE, *m.* Mending, darning; St.-Fr. *raccommodage.* Dial.—Loreauville, in Iberia Parish; Can.-Fr.; Berry, Norm.

RACMODER, *vb. tr.* Mend, patch; St.-Fr. *raccommoder.* Dial.—Iberia Parish; Can.-Fr.; Normandy, Saintonge, Anjou, Bretagne, etc.

RACOIN, *m.* Corner, nook; St.-Fr. *recoin.* Dial.—Iberia Parish; Can.-Fr.; Anjou, Bretagne, Norm.-Pic., and some other dialects.

---

[177] *Histoire,* II, 195.

RAITON, *m.* A little stingray (family *Dasyatidae*); formed from *raie*, "stingray," by the augmented diminutive suffix *-eton*; heard in New Orleans and along the Gulf Coast. Only the wings of the *raiton* are eaten. In the dialects of Normandy and Manche *raiton* likewise designates the young ray.[178]

RÂLE, *m.* The name bestowed on various species of rail and gallinule. The Sora Rail (*Porzana carolina* L.) is called *râle masqué*, "masked rail," because of its black face and throat. Another name is *ortolan, supra.* Other species of rail in Louisiana, such as the King Rail (*Rallus elegans* Aud.) and the Louisiana Clapper Rail (*Rallus crepitans saturatus Hensh.*) go indifferently by the name of *râle.* But the King Rail is also known as *le Grand Râle de Prairie;* the Louisiana Clapper Rail as *la Poule d'Eau,* though the latter name is regularly given to a different bird,[179] the coot, *supra.*

Râle Bleu is the Purple Gallinule (*Ionorsis martinicus* L.), known in English also as *marsh guinea* or *blue Peter.* The negroes are said to use its flesh in the preparation of gumbo.[180]

Râle Poule d'Eau, m., or *Poule d'Eau de Marais, f.,* "marsh water hen," is the name of the Florida Gallinule (*Gallinula galeata galeata* L.).

French *râle* is of uncertain origin.

RAMEAU, *m.* Magnolia (*Magnolia grandiflora* L.). As the leaves and branches of the magnolia are blessed by the priest at the services on Palm Sunday—*Dimanche des Rameaux*—some Acadians apply the term *rameau* to the magnolia itself. This usage of *rameau* may be observed at Loreauville, Iberia Parish. Those who use St.-Fr. *rameau,* "branch of a tree," in this way render "magnolia leaves" by *feuilles rameaux.* Cf. *bois de rameaux, supra.*

Some speakers designate the magnolia by St.-Fr. *magnolia*; others restrict this name to the Sweet Bay (*Magnolia glauca* L.). The latter is also called *laurier doux.*

---

[178] Rolland, *Faune,* XI (1910), 163.
[179] Cf. Audubon, *Birds,* V, 141.
[180] Audubon, *Birds,* V, 131.

RAT DE BOIS, *m.* Opossum.[181] Several species of opossum are found in Louisiana: *Didelphis virginiana pigra* (Bangs.); *Didelphis virginiana* (Kerr.); and perhaps *Didelphis mesamericana texensis* (Allen).[182]

The Choctaw name for the opposum is *shukáta*—literally "white hog," from *shukha,* "hog," and *háta,* "white."

+RAVET, *m.* Cockroach (family *Blattidae*); in France a popular substitute for Fr. *blatte.* The latter seems to be unknown in Louisiana.

Ravet is from Tupi Indian *arabé.* The earliest reference that I have found to the word is in Jean B. Dutertre's *Histoire Générale des Îles S. Christophe, de Guadeloupe, de la Martinique et Autres de l'Amérique* (Paris, 1654), page 389. After speaking of the large number of cockroaches and the damage inflicted by them, Dutertre concludes his description with the remark that chickens are extremely fond of these cockroaches—"*des ces ravets*"—and live on almost nothing else, growing fat on them more readily than on any other food.

Du Pratz's illustration of the cockroach is entitled *Laver;* his remarks on the cockroach begin, however, with the words *Le Lavert.*[183] De l'Ain, too, refers to these insects as "Les Laverts qui rendent désagréables le voisinage des bois."[184]

In the parish of Pointe Coupée *ravet* is sometimes pronounced as if written *ravert.*

RELIGIEUSE, *f.* Literally "Nun," Black-necked Stilt. See *avocat, supra.*

RIZ DE L'ÂNE, *m.* Water-grass or Cockspur grass; known locally as *Wild Millet* or *Wild Rice* (*Echinochloa Crusgalli* Beauv.). The stems and leaves of this plant are a favorite food of wild geese and many species of wild ducks.

ROITELET, *m.* Wren (family *Troglodytidae*). This word appears in Louisiana-French also as *rotelet;* and from the latter there has arisen, by reciprocal metathesis of *r* and *l,* the pronunciation *lo-tré.* One may note here that

---

[181] See Joutel, in Margry, III, 287; Charlevoix, *Histoire,* III, 134; Robin, *Voyages,* II, 337.

[182] See Arthur, *The Fur Animals of Louisiana,* pp. 77-78.

[183] *Histoire,* II, sketch facing p. 117; *ibid.,* p. 149.

[184] *Le Champ d'Asile,* pp. 94-95.

in the dialect of Picardy *oi* has the value of *o,* as in *do* for *doigt,* and *fro* for *froid.*[185] The term *le roitelet, huppé,* literally "the crested petty king," in which *roitelet* is a triple diminutive of French *roi,* "king,"[186] was applied to the European golden-crested kinglet (*Regulus cristatus* Charleton) and *roitelet* was subsequently bestowed on the European wren (*Troglodytes Europaeus* Vieillot). In an effort to explain the origin of the name, Du Pratz tells the story of an eagle which, on being attacked in a room by a wren, made no effort to defend itself.[187] According to a more popular fable, the fowls of the air once resolved to choose for their leader that one of their number which could fly highest. This feat was apparently performed by the eagle; but as a wren had concealed itself on the eagle's back during the trial flight, the name *roitelet* was immediately bestowed on the tiny bird. Six species of wren are found in Louisiana. Cf. *bènari* and *prie-dieu, supra.*

RONCE, *f.* Blackberry-Bush (*Rubus cuneifolius* Pursh.).

ROUPILLER, *vb. intr.* Doze; often used by the Acadians instead of sommeiller, "doze," "slumber"; found, too, in Canadian-French; derived from the French noun *roupie,* "snivel" (Gamillscheg). *Roupiller,* "to sleep," has existed in the colloquial speech of Paris since the seventeenth century.[188]

SABOT DE CHEVAL, *m.* Dichondra (*Dichondra carolinensis* Michx.).

+SACALAIT, *m.* *Sac à lait,* "milk bag," is the Louisiana name for the Crappie (*Poxomis annularis* Raf.), a name suggested by the silvery olive appearance of the fish, or by its beautiful white flesh. Similar formations in French are *sac à miel,* "honey-bag," *mouche à miel,* "honey-bee," *ver à soie,* "silkworm." The plural "les sacalés" is used by Baudry des Lozières.[189]

In Louisiana the final *t* of *sacalait* is silent and the word is pronounced by the French in French fashion; by the English approximately like *sackalay,* with the chief stress either on the first or on the last syllable.

SAC À PLOMB, *m.* See *plongeur, supra.*

---

[185] Kr. Nyrop, *Grammaire Historique de la Langue Française,*² I, 172.
[186] Diez, p. 671.
[187] *Histoire,* II, 110-111.
[188] L. Sainéan, *Les Sources de L'Argot Ancien,* I, 250.
[189] *Voyage à la Louisiane* (1802), p. 175.

The *sacalait* is found in the bayous, lagoons, and lakes of the State.

SANS-JOIE, *f.* See *grand héron bleu, supra.*

SARCELLE, *f.* Blue-Winged Teal (*Querquedula discors* L.). This bird has several names. In autumn, when the beauty of the bird's plumage is gone, it is called *La Sarcelle Automnière,* "Autumn Teal." *Automnière* is coined after the style of the adjective *printanière,* "spring (-like)", "vernal." In spring, when this bird is in full plumage, it is called *La Sarcelle printanière,* "Spring Teal." The blue-winged teal is said to have received these two names because it arrives in the State early in the fall and remains till late in the spring. Those members of this species which remain through the summer are known as *Sarcelles d'Été,* "Summer Teal." Yet another name is *Sarcelle Aile Bleue,* "Blue-Winged Teal."

The Green-Winged Teal (*Nettion carolinense* Gmel.), is the *Sarcelle d'Hiver,* "Winter Teal." Other names of this species are *Sarcelle du Nord,* "Northern Teal," *Sarcelle Aile Verte,* "Green-Winged Teal," and *Congo,* a designation that seems to have reference to the bird's black crest or to the black spots on its underparts.[190] Compare *Congo* in the sense of "moccasin," *infra.*

Two obsolete spellings are *Cercelles* (pl.)[191] and *Sercelles* (pl.).[192] The modern form of the plural is used by Lahontan.[193]

SAUTER, 1. *vb. tr. Sauter le fossé,* "to jump the ditch," *sauter les rapides,* "to descend (leap) the rapids"; found also in Canadian-French. 2. *vb. intr. Sauter à la corde,* "to jump the rope."

SAUTERELLE CHEVAL, *f.* The Lubber Grasshopper (*Dictyophorus reticulatus* Thunberg) of the Southern United States, often called "Georgia Hopper," is also found in Louisiana. To the Acadians the head of this grasshopper suggests that of a horse.[194]

SAVATES, *f. pl.* Slippers. Dial.—So.; Can.-Fr.

---

[190] Cf. Audubon, *Birds,* VI, 282, 287-288; Arthur, *Birds,* p. 40.
[191] Bossu, Pt. I, 110; Du Pratz, I, 242.
[192] Charlevoix, III, 156.
[193] *Mémoires,*[2] II, 47.
[194] Cf. Du Pratz, II, 144-145.

SERPENT MANGEUR D'OEUFS, *m.* The Yellow Chicken Snake (*Coluber obsoletus,* var. *quadrivitattus,* Holbrook), which takes its La.-Fr. name from its fondness for eggs.† These snakes are not poisonous.

SERPENT SONNETTES, *m.* 1. The Diamond-Back Rattlesnake (*Crotalus adamanteus* Beauvois). 2. The Banded or Timber Rattlesnake (*Crotalus horridus* L.). 3. The Southern Pigmy Rattlesnake (*Sistrurus miliarius* L.).

French *Serpent à Sonnettes,* "rattlesnake," shows ellipsis of the preposition *à* in Louisiana-French. Joutel has *serpent-sonnette* as early as 1685,[195] but *le serpent à sonnettes* appears in the works of Charlevoix, Du Pratz, Bossu, Duvallon, and De l'Ain.

The information that one gathers about the rattlesnake from the early explorers is at once curious and interesting. Thus, certain Indian tribes were accustomed to eat this snake, and even white men found its flesh palatable. William Bartram, while traveling in East Florida, killed near Fort Picolata a large rattlesnake whose body was cooked and served at the governor's table; for Governor Grant was very fond of the flesh of the rattlesnake.

Again, the Indian women are known to have pounded and swallowed the rattle, considering it a specific against the pains of childbirth; and they made the fat of the rattlesnake into an unguent for the treatment of rheumatism, an unguent that is said to have penetrated to one's very bones.

The Seminoles of Florida, on the other hand, never killed the rattlesnake, because they believed that the spirit of the snake would return and prevail upon its kin to avenge its death. That a similar belief prevailed among the tribes of Southwest Louisiana is made clear by the anonymous author of an *Essai sur Quelques Usages et sur l'Idiome des Indiens de la Basse Louisiane* (Howard Memorial Library, New Orleans). In this study, which was written at Opelousas in September, 1862, the word *sainti-oulou,* the equivalent of Choctaw *sintullo,* "rattlesnake," is treated, p. 31, as a compound of *sinti,* "snake," and *hullo,* "beloved," "sacred," "mysterious," etc., with the explanation that the Indians invested the rattlesnake with supernatural powers. This

† The same term is applied to the Blotched Chicken Snake (*Coluber obsoletus,* var. *confinis,* B. and G.).

[195] Cf. Margry, III, 167.

analysis of *sintullo* I am inclined to prefer to Gatschet's, in which the second element of the word is identified with Choctaw *ula*, "noisy," "rattling."[196] Be that as it may, there seems to be no doubt that the author of the *Essai* is right in his view of the attitude of the Indians toward the rattlesnake.[197]

SIFFLEUR, *m.* 1. The Common Hog-nosed Snake (*Heteredon platyrhinus* Latreille), also called *Spreading Adder, Puff Adder, Flat-headed Adder, Blow Snake,* and *Sand Viper.* 2. The Southern Hog-nosed Snake (*Heteredon simus* L.). The hog-nosed snake, when alarmed or angry, flattens the neck and head and hisses loudly. In many parts of America this perfectly harmless snake has long been mistaken for the poisonous Copperhead (*Ancistrodon contortrix* L.). Du Lac, for example, says that the only dangerous snakes in upper Louisiana are the rattlesnake (*le serpent à sonnettes*) and the whistler (*le siffleur*), which the English call *serpent cuivré,* "copperhead."[198] Bossu apparently makes the same mistake. "That snake which is called the *whistler* is about two feet long," he says, "but is so much more dangerous, because it is not so easily seen, being very little; so that the Indians and negroes often tread upon and are bitten by it: it has a prodigious wide mouth and when angry, it whistles at a terrible rate, and therefore the Indians call him *ho-huy,* that is, *whistler.*"[199] Bossu comments further on the powder with which an Indian doctor cured a soldier suffering from the bite of a copperhead.

SIROP DE BATTERIE, *m.* Open-kettle syrup. A *batterie* was one of the large iron kettles in which syrup and sugar were formerly made.[200]

SIRUGIEN, SIRURGIEN, *m.* Surgeon; with dissimilation of the initial consonant in St.-Fr. *chirurgien.* Dial.—Sw.; Can.-Fr.

SOLDAT, *m.* "Soldier." The Black-necked Stilt. See *avocat, supra.*

---

[196] *A Migration Legend,* II (1888), 193.

[197] References: Charlevoix, III, 159; Bossu-Forster, I, 363, 364; William Bartram, *Travels,* p. 261, footnote 267.

[198] *Voyages dans les deux Louisianes* (1805), p. 248.

[199] *Travels Through That Part of North America Formerly Called Louisiana,* translated by J. R. Forster, I (1771), 364-365.

[200] See the *Dictionnaire Général,* under *batterie,* and cf. Ducoeurjoly, *Manuel,* I, 118-119.

SOULIER SAUVAGE, *m.* Moccasin (shoe). Cf. *quantier, supra.*

+SOURIS-CHAUDE, *f.* Bat (*mammal*; order *Chiroptera*); Leather-Wing. Standard-French *chauve-souris* is also used in Louisiana, nor is it confined to the speech of the educated classes. *Souris-chaude* replaces *souris-chauve* in Canadian-French and a large number of the dialects of France.[201] Some of the Canadian woodcutters say that the bat sleeps in the hole of a tree during the winter and remains warm enough to defy the cold; hence his nâme *souris-chaude,* "hot mouse."[202] In reality the common people substituted *chaude* for *chauve* after they had ceased to comprehend the meaning of the compound *souris-chauve.*[203]

Nine species of flying mammals belonging to the order *Chiroptera* are found in Louisiana, though they vary in number from season to season and year to year, according to information kindly furnished me by my colleague, Dr. William H. Gates. Here are the nine:

Big-eared Bat—*Corynorhinus macrotus* (Le Conte).
Florida Bat—*Dasypterus floridanus* (Miller).
Free-tailed Bat—*Nyctinomus cynocephalus* (Le Conte).
Large Brown Bat—*Vespertilio fuscus* (Beauvois).
Leather-winged Bat—*Dasypterus intermedius* (H. Allen).
Little Brown Bat—*Myotis lucifugus* (Le Conte).
Red Bat (fall and spring migrant)—*Nycteris cinereus* (Beauvois).
Silver-haired Bat (rare)—*Lasionycteris Noctivagans* (Le Conte).
Twilight Bat—*Nycticeius humeralis* (Rafinesque).

Standard French *chauve-souris* or Acadian *souris-chaude,* like American English *leather-wing* or *leather-winged bat,* is a popular term for any mammal of the order *Chiroptera.*

SPATULE, *f.* V. Roseate Spoonbill (*Ajaia ajaja* L.), a bird that is now rarely seen on the coast of Louisiana. Du Pratz's description of the *spatule* shows that he has in mind this particular species of water fowl.[204]

Joutel mentions the *spatules* in January, 1686.[205]

---

[201] Cf. Rolland, *Faune,* VII, 7.
[202] Cf. L. de Montigny, *La Langue Française au Canada* (1916), pp. 15-16.
[203] A. Dauzat, *La Géographie Linguistique,* p. 77.
[204] *Histoire,* II, 116; cf. Du Pratz's illustration of this bird, *ibid.,* II, facing p. 98.
[205] See Margry, *Mémoires,* III, 215.

2. *Spatule* is likewise the name of the paddlefish, or Spoon-Bill Catfish (*Polyodon spatula* Walbaum). Its long spatula-shaped snout gave rise to the name. This fish, which is found in the Mississippi River and its tributaries, is used as food, and its roe is made into caviare.

SUCRERIE, *f.* Sugar-cane factory. In Canada *sucrerie* signifies an establishment used for the manufacture of maple sugar.

SUCRIER, *m.* An employee of a sugar factory; in Canada, of a maple-sugar factory.

SUSPECT, -ECTE, *adj.* Sensitive, susceptible. Dial.—Sw.; Can.-Fr.

TAC-TAC, *m.* Popcorn; popcorn candy. Evidently an echoic word; pronounced like American English *tock-tock*. *Maïs tactac* is "corn candy," made of parched corn and Louisiana molasses. St.-Fr. *tac-tac* is applied to the ticking of a clock or rapping of a knocker.

TAÏAUT, *m.* Hound; adapted from St.-Fr. *taïaut*, "tally-ho."

TAIRE, or TÈRE, *f.* Stingray or Stingaree (*family Dasyatidae*). This is the name applied to the stingray by the fishermen of Lower Louisiana. The same designation of the stingray is used in the dialects of Arcachon, Aunis, and Île de Ré.[206]

In New Orleans the stingray goes by the name of *raie*. The Creoles of that city use the "wings" of the stingray in preparing the dish called *raie au beurre noir*. Cf. *raiton, supra*.

Three well-known species of ray are the following: 1. Common Stingray, Clam-Cracker, or Stingaree (*Dasyatis centroura* Mitchill), found from Cape Cod southward. 2. Southern Stingray (*Dasyatis say* Le Sueur), common from New York southward. 3. Butterfly Ray (*Pteroplatea micrura* Schneider), from Massachusetts southward to the West Indies.[207]

TAMBOUR, *f.* 1. Drum, tambour. 2. Salt-Water Drum (*Pogonias cromis* Lacépède).

TAMPONNE, *f.* A stout, stumpy woman; found also in Canadian-French, and evidently adapted from Fr. *tampon*, "cork," "stopper," "plug."

---

[206] Rolland, *Faune*, XI, (1910), 170.

[207] See David Starr Jordan, *Manual of the Vertebrate Animals of the Northeastern United States*, p. 18.

TAOUBAS, *m.* Noisy gathering or reunion. Can this word, which Mr. G. L. Porterie reports to me from Marksville, be connected with Old French *tabois,* "noise"?[208]

TAPOCHER, *vb. tr.* Tap, strike, beat; a combination of St.-Fr. *taper,* "strike," "hit," and *talocher,* "cuff," "slap." Dial.—Sw.; Can.-Fr.

+TASSEAU, *m. Du tasseau* is the equivalent of "jerked beef." Formerly strips of deerskin and fish, too, were dried in the sunshine on a clothes line or wooden support. This word is adapted from St.-Fr. *tasseau,* "block," "bracket," "prop."

TILLER, *vb. tr. Tiller la mousse,* "to clean the (Spanish) moss."

'TIT, 'TITE, *adj.* Little, small; St.-Fr. *petit, petite.* Dial.—So.; Can.-Fr.; Norm.-Pic.

'TIT LAURIER, *m.* Red Bay, Sweet Bay, or Isabella-Wood (*Persea borbonia* Spreng.). The name is an aphetic form of *petit laurier.* The leaves of this tree are used in seasoning.

'TIT PAPE, *m.* Baltimore Oriole (*Icterus galbula* L.). *'tit pape,* "little Pope," is the name usually given in Pointe Coupée to the Baltimore oriole. Another name is *pape de bois.*[209] This bird is seen during the summer as far south as Baton Rouge.[210]

TIYON, *m.* A turban; a handkerchief worn about the head by colored women, and arranged in various styles—*tiyon chinoise* (Chinese), *tiyon créole,* etc.; corrupted from Fr. *tignon.*[211]

The change of "gn" to "y" appears also in *maquillon, supra.*

TOISE, *f.* An old French measure roughly equal to 6⅖ feet; formerly used in deeds and other court records, but now virtually obsolete in Louisiana-French. The word was Anglicized as early as 1598.

+TONDRE, *m.* Fungus collected for kindling. The source of this word, which is used in Pointe Coupée, is Norse *tundr,* "tinder." Found in Old French and Old Norman, *tondre, m.,* has been preserved in Canadian-French, Norman, and some other Modern French dialects. It is cognate with English *tinder.*[212]

---

208 See A. Tobler, in *ZRPh.,* XXX (1906), 743.

209 Audubon, *Birds,* IV, 48.

210 Arthur, *Birds,* p. 60.

211 See Lafcadio Hearn, *Gombo Zhèbes,* p. 9, footnote 5.

212 Cf. A. Sjögren, "Mots d'emprunt Norrois en Normand," *Romania,* LIV, 402-403.

Note *Bayu de la Chênière au tondre,* "Bayou of the oak forest abounding in tinder" (fungus), on a Spanish plan of the Ouachita district (1797),[213] *infra.*

+TOULOULOU, TOURLOULOU, *m.* Fiddler Crab (*Uca Mordax* Smith); corrupted from French *Tourlourou,* "foot soldier," by assimilation of *l—r to l—l.* Another Acadian form is *trouloulou,* which shows *r*-metathesis in the first syllable. Those Acadians who live at some distance from the sea-coast generally apply the term *tourloulou* to the larva of a tiger beetle; cf. *loulou, infra,* and *charlotte, supra.*

Tourlourou is the name of the crab (genera *Cancer* and *Portunus* Fabricius) in Brest, France; and the same name is bestowed on the crab by the French of the Antilles.[214]

Robin gives a lengthy description of a small crab which goes, he says, by the name of *tourlourou.*[215] This crab lives in holes which it digs near the water; its eyes are black and borne on tubes, so that it can see the better on both sides as well as to the rear. Furthermore, continues Robin, it strikes its claws together to give a signal of retreat to its companions, just as hares, when they wish to sound an alarm, strike the earth vigorously with their hind feet.

For an early reference to *tourlourous,* see Nicolas de la Salle's *Récit.*[216]

TOURNE-QUEUE, *m.* Wiggler, larva of a mosquito; used in some parts of Pointe Coupée Parish; literally, "turn tail."

TRAÎNASSE, *f.* A trail made through the marsh grass for the passage of canoes.[217] Cf. St.-Fr. *traînasse,* "creeping stalk" or "runner," "black couch-grass," "knot-grass"; "drag-net."

TRAÎNE, *f.* À *la traîne,* "in disorder." St.-Fr. *en desordre* has the same meaning. Dial.—Sw.; Can.-Fr.

TRIPOTER, *vb. tr.* To fondle a woman. Dial.—Sw.; Can.-Fr.; Berry, Nivernais, Norm. Sixteenth-century *tripoter,* "to scheme," "make a mess of," is connected with OF *triper, tréper,* "to stamp," "to dance."[218]

---

[213] *American State Papers,* Pub. Lands, II, 774 (ed. Gales and Seaton).
[214] Rolland, *Faune,* XII, 90.
[215] *Voyages,* I, 337.
[216] Margry, I, 561.
[217] Stanley C. Arthur, *The Fur Animals of Louisiana,* p. 253.
[218] Gamillscheg, *Wb.,* p. 867.

TRUITE VERTE, *f.* "Green trout"; the Louisiana term for the Large-mouthed Black Bass (*Micropterus salmoides* Lacépède).

+VEILLÉE, *f.* An evening party; a *soirée.* Dial.—So.; Can.-Fr.; Haut-Maine.

VEILLER, *vb. intr.* To pass the evening with. Dial.—So.; Can.-Fr.; Anjou, Berry, Nivernais.

VERGLAN, *m.* Sleet; corrupted from St.-Fr. *verglas,* a derivative of Low Latin "*vitriglacium* = Latin *vitrum,* "glass," and *glacies,* "ice." Gamillscheg, *Wb.*, p. 884.

VIOLON, *m.* The Red Head (*Marila americana* Eyt.); so called on account of the whistling sound of its wings.[219]
Violon also has its usual meaning—"violin"—in Louisiana-French.

VIRE DE BORD, *m.* Larva of a mosquito (family *Culicidae*); wiggle-tail; wriggler. *Vire de bord* signifies literally "turn around." Dial.—Sw.

VIRE-VIRE, *f.* 1. Western Willet (*Catoptrophorus semipalmatus inornatus* Brewst.). This bird's incessant activity is responsible for the La.-Fr. name, which is a double imperative from French *virer,* "to turn about."[220]
For the etymology of *virer,* see Gamillscheg.[221]
The willet's persistent cries have caused it to be named *Tell-Tale* in English.
2. Larva of a mosquito; cf. *gorgoyo, infra; vire de bord, supra; tourne-queue, supra.* Dial.—Sw.

VOLÉE, *f.* American Nelumbo or Lotus; in English also called "Water Chinquapin," "Duck-Acorn," "Great Yellow Water Lily," etc. (*Nelumbo lutea* Pers.). The seeds of this lotus are termed "*graines à volée*"—properly "flying seeds."

VOLIER, *m.* A flock of birds. St.-Fr. *volée.* Dial.—So.; Can.-Fr.; Bas-Maine, Norm., Orléanais.

VOYAGE, *m.* Load. Ex.: *un voyage de bois,* "a load of wood." Dial.—Sw.; Can.-Fr.

---

[219] Audubon, *Birds,* VI, 254.
[220] A. Darmesteter, *Mots Composés* (1894), pp. 226, 229.
[221] *Wörterbuch,* pp. 892-893.

II

THE FOREIGN ELEMENT

1. INDIAN WORDS

Historical—At the close of the seventeenth century, the early French colonists found the Lower Mississippi Valley and the adjacent territory in the possession of numerous Indian tribes, who are classified as members of four great linguistic families, the Caddoan, the Muskhogean, the Siouan, and the Tunican. Beginning slightly west of Pearl River and extending eastward through what is now Middle and Southern Mississippi, and reaching a line at some distance beyond the Tombigbee River, was the territory of the powerful Choctaw nation. The French soon entered into fairly intimate relations with the Choctaws, who at that time numbered about 15,000 souls, and who during the latter part of the eighteenth century drifted in bands, more or less numerous, across into Louisiana. From the Choctaw language the French borrowed more words directly than from any other Indian source, a fact that may be ascribed partly to the numerical superiority of the Choctaws over other Southern tribes, and partly to the close kinship of Choctaw with the Mobilian dialect. The *Mobilienne,* thus named by the French after Mobile, the great trading post of the Colonial Period, served as a medium of communication for all the tribes of the Lower Mississippi Valley,[1] and extended its influence as far north even as the mouth of the Ohio. It was as important to the Indians and white traders of the Colonial Period as French is today to the diplomatic

[1] Fort Louis de la Mobile, established by the French in 1702, on the river Mobile, was removed in 1710 to the present site of the city of Mobile. The Mobile Indians were a branch of the Muskhogean family. The tribal name *Mobile* may be connected with Choctaw *moeli,* "to paddle a canoe." The Choctaws call Mobile *Moilla.* See *A Dictionary of the Choctaw Language,* p. 262.

circles of Europe. To British traders it became known as the Chickasaw trade jargon, because of the close resemblance between the Chickasaw and the Choctaw or Mobilian vocabulary. Now the Mobilian is based chiefly on Choctaw, and contains indeed so much of the Choctaw vocabulary that this circumstance proved to be decisive in rendering the influence of Choctaw greater on the French language than that of any other Indian dialect. A few Choctaws still live in St. Tammany Parish, and four Choctaw families occupy the Whatley farms near Jena, in La Salle Parish. More than a thousand Choctaws are in Mississippi. In 1925 the Choctaw Nation in Oklahoma was estimated at 26,828. It should be borne in mind, furthermore, that the Mobilian was enriched by loans from the dialects of Algonquian tribes who inhabited the region lying to the north of the Southern Indian territory.

Besides the Choctaw or Mobilian element there is another class of significant Indian loans in Louisiana-French. These are the words, either Algonquian or Iroquoian in origin, which were brought to Louisiana by Acadians and Canadians, by missionaries, *voyageurs,* and *coureurs de bois.* The territory of the Algonquians formerly comprised almost all of Canada east of the one hundred and fifteenth meridian and south of Hudson's Bay, as well as that part of the United States lying east of the Mississippi and north of Tennessee and Virginia. In 1907 there were about 90,000 Algonquians, a majority of whom are now distributed at various points throughout Canada. At the coming of the white men the Algonquian territory surrounded that of the Iroquois, another extensive linguistic family, whose northern tribes once occupied the region extending from the shores of the St. Lawrence, Lakes Huron, Ontario, and Erie as far south as the present state of Maryland. The present population of the Iroquois is estimated at 16,000 or 17,000 souls, of whom two thirds are settled at various places in the provinces of Quebec and Ontario.

It is important to remember, in the next place, that the French first used the name *Acadie* to distinguish the eastern part of New France from the western, which began with the St. Lawrence Valley and was called *Canada*. The ancient province of Acadia comprises approximately parts of Maine and the province of Quebec, as well as the provinces of New Brunswick, Nova Scotia, and Prince Edward Island. When a settlement was effected in 1605 at Port Royal, now Annapolis, in Nova Scotia, by the Sieur de Monts, Champlain, and other noted Frenchmen, all this region formed the hunting grounds of Algonquian tribes known as the Abnakis, the Micmacs, and the Malecites. Survivors of these tribes still inhabit parts of the Ancient Acadia. Indian words, therefore, which survive in the Acadian dialect are likely to be of Algonquian origin; whereas those met with in the dialect of western Canada may be either Algonquian or Iroquoian.

Unfortunately, it is difficult to determine, from the writings of the French explorers, exactly when an Indian word reached Louisiana. Now and then, it is true, an Indian loan is mentioned in such a way as to prove beyond question that it was brought to the Lower Mississippi region long before any Acadian exile ever set foot on the soil of his new home. Thus Pénicaut speaks of *mitasses* as one of the presents given by Iberville in 1699 to the chiefs of five Southern tribes, and he adds that the Canadians in their party showed the Indians how to put on these *mitasses*, or "leggings."[2] In this connection one will recall that the edict of exile was not issued against the Acadians until 1755; and that perhaps ten years passed before any Acadians settled in Louisiana. Occasionally one comes across an Indian word in a work that was published after the arrival of some of the Acadians in Louisiana; but the reference to such a word simply fixes the *terminus ad quem*, and leaves us in the dark as to the *terminus a quo*. The writers on Indo-Canadian words are here of little help, being often content to say nothing about the particular locality in which Indian words are found. The exact provenience of these Indo-Canadian words is a problem that needs further investigation.

---

[2] Margry, V, 380.

The French language of Louisiana has drawn, as has been seen, on the vocabulary of the Choctaw or Mobilian, the Algonquian, and the Iroquoian dialects. It has also borrowed a few words from various other sources, notably Carib, Malay, Mexican, and South American. Some of these words came into Louisiana-French through the medium of Spanish, *supra.* One or two Malay words are here grouped with the Indian for lack of a more suitable place.

Let us look now at the Indian words used in Louisiana-French. That the total number of Indian loans is small will not surprise any one who reflects on the vast difference between the structure of the French language and that of an Indian dialect. Moreover, the French colonists, considering themselves in every respect superior to the Indians, naturally borrowed as a rule only those words that designate place-names and objects peculiar to the New World.

ACADIEN, -IENNE, *sb., adj. Acadien,* "Acadian," is formed from *Acadie,* the ancient French name of Nova Scotia. The exact origin of *Acadie,* which was early Latinized to *Acadia,* has never been solved.[3]

Acadien is often shortened to *Cadien* and the latter is frequently pronounced *Cajẽ. Cajẽ* may be derisive in tone, as not seldom in *Il est un Cajẽ,* "he is a Cajun," or in *il parle Cajẽ,* "he speaks Cajun."

AÇMINE, *f.* The fruit of the papaw tree; a syncopated form of *acimine.*[4]

An earlier form than Charlevoix's is *racemina* (1772), which is derived from Illinois (Algonquian) *rassimina,* a compound of *rassi,* "divided lengthwise in equal parts," and *mina,* "seeds."[5]

AÇMINIER, *m.* The Pawpaw Tree (*Asimina triloba* Dunal). The proper form is *acminier,* as used by Charlevoix, *Histoire,* III, 395. Du Pratz writes it *Asseminier.*[6]

Açminier and *açmine* (the fruit) are sometimes heard at Marksville, according to Miss Velma Barbin;

[3] Cf. Eugène Rouillard, *Noms Géographiques da la Province de Québec,* etc., (1906), pp. 17-18, for a summary of the various interpretations of the name; and my *Louisiana Place-Names of Indian Origin* (1927), pp. 2-3.

[4] See Charlevoix, *Histoire,* III, 395.

[5] Hodge, *Handbook,* I, 101. See *jasmine, infra.*

[6] *Histoire,* II, illustration facing page 20.

but the usual terms are *jasmine* and *jasminier*. *Jasmine* and *jasminier* are also used at Lafayette, I am informed by Miss Ann Spotswood Buchanan. Cf. *jasminier, infra.*

ACOLAN, *m.* I have not succeeded in finding any Creole or Acadian who is familiar with *acolan,* "petticoat"; but the word occurs, as Friederici has pointed out,[7] in Baudry des Lozières' *Voyage à la Louisiane* (1802), p. 211, where one reads of Indian women who wear "un petit jupon de drap qui pend jusqu'aux genoux, et qu'on appelle, à la Louisiane, *acolan.*"

Acolan is a corruption of Choctaw *álhkuna,* "gown," "dress for a lady." Dumont observes that the married women alone were permitted to wear the little skirt which they called *un Alconand.*[8] Perhaps some Creole of the older generation may remember this variant, which is much closer to the Indian source than *acolan.* The Indian word may have survived in the French language of Louisiana as late as 1862; for in that year the anonymous author of an *Essai sur Quelques Usages et sur l'Idiome des Indiens de la Basse Louisiane* gives, on page 56, the phrase *Vêtements de femme* as the equivalent of Indian *Alcouna.*

BABICHE, *f.* A rawhide, especially one that is hard and stiff; or also a strip cut from a rawhide, a thong. The word is used figuratively, too, as in the sentence *Il* (*elle*) *est raide comme une babiche,* "He (she) is as tough as a rawhide." My attention was first called to this word by Mr. Philip Brignac, of French Settlement, in Livingston Parish; subsequently his definition of *babiche* was corroborated by my colleague, Professor Frank Guilbeau, whose dialect was formed chiefly in the parish of St. Martin.

Canadian-French *babiche,* the immediate source of the La.-Fr. word, is defined as the term for a "narrow strip of leather, eelskin, etc.";[9] and it is said to be an aphetic derivative of Algonquian *sisibab,* "cord," or rather *sisibabish,* "a little cord.[10] Another highly probable source is Cree *Assababish,* the diminutive of *Assabab,* "thread.[11] Again, the Nipissing dialect has *nababish*

---

[7] *Hilfswörterbuch für den Amerikanisten* (1926), p. 1.

[8] *Mémoires Historiques de la Louisiane,* I (1753), 138.

[9] N. E. Dionne, *Le Parler Populaire des Canadiens Français* (1909), p. 48.

[10] M. le Senateur P. Poirier, "Des Vocables Algonquins, Caraïbes, etc., qui sont entrés dans la langue," in *Mémoires de la Société Royale du Canada,* Series III, Tome X (1916), 343.

[11] See Baraga, *Dictionary,* I, 298.

in the sense of a little strip of rawhide with which the Indians sew their moccasins; and Micmac has *abebe*, "rope." Lescarbot spells the word *ababich*, which he renders by "corde ou fil."[12] The French-Canadians use strips of eel skin in making snowshoes.

The La.-Fr. homonym *babiche*, as used contemptuously in such an expression as *une grosse babiche*, "a big mouth," or *Ferme ta babiche*, "shut your mouth," is connected with the echoic stem **bab-*, found in *babiller*, "to babble," *baboue*, "grimace," and similar French words. The French dialects of Vendée and the Centre have *babiche*, "lip"; the dialect of Mons has *babiches*, "big lips."[13] As to French *babiche*, "lap-dog," I note that it seems to be generally replaced in Louisiana by *caniche, f.*, literally "poodle-dog." This third *babiche* is a hybrid derivative of the stem **bab-*, "to babble," and French *barbichet*, "little poodle-dog."[14]

BACHOUCTA, *m.* Dye made from the foliage of the Smooth, Upland, or Scarlet Sumac (*Rhus glabra* L.). Some Acadians in the Southwest still color their yarn with this dye. The source of *Bachoucta* is Choctaw *bashukcha*, "sumac." The vowels and consonants in *Bachoucta* have the values assigned to them in French.

BATISCAN. The Canadians use *batiscan* as a mild oath to express surprise, regret, scorn, or discontent. Its Standard-French equivalent is *sapristi*.

Batiscan is apparently the same word as *Batiscan*, the name of a tributary of the St. Lawrence. Champlain mentions the Batiscan River as early as 1603.

In a dialect of the Montagnais, an Algonquian tribe living in Canada, *patiscan* signifies "vapor," "light mist." The same word is also said to be used in the sense of "dried meat," from which the Indians prepared their pemmican.[15]

Baraga derives *batiscan*—less plausibly, I think—from Cree *Tabateskan*, "split horn," "hanging horn," or from Cree *nabateskan*, "one horn."[16]

Canadian *batiscan* seems to be a rare word in Louisiana-French. My friend, Dr. E. O. Trahan, however, is familiar with *batiscan*, which he has heard in Southwest Louisiana.

---

[12] *Histoire de la Nouvelle France*, III (1612), 666.
[13] Wartburg, *Wörterbuch*, p. 192.
[14] Gamillscheg, *Wörterbuch*, p. 64.
[15] Eugène Rouillard, *Noms Géographiques*, p. 25.
[16] *A Dictionary of the Otchipwe Language*, Part I, 298.

BAYOU, *m.* The term *bayou* is generally applied to a sluggish stream that is smaller than a river and larger than a *coulée.* Historic Bayou Teche, however, is about 175 miles long, and it widens into a river near its junction with the Atchafalaya. Though a bayou may serve to connect one stream, or body of water, with another, a glance at a map of Louisiana will show that such a condition is far from being invariable. Moreover, a bayou sometimes changes the direction of its current according to the amount of rainfall in its vicinity. Standing on the bridge at Hope Villa, in Ascension Parish, one may see Bayou Manchac flowing eastward towards the Amite River; but when the Amite is swollen by heavy rains, the bayou sets westward towards its former source, the Mississippi. A bayou of course remains stationary when it attains, as Bayou Manchac often does, the same height as that of the stream into which it ordinarily empties.

Bayou, in spite of its formal resemblance to French boyau, "bowel," is not related to this French word. The sole origin of *bayou* is unmistakably Choctaw *bayuk,* "creek," "river."[17]

BOUCANE, *f.;* BOUCANER, *vb. tr., intr.;* BOUCANIÈRE, *f. Boucane* is the usual La.-Fr. equivalent of French *fumée,* "smoke." Thus one says, *La cuisine est remplie de boucane,* "The kitchen is filled with smoke"; *Il voit la boucane d'un bateau à vapeur,* "He sees the smoke of a steamboat."

The verb *boucaner* is a transitive, as in *boucaner de la viande, du poisson, du tabac,* "to smoke-dry meat, fish, tobacco"; an intransitive, as in *La cheminée boucane,* "The chimney smokes," *Le poêle boucane,* "The stove smokes," etc.

Boucanière is Louisiana-French for "smoke-house." With the termination of *boucanière* one may compare that of *cyprière,* "cypress forest," *pacanière,* "pecan grove," and similar forms. But if French *boucanier,* "buccaneer," is used in Louisiana, it has escaped my attention: its place is taken by French *pirate* or *flibustier.*

Boucan, m., Boucanerie, f., and *Boucanière* are Canadian-French designations of a "smoke-house." *Boucane* and *boucaner* are likewise common in Canadian-French, and the latter is found in the writings of the French explorers of the seventeenth century. Thus Nicolas de la Salle, in his description of the Cavelier de la

[17] Compare the writer's *Louisiana Place-Names of Indian Origin* (1927), p. XII, and the references there given.

Salle's discovery, in 1682, of the Mississippi, makes the following reference to a band of savages that La Salle's party encountered not very far south of the Oumas: "They fled to their village, leaving their fishing and a basket that contained a fish, a man's foot, and a child's hand, all smoked (*boucané*)."[18] Pénicaut, too, comments briefly on the manner in which the savages prepared their meat: "Their meat is ordinarily smoked or *boucanée*, as one says in that country."[19]

Boucan is not, as is generally thought, a Carib word. The French adventurers of the sixteenth century borrowed it from South-American Tupi, a dialect in which *bucán* signifies a wooden lattice frame for the smoking of meat.[20]

The verb *fumer*, "to smoke," is applied in Louisiana, as in France, to the act of smoking tobacco, a pipe, a cigar, etc.: *Fumer du tabac, une pipe, un cigare,* etc. Similarly, *Une personne qui ne fume pas,* "A person who doesn't smoke," is correct both in Louisiana and in France.

CANADIEN, -ENNE, *adj. Canadien* is naturally a familiar term in Louisiana-French, the Canada goose, for example, being commonly known as *l'oie canadienne* (*Branta canadensis canadensis* L.). Other names for this wild fowl are *l'outarde,* properly "the bustard," and *la barnache,* "the barnacle goose."

French *Canada, m.*, the geographical name from which the adjective is formed, is derived from Iroquois *kanata,* "city," "village," "camp."

CANARI, *m. Canari,* "clay pot," seems to have disappeared from the language of the Creoles, though it survives in the following negro-French refrain:

Ya pas bouillon pou vos, macommère;
Canari cassé dans difé (bis);
Bouillon renversé dans difé.
Ya pas bouillon pou vous, macommère;
Canari cassé dans difé.

("There's no soup for you, my gossiping friend;
The pot's broken in the fire;
The soup is spilled in the fire," etc.)[21]

---

[18] Cf. Margry, I, 560.
[19] Cf. Margry, V, 390.
[20] Georg Friederici, "Vier Lehnwörter aus dem Tupi," *Zeitschrift für Französische Sprache und Literatur,* LIV (1930), 177-180.
[21] Lafcadio Hearn, *Gombo Zhèbes* (1885), p. 30, footnote 2.

Marbot, the author of *Les Bambous* (new edition, 1869), notes on pages 36, 137, that *canari* occurs in the native dialect of Martinique, and John Bigelow finds the word in Haitian proverbs, such as

Moune connait ça qua bouilli nen canari li
("Every one knows what is boiling in his own pot")

and

Canari vlé rîé chôdier
("The earthen pot wishes to laugh at the iron pot.")[22]

Canari is a corruption of *canálli,* the Carib name of large earthen pots in which the Carib Indians made their wines.[23]

The Indian women of Louisiana also made large clay pots, in which enough sagamité was cooked at one time for two or three families.[24]

CANTAQUE, *m.* Smilax—*Smilax laurifolia* L., or perhaps *Smilax Bona-nox* L.; its large tuber served as food for the Indians and early settlers.[25] These tubers were reduced to powder and mixed with cornmeal or flour. *Cantaque* is still known to some of the older French natives of Southwest Louisiana. This word is derived from Choctaw *kantak,* "smilax." Compare Choctaw *kantak páska,* "brier-root (smilax) bread."

CASSINIER, *m. Cassinier* is the La.-Fr. name of the Yaupon (*Ilex Cassine* Walt. 1788, or *Ilex vormitoria* Ait.), a shrub or small tree, which thrives in Louisiana and from whose leaves the Indians of the Gulf Coast formerly prepared a famous black drink for use on all festive and ceremonial occasions. This black drink, named thus by British traders, was held in such esteem by the Southern tribes that they never went to war without drinking it in huge quantities. "All the Allibamons," says Bossu, "drink the Cassine; this is the leaf of a little tree which is very shady; the leaf is about the size of a farthing, but dentated on its margins. They toast these leaves as we do coffee, and drink the infusion of them with great ceremony. When this diuretic potion is prepared, the young people go to present it in

---

22 "The Wit and Wisdom of the Haytians," *Harper's Magazine,* Vol. 51 (1875), 585, 586.

23 R. R. R. Breton, *Dictionnaire Caraïbe-Français,* p. 107.

24 Pénicaut (1699), in Margry, V, 389.

25 *Annals of Congress,* 9th Congress, 2nd session (Dec. 1, 1806—March 3, 1807), p. 1107, footnote.

Calebashes formed into cups, to the chiefs and warriors, that is the honorables, according to their rank and degree. The same order is observed when they present the Calumet to smoke out of: whilst you drink they howl as loud as they can, and diminish the sound gradually; when you have ceased drinking, they take their breath, and when you drink again, they set up their howls again. These sorts of orgies sometimes last from six in the morning to two o'clock in the afternoon. . . .

"The women never drink of this beverage, which is only made for the warriors."[26]

Cassinier is derived from *cassine, f.*, the name given to the black drink by a Timucuan tribe of Florida. In the sixteenth century the Timucua formed the largest and most powerful Indian confederacy in Florida. Laudonnière gives the Indian name of the drink as *Casine*;[27] Le Challeux spells it *cassinet,* according to Paul L. J. Gaffarel's *Histoire de la Floride Française* (1875), p. 462; Francisco Pareja, citing Laudonnière and De Gourges, calls the drink *Cassine* and *Casine.* Cristobal Colon may have been acquainted with the yaupon, for which the Spanish is *casina.*[29]

I have not met any Creoles or Acadians who are familiar with *cassine,* or who brew the drink that the word denotes; yet as late as 1879 Chahta-Ima (Father Rouquette), in *La Nouvelle Atala,* p. 29, mentions *la cassine* as one of the trees of Louisiana. *Cassinier,* on the other hand, is still well known to the citizens of French Settlement, in Livingston Parish, and it has been heard occasionally by Mr. A. Lovell, whose address is Theriot, in Terrebonne Parish.

Charlevoix calls the yaupon. *Cassine, f.,* or *Apalachine, f.,*[30] deriving the latter term from *Apalachée,* the name of a native tribe of Florida which formerly occupied the region extending from the neighborhood of Pensacola eastward to Ocilla River. The chief towns of this tribe were near the sites of the present Tallahassee and St. Marks. *Apalachée* is from the Hitchiti dialect and signifies "those (people) on the other side, shore, or river."[31]

---

[26] Bossu-Forster, I, 249-250.

[27] French, *Hist. Coll.,* N. S. (1869), pp. 246, 247, 301.

[28] *Arte de la Lengua Timuquana* (1614), XII, XIII.

[29] Cf. D. Miguel Colmeiro, *Primeras Noticias acerca de la Vegetación Americana,* (Madrid, 1892), p. 24.

[30] *Plantes d'Amérique,* in *Histoire,* II, 29-30; *ibid.,* III, 449-450.

[31] Albert S. Gatschet, *A Migration Legend of the Creek Indians,* I, 74.

Personal names were freely bestowed on Indians who took prominent parts in black-drink festivals. Thus *Osceola*, the name of a famous Seminole chief, is literally Creek *Assi-yahola*, "Black-Drink Singer"; and a Chitimacha Indian is said to have been called *Wait'i-Kestmic*, "Pounding-up *Cassine*."[32] What is here even more pertinent is the fact that *Lacasine* was an Attakapas chief whose memory is perpetuated by the name of a large bayou in Southwest Louisiana, now spelled *Lacassine*, but formerly *Lacasine*, *Lacacene*, and *Cassine*.[33] The village of Lacassine, in Jefferson Davis parish, was apparently named after the bayou. How did the Indian acquire his name? Was it conferred on him by French settlers because he was a noted drinker of cassine, or because his village was situated among yaupon trees? Or, on the other hand, is his name merely a compound of the French article *la* and the French geographical term *cassine*, literally "cottage," "country house," a derivative of Low Latin *cassina?* Not a few Indians have received French names, such as *Antoine*, *Bernard*, *Louis* and *Celestin(e)*.[34] The latter view I believe to be correct.

On the yaupon and the drink called *cassine*, one may consult the following additional references: Du Pratz, *Histoire*, II, 45-46; William Bartram, *Travels* (1791), pp. 449-450; Thwaites, *Early Western Travels*, XVII, 50-51; Andrew Ellicott, *Journal* (1814), pp. 286-287; F. W. Hodge, *Handbook*, I, 150; *ibid.*, II, 1000 f.; John R. Swanton, *Bur. of Amer. Ethnology*, Bul. 73 (1922), 313, 374-375, 395-39; Georg Friederici; *Hilfswörterbuch für den Amerikanisten* (1926), p. 13; Caroline Dormon, *Forest Trees of Louisiana, and How to Know Them*, Bul. No. 15 (Department of Conservation), 69.

CHACTA, *m.* and *f.* *Chacta* is used not only in the sense of "Choctaw," but also in that of "small," inferior," as in *une cabane Chacta, un cheval Chacta*. The plural is *Chactas*.

I know of no grounds for the view that Choctaw *Chahta*, the source of French *Chacta*, is corrupted from

[32] John R. Swanton, in *Bur. of Amer. Ethnology*, Bul. 43 (1911), 353.

[33] Cf. *American State Papers*, Public Lands, III, 92, 105, 114, ed. Gales and Seaton; *ibid.*, III, 154, ed. Green; Darby's map of Louisiana, 1816; La Tourette's map of Louisiana, 1846.

[34] See *American State Papers*, Public Lands, III, 92, 93, 99, 239, 249, ed. Gales and Seaton.

Spanish *chato,* "flat," though it is true that the Choctaws were accustomed to flatten the heads of their infants.

It was customary for other Southern tribes to flatten the heads of infants. "As they were looking for him [Prudhomme] they fell in with two Chikasas savages, whose village was three days' inland," says Tonti. "They have 2,000 warriors, the greatest number of whom have *flat heads,* which is considered a beauty among them, the women taking pains to flatten the heads of their children, by means of a cushion which they put on the forehead and bind with a band, which they also fasten to the cradle, and thus make their heads take this form. When they grow up their faces are as big as a soup plate. All the nations on the sea-coast have the same custom."[35]

CHAGANON, CHAOUANON, *m.* A bob-tailed chicken, literally a "Shawnee chicken." The Algonquian tribe known as the Shawnee formerly inhabited South Carolina, Tennessee, Pennsylvania, and Ohio. Gatschet gives their name as *sáwano,* "southerner," with the plural *sawanógi.* Two Menominee forms for "south," "southerner," are *sawano* and *shawano.*[36] Why the term "Shawnee" was conferred on a bob-tailed chicken is not clear.

Tonti uses the form *Chaganon*—once *Chagenon*—in his *Mémoire;* but he has *Chaouanou* alone for "Shawnee" in his *Nouvelle Relation.*[37]

It may not be without significance in the evolution of La.-Fr. *Chaganon* that *Chaguanos* (1841) and *Saguanós* (1831) have been recorded as Spanish for "Shawnees."[38]

+CHAOUI, m. The earliest reference that I have found to *chaoui,* the La.-Fr. name of the raccoon (*Procyon lotor lotor* L.), is in Duvallon's *Vue de la Colonie Espagnole* (1803), 101, where *le chaoui* as well as *le pichou* is classed as a species of fox.

When an Acadian wishes to distinguish the dark raccoon of the cypress swamps from the slightly redder or yellower raccoon of the marshes, he calls the former

[35] French, *Hist. Coll.* (1846), p. 60.

[36] W. J. Hoffman, in *Bur. of Amer. Ethn., Rep. XIV,* Pt. 1 (1893), 311, 325.

[37] See French, *Hist. Coll.* (1846), pp. 69, 71, 72, 74, 75, 77; and *Relations de la Louisiane . . . ,* pp. 183, 188.

[38] See F. W. Hodge, *Handbook of North American Indians,* II, 537.

un chaoui cyprière, "a cypress-swamp raccoon." The number of raccoons taken in Louisiana during the season of 1926-27 reached the remarkable total of 127,-862.[39]

Chaoui is derived from Choctaw or Mobilian *shaui,* "raccoon." The first syllable of *chaoui* sounds like French *chat,* "cat," except that the Acadian "a" is a little more retracted than the French front "a"; the second syllable is exactly like French *oui,* "yes"; and the stress lies on the second syllable.

The term *chat sauvage,* by which the early French explorers designated the raccoon, is obsolete in Louisiana; compare, however, *chat, supra.*

CHOC, *m.* Blackbird. *Choc* is pronounced either like English *chock,* or like American *chock* with an unrounded "o." *Choc* is a general term for various species of blackbird. *Choc de bois* designates clearly the Florida grackle; *choc de prairie,* the boat-tailed grackle; and *choc aile rouge,* the red-winged blackbird. *Choc* is found, too, in *pape choc,* one of the names of the orchard oriole. *Pape* is merely the French word for "pope."[40]

I am confident that *choc* arose in imitation of the birds' notes. Nevertheless, I mention the word here because of the bare possibility that it was corrupted from Atakapa *ts'ok,* "blackbird." The apostrophe in *ts'ok* represents the glottal stop.

Parisian *choc,* likewise an echoic word, but related to *chic,* signifies "high life" as well as "a young gentleman of fashion." Compare the La.-Fr. derisive *un beau choc,* "a fine fellow." [41] *Choc* is also extremely common in the phrase *bien choc,* "quite tipsy."

CHOUPIQUE, *m.* The Bowfin (*Amia calva* L.). *Choupique* is almost the only name given in Louisiana to this fish even by those who cannot speak French. Another term sometimes heard is *poisson de marais, m.,* "swamp fish."

The choupique is commonly thought to be of little value as food, but its flesh, if properly salted and smoked, is said to have a delicious flavor.

Choupique is a derivative of *shupik,* "mudfish," the name bestowed on the bowfin by the Choctaws.[42]

---

[39] Stanley C. Arthur, *The Fur Animals of Louisiana,* Bul. No. 18 (Louisiana Department of Conservation, November, 1928), 410.

[40] Cf. Stanley C. Arthur, *The Birds of Louisiana* (1918), pp. 60, 61.

[41] L. Sainéan, *Langage Parisien,* p. 460.

[42] For further information see *The Fresh-Water Fish of Louisiana,* Bulletin 4 (Louisiana Department of Conservation, November, 1917), 15-16; and the writer's *Louisiana Place-Names of Indian Origin* (Louisiana State University Bulletin, February, 1927), pp. 24-26.

CHOUQUECHI, *m.* *Chouquechi* is used at Marksville, Avoyelles Parish, as the name of the cushaw, a variety of Crookneck Squash (*Cucurbita moschata* Duchesne), according to Mr. G. L. Porterie, of Marksville. The same term is sometimes heard in the Leonville neighborhood, parish of St. Landry.

Chouquechi is pronounced in two syllables and with the vowels and consonants as in French. *Chouquechi* is clearly an adoption of Choctaw *shukshi,* "watermelon," though the Indian word has changed its meaning in the transition to French. The Indian tribes of Lower Louisiana cultivated the pumpkin, the watermelon, the gourd, and the cushaw.

Another term for the "cushaw" is *giraumon patate, m.,* literally "potato pumpkin," which is heard, for example, at Breaux Bridge, False River, French Settlement, Houma, Labadieville, and St. Martinville. Other less popular terms for the "cushaw" are *coucroche, m.,* "crooked neck," which is very common in the eastern part of St. Landry; *giraumon confiture, m.,* "preserve-pumpkin," which is occasionally used at Opelousas, Houma, Labadieville, and doubtless other towns; and *cushaw,* which has been adopted from English and generally pronounced like French *coucha, m.,* by the farmers of Evangeline Parish. The information about *cushaw* I owe to the kindness of Mr. L. L. Perrault, of Opelousas. I have myself heard *cushaw* pronounced as in English by natives of Pointe Coupée. *Cushaw,* which is also written *cushaw* and *kershaw,* came into English from Virginia Algonquian *escushaw*; compare Cree *askisiw,* "it is raw or green." In some parts of the Southwest *cacha, m.,* with a French pronunciation, is the usual term.

Yet another term that is often used in Pointe Coupée for the cushaw is *giraumon (à) cou, m.,* "neck pumpkin." It reminds one of Du Pratz's comparison of the cushaw to a hunting horn. Du Pratz, however, does not distinguish the cushaw from the pumpkin, including both under the term *giromons,* "pumpkins." After observing that one kind of pumpkin is round, he says that another kind is shaped like a hunting horn, is sweeter and firmer, contains fewer seeds, and keeps longer than the other. His term *corps de chasse,* by the way, is erroneous for *cor de chasse,* "hunting horn." He also mentions several ways in which *giromons*, "cushaws," were cooked, dwelling upon the fact that they were fashioned like pears or other fruit and preserved with sugar.[43]

Standard French *giraumon(t)*, *m.*, the usual Louisiana-French term for "pumpkin," the fruit of the vine *Cucurbita pepo* (L.), is occasionally followed by the word *boeuf* (Livingston Parish), which then has the force of an adjective, "big," "enormous," "extraordinary." As *boeuf* is here invariable, the plural is *les giraumon(t)s boeuf*. A similar usage of *boeuf* prevails in Canada and in the colloquial speech of France. The final *f* is pronounced in *boeuf*.[44]

\+ *Giraumon(t)* is from Tupi *geromú, jurumú.*

The Creoles also use St.-Fr. *citrouille* for "pumpkin," and St.-Fr. *potiron* for "cushaw."

+GRIVE CHÉROKI(S), *m.* Towhee, Cherokee Robin, or Swamp Robin (*Pipilo erythrophthalmus erythrophthalmus* L.). As this bird becomes very fat in winter, it is also called *grasset* or *grassel*, "fatty," "plump."[45]

St.-Fr. *grive*, "thrush," is used in Louisiana-French as the name of the American Robin (*Planesticus migratorius migratorius* L.).

The original settlements of the Cherokee Nation, a powerful Iroquoian tribe, were on the head waters of the Savannah and Tennessee rivers.

Chéroki(s) is thought to be a derivative of Choctaw *Chalákki*, "Cherokee," which is in turn a corruption of Choctaw *Chiluk-okla*, "Cave dwellers," the term alluding to the fact that some Cherokees formerly lived in caves. Pénicaut spells the tribal name *Cheraquis* in 1659.[46]

JASMINE, *f.* The fruit of the Pawpaw Tree (*Asimina triloba* Dunal). Compare N. Bossu's comment, in *Nouveaux Voyages*, Pt. II (1768), 154:

"The Jasmine has the form and color of a lemon; it is odoriferous, and tastes like fig bananas; its seeds resemble beans. The jasmine is poisonous to hogs."

Under the name *la jasmine* Bossu clearly refers to the fruit of the papaw. He is mistaken, however, in thinking that it is poisonous to hogs.

---

[43] *Histoire*, II, II.

[44] Cf. N. E. Dionne, *Le Parler Populaire des Canadiens Français* (1909), p. 80; L. E. Kastner and J. Marks, *A Glossary of Colloquial and Popular French* (1929), p. 47.

[45] Cf. Audubon, *Birds*, III, 168.

[46] Margry, V, 404.

The initial *j* in *jasmine* may be due to popular confusion with French *jasmin*, "jasmine," or to dissimilation of *z-s* to *"j"-s* in the plural combination *les acimines*; *cf. açmine, supra.*

In a somewhat similar manner folk etymology developed obsolete French *danser les jolivettes* from *danser les olivettes* "to dance the olive dance."[47]

The word *Natchitoches*, I recall here, which is familiar as the name of a town and parish in Louisiana, is Caddo Indian for "papaws."

JASMINIER, *m.* The Papaw tree; cf. *jasmine, supra.* Miss Velma Barbin, of Marksville, first called my attention to the fact that *jasminier* and *jasmine* are still used in Louisiana-French.[48]

LATANIER, *m.* Pénicaut observes in 1699 that the cabins of the Pascagoula Indians "were made of earth, and of a round shape, somewhat like our wind-mills, the roofs being generally covered with bark; but some were covered with a species of leaf, which is called, in this country, *latanier* (*palmetto*), a shrub peculiar to the country."[49] The Indian women, according to Du Pratz, made of the palmetto leaves hats as light as an ounce, hooded coats for themselves, and other pretty things.[50]

The huts of fishermen, hunters, and loggers are still sometimes covered with the leaves of the dwarf palmetto (*Sabal Adansonii* Guerns.), a low gregarious palm, with large fan-shaped leaves, which is extremely abundant in Southern and Lower Louisiana. It is Robin's *Palmier nain*, "dwarf palm," or *Latanier.*[51]

A bayou by the name of *Latanier* is situated not far from the village of Richland, in Rapides Parish. See survey T 3 N, R 1 E, La.-Mer., 1807.

Seventeenth-century *latanier*, which was Latinized to *Latania* by Commerson in 1789, is a French derivative of Carib *aláttani*, the name of a small fan-leaf palm.[52]

---

[47] Cf. A. Thomas, *Romania*, XXVIII, 193-194.

[48] Note *jasseminier*, in Duvallon, *Vue de la Colonie Espagnole*, p. 112, and in De L'Ain, *le Champ d'Asile* (1819), p. 74.

[49] See B. F. French, *Historical Collections*, N. S. (1869), p 49; Margry, V, 389 ff.

[50] *Histoire*, II, 48.

[51] *Voyages*, III, 337 ff.; cf. C. S. Rafinesque, *A Flora of Louisiana* (1817), p. 16.

[52] Breton, *Dictionnaire Caraïbe-Français*, pp. 243-244.

MARINGOUIN, *m.* *Maringouin,* "mosquito," is a derivative of South American Tupi and Guarani *marigoui* or *maringouin.* For references on the history of *maringouin,* see especially Friederici, *Hilfswörterbuch,* p. 61.

The earliest example of *maringouin* recorded by the *Dictionaire Général* is taken from the *Relation des Missions* (1655) of Pierre Pelleprat, a Jesuit missionary to Mexico and the West Indies. But in 1632, nearly a quarter of a century before the appearance of Pelleprat's work, Paul Le Jeune speaks of being nearly devoured by the *maringouins* in New France [Canada];[53] and Pierre Boucher, in 1664, says that he regards the *Maringouins,* along with the hostile Iroquois, as the two chief disadvantages of residence in that country.[54] Even more convincing evidence of the Canadians' familiarity with *maringouin* is furnished by a Canadian folk song, a stanza of which runs as follows:[55]

Si les maringouins te réveillent
De leurs chansons,
Ou te chatouillent l'oreille
De leurs aiguillons,
Apprends, cher voyageur, alors
Que c'est le Diable
Qui chante tout autour de ton corps
Pour avoir ta pauvre ame.

Maringouin was not long in making its way down the valley of the Mississippi. Thus the Cavelier de la Salle suffered, according to his own statement, little annoyance from *maringouins* in the country of the Miami Indians.[56] Pénicaut, however, who in 1699 was sailing along the Gulf Coast, had a different story to tell: "We hurried off an hour before daybreak," he said, "to get rid of the annoyance of swarms of small flies or *cousins,* which the Indians call *Maragouins,* and which puncture even to the drawing of blood."[57] This statement of Pénicaut's seems to warrant the conclusion that Southern tribes borrowed *maringouin* from the Canadian travelers—just as the Choctaws adapted *shapo,* "hat," from French *chapeau* and *wak,* "cow,"

[53] *Jesuit Relations,* V, 36.
[54] Benj. Sulte, *Pierre Boucher et Son Livre,* p. 164.
[55] See *Roy. Soc. of Canada,* Trans., II, (1896), 97.
[56] Margry, I, 465.
[57] French, *Historical Collections,* N. S., I (1869), 44; cf. Margry, V, 384. Note, too, Iberville's reference to the *maringouins,* Margry, IV, 188.

from Spanish *vaca*—or that *maringouin* had early come up the South American coast and reached Louisiana by way of the Antilles. Doubtless this novel word was brought to the lower Mississippi valley not only from Canada but also from the islands. A Haitian proverb runs *Toute cabinette gagne maringouin a yo*, "Every closet has its mosquito," that is, "There's a skeleton in every closet," which my colleague, Professor James F. Broussard, a master of Parisian French, Louisiana-French, and the negro patois, renders for me into the negro-French of Louisiana by *Tout cabinet gẽ maringouin.*[58]

Though *maringouin* and Standard-French *moustique* are both used in Louisiana, they do not signify the same thing in every part of the State, nor are they everywhere equally common. The distribution and the meaning of the two words are indicated, with a reasonable degree of accuracy, in the following tables:

TABLE I

Maringouin, "mosquito."

Place	*Parish*
Colfax	Grant
Grant	Allen
Lake Charles	Calcasieu

TABLE II

Moustique, "mosquito."

Place	*Parish*
Baton Rouge	E. Baton Rouge
Clinton	East Feliciana
Destrehan	St. Charles
Gramercy	St. James
Louisa	St. Mary
Mandeville	St. Tammany
Pilot Town	Plaquemines
Pointe à la Hache	Plaquemines

[58] Cf. John Bigelow, in *Harper's Magazine*, LI (1875), 438.

TABLE III

Maringouin and *Moustique*
"Mosquito"

Place	*Parish*
Bayou Goula (*Maringouin* is rare and low colloquial)	Iberville
Des Allemands	Lafourche
Franklin (*Moustique* is the more common)	St. Mary
Golden Meadow (*Maringouin* is rare)	Lafourche
Gueydan	Vermilion
Houma (*moustique* is rare)	Terrebonne
Lafayette (*maringouin* is low colloquial)	Lafayette
Mansfield	De Soto
Marksville (*maringouin* is less common and often low colloquial)	Avoyelles
Napoleonville	Assumption
Natchitoches (*maringouin* is rare)	Natchitoches
Paradis	St. Charles
Plaquemine	Iberville
St. Bernard (*maringouin* is rare)	St. Bernard
Thibodaux	Lafourche
Ville Platte	Evangeline

TABLE IV

Maringouin, "large swamp mosquito"; *moustique,* "small house mosquito."

Place	*Parish*
Bunkie	Avoyelles
Dutch Town	Ascension
French Settlement	Livingston
La Place	St. John Baptist
New Iberia	Iberia
New Orleans	Orleans
Opelousas	St. Landry
St. Martinville	St. Martin

TABLE V

Maringouin, "mosquito"; *moustique,* "small black gnat."

Place	*Parish*
Addis	W. Baton Rouge
Maringouin	Iberville
New Roads	Pointe Coupée

TABLE VI

Maringouin, "wiggletail"; *moustique,* "mosquito."

Place	*Parish*
St. Francisville	West Feliciana

Mangeur Maringouins, "mosquito eater," is one of the names of the Nighthawk or Bull Bat (*Chordeiles virginianus virginianus* Gmel.) and the Florida Nighthawk (*Chordeiles virginianus chapmani* Coues). The Chuck-Will's-Widow (*Antrosfomus carolinensis* Gmel.) is also called *Mangeur Maringouins.*[59]

Can.-Fr. *Mangeur de Maringouins* signifies "Nighthawk."

Here and there in Louisiana, Standard-French *cousin* is occasionally used as a general term for the "mosquito."

Finally, *Maringouin* designates a town and a bayou in Iberville Parish.

MATACHÉ – ÉE, *adj.* This adjective is used in such expressions as *un chien mataché,* "a spotted dog," *une vache matachée,* "a spotted cow," *les cochons matachés,* "the spotted pigs," etc.

Father Du Poisson, writing to Patouillet in the first quarter of the eighteenth century, says that *un peau mataché* is a skin painted in divers colors by savages, a skin on which are represented calumets, birds, and beasts; and he comments, furthermore, on the appearance of a group of savages "arrayed as for a ceremony, carefully *mataché*—that is, with the whole body painted in different colors."[60] Again, Dumont observes that the Indian women are passionately fond of vermilion, which they use for the purpose of besmearing themselves—*pour se mattacher*—applying it not only to the face, but sometimes also to the top of the shoulders and the breast[61] *Matachiaz,* a noun related to *mataché,* is the equivalent of "necklaces, scarfs, and bracelets," according to Lescarbot (1612-1614).[62] Champlain declares that among the northern tribes *matachias* is the name given to bits of shell polished and strung together in beads.[68]

---

[59] Cf. Stanley C. Arthur, *The Birds of Louisiana,* Bul. 5 (Louisiana Department of Conservation, January, 1918), pp. 54, 56.

[60] *Jesuit Relations,* LXVII, 256; *ibid.,* LXVII, 251.

[61] *Mémoires Historiques,* I (1753), 155.

[62] *Jesuit Relations,* II, 134.

[63] *Jesuit Relations,* II, 294, note 17.

In Canadian-French *mataché* also signifies "spotted," and it is from Canada that the word must have been brought to Louisiana. Though the exact source of *mataché* has thus far eluded my search, the word seems to be connected with Algonquian *mat-*, a prolific stem that expresses the general idea of passing from action to inaction, as in *mataton,* "to carry a canoe to the water," *matadjimo,* "to begin to speak," *mataige,* "to scrape skins,"—in Ojibway, *madaige,* and in Cree, *mâtahwew.*

The Canadians may have misunderstood the meaning of Cree *mâtahwew,* "to scrape a skin," and corrupted it to *mataché,* applying the term to the colors with which a skin was painted. Perhaps, however, the original signification of the Algonquian term is no longer clear. Thus William Strachey, as A. F. Chamberlain has pointed out, renders English "Perle" by the Indian *Matacawrak* and "a red dye" by the Indian *Mataquiwun,* in the supplement to a *Historie of Travaile into Virginia Britannia.*[64]

Leo Wiener connects *matachiaz* with French *matasse,* "raw silk"—in other words, "a silk string of beads."[65]

The striking resemblance between *mataché* and Span.-Port. *matizar,* "to color," "to beautify,"—cf. Span. *matizado,* "variegated,"—cannot escape the attention of Romance scholars. This resemblance cannot but be purely accidental.

Mr. Émile Picou, of Houma, in Terrebonne parish, first explained to me the meaning of *mataché.* Since my conversation with him I have heard the word in many other parts of Louisiana—in the parishes of East Baton Rouge, Pointe Coupée, Livingston, Iberia, Assumption, St. James, St. Landry, St. Martin, Lafourche, Jefferson, Orleans, and Plaquemines. *Mataché* is probably used wherever French is spoken in Louisiana. The transition in meaning from the Indian "painted in divers colors" to the Canadian "spotted" is easy and natural. The substantive *matachias* seems not to have been preserved in Louisiana-French—nor the verb *se matacher* either.

MICOINE, *f.* Audubon says that he cannot trace the etymology of *Micoine,* the name by which the Creoles of Lower Louisiana designate the Shoveler Duck (*Spatula clypeata*

[64] *American Notes and Queries,* II (1888), 3.
[65] *Africa and the Discovery of America,* II, 253.

L.).[66] The word is of Indian origin. Lahontan observes that the *Micoine* is a wooden spoon, made with a curved knife, a *Coutagan,* by the savages of Canada.[67] He also gives *Mickouan* as the Algonquian term for a spoon.[68] Again, Du Pratz notes that the savages eat their *Sagamité,* as one eats soup, with a utensil made of a buffalo horn, which is cut in two and fashioned almost like a spoon.[69] Bossu, too, declares that the Indians make *Micouenes* or spoons, as well as powder horns, out of the buffalo horn.[70]

Canadian-French *micoine* or *micoinée, f.,* "large spoon," is corrupted from Algonquian *emikwan,* the name of a wooden spoon made in various shapes and sizes.[71] The Canadians brought the word to Louisiana and applied it to the shoveler duck, whose bill is wide enough at the end to scoop up the mud in the manner of a spoon. *Micoine*—I have never heard *micoinée*—maintains its French pronunciation, *mi-* riming with French *si* and *-coine* with French *moine.* The stress is on the second syllable. It may not be without interest to recall that the Biloxi-Indian word for "hoe" is *mikõni.*

MITASSES, *f. pl.* Leggings, puttees, as in *une paire de mitasses,* or, in a transferred sense, as in *une poule à mitasses,* "a hen with feathers on its legs." The word is well known among the French of Louisiana.

In 1699 Pénicaut describes the *mitasses* as garments made of half a yard of cloth, cut in two and sewed together like a pair of stockings, through which the Indians pass their legs.[72] Baudry des Lozières observes that the *mitas* which are worn by the Indian men in winter are a kind of gaiter, made of very fine skin and ornamented with little bells, which make a good deal of noise when their wearers are walking.[73] Other references to the word are not rare: compare *mytes,* Pénicaut (Margry, V, 446); *Mitas,* Lahontan, II, 223; *Mitasses,* Du Pratz, II, 196; *une paire de superbes mitasses,* Du Lac, p. 327, and *Mitasses,* p. 349.

[66] *The Birds of America,* VI (1859), 293.
[67] *Mémoires de l'Amérique Septentrionale,*[2] II (1728), 215.
[68] *Op. cit.,* II, 225.
[69] *Histoire,* III, (1758), 9.
[70] *Nouveaux Voyages aux Indes Occidentales,*[2] II (1768), 161.
[71] Lacombe gives Cree *emikkwân;* Baraga, Ojibway *êmikwân;* Cuoq, Nipissing *emikwan.*
[72] See B. F. French, *Hist. Coll.,* N. S., (1869), 40; Margry, V. 380.
[73] *Voyage à la Louisiane* (1802), p. 210.

Mitasses came into Canadian-French from Algonquian (Nipissing or Cree) *mitas*, "leggings," and reached the Gulf Coast more than half a century before the edict of exile was issued, in 1755, against the Acadians. The word is found in several Algonquian dialects, two curious forms being Ojibway *Mittaous*—or *Midass*, according to Baraga—and Menominee *mitiqsan*.[74]

ORANG-OUTANG, *m*. Standard French *Orang-Outang*, the name of an anthropoid ape (*Pithecus satyrus* Geoffroy), inhabiting Borneo and Sumatra, is also used in Louisiana and Canadian-French. The French word is derived from Malay *Orang* (*h*)*utan*, "man (of the) woods," that is to say, "wild man," "jungle-dweller," the native designation of a member of a savage race. Either in jest or through misapprehension the name was given to the ape by Europeans of the seventeenth century.[75]

The first vowel of *orang-outang* is often elided in the Acadian pronunciation. This word doubtless found its way into Louisiana-French from Canada as well as from France.

OUAOUARON, *m*. Lafcadio Hearn cites *ouaouaron*, the La.-Fr. word for the bullfrog (*Rana catesbiana* Shaw), as a delightful and absolutely perfect example of onomatopoeia.[76] This word, however, was not coined in Louisiana; for it is found, as Sagard points out, in the Huron dialect, where it takes the form *ouraon*, "gros grenouille."[77] J. A. Cuoq, too, renders Iroquois *iotskwarhohon* by *Il y a bruit de grenouilles; on entend coasser les grenouilles*; and he gives *wararon* as the correct Iroquois name for the bullfrog.[78] There is no doubt, then, that Huron *ouraon* and Iroquois *wararon*, which are alike imitative of the bullfrog's notes, were corrupted by the French of Canada and brought by them to Louisiana in the form *ouaouaron*.

Ouaouaron is pronounced as a French word—usually *wawarõ*, but sometimes *warwarõ* (Ouararon)—with the stress in each case on the open nasal "o" of the final syllable. The latter pronunciation is said to be the more refined.

---

[74] See, respectively, Des Lozières, *Voyage*, p. 357; W. J. Hoffman, in *Bureau of American Ethnology*, Rep. 14, Pt. 1 (1893), p. 304.

[75] Gamillscheg, *Wb.*, p. 650, cites E. Littmann, *Morgenländische Wörter im Deutschen*,[2] pp. 128 ff.

[76] *Gombo Zhèbes* (1885), p. 14, footnote 4.

[77] *Le Grand Voyage du Pays des Hurons*, II, 229.

[78] *Lexique de la Langue Iroquoise* (1882), p. 140, footnote; *ibid.*, p. 156.

French *grenouille,* generally pronounced by the Acadians as if it were written *grounouille* or *gounouille,* signifies in Louisiana any small green frog; it is never used in Acadian, so far as I know, as a designation of the bullfrog.

PACANE, *f.* 1. The pecan nut. Cf. *pacanier, infra.*

The nuts of the pecan tree are more delicate than those of France and less oily, says Du Pratz; their flavor is so fine that the French make pralines of them as good as those of almonds.[79]

The pralines of Louisiana are too well known to require description. Perhaps it should be noted, however, that *praline* is often pronounced as if it were written *plarine;* and that *praline* has helped to render famous the Maréchal du Plessis-Praslin (1598-1675), whose chef was the first to make the candy bearing this nobleman's name. 2. The Least Sandpiper (*Pisobia minutilla* Vieill.). The name *pacane,* "pecan," is conferred on this bird by hunters and guides of South Louisiana because of its small size and color. It is also called *la petite bécassine,* "the little snipe."

Pacane is derived from the generic name for a hard-shell nut in the Algonquian dialects. Compare Cree *pakan,* "nut," and Ojibway *pakan,* "nut," "walnut"; *pagan,* "hazel nut." Though *pacane* is also found in Canadian-French, the immediate source of the Louisiana word is doubtless to be sought in the Mobilian, which took the name from some Algonquian dialect.

La pacane amère is a La.-Fr. term for the bitter pecan, the fruit of the Water Hickory (*Hicoria aquatica* Britt.), as well as for the pignut, the fruit of the species *Hicoria glabra* Britt. and *Hicoria cordiformis* Britt.

PACANIER, *m.* "Parmi les fruitiers, qui sont particuliers à ce pays, les plus remarquables sont les Pacaniers, les Aciminiers, & les Piakiminiers," writes Charlevoix in October, 1721, describing the country inhabited by the Kaskaskia, once the leading tribe of the Illinois confederacy.[80] Of the trees that he mentions here, two are the pecan and the persimmon; the other variety, which he calls *Aciminiers,* is the North American Pawpaw (*Asimina triloba* Dunal), though the Acadians of the present day usually speak of this tree as *le jasminier*

[79] *Histoire,* II, 26.
[80] *Histoire,* III, 417.

and of its fruit as *la jasmine, supra.* In M. Lézermes's *Catalogue Alphabétique des Arbres et Arbrisseaux* (Paris, 1788), p. 15, *Assiminier* is given as the name of the pawpaw tree; but Standard-French *asiminier* is likewise applied to the West-Indian tree known in English as the Sour-Sop (*Anona muricata* L.). A year and a half before Charlevoix's statement—on May 1, 1720, to be exact—La Harpe, describing his expedition to the Caddo country, gives a lengthy list of the trees he saw there, among which he names the *paganiers* and the *plaqueminiers.*[81]

The pecan tree (*Hicoria pecan* Engl. and Graebn.) grows wild in Louisiana, and produces small nuts with sweet kernels; the cultivated pecan, said to be *seeded* or *grafted,* bears much larger nuts of a very fine flavor. The wild pecan is sometimes called *le pacanier sauvage,* or *le pacanier d'aventure,* in contrast with the cultivated variety—*le pacanier greffé* ("grafted"). The bitter pecan or water hickory goes by the name of *le pacanier amer;* so, too, does the pignut, a name generally given to two species of hickory (*Hicoria glabra* Britt. and *Hicoria cordiformis* Britt.).[82] Robin's name for the bitter pecan is *Noyer pacanier amer.*[83]

Ordinarily *le noyer* is the Black Walnut Tree (*Juglans nigra* L.), or the wood of that tree; sometimes, however, it is used as the name of the Hickory (*Hicoria*). When the one is to be distinguished from the other, such terms as *noyer blanc,* "white hickory," and *noyer rouge,* "red hickory," are employed, according to Mr. E. Parent, Jr., of French Settlement. But in Pointe Coupée the hickory is usually called *ikri, m.,* and in Assumption Parish it is *ikré,* both words clearly being deformations of English *hickory.*

Robin describes the black walnut tree as *le Noyer à Fruit noir;* Charlevoix calls it more simply *noyer noir.*[84] Du Pratz groups both the black walnut and certain species of hickory under the name *noyers.*[85]

Pacanier is formed from *pacane, supra,* by the addition of *-ier.* Compare La.-Fr. *La pacanière,* "the pecan grove."

---

[81] See Margry, VI, 265.

[82] Cf. *Coteau Pacaniers Amers,* Survey T 14 S —R. 18 E., SE Dist. La., West of Miss. River.

[83] *Voyages,* III, 511.

[84] *Voyages,* III, 509-510, and *Histoire,* II, App. 48 ff., respectively.

[85] *Histoire,* II, pp. 24-26.

PATASSA, *m.* *Patassa,* a derivative of Choctaw *patàssa,* "flat," as used in the phrase *nàni patàssa,* "flat fish," is the generic name of the various species of sunfish that inhabit the fresh waters of Louisiana. Du Pratz, who gives the etymology of the word correctly, observes that the patassa is the *gardon* of the New World.[86] The plural "les patassas" is used by Baudry des Lozières.[87] *Patassa* is pronounced as a French word; but those persons who do not speak French refer to the sunfish by the erroneous term "perch."

At least eight species of sunfish are found in Louisiana; among these the most important are the Bluegill (*Lepomis pallidus* Mitchill), the Scarlet Sunfish (*Lepomis miniatus* Jordan), the Red-breasted Bream (*Lepomis auritus* L.), the Round Sunfish (*Centrarchus macropterus* Lacépède), and the Green Sunfish (*Lepomis cyanellus* Raf.).[88]

PICHOU, *m.* The bob-tailed wild cat, an animal known also as the bobcat, or Bay Lynx (*Lynx rufus Guldenstaed and Lynx rufus floridanus* Raf.). In November, 1721, Charlevoix uses the plural *Pijoux* for two species of wild cats: the one with a short tail, which is the common American wild cat; and the other, a larger animal that goes by the name of *cougar* or *puma* (*Felis concolor* L.). The latter is called also *catamount, mountain lion,* and *American lion.* Du Pratz, too, describes the *Pichou,* remarking that it is smaller than the tiger, has a beautiful skin, and is very destructive of poultry; but his illustration of the animal is interesting chiefly because of its total lack of resemblance either to the wild cat or to the cougar.[89]

The wild cat is still met with in the dense forests of Louisiana, whereas the cougar is now almost extinct. The La.-Fr. name for the cougar is *chat-tigre, m.* Duvallon calls the cougar *le tigre Américain.*[90]

Pichou, which is pronounced strictly as a French word, seems to have reached Louisiana in two ways: first, through Mobilian *pishu,* "wild cat," which is taken from Ojibway *bishi, pishiu,* "lynx," or from Menominee *pisheu, "cougar";*[91] and secondly, through Canadian

[86] *Histoire,* II, 156.
[87] *Voyage,* p. 175.
[88] *Louisiana Today* (1924), p. 76.
[89] Cf. Charlēvoix, III, 407; Du Pratz, II, 92; Duvallon, p. 101.
[90] *op. cit.,* p. 100.
[91] Cf. W. J. Hoffman, in *Bureau of American Ethnology,* Rep. 14 (1893), Pt. I, p. 310.

travelers, who borrowed it from Cree *pisiw*, "lynx," or from Nipissing *pishiu*, "lynx," the latter being written *piciw* in Cuoq's *Lexique de la Langue Algonquine*, p. 335, with the translation "loup-cervier," the French term for the Canada lynx (*Lynx canadensis* Geoffroy).

In Canadian-French the word *pichou* designates, as Clapin observes, a person who is ugly or malicious, the phrase *laid comme un pichou* being especially common.[92] In Louisiana an expression often heard is *méchant comme un pichou*, "bad as a wild cat."

From *pichou* has perhaps been formed La.-Fr. *pichouette, infra.*

It is worth adding that Mobilian *pishu* is entirely different from the Choctaw name for the wild cat—that is to say, *shakbatina*, which is formed from Choctaw *shakbona*, "brown," "dusky."

The Choctaw term is appropriate; for the wild cat is reddish-brown in autumn and winter, and ashy-brown in spring and summer, according to Audubon and Bachman.[93] Compare Latin *rūfus*, which in the scientific term for the wild cat signifies "reddish" of various shades.

PICHOUETTE, *f. Pichouette*, formed perhaps from *pichou*, *supra*, with the aid of the diminutive suffix *-ette*, signifies a "bad little girl," the word being often used in such an expression as *C'est une* (*petite*) *pichouette*, "She's a bad little rascal."

Pichouette must not be confused with La.-Fr. *chouette*, "darling," a term of endearment that is related not to French and La.-Fr. *chouette*, "screech owl," but through the Norman dialect to Old French *souef*, "sweet," "gentle" (Gamillscheg). "Ma petite chouette," one says in Louisiana.

Canadian-French *chouette*, too, has the force of *amie*, "sweetheart," and also, like Continental French, of the adjectives "fine," "splendid," "classy." An example of the latter usage is *Cela est chouette.*

The Indian source of *pichouette* is rendered very dubious by the existence, in Southern France, of the personal names *Pichio, Pichon, Pichot,* and *Pichou,* which L. Larchey renders by (1) *petit enfant, mince, nouveau-né,*; (2) *pie, blanc et noir.*[94] *Pichon* is also a saint's name, equivalent to Latin *Picio*. Moreover,

---

[92] *Dict. Canadien-Français*, p. 245.
[93] *The Quadrupeds of North America*, I, 2.
[94] *Dictionnaire des Noms* (Paris, 1880), p. 375.

Pichon signifies "a fish," or "fisherman," in the district lying between Douai and Lille, in Northern France[95]

Pichon, Pichot, and *Pichou* are Canadian family names.[96] Of the three *Pichou* especially is common in Louisiana.

PICOUETTE, *f.* Some Acadians, according to my colleague, Mrs. Judith Major, designate a thin, ill-tempered child by the term *picouette,* saying *c'est une picouette.* The origin of this term is obscure; perhaps it is related, with change of suffix, to Canadian-French *picouille, f.,* "an animal extremely thin, emaciated," which is formed from the Algonquian stem *pīko-,* "broken," "shattered," "torn."

PLAQUEMINE, *f.* The fruit of the persimmon tree is called *plaquemine*; the tree itself, *le plaqueminier,* a word which ends in the familiar suffix *-ier. Plaquemine* came into Louisiana-French, through the Mobilian dialect, from Illinois *piakimin,* "persimmon."[97] The names for the persimmon tree and its fruit are known to all the French inhabitants of Louisiana.

In Choctaw the persimmon is *ũkof ápi.*

An early reference to the food prepared from persimmons by Indian women is made by Henry de Tonti, who speaks, on November 14, 1684, of "des pastes d'un certain fruit qu'ils appellent *Paquimina,* lequel est fort bon."[98]

PLAQUEMINIER, *m. Plaqueminier* is the name of the persimmon tree (*Diospyros virginiana* L.), which grows almost everywhere in the State. Charlevoix gives the name as *Piakiminier* or *Plakminier de la Floride;*[99] and Du Pratz notes the French change of *Piacminier* to *Placminier.*[100] On May 1, 1720, La Harpe uses the modern spelling, in the plural *plaqueminiers.*[101]

For the origin of *plaqueminier,* see *plaquemine, supra.*

SACACOUA, *m.*; SASACOUA, *m.* These words signify "hubbub," "racket," "uproar," "confused cries," "shouts," as defined for me by Messrs. F. V. Brignac, V. Guitrau,

---

[95] See Charles Bonnier, *Uber die Französischen Eigennamen in Alter und Neuer Zeit* (1888), p. 14; cf. also Alice Sperber, "zur Bildung Romanischer Kindernamen," *ZRPh., Beih.,* XXVII, 152 ff.

[96] N. E. Dionne, *Les Canadiens-Français* (1914), p. 484.

[97] See my *Louisiana Place-Names of Indian Origin* (1927), pp. 50-51.

[98] Margry, I, 601.

[99] *Histoire,* II, App., 37; cf. *Piakiminiers, ibid.,* III, 395.

[100] *Histoire,* II, 18.

[101] Margry, VI, 265.

and A. Vicknair, all of French Settlement, Livingston Parish. *Sacacoua* has nothing to do with French *saccage,* "confusion," "jumble," but is of Algonquian origin: compare Cree *Sâkowew,* "to utter cries of joy or encouragement," Nipissing *sakwatam,* "to utter cries," and *sakakwa,* "thick forest," words containing the stem *sak-,* "numerous," "close together," "serrated." *Sacacoua* is pronounced as if written *sakakwa,* the stress normally falling on the last syllable. That Algonquian *sakakwa* was adopted by the French of Canada, to whom it is still familiar and by whom it was brought to the lower Mississippi valley, is evident from the occurrence of the form *sacacayou* in Nicolas de la Salle's narrative of an encounter with a body of Natchez Indians: "Ils firent le sacacayou, la huée," he says, obviously assigning to *sacacayou* the sense of "war-cry."[102] The ending of *sacacoua* is apparently due to confusion with that of *sasacoua, infra.*

SASACOUA, *m.* Another Canadian-French word of the same signification as *sacacoua* is also used in Louisiana—namely, *sasacoua,* which was adopted by the Canadians from Algonquian (Nipissing) *sasakwe,* "to utter piercing cries"; compare Ojibway *sassakwe,* "to shout with joy," Cree *sâkowew, sâsâskwew,* "to utter cries of joy, of encouragement." The form *sasocoüest* is found in Father Membré's narrative of La Salle's voyage down the Mississippi. "Having sailed forty leagues till the third [or 13th] of March [1682]," writes Membré, "we heard drums beating and sasocoüest (war-cries) on our right. Perceiving that it was an Akansa village, the Sieur de la Salle immediately passed over to the other side with all his force, and in less than an hour threw up a retrenched redoubt on a point, with palisades and felled trees, to prevent a surprise and give the Indians time to recover confidence."[103] *Sasacoué* is a Canadian-French variant.

Sacacoua is used at Bayou Goula, Convent, French Settlement, Jonesville, and Kinder; *sasacoua,* at Clinton, Loreauville, Marksville, and New Iberia; in the parish of Pointe Coupée and in the city of New Orleans. Obviously, a city as large as New Orleans may also num-

[102] Margry, I, p. 557.

[103] Isaac J. Cox, *The Journeys of René Robert Cavelier, Sieur de la Salle,* I, 136.

ber among its residents some who are familiar with *sacacoua* rather than with *sasacoua.* But in many communities neither form of the word is known.

Folk etymologists are inclined to resolve *sacacoua,* which is pronounced *sakakwa,* into *sac à quoi,* and sometimes they apply the term to a braggart, taking *C'est un sacacoua* to be the equivalent of "He's a windbag." Ordinarily, however, *sacacoua* as well as *sasacoua* has the same meaning as *tapage* and *vacarme,* "great noise," words which are naturally as common in Louisiana as they are in France.

SACAMITÉ, *f.* *Sagamité* is the name of the hominy or porridge that the Indians made of coarse Indian corn; with this hominy they sometimes boiled meat, or fish, or beans. The popularity of this dish attracted the attention of many early explorers of the New World. Bossu once dined with the Peoria Indians on bears' paws, beavers' tails, and a kind of bread which the Indians called *pliakmine.* (Cf. *Plaquemine, supra.*) "I likewise eat," he says, giving further details about the dinner, "of the dog's flesh through complaisance, for I have made it a rule to conform occasionally to the genius of the people with whom I am obliged to live, and to affect their manners, in order to gain their friendship: they likewise brought in a dish of boiled gruel, of maize flour, called *sagamité,* sweetened with syrup of the maple tree; it is an Indian dish which is tolerably good and refreshing. At the end of the repast they served a desert of dry fruits which our Frenchmen call *bluets* (huckleberries; blueberries), and which are as good as Corinth raisins: they are very common in the Illinois country, which is red all over with them in the season. The village of the Peorias is situated on the banks of a little river, and fortified after the American manner, that is, surrounded with great pales and posts.[104]

No Indian tribe, one should observe, ever conferred the name *sagamité* on its hominy. As early as 1632, however, the word *sagamité* appears in Canadian-French through a misapprehension of the meaning of Ojibway *kisagamitew* or of a similar form in some other Algonquian dialect. Algonquian (Nipissing) *kijagamite,* according to Cuoq, signifies "the liquid (or water) is hot," the component elements being *agami,* "beverage or soup," and *Kiji . . . ite,* "to be boiled." Algonquian

[104] Bossu-Forster, I, 189.

Kij signifies "heat" or "hot." Lacombe, p. 708, has "*Sagamite* (Cris) pour: *Kisagamitew,* 'C'est un liquide chaud.'" The French Canadians, taking *kijagamite* or *kisagamite* to be the Indian for "porridge," corrupted the word into *sagamité. Sagamité* ultimately found its way through Mobilian to Louisiana, where in the form *sac(c)amité,* "hominy," it is still used by the French. The pronunciation, of course, is French. Another term for *sacamité* is *le gros gru.*

The eighteenth century saw the evolution of such English forms as *shaggamitie, sagamitty,* and *sagamite;* the nineteenth century, *sagamity* as well as *sagamité.* The preferable spelling in English is now *sagamité.*[105]

SOCO, *m.* The French of Louisiana are all familiar with *soco,* the name of the Southern Fox-grape or the berry of the muscadine (*Vitis rotundifolia* Michx.). This grape, which is still fairly common in the forests of Louisiana, is large and round, with a tough skin and a somewhat musky flavor. The jelly made from the muscadine is highly prized. The vine is known as *la liane de soco.* The scuppernong, a variety of the muscadine, is called *soko* or *soko blanc,* "white muscadine."

Choctaw *suko,* "muscadine," is the source of the word. The fact that *suko* has become La.-Fr. *soco*—pronounced *sokó*—doubtless reflects the well-known tendency of Choctaw "u" to interchange with "o," as in *fuka, foka,* "residence," *humma, homma,* "red," *shukulbi, shokolbi,* "nook," *sukolichi, sokolichi,* "to tap," and numerous other words.

\+

TAFIA, *m.* A spirituous liquor obtained from molasses, sugar cane, and brown sugar. Du Pratz speaks of the ardor with which the negroes worked when he promised them "un coup de Tafia."[106] Duvallon observes that the favorite drink of the colonists was *tafia* in which there had been preserved the fruit of the wild cherry tree.[107] The popularity of *tafia* is also attested by the author of *Le Champ d'Asile* (1819), p. 73, note 3.

Mr. L. T. Fontenelle, of Pointe à la Hache, and Mr. L. Falgout, of Raceland, inform me that the word *tafia* is fast becoming obsolete. As late as 1880, however, George W. Cable mentions the syrup and tafia that were

---

[105] Cf. J. A. Cuoq, *Lexique de la Langue Algonquine,* pp. 15-16, 156; F. W. Hodge, *Handbook of American Indians,* II, 407; the *New English Dictionary,* under *sagamité.*

[106] *Histoire,* I, 347.

[107] *Vue de la Colonie Espagnole* (1803), p. 113.

made from sugar cane;[108] and *tafia* undoubtedly survives in the Louisiana proverb, *Le tafia dit toujours la vérité,* "Tafia always tells the truth." Nowadays, however, Du Pratz's *un coup de Tafia* is ordinarily replaced by *un coup de whisky,* a phrase that the Acadians pronounce *ẽ kud wiski* (or *uski*). Here *ẽ* represents the sound of "a" in English *bat* nasalized, and the other letters have the same values as in French.

Tafia is of obscure origin. Though given in 1722 as a native name in the West Indies—"Les sauvages et les nègres l' appellent tafia"[109]—it is, nevertheless, recorded in Malay dictionaries and must have been widely known not only in the West but also in the East. It was admitted to the French Academy in 1762, and is found in English as early as 1777.[110]

From *tafia* has been formed La.-Fr. *tafiateur, m.,* "drunkard."

TAÏQUE, *f.* *Taïque,* "squaw," is an adaptation both in form and in meaning of Choctaw *tek,* "female," a word which regularly designates the female gender. Thus *isi* is the Choctaw for "deer," whereas *isi tek* signifies "doe." *Taïque* forms the second element in *Faquetaïque,* the name of a prairie in St. Landry Parish and a derivative of Choctaw *fakit tek,* "turkey hen." *Taïk* and *taik* are the spellings used by the anonymous author of an *Essai sur Quelques Usages et sur l'Idiome des Indiens de la Basse Louisiane*—see page 26 *et passim*—which was written at Opelousas in 1862. On page 41 of this essay *taïk* is several times rendered by *femme.* The Howard Memorial Library, in New Orleans, has a copy of this interesting study.

Taïque, which is pronounced strictly in French fashion with the stress on the second syllable, is often employed in a derogatory sense, such an expression as *Elle est mechante comme une taïque,* "She's as bad as a squaw," being not uncommon in Livingston Parish as well as in Lower Louisiana. I have also heard it in the city of New Orleans.

Some Acadians, unfamiliar with the original meaning of *taïque,* use *méchante comme une taïque* with the force merely of *très méchante*; others, equally ignorant

[108] *The Grandissimes,* XVIII, 197.
[109] Jean B. Labat, *Voyage aux Iles de l'Amérique,* III, 410.
[110] See *A New English Dictionary,* under *tafia.*

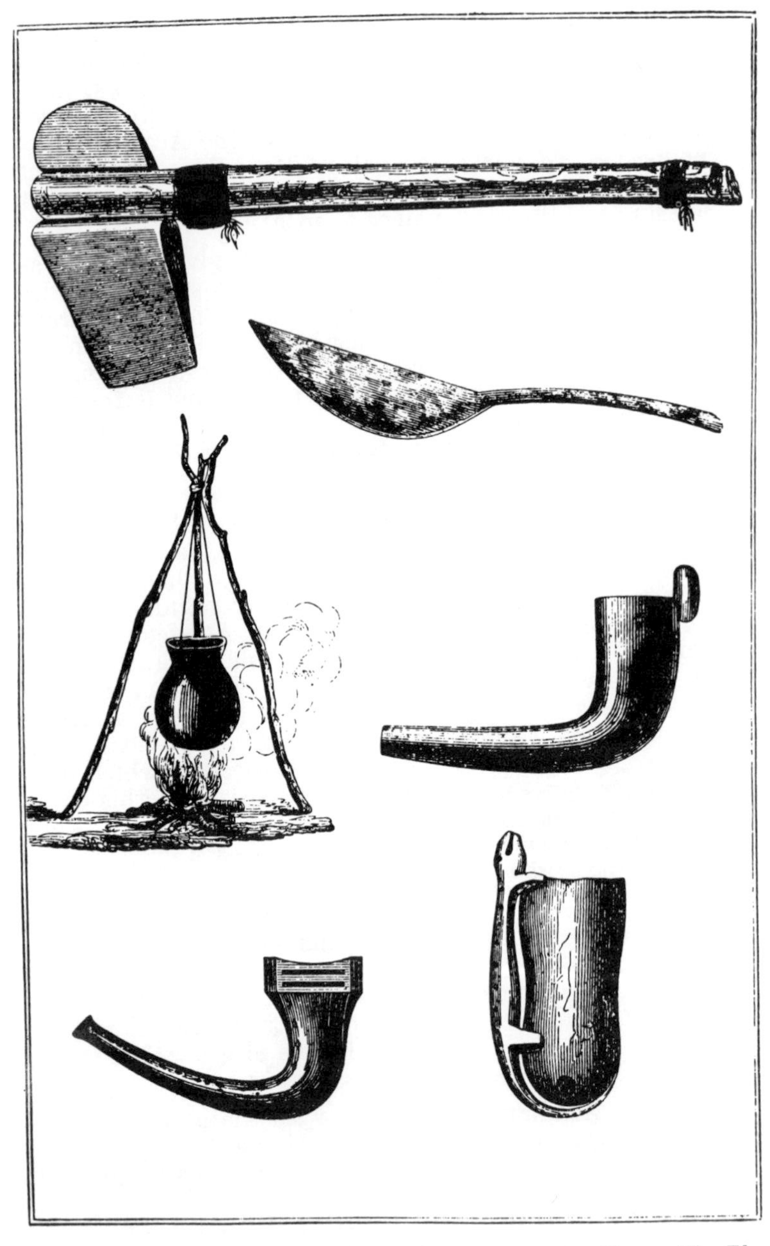

Indian Tomahawk, Kettle, Spoon, Pipes, etc. From Brownell's *The Indian Races of North and South America*, p. 30.

of the source of *taïque*, assign to it the sense of "a person with long, disheveled hair," saying, for example, *Elle est (comme) une taïque.*

TOMAHAWK, *m.* In Louisiana-French *tomahawk* is rare, being heard, so far as I know, at French Settlement alone, where it signifies "an old hatchet." In Canadian-French it signifies "war-club," and in Chateaubriand's *Atala* (1801) it appears in the sense of "war-ax."

Tomahawk, a word applied to the Indian war-ax, and erroneously also to the war-club, came into English from Virginia Renape *tomahak*, Captain John Smith defining *tomahacks* in 1612 as "axes." Renape *tamahak* is shortened from *tamahakan*, "cutting utensil," which is cognate in turn with Micmac *tumigan*, "ax," Abnaki *tamahigan*, Mohegan *tummahegan*, and similar forms in some other Algonquian dialects.[111] As late as 1874 Lacombe derives Canadian-French *tomahawk* from Cree *otomahuk*, "knock him down," or *otamahwaw*, "he is knocked down"; but Standard French borrowed the word from English, and such, too, is, in all probability, the medium through which *tomahawk* reached the French dialect of Canada as well as that of Louisiana. The English form, at any rate, must have helped the Indian word to fix itself in the latter two dialects.

The early French explorers applied the term *casse-tête, m.*, first, to the Indian war-club, and afterwards to the little ax that the Indians obtained from white traders. La Salle, awaiting in 1679 the approach of a band of twenty savages, remarks that they were armed with muskets, axes, bows, arrows, and a kind of club called *casse-tête*.[112] Charlevoix, too, defines *casse-tête* as a little club of very hard wood, terminating in a round head with a sharp edge; but he observes further that the same name was subsequently given to little axes which the savages had substituted for the wooden clubs, and which consequently rendered combats more sanguinary.[113] Again, in one of the drawings in Lahontan's *Mémoires*, the war-club is described as a *Casse-tête*, and the war-ax is distinguished from it merely by the use of the adjective *petit*.[114]

[111] W. J. Gerard, in *The American Anthropologist*, X, N. S. (1908), 277.
[112] Margry, I, 453-454.
[113] *Histoire*, III (1744), 222, 238; cf. Du Pratz, II, 200-201 (misprinted 190-191).
[114] Lahontan, *Mémoires*,[2] II (1728), facing page 193.

The information derived from Charlevoix and Lahontan is especially interesting because of the light that it throws on the meaning of *casse-tête* in Louisiana-French. In this dialect *casse-tête,* literally "break head," is the only word that corresponds to English *hatchet. Hache,* on the other hand, invariably renders English *ax.*

+TOPINAMBOUR, *m.* Jerusalem Artichoke (*Helianthus tuberosus* L.), and its edible tuber.

French *topinambou* originally designated the name of a native people of Brazil. From *topinambou* was formed *topinambour,* which received the meaning of artichoke because the plant is thought to have been first observed in the land of this Brazilian race. The Jerusalem artichoke was cultivated by Indian tribes of the Mississippi Valley before the discovery of the New World.†

Topinambour is found in Canadian as well as in Continental French. In the seventeenth century it made its way into English, in which it is now written *topinambou, -bour, -bar.*

In the parish of Iberia *topinambour* is usually pronounced *toupinambour.*

For an excellent comment on the etymology of *topinambour,* see O. Nobiling, "Beziehungen zwischen Europaischen und Amerikanischen Sprachen," *Revue de Dialectologie Romane,* I (1909), 428.

2. GERMAN WORDS

German influence on Louisiana-French is virtually confined to personal and geographical names. The German colonists who settled, between 1719 and 1722, on the west bank of the Mississippi, from twenty-five to thirty-five miles above New Orleans, extended their holdings, especially after 1728, to the other bank as well as farther up and down the river. The best known of their villages was named *Carlstein* after Karl Friedrich d'Arensbourg, who was commander of the German Coast for more than forty years; it occupied the site of the present village of Lucy, in the parish of St. John the Baptist.[115] At some distance

† Clark Wissler, *The American Indian,*[2] p. 15.

[115] L. F. Laurent, "History of St. John the Baptist Parish," *Louisiana Historical Quarterly,* VII, No. 2 (April, 1924), 328.

south of Lucy are situated Lake des Allemands, Bayou des Allemands, and the village of Des Allemands.

The settlements of the Germans gave rise to the term *Côte des Allemands or Côte Allemande,* "German Coast," which was applied to land along the banks of the Mississippi in the parishes of St. Charles and St. John the Baptist. The German Coast received various accessions, notably from Lorraine in 1754, and from Swiss soldiers employed in Louisiana by the French authorities. As early as 1721 seventy Germans settled below English Turn on the Mississippi; other German families were scattered up the river above New Orleans. In 1774 a large number of Germans came from Maryland and made their homes in the vicinity of Manchac, an old post fourteen miles by river below Baton Rouge. Further details on early German immigration to Louisiana are given in J. Hanno Deiler's well-known volume entitled *The Settlement of the German Coast of Louisiana* (Philadelphia, 1906).[116]

The remarkable changes suffered by the German family names at the hands of the French and Spanish officials receive adequate treatment in Deiler's study. The following are some typical transformations, in which the original German form precedes its Romance counterpart:

Bertram—Spanish *Beltram.*
Graef (in)—*Crevine.*
Heidel—*Aydel, Jaidel, Keidel, Hedelle, Idel, Etdell,* now *Haydel.*
Himmel—*Hymel, Ymelle.*
Kerner—*Cairne, Kerne,* etc., and Spanish *Quernel.*
Kleinpeter—*Clampetre, Cloinpetre,* now again *Kleinpeter.*
Nolte, Jacob Wilhelm—Spanish, *Villenol, Don Santiago.*
Rommel—*Rommelle, Romle, Rome,* etc., and Spanish *Romo.*
Schaf—*Chauff, Skoff,* etc., now *Chauffe.*
Schoen—*Chaigne, Chesne, Chin.*

Zweig, proving too difficult for the French tongue, was merely translated into *Labranche.* But the most baffling

[116] See also George C. H. Kernion, in the New Orleans *Item-Tribune,* Sunday, December 16, 1928, p. 7.

name of all seems to have been *Scheckschneider,* for which Deiler records twenty-seven different forms:[117] it is now usually written *Schexnayder* or *Schexnaydre.* As the earliest form is *Scheckschneider,* this name cannot signify either "Jake Schneider" or "Six Schneiders," the one interpretation like the other being the product of folk etymology. The second element of the name is clearly German *Schneider,* "tailor," whereas the first, which alone presents any difficulty, is connected with German *scheckig,* a term applied to one whose hair or beard is beginning to be streaked with gray. The corresponding French term is *grisonnant.* I note, however, that Adolf Socin takes Middle High German *Scheko* for a nickname signifying "dressed in striped clothes."[119]

It is, furthermore, important to remember that the early German colonists pronounced German, as Deiler has pointed out, after the fashion of their native dialects. Con- +sequently the view that *Teche,* the name of the well-known bayou in Southwest Louisiana, is a corruption of *Deutsch* should not be lightly dismissed;[120] for in many dialects of South Germany *Deutsch* is pronounced as if written *Teitsch,*[121] *d* having the value of *t* and the dipthong "eu" being unrounded to "ei."

The natives of the Teche country, however, maintain that *Teche* is derived from an Indian word meaning "big snake." The meaning of *Teche* must as yet be considered obscure.

Nevertheless, there remains the possibility that some early settler named the Louisiana bayou after the Tech, a small river which descends from the Pyrénées-Orientales and empties, near Ceret, into the Mediterranean.

---

[117] *Ibid.,* p. 126.

[119] *Mittelhochdeutsches Namenbuch* (1903), p. 438.

[120] Norman Walker, "The Geographical Nomenclature of Louisiana," *The Magazine of American History,* X, No. 3 (1883), 215.

[121] Otto Behaghel, *Geschichte der Deutschen Sprache*[4] (1916), pp. 154-155; 254-255.

3. ENGLISH WORDS

Historical.—As early as 1765 or 1766 colonists from North Carolina had settled in the vicinity of Baton Rouge, and before the outbreak of the Revolution other immigrants from the colonies had established themselves along the Mississippi between Natchez and Manchac. During the Revolution many Tories fled to the Spanish province of West Florida, and some of them found refuge in a place that they are said to have named Galveztown, as a token of their gratitude to Governor Bernardo de Galvez.[122]

To the English and American inhabitants of Galveztown there were added in 1778 about three dozen Spanish colonists, who were among the immigrants sent over at the expense of the Spanish crown from the Canary Islands. But Galveztown did not prosper; it fell into early decay, and almost all traces of its site on the right bank of the Amite River, just below the mouth of Bayou Manchac, have long since disappeared. The present village of Galvez, in Ascension Parish, occupies a site two miles distant from that of the extinct Galveztown.[123]

After the purchase of Louisiana by the United States in 1803, immigration from various parts of America became so great that by the middle of the nineteenth century the American sugar planters in Louisiana almost equaled in number those of Creole descent, the former being estimated at 710 and the latter at 751.[124] In 1832 Timothy Flint, it is true, had been inclined to consider the American element numerically inferior to the Creole in New Orleans;[125] but by 1830 the business rivalry between Creole and American had become so keen that the city was actually divided into three parts, each with its own board of aldermen, though the three municipalities were all governed by one mayor and council.[126]

---

[122] Alcée Fortier, *History of Louisiana*, II, 61; Judge Carrighan, "The Parish of East Baton Rouge," *De Bow's Review*, XI, N. S., 253.

[123] See V. M. Scramuzza, "Galveztown," *La. Hist. Quar.*, XIII, No. 4 (October, 1930), 553-609.

[124] V. Alton Moody, "Slavery on Louisiana Sugar Plantations," *La. Hist. Quar.*, VII, No. 2 (April, 1924), 201.

[125] *History and Geography of the Mississippi Valley*[2] (1832), p. 267.

[126] Grace King, *Creole Families of New Orleans* (1921), p. 43.

The influence of English on Louisiana-French is very strong, and this influence is steadily increasing. The time will inevitably come when French will no longer be spoken in Louisiana; for Creoles and Acadians alike are prone to discard their mother tongue, largely because they are compelled in their youth to acquire English in the classrooms of the public schools of the State. As the English loans, however, are easily recognized, they need not detain us long. Here are some typical examples:

ACRE, *m.* From English *acre.* Dial.—So.; Can.-Fr. Cf. *arpent, infra.* Pronounced in French fashion.

ADRESSER, *vb. tr.* From English *address: adresser la parole = prononcer un discours,* "deliver a speech." Dial.—So.; Can.-Fr.

AGENT. From English *agent.* Dial.—So.; Can.-Fr. Pronounced in French fashion.

ANXIEUX, EUSE *adj.* English *anxious.* Dial.—So.; Can.-Fr.

APPLICATION, *f.* English *application;* request. *Faire application* is equivalent to St.-Fr. *faire une demande,* "to make a request"; *sur application,* "on request," is St.-Fr. *sur demande.* Dial.—So.; Can.-Fr. Pronounced like a French word.

APPOINTMENT, *m.* Appointment; engagement, rendezvous. From English *appointment.* Dial.—So.; Can.-Fr. Pronounced like a French word.

BAD LOQUE, *m.* From English *bad luck.* Dial.—Sw.; Can.-Fr.

BÉQUINE, *m.* From English *bacon.* Dial.—So.; Can.-Fr. Standard French has *lard,* "bacon."

BOFLO, *m.* Corrupted from English *buffalo;* dialect of Pointe Coupée; pronounced as if written *beaufleau.*

BOSS, *m.* Master; from English *boss,* the latter being a derivative of Dutch *baas,* "master" originally "uncle." cf. Ger. *Base,* "female cousin."

BOUILLOIRE, *m.* Steam boiler. From English *boiler.* Dial.—Sw.; Can.-Fr.

BULL-EYE, *vb. tr.* To hunt animals with a bull's eye lantern, as in the phrase "bull-eye des caïmans" (alligators). Dial.—So.

CHARGER, *vb. tr.* and *intr.* To charge; to fix a price; to make an entry to one's debit. This verb, derived from English *charge,* is used in the South and Southwest in such expressions as *charger trop cher, charger trois piastres* ("dollars"), *il m'a chargé une piastre, je vous l'ai chargé,* "I have charged it to you." *Charger* was brought to Louisiana by the Acadians, and is pronounced like a native French word.

COQ GA-IME, *m.,* Game cock. *Ga-ime,* from English *game,* is heard in Lafayette, Louisiana; *gam,* rhyming with English *jam,* in Pointe Coupée, where *coq batailleur* is used as well as *coq gam.* In Breaux Bridge *coq de bataille* is very common, by the side of the curious form *coq ga-ine. Ga-ime* and *ga-ine* are pronounced like French words.

CORRECT, -TE, *adj.* From English *correct.* Dial.—So.; Can.-Fr.

COUPER, *vb. tr. Couper les gages,* "to cut the wages." Dial. —Sw.; Can.-Fr.; merely a translation of the corresponding English term.

DÉPÔT, *m.* Railway station. From English *depot.* St.-Fr. *dépôt* signifies "warehouse." Dial.—So.; Can.-Fr.

DISGRACE, *f.* Disgrace, dishonor. Pronounced in French fashion, with *s* like *z.* Dial.—Sw.; Can.-Fr.

DURS TEMPS, *m. pl.* A literal translation of English "hard times." Dial.—Sw.; Can.-Fr.

FERRY, *m.* Ferry; pronounced as a French word, with *y* like French *i;* heard at Port Vincent, in Livingston Parish, and also in the Southwest.

In Canadian-French *ferry* is pronounced *ferrai.*

GODDAM, GODDEM, *m.* One of the names of the Ruddy Duck (*Erismatura jamaicensis* Gmel) : in Standard French a nickname for an Englishman. Dial.—South Louisiana, especially the coast region.

GROCERIE, *f.* Grocery. From English *grocery.* Dial.—So.; Can.-Fr.

GROCERIES, *f.* Groceries. From English *groceries.* Dial.—So.; Can.-Fr.

IKRÉ, IKRI, *m.* Corrupted from English *hickory.* Dial.—*Ikré* in Assumption Parish.

INTRODUIRE, *vb. tr.* To introduce one person to another. This signification of the verb is taken from English *introduce.* Dial.—Sw.; Can.-Fr.

MARCHANDISES SÈCHES, *f. pl.* A translation of English *Dry Goods.* The designation of a store handling dry goods or novelties. Dial.—Can.-Fr. Extensively used in Louisiana-French.

PIE, *m.* Pie, as in *un morceau de pie,* "a piece of pie"; widely used and pronounced as in English.

SAY-SO, *m.* English "say so," used in various ways. *Un say-so de crème,* for example, is the equivalent of "a cone of ice-cream."

RED SNAPPER, *m.* An important salt-water fish of the Gulf Coast (*Lutianus campechanus* Poey). La.-Fr. *poisson rouge,* "Red fish," is the name of another salt-water fish (*Sciaenops ocellata* L.), found in the waters of the South Atlantic Coast.

REMARQUES, *m. Passer des remarques,* "to pass remarks." A literal translation of the English term. Cf. St.-Fr. *faire des observations.* Dial.—Sw.; Can.-Fr.

STEAK, *m. Steak:* Standard French has *bifteck.* Dial.—So.; Can.-Fr.

TICKET, *m.* From English *ticket;* pronounced approximately *tickette*; equivalent in meaning to St.-Fr. *billet,* and widely used in French Louisiana as well as in Canadian-French.

TRACK, *f.* Railway track, race course, etc. English *track.* Widely used; Can.-Fr. Pronounced like Fr. *trac,* "track of animals," "pace" (of horses, etc.).

WAGUINE, f. A spring wagon. English *wagon. Waguine* is pronounced like a French word. Popular everywhere in Louisiana and found in Canadian-French.

4. AFRICAN WORDS

Besides the dialects of the Creoles and the Acadians there has been developed in Louisiana a patois which is spoken by many colored people, and which has undergone so many violent changes that it is virtually unintelligible to one who is quite at home in Standard French. Some white natives of Louisiana, it is true, speak good French, Acadian, and the negro-French patois with almost equal facility.

A specimen of the negro patois will be found on page 148, *infra*.[127]

When the Company of the Indies surrendered its charter of Louisiana to the crown of France in 1731, there were only about two thousand negroes in the whole province of Louisiana.[128] This number was steadily increased in North America until after the outbreak of the Civil War. Before the end of the War, however, the African slave-trade was altogether suppressed. As early, indeed, as 1807, President Jefferson had approved Senator Bradley's bill prohibiting the importation of slaves into any port or place within the jurisdiction of the United States from and after January 1, 1808.[129]

Nevertheless, in 1809, the year after French troops had occupied Madrid, the French were exiled from the Spanish colonies, and the United States government undertook the task of transporting to New Orleans 6,060 souls; of these 1,887 were whites, 2,060 were free blacks, and 2,113 were slaves. In August of the same year there arrived some 1,484 more refugees, of whom at least 884 were slaves.[130] These slaves accompanied their masters from Cuba by permission of the United States. On the other hand, the smuggling of slaves into America continued steadily, so that by 1860 the number of slaves in Louisiana had increased to 326,726, and the colored people who had been made free reached a total of 18,527. At that time the population of the State was estimated at 708,002. Most slaves came from a belt of land extending along the western coast of Africa from Cape Verde southward through the Congo region; some were brought from the interior of Africa.[131]

---

[127] See Alfred Mercier, *Étude sur la Langue Creole en Louisiane* (no date); Alcée Fortier, *Louisiana Studies*, pp. 134-147, a reprint of "The French Language in Louisiana and the Negro-French Dialect," *Transactions of the Modern Language Association of America*, I (1886), 96-101. Cf. *Romania*, XV, 635.

[128] Cf. Fortier, *History of Louisiana*, I, 101; Sir Harry H. Johnston, *The Negro in the New World*, p. 137; Carter H. Woodson, *The Negro in Our History*,[5] p. 87.

[129] W. E. B. Du Bois, *The Suppression of the African Slave-Trade to the United States of America* (1904), pp. 108, 192.

[130] L. M. Perez, "French Refugees to New Orleans in 1809," *Publications of the Southern History Association*, IX, No. 5 (1905), 293-310.

[131] John R. Commons, *Races and Immigrants in America* (1907), p. 39; Newbell N. Puckett, *Folk Beliefs of the Southern Negro* (1926), p. 3.

The Company of the Indies established for its African slaves a corral across the river from New Orleans, where Algiers is now situated. This corral was called the "Plantation of the Company"; it was in reality a slave prison, says Henry P. Dart.[132]

In 1719 the first cargo of African slaves—500 in number—reached Louisiana.[133]

African loans to Louisiana-French are necessarily limited in number; for the negro slaves were obviously compelled to learn the language of the ruling class, and hence must rapidly have abandoned or forgotten their native dialects. The negro-French patois is composed of a highly corrupt French vocabulary, some native African words, and a syntax for the most part essentially African. The following are some of the African words that have made their way into Louisiana-French:

BAMBOULA, *f.* 1. A drum of bamboo. 2. A dance performed to the beat of this drum. *On fait la bamboula* is Acadian for the modern "They are making whoopee."

Bamboula is thought to have been derived from Fr. *bambou* by the negroes of Haiti, and *bambou* is perhaps ultimately from Malay *samambu,* "Malacca cane," through the intermediate form *mambu* (Weekley). E. Littmann, however, suggests that *bambus,* which is the German cognate, may be of Indian (*Hindoostan*) origin;[134] and the *New English Dictionary* cites *bănbŭ* or *banwu* from the Kanarese of India as the possible source of the Malay word.

Bambou and *bamboula* are both found in Standard French as well as in the French dialects of Louisiana.

+CALA, *m.* A sweetened rice cake, served with the morning *café au lait,* and formerly sold by the Creole negro women in the French Quarter of New Orleans. These women are said to have advertized their cakes to the cry of "bel (les) calas tout chauds."

The apparent discrepancy between the gender of *belles* and that of *calas* or *chauds* requires a word of

[132] "The Slave Depot of the Company of the Indies at New Orleans," *Louisiana Hist. Quarterly,* IX, No. 2 (April, 1926), pp. 286-287.

[133] See Henry P. Dart and Alfred G. Sanders (translator), "The First Cargo of African Slaves for Louisiana, 1718," *Louisiana Historical Quarterly,* XIV, No. 2 (April, 1931), 163 ff.

[134] *Morgenländische Wörter im Deutschen,*[2] (1924), p. 129.

explanation. Though the negro-French adjective is regularly masculine in form, *belle* serves for the masculine and the feminine gender, because negro-French *beau* is a substantive only, signifying "sweetheart," "beau."

Recipes for *calas* are given in the *Picayune Creole Cook Book,*[6] page 165, and in Célestine Eustis' *La Cuisine Créole à l'Usage des Petits Ménages* (1928), p. 108.

The rice-cake batter is fried in boiling lard deep enough to prevent the cakes from touching the bottom of the pan. My friend, Mr. J. St. Clair Favrot, therefore, suggests that *cala* is nothing but a corruption of *calé,* the past participle of *caler,* a verb which in Louisiana and Canada has the force of French *enforcer,* "to sink," "to plunge." Compare a similar usage of *caler* in the dialect of Poitou. The *calas,* then, are thus called, because they are plunged into boiling lard. I am myself of the opinion that the word is of African origin. In the Duala (Bantu) dialect of Cameroon rice is called *wond'a bakala,* "beans of the Europeans."[135] Whether *cala* is an aphetic form of this term must obviously rest on conjecture. Again, in the Malinke dialect of Senegal *Kala* is applied to various objects.[136]

In the Mande dialect, too, of Western Sudan, the Upper Niger, and the region to the south, *kala* signifies a bow (for shooting), a knife-handle, a stalk, a bough.[137] The word is probably African, though its exact source is as yet unknown.

As the negro women carried the *calas* in baskets on their heads, *cala* is sometimes used sarcastically in the sense of a hat.

CALALOU, *m.* This word is used in Pointe Coupée in such a phrase as *je lui ai fait manger du calalou,* "I have made him eat calalou"—that is, "I have got even with him." *Calalou* is apparently not found elsewhere in Louisiana; nor has it, strange to say, any other meaning in Pointe Coupée than that which has just been noted.

The West Indian *calalou* is a thick soup or stew, made almost exactly like the Louisiana *gombo.* Here is Turiault's recipe for the *Calalou* of Martinique:

---

[135] A. Seidel, *Die Duala-Sprache in Kamerun,* pp. 41, 63.

[136] *Dictionnaire Français—Malinké et Malinké-Français,* p. 130.

[137] E. Péroz, *Dictionnaire Français-Mandingue,* p. 124.

"Fameux ragoût créole dans lequel entrents des bourgeons de giraumon, du pourpier, du gombo, des feuilles d'amaranthe, de l'oseille de Guinée et autres herbages, une volaille, un morceau de jambon, des crabes, des écrevisses, du jus de citron et surtout beaucoup de piment."[138]

In Haitian-French *calalou gombo* is the popular name of the okra plant (*Hibiscus esculentus* L.).[139]

Carlos Gagini observes that the *calalú* of Costa Rica is the *Phytolacca decandra* L., a plant which is known in English as *Poke, Scoke,* or *Pigeon-berry.* It is also called *Inkberry, Redweed, Red-ink plant, Pocan-bush, Coakum, Cancer-jalap, American nightshade,* and *Pokeweed.*[140]

C. Suárez gives the Cuban-Spanish *calalú, m.,* first, as the name of a species of wild plant belonging to the family *Amaranthaceae;* and secondly, as the name of a soup made with various vegetables, among which is the *calalú.*[141] The plant that he mentions is probably the spiny amaranth (*Amaranthus spinosus* L.).

F. Ortiz traces Cuban-Spanish *calalú* to the African *colilú,* a Mandingo name of an edible plant resembling spinach.[142] The French language of Louisiana may have received the word from African slaves as well as from French refugees and Spanish settlers.

CALINDA, *m.* An immodest African dance, in which the men formed in one line and the women, facing them, in another. The *calinda* and other voodoo dances were banished from Congo Square by the city of New Orleans about 1843.[143] The *calinda,* however, has long been popular in the West Indies. Speaking of the African slaves of the French Antilles, Père Labat says, "That which pleases them best and is their most common diversion is the *calenda,*" a dance which he believes was brought from the region of Arada on the coast of Guinea.[144]

---

[138] *Etude sur le Langage Créole de la Martinique,* p. 488.

[139] *Identification des Plantes d'Haiti,* p. 9.

[140] *Diccionario de Costarriqueñismos,* p. 81. Gagini cites H. Pittier, *Ensayo sobre las Plantas Usuales de Costa Rica.* Washington, D. C., 1908.

[141] *Diccionario de Voces Cubanos,* p. 95.

[142] See *Glosario,* p. 94, and the references there given.

[143] H. E. Krehbiel, *Afro-American Folksongs*[4] (1914), p. 116.

[144] *Nouveau Voyage aux Isles de l'Amérique,* IV (1742), 463; quoted by Ortiz, *Glosario,* p. 107.

Du Pratz records the dance as the *caleinda.*[145] J. Turiault cites it as *calinda* or *caleinda* from the negro-French dialect of Martinique.[146]

Ferdinand Ortiz has tried to show that Cuban-Spanish *calinda* is of African origin, the word being identical with Cuban-Spanish *caringa,* the name of an ancient region and of a river in the Kongo region. Ortiz regards Cuban *caringa* as a corruption of *calinda*: both words signify a dance.[147] The orthography of *calinda* points to a Congo source: cf. Congo *empinda,* "pinder," "peanut," *emfinda,* "wood," and *oluinda,* "lamp." Hearn's suggestion of Spanish *que linda,* "how beautiful," as a possible source of *calinda* rests on folk etymology.[148] Even more preposterous is W. W. Newell's association of the word with Latin *calendae,* "kalends."[149]

Danser le calinda is the La.-Fr. term for "to dance the calinda."

CONGO, *m.* The name *Congo* is given by most Creoles and Acadians to the poisonous Water Moccasin, or Cotton-Mouth Moccasin (*Ancistrodon piscivorus* Lacépède) ; by others to a bluish-black eel-like amphibian (*Amphiuma means* Garden), which, though quite harmless, is considered deadly by the common folk. Both reptiles are common in Louisiana. Duvallon classes *"le Serpent Congo"* with *"le Serpent à sonnettes,"* "rattlesnake," as the two most dangerous snakes in Louisiana.[150]

Congo, a name first given to negroes from the Congo region of Africa, was afterwards bestowed on objects or animals of a dark or black color. Thus *Le Congo* is a negro dance; and *Sarcelle Congo, f.,* is one of the names of the green-winged teal (*Nettion carolinense* Gmel.).

In the Mandingo language of Western Sudan, the Upper Niger, and the district to the south, the word *Congo,* signifying "country," "forest," or "mountain," was first conferred on a vast territory in Africa; subsequently the same name was used instead of *Zaire,* the term by which the Portuguese designated the great river running through the Congo region. The present Congo name, however, of the river is *Enzadi,* "the

---

145 *Histoire,* I, 352.

146 *Étude sur La Langue Créole de la Martinique* (1874), pp. 410, 411, 422, 423.

147 *Glosario,* pp. 107-109, 540.

148 *Gombo Zhèbes* (1885), p. 32.

149 *Journal of American Folklore,* IV, 70.

150 *Vue de la Colonie Espagnole* (1803), p. 105.

river," of which *Zaire* is a corruption.[151] The original meaning of *Kongo* seems to have been "iron spear," a name afterwards given to territory acquired by war-like tribes who made use of this weapon.[152] In far Western Kongo, at any rate, the word for "hunter" is *n-Kongo*. But Duala *Kongo* (*Koñgo*) signifies "plantation."[153]

+COUCHE-COUCHE, *m.* Corn-meal dough sweetened with sugar and fried brown. It is served with milk or eaten at breakfast with coffee.

St.-Fr. *couscou*—in the eighteenth century written also *cuzcuz, cousse-couche* and *couche-couche*—was borrowed from the African slaves of the West Indies. The ultimate source of the word is the same as that of Fr. *couscous*, an Arabian dish of meat-balls and flour, which is borrowed from Arabic *kuskus,* itself a derivative of Arabic *kaskasa,* "to pound small." Du Pratz uses the form *couscou.*

GOMBO, *m.* Originally the okra plant (*Hibiscus esculentus* L.), from Congo *quingombo,* "okra"; now applied to any thick soup in which the okra pod is an ingredient, such as *gombo févis,* "okra gumbo," *gombo aux crabes,* "crab gumbo," and *gombo aux huîtres,* "oyster gumbo"; or to other kinds of gumbo thickened with a powder prepared from sassafras leaves. This powder goes by the name of *filé,* the past participle of French *filer,* "to twist"; hence *gombo filé* signifies properly "ropy or stringy gumbo."

Gombo is also applied to a heavy, sticky soil and to the negro-French patois. The English form *gumbo* is widely used in Louisiana.

GRIS-GRIS, *m.* An object worn as a protective charm against evil, or used, on the other hand, for the purpose of inflicting injury. *Faire un grig-gris* is "to make a charm," either for good or for evil purposes. *Gris-gris* also has the force of a transitive verb, "to voodoo, bewitch, cast a spell over," as in *elle m'a gris-gris,* "she has bewitched me." As *gris-gris* is commonly associated with voodoo rites, it is generally believed to be of African origin. In Senegal, indeed, the word designates any kind of

---

[151] See Alexander Knox, *Glossary of Geographical and Topographical Terms* (1904), pp. 206, 408.
[152] H. H. Johnston, *A Comparative Study of the Bantu and Semi-Bantu Languages,* II (1922), 106, footnote 1.
[153] Leo Wiener, *Africa and the Discovery of America,* I, 161.
[154] *Histoire,* I, 351.

amulet;[155] in the Mandingo dialect *grigri* or *girigiri* signifies "to shake," "to tremble," a term that was also used in the sense of evil spirit or charm.[156] In Spain, where the word is also found, it is the name of a relic containing the names of certain saints and worn as a talisman by the Moors. Thus the word traveled to Louisiana not only from Africa, doubtless by the way of the Spanish West Indies, but also directly from Spain. The ultimate source of *gris-gris* is Arabic *hirz acihr,* "amulet of enchantment."

Gris-gris were made and used in various ways by the voodoos of New Orleans. Marie Laveau, a noted voodoo queen, concocted a gris-gris of salt, gunpowder, saffron, and dried dog dung; she carried, too, a rabbit's foot, a magnet, and some gold ore. Balls as large as oranges were fashioned of gaudy feathers and secreted in a pillow or in a bed; a cross of wet salt or a small coffin was placed on a porch or doorstep, the former pointing to trouble and the latter indicating death. Among the *gris-gris* that protect against evil or bring good luck a favorite was, and is, a dime with a hole in it, which is often worn about the ankle.

+JAMBALAYA, *m.* A Spanish-Creole dish made with rice and some other important ingredient, such as shrimp, crabs, cowpeas, oysters, sausage, chicken, or turkey. A jambalaya may consist, too, chiefly of rice and the remnants of beef, pork, or game. Favorite recipes are *jambalaya à la Créole, jambalaya aux chevrettes* (shrimp), *jambalaya aux crabes,* and *jambalaya aux congris* (cowpeas).

Jambalaya is pronounced in French fashion as a rule. Occasionally, however, the initial consonant is sounded like "j" in English *jam.* The word has been Anglicized as *jumbal(l)aya.*

I can suggest no plausible source for *jambalaya.* Can it be related to Congo *chimbolo, zimbolo,* "bread," "biscuits"?[157]

NÈGRE BAMBARA, *m.* A light-hearted negro; one free of care and indifferent about his appearance. *Un nègre Bambara* is used in St. Landry Parish and doubtless elsewhere in the Southwest.

---

[155] *Mélusine* for March, 1888, p. 57; cited by W. W. Newell, *Journal of American Folklore,* II, (1889), 44.

[156] Leo Wiener, *op. cit.,* III, 129-130.

[157] Craven and Barfield, *English Congo and Congo English Dictionary* (1883), p. 149; Ortiz, *op. cit.,* p. 173.

Two interpretations of *Bambara* are possible. It may signify, first, a negro who came from the Bambara tribe, which inhabits Western Sudan and the region of the Upper Niger. As the Bambara tribe is a member of the Mandingo nation, and as Mandingo *bamba* signifies "crocodile," we may interpret *Bambara* as the "people whose idol or fetish is a crocodile."[158]

The objection to this analysis of Bambara lies in the apparent discrepancy between the literal meaning of *Bambara* and that assigned to the word in Louisiana. It is a fact that Cuban-Spanish *Bambara* has the natural signification of "member of the Bambara tribe," or "pertaining to the Bambara tribe." Perhaps *Bambara*, to state a second possibility, has been confused with Spanish and Cuban-Spanish *bambarria*, which signifies (1) "fool" (colloquial) and (2) "an accidental but successful stroke at billiards." *Bambarria* is derived by the *Diccionario de la Lengua Academia* from *bamba*, which springs in turn from the stem of Latin **bambus, -a, um,* "stammering"; then "foolish."[159] But *Bamba*, which has the second meaning assigned to *Bambarria*, is connected by Ortiz with Congo *Mbamba*, "gambling," or perhaps with Mpongwe *bumbua*, "to obtain something unexpectedly, without effort."[160] The Mpongwe language is spoken in the French Congo, along the lower Ogowe and Gabun rivers.

NIAME-NIAME, *m.* 1. "Food," as in *c'est du bon niame-niame*; 2. *vb. tr.* and *intr.* "to eat," as in *je vais niame-niame la pomme; je vais niame-niame.*

In most Bantu dialects *nyama* or *inyama* signifies "meat"; in Northwestern Bantu *nya* is the stem of the verb "to eat."[161] In Central Africa *niam-niam* is used in the sense of "cannibals," a term applied to the tribes inhabitating the plateaux between the Ubangi River, the upper Bahr el Ghazal, and the upper Shari River.[162]

It is interesting to note that the Gullah (Angola-Bantu) dialect of South Carolina makes use of the verb *nyam* or *nyam-nyam*, "to eat";[163] and that Afro-Cuban

---

[158] Cf. Alex. Knox, *Glossary of Geographical and Topographical Terms*, p. 32; E. Péroz, *Dictionnaire Français-Mandingue*, p. 25.

[159] Cf. Körting, *Wb.*, pp. 138-139.

[160] *Glosario*, pp. 41-42.

[161] Sir H. H. Johnston, *A Comparative Study of the Bantu and Semi-Bantu Languages*, I, 90, 119, 622, *et passim;* II, 181, 533.

[162] Alex. Knox, *Glossary* (1904), p. 280.

[163] A. E. Gonzales, *The Black Border* (1922), p. 315.

Spanish has the substantive *ñami-ñami f.*, "food."[164] Perhaps Bantu *nyama*, "meat," reached Louisiana by way of Cuban-Spanish.

OUANGA or WANGA, *m.* A charm; from Southwest African *owanga*, "witchcraft"; compare Angola *wanga*, "magic," and western Zambesia *Vuañga*, "witchcraft."[165] Here, too, should be noted Congo *mbwanga*, a charm consisting of a bundle of aromatic powder, used as a cure for headache; or a charm made of a bundle of powder, bits of leaves, serpents' heads, birds' beaks, etc., having power to produce or avert disease.

From *ouanga* has been formed La.-Fr. *ouangateur* (*wangateur*), *m.*, "conjurer," "voodoo-doctor," with the feminine *ouangateuse* (*wangateuse*). These terms are well known in New Orleans; they are also used in St. Martinville, and perhaps elsewhere in South Louisiana.

The Congolese use various charms to protect themselves against the witches whom they believe to be responsible for sickness, misfortune, and death. If a man becomes seriously ill, the *nganga a moko*—"arms-doctor"—pretends to find out who is bewitching the patient. If the man dies, the *nganga a ngombo*—"witch-doctor"—is summoned, who shortly declares some one guilty of causing the patient's death. The accused is compelled to drink poison in order to prove his innocence; if he happens to survive, he is freed, and the witch-doctor is fined or receives no fee.[166]

Cuban Spanish *uangá, m.*, "witchcraft," is likewise of African origin.[167]

The resemblance between *ouanga* and French *onguent*, "salve," which W. W. Newell considers significant, is purely accidental.[168]

VOUDOU, *sb. m.* and *f.* A negro sorcerer or witch; a practicer of voodoo rites, consisting of enchantment, charms, and witchcraft, which are all imbued with African customs and superstitions: *il est un voudou*, "he is a voodoo"; *elle est une voudou*, "she is a voodoo"; *la danse des voudoux*, "the dance of the voodoos." 2. *adj.* Of or pertaining to voodooism or a voodoo: *une danse*

[164] Ortiz, *Glosario*, pp. 373-374.

[165] Sir H. H. Johnston, *Comparative Study*, I, 343, 358, 369.

[166] The Rev. W. Holman Bentley, *Dictionary and Grammar of the Kongo Language* (1887), pp. 345, 504-505.

[167] Cf. Ortiz, *Glosario*, p. 468.

[168] *Journal of American Folklore*, II (1889), 43-44.

voudou, "a voodoo dance"; *la religion voudou,* "the voodoo religion."

The formal observance of voodoo rites is now quite rare, if not virtually extinct, in Louisiana; but the persistence of such terms as *gris-gris* and *ouanga* shows how deeply the voodoo cult has modified the beliefs of many negroes and illiterate whites. With the death of Marie Laveau, a noted voodoo queen, "voudouism all but disappeared from New Orleans. The little that is practiced today assumes a harmless form; a few chicken bones placed on a doorstep, a black cross-mark on the front board, a bright red powder sprinkled on the banquette; these are the last vestiges of the once-dreaded *gris-gris.*"[169] Marie Laveau was born on February 2, 1827, the illegitimate child of Jacques Paris's widow, and one Christophe Glapion, both free mulattoes. She resided for a long time in a cabin on Bayou St. John, and here she made the "gris-gris" that she sold as cures for various diseases or as charms to protect the purchaser against this or that calamity. In 1884 she is said to have been living in a shanty on the bank of Lake Ponchartrain. She is buried in the old St. Louis cemetery of New Orleans.

Lyle Saxon gives a vivid description of a voodoo ceremony that he attended in 1928.[170] As he tried in vain, however, for many years to ascertain whether voodooism was still practised in Louisiana, his experience seems to verify the conclusions of N. N. Puckett, who, writing of voodooism in New Orleans, declares that "the closest search fails to reveal any underlying organization; and real 'hoodoo-men,' who inspire the fear and patronage of superstitious clients, have confided to me that they have long wished to join the voodoo society, but years of residence in New Orleans have failed to bring to light the existence of any such."[171]

Nevertheless, a New Orleans family recently found a large cross of damp salt on the front porch of their home. The voodoos—or "hoodoos," as they are often called—regard a cross of salt as a symbol of impending misfortune; and consequently Hilda Phelps Hammond, writing in the New Orleans *Times Picayune* for Sunday, October 5, 1930, argues that voodooism, brought to

[169] G. William Nott, *Marie Laveau,* The New Orleans *Times-Picayune* (Nov. 19, 1922), Magazine Section, p. 2.

[170] *Fabulous New Orleans* (1928), pp. 309-322.

[171] *Folk Beliefs of the Southern Negro* (1926), pp. 190-191.

Louisiana from the African coast by way of the West Indies, still exists in New Orleans despite the efforts of the municipal authorities to stamp out this abominable cult.

A popular voodoo chant is composed of the following lines:

> L'appé vini, li Grand Zombi;
> L'appé vini pou to gri-gri.
> ("He is coming, the great Zombi;
> he is coming for your gris-gris.")

Voudou is borrowed from African (Dahomey) *vodũ* "fetish." In the related Ewe dialect the word signifies " a god," "a supernatural being," "an object regarded as a fetish."[172] The fact that the Waldensians were accused of sorcery has led some writers to derive *voudou* erroneously from French *vaudois*, "Waldensian," "sorcerer."

Numerous publications on every phase of voodooism are cited in the bibliography of N. N. Puckett's *Folk Beliefs of the Southern Negro,* (1926), pp. 583-598. George W. Cable's articles in the *Century Magazine* for February and April, 1886, are especially valuable, the one dealing with "The Dance in Place Congo" and the other with "Creole Slave Songs."

ZINZIN, *m.* Baldpate or American Widgeon (*Mareca americana* Gmel.). This term is evidently considered imitative of the baldpate's shrill notes, which to Audubon's ear sounded somewhat like the word *sweet.*[173] *Zinzin* is pronounced strictly in La.-Fr. fashion: *zẽ-zẽ.*

Zinzin is of African origin. In Angola the word for "bird" is *zinzila;* that for "fowl" is *sanse* or *sanisi.* In the language of the Yombas, who reside between Dahomey and the Lower Niger, *sinsin* signifies "fly" (insect). Furthermore, in the Kongo dialect a "chicken" is *nsusu,* and west of the Zambesi a "sparrow" is *zune. Zinzin* must therefore be regarded as a La.-Fr. adaptation of some Bantu word for "bird," or "fowl," or insect." This view is corroborated by the existence of Cuban-Spanish *zunzun,* the name of a species of humming bird, which Ferdinand Ortiz traces to *susu,* the Mandingo-Malinke term for "mosquito."[174]

---

[172] Ortiz, *Glosario,* pp. 470-471.

[173] Audubon, *Birds,* VI, 259.

[174] *Glosario,* pp. 506-508: cf. Johnston, *Comparative Study,* I, 366, 674; 674; II, 105, 301.

ZOMBI, *m.* Ghost, apparition. In Pointe Coupée *zombi* is pronounced like a French word of the form *jombi.* The substitution of "j" for "z" probably indicates the popularity of the word, initial "z" being almost wholly confined to literary loans in French. *Faire zombi* (*jombi*) signifies "to play possum," for a *zombi* is naturally associated with the opossum's habit of feigning death.

The source of *zombi* is Congo *Onzambi, Nzambi* (Angola), "God." The Pointe Coupée form may point to Central Congo *jambi,* in which *j* is equivalent to French *j.*[175]

In Haitian-French *zombi,* "devil," forms an element of some plant-names, such as *Callebasse Zombi* (*Enallagma cucurbitana* L.), *Corossol Zombi* (*Annona montana* Macf.), *Latanier Zombi* (*Coccothrinax anomala* Becc.).[176]

In the negro-French dialect of Martinique, *zombi* signifies "devil."[177]

5. SPANISH WORDS

Historical—The Spanish element in Louisiana-French consists chiefly of words that found their way into Standard French through the early Spanish Conquests in the New World. Such words have come from the Carib of the West Indies and the Northeast Coast of South America, the Arawakan of South America, the Nahuatlan (Aztec) of Mexico, and the Kechuan, this last being the language of the ancient Inca empire and nowadays that of Indian tribes in Peru.[178]

Some words, ultimately of Indian origin, are seldom heard in popular speech, but are almost wholly confined to commercial, technical, or literary usage. Many of them came through Spanish into French; most of them appear both in English and in Standard French; hence their origin and signification can as a rule be found in reputable French or English dictionaries, as well as in publications like W. F. Schmidt's *Die Spanischen Elemente im Französischen*

[175] Johnston, *Comparative Study,* II, 307.

[176] See *Identification des Plantes d'Haiti par Leurs Noms Créoles,* Bul. 18, (Avril, 1930), 9, 11, 16.

[177] J. Turiault, *Étude sur la Langue Créole de la Martinique* (1874), p. 488.

[178] Cf. Menendez Pidal, *Manual de Gramática Histórica Española*[4] (1918), pp. 32-34.

Wortschatz (1914), Rudolf Grossmann's *Das Ausländische Sprachgut im Spanischen des Rio de la Plata* (1926), and Georg Friederici's *Hilfswörterbuch für den Amerikanisten* (1926).

Some of the most important of the loans from Spanish are *alpaca, ananas, cacique, coyote, lama* (Sp. *llama*), *mangle, manioc, tamalé, and tapioca.* Among these words *alpaca, ananas,* and *tapioca* are quite common; *coyote* is pronounced *kayót;* and *tamalé, m.,* which is generally pronounced in French fashion, and may have been borrowed by the French of Louisiana from English *tamale,* seems to be gaining in popularity. Mexican-Spanish *tamál*—pl. *tamáles*—the source of the English word, is an adoption of Nahuatlan *tamalli,* and may indeed be the real origin of the Louisiana-French word.

Some other traces of Spanish influence lead back to Franco-Spanish rivalry in the Southwest during the latter part of the seventeenth and the beginning of the eighteenth century. When St. Denis had established Fort Natchitoches in 1714, the Spanish government met this advance by founding a mission among the Adai Indians in 1716 and erecting an outpost in 1721 where the town of Robeline is now situated. Near Robeline a bayou is designated as *Adois,* a corruption of the tribal name *Adai,* "brushwood." In the seventeenth century the Sabine River was known to the Spaniards as *Rio Sabinas, infra.* Owing to the lack of early surveys it is difficult to fix the exact age of certain place-names of Spanish origin in the western and southwestern areas of Louisiana; but such names as *Bayou S. Patricio, Bayou Lenan, Bayou Negreet, Bayou Toro,* and *Bayou Anacoco* are probably not much older than the period of Spanish domination (1762-1803).

In 1778, during the administration of Governor Bernardo de Galvez (1777-1785), Spanish immigrants from the Canary Islands were established on Bayou Terre-aux-Boeufs, at Galveztown, and in the Valenzuela district along the banks of Bayou Lafourche. The descendants of those who settled in the Delacroix region, southeast of New

Orleans, are known as *Islingues*, "Islanders," from Spanish *Isleños*.[179] Another group of Spanish immigrants founded the settlement of New Iberia, on Bayou Teche, in 1779. But the town of New Iberia was not laid off until 1835.

The village of Barton, situated about 3 miles below Donaldsonville, is inhabited largely by descendants of early Spanish settlers. In Barton Spanish is the language of the older generation. See Sidney A. Marchand, *The Story of Ascension Parish*, p. 114.

Various Spanish place-names are more important for the historian than for the linguist. Thus St. Joseph, a lake in Tensas Parish, bears the first name of *José Vidal*, who was commandant of the post of Concordia from 1798 to 1803. The town of Vidalia, as well as Bayou Vidal, perpetuates his family name. Again, Spanish Fort, founded by Carondelet near New Orleans in 1770, was formerly called Fort San Juan. More interesting perhaps than the foregoing names, *Colyell Bay*, in Livingston parish, recalls the career of Francisco Collel, a young Spanish (Catalonian) officer who served under Galvez in the campaign of 1779-1781 against the British forces in West Florida.

It is not merely by old Indo-Spanish loans and geographical or family names that the Spanish element in Louisiana-French may be distinguished: the same element is evident in certain words, some of which found their way, during the Spanish régime or later, into the popular Louisiana-French vocabulary. The following list includes examples of both early and of late loans as well as one or two loans that may be from Portuguese:

ACAJOU, *m.* *Acajou* is the name of the wood of the mahogany tree (*Swietenia mahagoni* L.). Canadian-French uses this word in the same sense as well as *mahogané*, *m.*, an adaptation of English *mahogany*. I have not heard the latter in Louisiana-French.

Standard-French *acajou* is derived, probably through Portuguese *acajú*, from Brazilian Tupí *acaju* or *acaiu*, the name applied to the fruit of the tropical tree *acaiba*

[179] Cf. Alcée Fortier, "The Isleños of Louisiana and Their Dialect," *Louisiana Studies* (1894), pp. 197-210.

(*Anacardium occidentale* L.). French *acajou* is the source of English *acajou* and *cashew*.†

ANANAS, *m.* *Ananas,* Louisiana-French, Canadian, and Standard French for the pineapple plant and fruit, is derived, through Spanish *ananas* or Portuguese *ananáz,* from Guaraní *anāña,* "pineapple fruit," and *nānā,* "pineapple plant." *Ananas* is not, as is sometimes stated, of Peruvian origin; in Peru the Kechuan name for the pineapple plant and fruit is *achupalla.*[180]

American-Spanish has substituted *piña* for Standard-Spanish *ananas,* because of the resemblance of the pineapple to a pine cone.

BACALAO, *m.* Codfish (*Gadus morrhua* L.). A well-known recipe is called *Bacalao à la Vizcaína,* properly "Biscayan Codfish." Spanish *bacalao* signifies "codfish."

BANANE, *f.*; BANANIER, *m.* *Banane,* "banana," and its derivative *bananier,* "banana tree," are used in Louisiana as well as in France. French *banane* is borrowed from Sp. *banana.* The ultimate origin of *banane* is obscure. The *Dictionnaire Général* traces *banane* to the dialects of India. The *New English Dictionary* considers the word an adoption of Spanish and Portuguese *banana,* the fruit, and *banano,* the tree, which De Orta gives in 1563 as the native Congo terms in Guinea. *A Glossary of Anglo-Indian Words and Phrases*[2] (London, 1903) calls attention to the fact that the coincidence of the name *banana* with the Arabic *banan,* "fingers or toes," and *banana,* "a single finger or toe," can hardly be accidental.[181] I believe the Congo source to be the most plausible.

Oviedo Y Valdes, who visited the New World as early as 1514, declares that the banana was brought to America in 1516 by Brother Tomas de Berlanga.[182]

BAJO, *m.* A man of little culture; a common laborer; a person of humble origin; used in the Southwest; borrowed from the Spanish adjective *bajo,* "low," "common," etc., which springs from Low Latin *bassus, -a, um.* La.-Fr. *bajo* is pronounced like a French word, except that the medial *j* sounds like *j* in English *June.*

---

† Cf. Friederici, *Hilfswörterbuch,* pp. 1, 16.

[180] W. W. Skeat, *Notes on English Etymology* (1901), p. 4.

[181] Quoted by Ernest Weekley, *An Etymological Dictionary of Modern English* (1921), p. 109; cf. E. Littmann, *Morganländische Wörter im Deutschen,*[2] p. 152.

[182] See Erland Nordenskiöld, *Comparative Ethnographical Studies,* No. 5 (1922), pp. 70-71.

BOSSAL or BOSSALE, *m.* 1. Halter for a horse or other animal; pronounced as if written *beau-sále*; derived from Sp. *bozal*, "muzzle worn by horses, dogs," etc.; "headstall for a horse." Dial.—Pointe Coupée.

2. *Adj.* and *n.* A term applied long ago in New Orleans to a negro slave newly landed in Louisiana. This meaning of the word was brought from Santo Domingo: Ducoeurjoly defines *des nègres bossales* as those who were *nouvellement débarqués.*[183] Sp. *bozal*,, whence has come *bossale* (2), signifies "a newly imported negro slave." The source of Sp. *bozal* is Italian *barbazzale*, "curb-chain." *REW* 944.

BRÈME, *f.* Eggplant, the fruit of *Solanum melongena* (L.); shortened from Sp. *berenjena*, "eggplant," with change of the first *-n* to *m* under the influence of the initial *b*. St.-Fr. *aubergine*, "eggplant," is occasionally heard in New Orleans; *bérégène* and *aubergine* are found in Haitian-French for the "eggplant."

CABRESSE, *f.* A rope made of horsehair; used in the parish of St. Landry. *Cabresse* is adapted, with metathesis of the *r* and change of suffix, from Sp. *cabestro*, *m.*, "halter," which signifies a "rope made of hair," in the dialect of the Southwestern United States.[184] The ultimate source is Low Latin *capistrum*, "halter."

CACAO, *m.* Standard-French *cacao*, "cacao," "cocoa," is a bookish word for all except the educated Creoles.

Cacao is borrowed from Sp. *cacao*, the name of a tropical tree (*Theobroma cacao* L.), or its seed; and Sp. *cacao* is shortened in turn from Nahuatl *cacauatl* or *cacahuatl*, "cocoa-bean," in which *-tl* is the ending seen in numerous other words like *atl*, "water," *tepetl*, "mountain," and *tetl*, "stone." *Cacauatl*, whatever its elements may be, cannot be resolved into *caca-uatl*, "caca-tree," as has been done by the *New English Dictionary*, *v. cacao.*[185] Antonio Peñafiel, I note in this connection, considers *cacao* a shortened derivative of Nahuatl *cacahuacuahuitl*, which is clearly a compound of *cacahuatl*, "cocoa-bean," and *cuahuitl*, "tree."[186]

The seeds of the cocoa-tree form the principal ingredient in the manufacture of chocolate, and served the ancient Mexicans in lieu of money.

---

[183] *Manuel des Habitans de Saint-Domingue*, I, 35.
[184] Sylva Clapin, *A New Dictionary of Americanisms*, p. 90.
[185] Cf. W. W. Skeat, *Notes on English Etymology* (1901), p. 331.
[186] *Nomenclatura Geográfica Y Etimológica de Mexico* (1895), II, 47.

CACHIMBO, *m.* A smoking-pipe, formerly made of clay; pronounced as a French word; adapted from American-Spanish *cachimbo, m.,* a "smoking-pipe."[187] *Dial.*—Pointe Coupée; parish of St. Mary.

In Argentina this word takes the form *cacimba*; in Cuba and Costa Rica, *cachimba.*[188]

The immediate source of the American-Spanish *cachimbo* is Portuguese *cachimbo,* "pipe," rather than Spanish *cachimba.* Be that as it may, the word was certainly brought to the New World by African slaves. In Zanzibar opium is called *kasumba;* among the Congos the pipe is *kashiba.* The source of the African terms is Arabic *qusabah* or *qassibah,* "pipe." Cf. Arabic *qasab,* "reed."[189]

It is not surprising to find *cachimbo* and other Spanish loans in the dialect of Pointe Coupée. There exists a list of the Spanish garrison at Pointe Coupée in 1766; and instructions are known to have been issued for the commandant of *Punta Cortada* in 1770.[190]

CACHOUQUE, *f.* A dowdy woman; one whose dress lacks style. *Une vieille cachouque* is a popular phrase. This word is derived from American-Spanish *cuchuqui,* a person or thing extremely dirty. *Cuchuqui* is formed from Sp. *cuchi,* which signifies "pig" in Peru and Salvador;[191] and *cuchi* is corrupted from Sp. *cochino,* "pig."

Cachouque is said to be used at Breaux Bridge. The word is pronounced as in French except that the medial "ch" has the value of Spanish "ch."

+CAÏMAN, *m.* Alligator (*Alligator Mississippiensis* Daudin). Most Creoles and Acadians apply the term *caïman* to a large alligator with prominent scales, reserving *cocodrie, m.,* for a smaller type, quite slender and covered with scales that are nearly smooth. Some French natives, however, do not distinguish *caïman* from *cocodrie, m.;* others use Standard-French *crocodile* as the name of every kind of alligator. During the season of 1924 more than 21,000 alligators are said to have been killed in Louisiana for their hides.[192]

---

[187] Ciro Bayo, *Vocabulario Criollo-Español, Sud-Americano,* p. 41.

[188] Cf. C. Suárez, *Diccionario de Voces Cubanas,* p. 88; C. Gagini, *Diccionario de Costarriqueñismos,* p. 79.

[189] Leo Wiener, *Africa and the Discovery of America,* I, 112-113.

[190] Cf. Roscoe R. Hill, *Descriptive Catalogue of the Documents Relating to the History of the United States in the Papeles Procedentes de Cuba . . . ,* pp. 128, 480.

[191] Cf. C. Bayo, *Vocabulario Criollo-Español Sud-Americano,* p. 66.

[192] Stanley C. Arthur, *The Fur Animals of Louisiana* (1928), p. 183.

The Building of a Canoe. From *Relations de la Louisiane*, page 45.

French *caïman* comes through Sp. *caïman* from Carib *acáyouman,* "alligator," "crocodile." The form *caymanes* is found in French as early as 1587, being used in that year by Fumée, in his *Histoire Générale des Indes,* p. 95; "Cocodrilles, lesquels ils appellent en leur langue Caymanes."[193]

La.-Fr. *cocodrie* results from an effort to adjust the spelling to the present pronunciation *kokodrí,* which has descended, slightly corrupted, from French *cocodrille.* As early as the thirteenth century French *crocodile* was sometimes altered to *cocodrille* through metathesis of *r* and change of suffix. Cf. *cocodrie, infra.*

CANNIBALE, *m.* Standard-French *cannibale,*" "cannibal," is well known in Louisiana, but the derivative *cannibalisme, m.,* is scarcely used except by the educated class.

Spanish *canibal, adj.* and *n.,* the source of French *cannibale,* is a dialectal variation of *caribal,* Columbus using the plural *Canibales* as well as *Caribales* and *Caribes* to denote the Caribs, a fierce nation of the West Indies, who are recorded by foreigners to have been "man-eaters." Among the natives themselves, however, *Caribes* is said by Oviedo to have signified "brave and daring." Breton, *Dict. Car.-Fr.,* p. 105, gives *Callinago* as the true name of the West-Indian Caribs.[194]

CANOT, *m.* Standard French *canot* is now rarely heard in Louisiana, the most usual designation for a canoe or dugout being *pirogue, infra.* Other La.-Fr. names for small, flat-bottomed boats, constructed of planks, are French *chaland* and *péniche. Chabec, m.,* the equivalent of French *chébec,* is used sometimes for a small boat with a pointed bow, sometimes for a lugger. For "lugger" some Acadians employ, strange to say, the diminutive *une canotte.* French *esquif, m.,* "skiff," and English *skiff, m.*—the latter pronounced like *esquif* without the initial vowel—are other terms for a small boat.

Pénicaut gives in 1699 the following description of the manner in which the Southern Indians made their canoes before the coming of the white man:

"Nevertheless, up to that time, their canoes (Canots), with which they went from place to place upon the river, were made with the aid of fire, built at the foot of a cypress and kept up until the tree fell to

[193] Quoted by W. F. Schmidt, *ZRPh., Beiheft,* LIV, 149.

[194] Cf. The *New English Dictionary,* under *cannibal*; W. W. Skeat, ***Notes on English Etymology*** (1901), p. 30.

the ground. They then burned it off at the desired length. When they had burned the tree sufficiently for their purpose, they extinguished the fire with moist earth, and scraped out the tree with large thick shells. They then washed the canoes with water so as to give them a fine polish. Some canoes are twenty-five or thirty feet long; others vary in length according to the uses for which they are intended."[195]

The boats that Pénicaut here calls *canots* would now usually be known as *pirogues*. Indeed, Charlevoix in 1721 distinguishes the light Algonquian birch-bark *Canots* from the heavier *Pirogues* hollowed from the trunks of trees.[196]

The ultimate source of Sp. *canoa,* whence has come French *Canot,* has been sought in Carib *canáoa,* "pirogue."[197] Leo Wiener, however, has suggested that Sp. *canoa* is actually the source of the Carib word; and that *canoa* is in all probability due to a misreading of the Latin plural *scaphas,* "skiffs," found in Columbus's first letter.[198]

+
+CAOUANE, *f.* The name *caouane* is applied to the fresh-water alligator snapping turtle (*Macrochelys lacertina* Schweigger), which ranges from western Texas to western Florida and as far north as Missouri. It frequents the muddy bottoms of streams and the waters of swamps, and attracts its prey by waving a white piece of flesh which grows near the base of its tongue. This species of turtle attains a weight of 140 pounds; and the jaws of a large specimen are said to be strong enough to crush a man's hand or foot.[199] Owing to the remarkable size of its head, which may measure nearly or quite twenty-five inches in circumference, the alligator turtle is commonly known as a "loggerhead."

Standard French *caouane* is the designation of the enormous loggerhead turtle of tropical and semi-tropical seas—the *Thalassochelys caretta* (L.).

Caouane is of obscure origin. Perhaps it came into French, through the medium of Spanish, from a West-Indian dialect. In 1665 Breton gives the Carib names of three kinds of marine turtles: *Catállou,* or "tortue

[195] Cf. Margry, V, 381.
[196] *Histoire,* III, 192, 404.
[197] Cf. Karl Nyrop, *Grammaire Historique,* III, 142.
[198] *ZRPh.,* XXXIII, 529 ff. Cf. O. Nobling, in *Revue de Dialectologie Romane,* I, 428.
[199] R. L. Ditmars, *The Reptile Book* (1908), p. 18.

franche"; *Hálata,* or "Caoüànê"; and *Cárarou,* or "*caret.*"[200] An imperfect clue to the source of the word is found in Philip A. Nemnich's *Alllegemeines Polyglottenlexikon der Naturgeschichte,* II (Hamburg-Halle, 1793), 1436, where the Spaniard Cepeda is cited as the author of the assertion that Americans and travelers call a certain species of sea turtle a *caouane.*[201]

CARABAS, *m.* An ugly hat; changed in meaning from St.-Fr. *carabas,* "a large old coach," which is a loan from Norman and West-French *carabas. Carabas* is derived from Fr. *carabe,* "a wicker canoe covered with skins; a sedan-chair." *Carabe* is in turn from *caraba,* a kind of vessel used in the waters of the Levant; Low Latin *carabus,* "canoe," is the source of the Spanish word (Gamillscheg).

Carabas, which is used in parts of Southwest Louisiana, retains the final *s*-sound in Louisiana-French.

+CARANGUE, *f.* Amber fish (genus *seriola*). *Carangue,* "West-Indian mackerel," came into seventeenth-century French from *Caranga* (Gamillscheg). *Carangue* is used by the fishermen in South Louisiana.

CARGAISON, *f.* A load; an adaptation in the Southwest of Sp. *cargazon,* "cargo of a ship." The *s* of the final syllable sounds like *s,* not like *z.*

CHAMPOURA, *m.* A festive, convivial occasion. The word is pronounced as in French, except that the initial consonant is like Spanish "ch." Cf. *champurrado,* "jargon," etc., and *champurrar* or *chapurrar* "to mix liquors," etc. In the popular speech of France *champoreau* signifies a mixture of coffee and brandy or rum; from *champorro,* "mixture."[202]

At French Settlement, in Livingston Parish, *champoura* or *champara* signifies the odds and ends of vegetables, or different kinds of vegetables, cooked together. Sp. *champurra* is said to be echoic in origin; but compare Malay *champur,* "mixing," and *champurkan,* "to mix."

CHARARA, *f.* Weak coffee. This word is used in Pointe Coupée, according to Mr. D. S. Wogan, of New Orleans; and in St. James Parish, according to Miss Yolande Dicharry, of Gramercy. *Charara,* pronounced with

---

[200] *Dict. Car.-Français,* p. 409.

[201] See Dietrich Behrens, *Beiträge zur Französischen Wortgeschichte und Grammatik,* p. 354.

[202] L. Sainéan, *Langage Parisien,* p. 160.

Spanish "ch," but in other respects like a French word, may perhaps be echoic in origin—imitative of the sound heard when coffee is dripped too fast. Far more probably, however, *charara* is a corruption of Sp. *chorrera,* "spout or place whence liquids drop."

CHAURICE, *f.* A sausage made of pork, highly seasoned with spices and very hot with pepper, both black and red. The casings for this sausage are taken from the entrails of sheep.[203]

La.-Fr. *chaurice* is borrowed from Sp. *chorizo,* "pork-sausage," but owes its ending to that of Fr. *saucisse,* "sausage." *Chaurice* is pronounced with Spanish "ch"; otherwise as in French.

CHIPOLATA, *f.* A stew, a ragout; borrowed by Standard French from Sp. *chipolata* and also used in Louisiana. A goose (*oie*) may be cooked *à la chipolata. Chipolata* is pronounced as a French word.

CHOCOLATE, *m.* Standard-French *chocolate* is, of course, used in Louisiana, as in *une tasse de chocolate,* "a cup of chocolate." The French hunters of Lower Louisiana designate the female and young of the Marsh Hawk (*Circus hudsonius* L.) by *chocolatière,* "chocolate pot," because these birds are brownish-black above and rusty with dusky streaks on the breast and sides.[204]

French *chocolate* is derived from Sp. *chocolate,* and the latter is adapted from Mexican (Nahuatl) *chocolatl,* which Simeon, quoted by the *New English Dictionary* v. *chocolate,* explains as "an article of food made of equal parts of the seeds of cacao and those of the tree called *pochotl*" (*Bombax ceiba* L.). All efforts to resolve *chocolatl* into its constituent elements have failed, Friederici, in his review of Lokotsch, has very properly pointed out.[205] *Chocolate* has no connection either with *cacao,* or with *cocoa,* the English corruption of the latter word.

COLIBRI, *m.* Standard-French *colibri* is one of the La.-Fr. names of the Ruby-throated Humming-Bird (*Archilochus colubris* L.), the only species that is seen in Louisiana. A more common name is *oiseau-mouche,* literally "fly-bird," which is also found in Standard French. In Canadian-French the term *oiseau à mouche,* as well as *colibri,* is said to be used.

---

[203] *The Times-Picayune Cook Book,*[6] p. 101.

[204] Cf. Stanley C. Arthur, *The Birds of Louisiana,* p. 47.

[205] *Sonder-Abdruck aus den Göttingischen Gelehrten Anzeigen,* Nr. 7-8 (1927), p. 303.

At French Settlement, Livingston Parish, the most usual term for the humming-bird is *le baron,* properly "the baron"; in Pointe Coupée, *oiseau de fleurs.*

Colibri is said to come through Sp. *colibri* from the Carib name of the humming-bird.[206] Breton, however, does not treat *colibri* as a Carib word; on the contrary, he records *alamoinchay* for a colibri with a red breast, *manléchi* for another species with a beautiful crest, and *ierèttê* or *yerettê* for a third species with no crest at all.[207]

CONGRI, *m.* A dish of rice and cowpeas (seed of the plant *Vigna sinensis* L.). This word appears in *jambalaya au congri, m.,* the name of a dish for which *The Picayune Creole Cook Book*[6] p. 163, gives the following recipe:

1 cup of rice
I pint of cowpeas
1 large onion.
½ pound of salt meat
1 square inch of ham

In the eastern part of Cuba, *congri, m.,* is the name of a dish composed of kidney beans and rice. Throughout the island, however, this dish is generally called *moros y cristianos,* "Moors and Christians," the first word of this term referring to the color of the beans and the last to that of rice.

Ortiz, to whom I am indebted for this comment on *congri,* believes *congri* to be of African origin, but cannot trace the word to its exact source.[208]

COPAL, *m.* The explorer La Salle is said to have been the first to use *copal* as the designation of the Sweet-Gum Tree (*Liquidambar styraciflua* L.). Joutel writes in March, 1687:

"We found the country pleasant enough about that river [probably the Trinity, in Texas], though the land did not seem to be any of the best; but still it was delightful to the eye, well planted with fine trees of several sorts, among which is one that M. De La Salle had named Copal, being very beautiful, the leaves of it between those of the maple and the lime trees in resem-

[206] Cf. the *Dictionnaire Général* and R. Menendez Pidal, *Manual de Gramática Histórica Española*[4] (1918), p. 33.

[207] *Dict. Car.-Fr.,* pp. 26, 293; cf. Friederici, in his review of Lokotsch, *Göttingische Gelehrte Anzeigen* (1927), p. 299.

[208] Fernando Ortiz, *Glosario,* p. 127.

blance, and from it comes a gum of a very agreeable scent."[209]

Spanish *copal*, from which Standard French took the word in the seventeenth century, is a derivative of Aztec *copalli*, the generic name for resin, yielded by various trees and used by the Mexican Indians for incense in their temples. Louisiana-French has, so far as I know, no other name than *copal* for the sweet gum tree.

CORRAIL, *m.* Enclosure; *mettre au corrail*, "to shut up (animals) in an enclosure"; from Sp. *corral.*

CUARTEE, *f.* Two cents and a half; from Sp. *cuartillo*, the fourth of a *real.* Ex.: *Une cuartee* (*de*) *sucre. Cuartee* is pronounced as if it were French *kwarti.* Dial.—Formerly popular in New Orleans.[210]

ESCALIN, *m. Escalin* is rarely heard apart from its occurrence in the phrase *six escalins*, "seventy-five cents." *Un escalin* is, then, the equivalent of twelve and one-half cents in Louisiana-French.

French *escalin* is a derivative of Dutch *schelling*, with which English shilling is cognate;[211] but as Spanish has borrowed *escalin* from French, the popularity of this word in Louisiana may be largely ascribed to Spanish influence. Moreover, the absence of *escalin* from Canadian-French indicates rather a Spanish than a French source for the appearance of the word in Louisiana.

+

+GOFIO, *m.* Toasted cornmeal. Spanish *gofio* is used in the Canary Islands, Cuba, Porto Rico, and Argentina.[212]

The ultimate source of *gofio* seems to be unknown. *Gofio* is found in the *Historia de los Reyes Catholicos* of Andrés Bernáldez, who died in 1513.[213]

GORGOYO, *m.* Wiggler, wriggler, or wiggle-tail; the larva of a mosquito (family *Culicidae*). *Gorgoyo* is a corruption of Sp. *gorgojo*, "grub, mite, weevil, "which is a derivative of Latin *curculio*, "weevil." Dial.—Parish of Lafayette. See also *tourne-queue, vire de bord*, and *vire-vire.*

+GRÈGUE, *f.* A drip coffee pot. *Grègue* is an adaptation of Cuban-Spanish *greca*, which is used in the same sense.[214]

---

[209] B. F. French, *Historical Collections* (1846), p. 145; cf. Margry, III, 335.
[210] See Magda Chalaron, in *The Newcomb Arcade*, X, 77.
[211] Cf. Gamillscheg, *Wb.*, p. 379.
[212] C. Suárez, *Diccionario de Voces Cubanas* (1921), p. 249. Cf. C. Bayo, *Vocabulario Criollo-Español Sud-Americano*, p. 91.
[213] J. C. Y. Frauca, *Vocabulario Medieval Castellano* (1929), p. 86.
[214] Suárez, *Diccionario*, p. 252.

French émigrés must have brought the word to Louisiana. *Greca* is merely the feminine of the Spanish adjective *greco*, "Greek," employed as a noun, and apparently signifies a coffee pot made in Greek style.

HAMAC, m. Standard-French *hamac*, "hammock," is derived from Sp. *hamaca*, and the latter is a loan from Carib *amaka*. *Hamac* is used in Canadian-French.

In Louisiana *hamac* is treated as a feminine. Linking, too, takes place, as in *les hamacs*, and the vowel of the article *la* is elided, as in *l'hamac*. Here Standard French has neither linking nor elision.

HERBE À MALO, *f*. A species of water-plantain (*Alisma odorata* Raf.). Its leaf is applied to wounds and inflamed surfaces for its soothing effect. Hence Robin regards the name as the equivalent of *herbe contre tout mal.*[215] Compare:

> "And plantain ribb'd, that heals the reaper's wound."
> (Shenstone, *The Schoolmistress*, st. 12.)

At Lafayette and some other places in Southwest Louisiana, the French apply the name *Herbe à malo* to the plant called "Lizard's-Tail," Swamp Lily," or "Breast-Weed (*Saururus cernuus* L.). Tea is made from the roots of this plant and given to teething children.

The Spanish adjective *malo*, "bad," "evil," is used as a substantive in *herbe à malo*.

KAÏAC, *m*. This word signifies a "big, powerful fellow," a "roughneck," according to my friends at French Settlement. A diminutive formation is *kaïacot, m.*, a "tough little fellow." La.-Fr. *kaïac* has been changed in form and meaning from Standard-French *gaïac*, the name of the lignum-vitae tree (*Guajacum officinale* L. and *Guajacum sanctum* L.). Canadian-French has *kaïac* in the sense of "lignum vitae," as in the phrase *une toupie en kaïac*, "a spinning-top of lignum-vitae wood." The final consonant in *kaïac* has the value of *k*.

French *gaïac* is derived from Sp. *guayaco*, which is taken in turn from the name of the lignum-vitae tree in the Arawakan dialect of Haiti.[216]

La.-Fr. *kaïac* must not be confused with another Canadian-French word of the same form—a word

[215] *Voyages*, III, 340; cf. Rafinesque, *Flora*, p. 17.
[216] See the *New English Dictionary*, under *guaiacum*.

which signifies "a man's boat," built and used by the Eskimos. This homonym came into Canadian-French from Eskimo *kaïak*, "a man's boat." The Eskimo for "a woman's boat" is *umiak*.[217]

LAGNIAPPE, f. A trifling gift presented to a customer by a merchant, or, by extension, any kind of gratuity that may be regarded as thrown in for good measure. Thus a column in the New Orleans *Times-Picayune* has long borne the heading *Lagniappe*. But though the name survives everywhere in Louisiana, the merchants have largely abandoned the custom of giving lagniappe.

As an English word *lagniappe* is pronounced *lanyap*, with the stress usually on the second syllable, but sometimes on the first; the first "a" has the value of that in *land*, and the second of the vowel in *gap*. As a French word *lagniappe* is pronounced in French fashion, except that the palatal "gn" is often replaced by the sound of *ny*.

Lagniappe is composed of the French *la*, "the," and a French adaptation of Spanish *ñapa*, which is taken in turn from Kechuan *yapa*, "a present made to a customer." From Peru the word was carried to other parts of South and Central America, appearing as *ñapa* in Venezuela, Bogota, Costa Rica, and Columbia, but maintaining the form *yapa* in Ecudor. *Ñapa* is heard in the eastern part of Cuba, but this word is replaced by *contra, f.*, in the rest of the Island. In Spain the word for *lagniappe* is *adehala, f.*[218]

LOULOU, *m.* A worm; the larva of a tiger beetle (family *Cicindelidae*); known in Louisiana as a "doodle" or "doodle-bug," but in some other parts of the South as a "camel," by reason of the slight hump on its back; a cutworm; the larva of the botfly, or the swelling produced in the skin of a rabbit or other animal by the larva of this fly. Cf. *roulo, infra.*

+MAÏS, *m.* *Maïs* seems to be the only word that the French of Louisiana use for Indian Corn (*Zeo mays* L), though the term *bled d'Inde* is by no means rare in the writings of the early French explorers, and like *blé de Turquie*, was once a popular expression in France for the same

---

[217] Cf. Hodge, *Handbook*, I, 156; Pascal Poirier, *Des Vocables Algonquins*, p. 350.

[218] Cf. E. W. Middendorf, *Wörterbuch des Runa Simi oder der Keshua Sprache* (1890), p. 109, footnote 3; Carlos Gagini, *Diccionario* (1919), p. 189; R. C. Cuervo, *Apuntaciones Criticas* (1914), p. 666; and Constantino Suárez, *Vocabulario Cubano* (1920), pp. 148-149, 381.

plant or grain. For *bled d'Inde* see La Salle's *Relation,* in Margry, I, 532, 542; for *mahis,* Nicolas de la Salle's *Récit,* in Margry, I, 556; and for *maïs, ou bled de Turquie,* des Lozières's *Voyage,* p. 360. Charlevoix has the form *maïz* (*Histoire,* III, 405). Both *maïs* and *blé d'Inde* are still heard in Canadian-French.

In Louisiana-French the *s* of *maïs* is always silent—silent even before the initial vowel of a following word, as in *le maï(s) est bon.*

French *maïs* is a sixteenth-century derivative of Sp. *maïz,* which is identical with Arawak *marisi* and Carib *marichi.*

MANGO, *m.* Mango, the fruit of the Mango-Tree (*Mangifera indica* L.). The term "Pickled mangoes" is translated as *des Mangos confits au Vinaigre.* The etymology of La.-Fr. *mango* is as follows: Spanish *mango,* Portuguese *manga,* Malay *mangga,* Tamil *mān-kay* *mān* = mango-tree plus *kay* = fruit). *Mango* is used in New Orleans.

+**MAQUECHOU,** *m.* A dish made of young corn cut from the cob and smothered with onions. Such is the meaning assigned to *maquechou* by most of my informants. Some of my friends, however, insist that *maquechou* is a thick soup in which corn is the principal ingredient. Finally some Acadians make *maquechou* of cabbage and give the name as *moque-chou,* "mock cabbage."

The origin of *maquechou* is obscure. The Choctaw word for "soup" is *okchi;* but the Choctaws who live near Lacombe, in St. Tammany Parish, assure me that they are not familiar with *maquechou.*

The substitution of the familiar French *chou,* "cabbage," for the novel *-chi* of the Indian word could readily be explained. Why should *ok-,* however, give way to *maque-?*

Marichi, the Carib for "Indian corn," is too remote in form to be considered the source of *maquechou.*

Again, one may recall American-Spanish *máchica,* from which *maquechou* may have been corrupted by folk etymology. *Máchica* is derived from Kechuan *machca,* cornmeal toasted and mixed with sugar and cinnamon.[219]

One last guess at the origin of *maquechou.* Is this word merely a corruption of dialectal *maigrichou,* "a thin child," "a small, delicate man"?

---

[219] Cf. Middendorf, *op. cit.,* p. 559.

Maigrichoux is found in Canadian-French in this sense, and *magre* is dialectal French for *maigre*.[220] Cf. *Maigrichon, -onne, adj.*, "a little too thin" (*Dict. Gén.*).

In Acadian-French final *-re* is regularly silent, and the *g* of *maig-* or *mag-* would normally be unvoiced before *-chou.*

The transfer in meaning from "thin child," to "soup," may be explained by the fact that *maquechou* is made without meat, and therefore may be classed among *potages maigres* or *soupes maigres,* which are greatly in vogue among the French of Louisiana during the Lenten season.

It is a remarkable coincidence that the word for "grapes" in Biloxi Indian is *maktcuhi.*

Maquechou is well known at French Settlement, in Pointe Coupée, and in the Southwest.

MAYOC, *m.* Starch; corrupted from French *manioc* or *magnoc. Manioc* is derived *from Tupí* (Brazilian) *mandioca,* "the root of the Cassava" (*Manihot utilissima* Pohl), through the medium of Spanish and Portuguese *mandioca.* Meal is made from the roots of the Cassava plant.

French *manioch* is found in Claude d'Abbeville's *Mission en Maragnan* (1614), p. 229. See *manioc,* in the *New English Dictionary.* The form *magnoc* is used by Breton (1665).[221]

MEXICAIN, *m.* Fulvous Tree Duck (*Dendrocygna fulva* Gmel.). As this duck usually spends the winter in Mexico, the French of Lower Louisiana have named it *Mexicain,* "Mexican."

Mexicain is the equivalent of Sp. *Mexicano,* now spelled *Mejicano.* Aztec *Mexico,* "place of the war-god named *Mexitli,*" is the source of Sp. *México,* from which *Mexicano* was formed. The termination *-co* signifies "place of."[222]

OURAGAN, *m.* Standard-French *ouragan,* "hurricane," is found both in Louisiana and in Canadian-French. The word is a derivative of Sp. *huracan,* "hurricane," which springs in turn from Carib *hurakan,* the native name of the storm god.

PAGAILLE, *f.* Standard-French *pagaie,* "paddle," is usually pronounced in Louisiana as if it were written *pagaille.*

---

[220] Cf. Gascon *magre,* Lespy et Raymond, *Dict. Béarnais,* II, 38.

[221] *Dict. Car.-Fr.,* pp. 328, 329.

[222] See Egli, *Nomina Geographica,*[2] pp. 602-603; Peñafiel, *Nomenclatura Geografica,* I, 214; II, 135, 170-171

The same pronunciation is heard in Canadian-French. Louisiana-French, like Standard French, also has *pagayer*, "to paddle," and *pagayeur, m.*, "paddler." *Pagaille*, a kind of short oar with a broad blade at one end, is used for propelling a canoe or small boat.[225]

Spanish *pagaya* designates a paddle with a broad blade at each end. This kind of paddle is used by the Filipinos. *Pagaya* is derived from the Malayan language of the Molukka Islands (East Indies); and French *pagaie* is probably adapted from the Spanish word.[226]

PAPEGAI, *m.* A bird of wood used as a target. Shooting at the *papegai* was formerly a popular amusement with Creole and Acadian, according to Lubin F. Laurent.[223] The custom, brought over from France, survives among the French of the rural districts in Louisiana. Another La.-Fr. form is *papegau*. Cf. *pategau, supra.*

Old and Middle French *papegai* and *papegaut* have been displaced in Standard French by *perroquet*, "parrot," except in the sense of a pasteboard or wooden bird used as a target. *Papegai* is from Spanish *papagayo*, and the latter is from Arabic *babbaghâ*. *Papegau* is from a popular Arabic form *babagâl*.[224]

PATATE, *f.* The La.-Fr. term for the sweet potato, the fruit of the vine *Batatas* (or *Ipomoea*) *batatas* (Lamb.), is *la patate douce;* the Standard-French term is simply *patate*. The Acadians also use *la patate jaune*, "the yellow sweet potato," to distinguish a variety of potato from the yam—La.-Fr. *la patate yamme*, or *la yamme*—a name given to any soft-fleshed variety of reddish-yellow sweet potato.[227]

Patate is borrowed from Spanish *patata*, "potato," and *batata*, "sweet potato," for which the source is said to be the Haitian *batata*, "sweet potato."

The French of Louisiana call the Irish potato *la patate anglaise*, "the English potato," and sometimes, as in Standard French, *la pomme de terre*. *La patate*

[223] See *The Louisiana Historical Quarterly*, VII, (April, 1924), 323; Fortier, *Louisiana Studies* (1894), p. 129; and, for the practice in France, Lespy et Raymond, *Dictionnaire Béarnais*, II, 122.

[224] See Wartburg, *Wörterbuch*, p. 195; and Gamillscheg, *Wörterbuch*, p. 666.

[225] Compare Charlevoix's "ces petites pagayes," *Histoire*, III, 404; and Du Pratz's "Pagaies," *Histoire*, II, 189.

[226] Cf. Friederici, *Hilfswörterbuch*, p. 73.

[227] Cf. H. C. Thompson, *Sweet Potato Production and Handling* (1929), p. 70.

ronde, "the round potato," is another term that is occasionally used for the Irish potato. The cushaw is often called *le giraumon patate,* "the potato pumpkin." Cf. *chouquechi, supra.*

PIROGUE, *f.* Pirogue is the regular word for a dugout, but is often loosely applied also to any other kind of small boat. For *chaland, péniche, esquif,* and *chabec,* compare the remarks under *canot, supra.*

Du Pratz described the pirogue as the trunk of a tree which the Indians hollowed out in the shape of a small boat (*Batelet*), and made large enough to hold from two to ten persons. Before acquiring hatchets and axes from the French, the Indians used to burn out the trunk and protect certain parts of it from the fire by means of layers of mud. The French, too, constructed pirogues, some capable of accommodating fifty men.

In Louisiana pirogues were made either of the cypress tree (*Taxodium distichum* Rich.) or of the gigantic Southern cottonwood (*Populus deltoides virginiana* Sudw.); in Arkansas, however, they were made of black walnut. C. S. Rafinesque observes that pirogues more than forty feet long and six feet wide were fashioned from a single trunk of the cottonwood. The Southern cottonwood attains a diameter of seven feet. Pirogues are still by no means uncommon in Louisiana.[228]

Standard-French *pirogue* is derived, through the medium of Sp. *piragua,* from the Carib dialect of the mainland.[229] Canadian-French, too, has *pirogue.*

POBON, *m.* An earthen jar; corrupted from Sp. *porron,* a kind of jar. St.-Fr. *bocal* and St.-Fr. *jarre* (from Prov. *jarro*) are used in a similar sense, and all three may be heard at St. Martinville.

POMPANO, *m.* Common Pompano (*Trachinotus carolinus* L.), a highly-prized fish of the South Atlantic and Gulf Coast waters. *Pompano* is corrupted from Sp. *pampano,* "vine tendril," a name applied to a fish of the family *Stromateidae* because of its color. Sp. *pampano* is derived from Latin *pampinus,* "vine tendril."

RACACHA, *m. Racacha* is used along the Gulf Coast and in the city of New Orleans as the name of the Bur-Grass or Hedgehog Grass, commonly called *sand-spur* or *sand-*

---

[228] Du Pratz, I, 107, footnote 1; II, 32-34, 188-189; Bossu, II, 10-11; Robin, III, 521 ff.

[229] See Friederici, *Hilfswörterbuch,* p. 80 ff.

bur (*Cenchrus tribuloides* L.). But in Pointe Coupée, Livingston, Ascension, Assumption, and some other parishes this word signifies a large spur worn by a horseman. Some Acadians apply the term *racacha* to an old horse or to an old man.

Racacha has found its way into English, and is used in the sense of "sand-spur" as far west as Texas, and perhaps farther. In Alabama it distinguishes the burgrass from the Small Burgrass (*Cenchrus carolinianus* Walt.), the latter being usually known as the *sand-spur.*

Some time ago I wrote to the director of the Museo Nacional of Mexico City, and asked whether the word *racacha* is found in Mexican Spanish, at the same time expressing the opinion that *racacha* is corrupted from *arracacha,* which is a Spanish derivative of Kechuan *rakacha.* Professor I. Ochotereno, of the Instituto de Biologia, in Mexico City, answered my letter with the statement that six kinds of the genus *arracacia* are found in Mexico, and that the term *rakacha* is given in divers countries of South America to these edible plants. Neither *arracacha* nor *rakacha* [*racacha*], he added, is used in Mexican Spanish.

Sp. *aracacha, f.*, is the name of a plant resembling the yucca in form, with an edible root sweeter and less mealy than the potato. This plant, known to botanists as *Arracacia xanthorrhiza* (Baner.), goes in Peru by the Kechuan name of *rakacha.* In Colombia it is called *arracacha;* in the Antilles either *aracacha* or *saracacha.* Diego Palomino, in his *Relación* written at Chacapoyas in 1549, mentions a large number of plants and vegetables, which he found in Peru, and among which he includes the *racacha.*[230]

Louisiana-French adopted *racacha* from Sp. *ar(r)acacha,* and English seems to have taken the word from French, or perhaps from Spanish. The ultimate source, as noted already, is Kechuan *rakacha. Racacha* is pronounced as a French word, except that *ch* has the value of Spanish *ch.* In English the stress falls on the first syllable; otherwise the English pronunciation of the word is like the Louisiana-French. The original meaning of *racacha* in Louisiana must have been *sand-bur,* whence was developed that of *spur,* owing to the

[230] See Erland Nordenskiöld, *Comparative Ethnographical Studies No. 5,* p. 68.

fancied resemblance between a bur and a horseman's spur. From *spur* to *an old horse* that needs spurring the transition in meaning was easy. Last of all, arose the meaning of *an old person.*

As the designation of *spurs, racachas* occurs in a negro-French refrain, which my friend and colleague, Professor H. A. Major, records for me as follows:

> Lendenmain matin Médo di moin
> Mo chien apé mégri.
> Dépi milat-là rentré dans la cou-là,
> Yé na pi des os pu chats.
> Mo mõnte mo chwal
> Mo mette mo racachas;
> mo ku dans la pleine Mogane
> Mo chwé kana, mo chwé ramyé,
> Mo fu pa mal la misé.

Here is Professor Major's translation of this refrain:

> Le lendemain matin Médor m'a dit,
> Que mon chien maigrit.
> Depuis que ce mulatre-là est entré
> dans cette cour-là,
> Il n'y a plus d'os pour les chats.
> Je monte sur mon cheval, je mets mes
> racachas,
> Je vais dans la savane Morgan:
> Je tue des canards, des ramiers,
> Je me fiche de la misère.

After I had completed the foregoing remarks on *racacha,* I came across Provençal *raca,* "horse," which Diez, p. 663, connects doubtfully with Old Norse *rakki,* "dog," the equivalent of Old English *raecc,* "hunting-dog." Perhaps *raca* is related to French *racquassure,* which Jean Palsgrave translates in 1530 by "rackyng of a horse in pace."[231] The etymolgy, however, of *racquassure* seems to be unknown. *Raca,* according to Professor H. A. Major, is found in Louisiana-French, as in the phrase *un vieux raca,* "a worthless old horse." But *raca* is not connected, in my opinion, with *racacha,* though the former may indeed be largely responsible for the use of the latter in the sense of "an old horse."

---

[231] *L'Éclairissement de la Langue Française,* éd. Génin (Paris, 1852), p. 260.

The Kechuan source of *racacha* is proved not only by the absence of any such suffix as French *-cha,* but also by the pronunciation assigned to the "*ch*" of the last syllable.

ROBAL, *m.* Kingfish (*Menticirrus americanus* L.); from Sp. *robalo,* the name of several marine fishes of the West Indies, especially the Snook or Robalo (*Centropomus undecimalis* Bloch).

ROULO, *m.* This word is used in the same sense as *loulou,* I am informed by Mr. E. E. Pavy, of Opelousas, and Mr. Paul Goux, of Marksville. *Roulo* seems to be taken from Sp. *rulo,* "ball," or *rulo,* "a printer's ink-roller," and *loulou* is corrupted from the same source. Rudolph Lenz observes that Chilean Spanish *el lulo,* which signifies anything long and round, is probably derived from Spanish *rulo;* but that certain Indian etymologies are not remote.[232]

Loulou is not the same word, I think, as colloquial French *loulou,* "darling," a reduplicated form of *loup,* "wolf." Another etymology suggests itself for *loulou*: this word may be quite simply an aphetic form of *tourloulou, supra.*

SAVANE, *f.* In Louisiana *savane* signifies "pasture land"; in Canada, "wet or swampy ground"; in France, "prairie," "treeless plain." *Savane* is a sixteenth-century loan from Sp. *zavana, çavana,* which Oviedo declares in 1535 to be of Carib origin. The source of the Spanish word is, indeed, to be found in the Arawakan dialect of Haiti.[233] Modern Spanish has *sabana,* "plain," with the original stress retained on the second syllable.

SOUTADAIRE, *f.* A saddle blanket; formerly common in the Southwest, but now rare; still used at French Settlement and in Ascension Parish. Adapted from Sp. *sudadero, m.,* "saddle blanket."

TOMATE, *f.* *Tomate,* "tomato," came into eighteenth-century-French from South-American Spanish *tomate,* which is in turn an adaptation of Nahuatlan *tomatl.* Both Canadian-French and Louisiana-French use the word *tomate* for the well-known fruit and plant.

+YAMME, *f.* A kind of sweet potato. Standard French *yam, m.,* is recorded by Littré from 1876; but the French

[232] See "Die Indianischen Elemente im Chilenischen Spanish," *Beiträge zur Romanischen und Englischen Philologie* (*Festgabe für Wendelin Foerster,* 1902), p. 21; and *Lenz's Diccionario Etimolojico,* pp. 440-441.

[233] Friederici, *Hilfswörterbuch,* p. 88.

plural *jammes* is found, according to the *New English Dictionary, v. yam,* in *Bosman's Guinea,* I, 7, as early as 1705. In Louisiana *yamme* is treated as a feminine, and is almost always pronounced without preceding linking or elision, as in *des yammes, la yamme.* A form *iamme,* as in *des iammes, l'iamme,* with preceding linking, respectively, elision, is not very common. La.-Fr. *Iamme* is merely a dialectal pronunciation of *yamme* or of French *igname, infra.* Compare the somewhat similar *tiyon* for *tignon, supra.*

From Portuguese *inhame* or Middle Spanish *iñame* (now *ñame*) has come French *igname,* "yam," the earliest example of which dates from 1575. Some cultivated Creoles use *igname* instead of the more usual La.-Fr. *yamme,* a later, corrupted form.

The Portuguese and Spanish forms are derived from West African *niami, niambi,* the designation in the French Sudan of a species of dioscorea. Compare Mandingo *nyambo,* Malinke *nyeme ku, ku nyambi,* Bambara *niambi,* Wolof *nyambi,* all names of a wild yam. The source of the African terms is the Arabic ǵambah, "yam-like root."[234]

6. ITALIAN WORDS

What influence the large and rapidly increasing Italian element in Louisiana will exert on the French language of the State, it is difficult to foresee. Such terms as *Polenta des haricots,* "bean polenta," and *chou broccoli,* "broccoli," are heard in Louisiana, but Italian *polenta* and *broccoli* are inherited from Standard French. So, too, is *piastre,* a name applied to the Spanish *peso duro,* dollar or piece of eight, and extensively used in South Louisiana as the equivalent of "dollar." The popularity of the *piastre* was established long before the transfer of Louisiana to Spain. As early, indeed, as the first quarter of the eighteenth century *piastres* were brought from Pensacola to Mobile and from the Spanish settlements in the Southwest to the French post at Natchitoches.[235]

---

[234] I follow Wiener here, *op. cit.,* I, 226, 228-229; but on the difficult word *yam,* see also Skeat, *Notes on English Etymology,* pp. 323-324; Weekley, *An Etymological Dictionary of Modern English,* p. 109; Ortiz, *op. cit.,* under *ñame,* pp. 371-373.

[235] Cf. Dumont, in French, *Historical Collections* (1853), p. 28; and Henry E. Chambers, *A History of Louisiana,* I, 158-159.

Canadian-French *piastre* is approximately equal to five francs.

The Italian *piastre*, the source of French *piastre*, originally signified a piece or leaf of metal.[236]

Standard-French *dollar*, a loan from English, is looked upon as a bookish word in Louisiana.

Chassepareille (= *salsepareille*) has been discussed *supra*.

---

[236] For Italian words in French, see Nyrop, *Grammaire*, I, 53-57, 87, 100-101.

III

GEOGRAPHICAL NAMES

The geographical nomenclature of Louisiana exhibits the same variety as that which may be observed elsewhere in the world. A large number of names are originally those of early settlers, famous men, saints, tribes, and nations. Many other names are drawn from the animal or the vegetable kingdom. Not a few, again, are based on some striking feature of the landscape, or on some local incident, the latter more often trivial than remarkable. Some names are simply imported from the Old World; others are taken from the Bible or the classic languages. Abstract and fanciful names, together with mechanical or even distorted formations, are not unknown. Finally, the orthography, meaning, and pronunciation of some place-names have been seriously corrupted through ignorance of the exact primitive sources.

Space is available for only a small number of the Romance place-names of Louisiana. The Indian names that are here included are mainly supplementary to my former studies of a similar subject. In the following list the Indian names are given first, then the French, and lastly the Spanish.

1. INDIAN PLACE-NAMES

ACASA. The bed of Lake Acasa in the southern part of Natchitoches Parish has long been dry. In 1687 Joutel mentions the *Nacassa* or *Nakasas,* an Indian tribe that Bienville and St. Denis encountered while they were exploring the valley of Red River in 1700.[1] The Nakasas were still residing in the region of Red River as late as 1741, but they moved to Texas in the second half of

[1] See Margry, *Mémoires,* III, 409; IV, 439.

the eighteenth century.[2] The meaning of *Nacassa*, clearly the source of *Acasa*, is unknown.[3]

CABANOSÉ. *Cabanosé* is the name of a plantation at St. James, in St. James Parish. The same name was formerly applied to St. James Parish as well as to a bayou that drains the northern part of Lafourche Parish and empties into Bayou Boeuf in Township 14 S—R. 18 E., West of the Mississippi River. The upper part of this stream is now generally known as *'Tit* (=Petit) *Chackbé;* the lower, as *Grand Bayou. Cabanosé* is pronounced as a French word, except that its *s* retains the value of *s*, I am informed by Mr. Morille Kliebert, of Vacherie. For *Chackbé,* see *Chegby*.

My former effort to trace the origin of the strange name *Cabanosé* proved to be fruitless.[4] The second part of the name, indeed, can be nothing but the familiar Choctaw *anusi* or *anosi,* "to sleep there," an element appearing in compounds like *ofanusi,* "dog kennel," *pàchanusi,* "pigeon roost," and many others. But the first part of the name remained perplexing, in spite of Dr. John R. Swanton's cautious and yet plausible guess at Choctaw *kàbaha,* "blacksmith," as its possible source. The etymology of *Cabanosé* might never have been solved but for the courtesy of Mr. Frank H. Waddill, of New Orleans, who wrote me, on February, 1930, a highly significant fact about the seal on the official correspondence of Michel Cantrelle, the first civil and military commandant, under the Spanish régime, of the old county of Acadia, after 1807 officially known as the parish of St. James. Cantrelle, it seems, addressed his letters from *Cabahan-nocée,* a name that he applied to his plantation situated on the west bank of the Mississippi River, opposite the present site of Convent. Under this name there appears on his writing paper a small oval, the center of which is occupied by the picture of a duck hanging by its neck on a cord, over a field of marsh grass. The figure of the duck is almost entirely surrounded by the name *Michel Cantrelle,* printed in bold letters. Numerous documents in Cantrelle's hand were formerly kept in the office of the clerk of the court at Convent; these were destroyed by fire

[2] F. W. Hodge, *Handbook of American Indians* (1910), II, 6.

[3] Cf. *The Louisiana Historical Quarterly,* XI, No. 3 (July, 1928), 449.

[4] For variant forms and the application of the name, see my *Louisiana Place-Names of Indian Origin* (1927), pp. 13-14.

some years ago. Such is the gist of Mr. Waddill's comments on Cantrelle and *Cabahan-nocée.*

The meaning of *Cabahannosé,* or *Cabanosé,* now becomes clear. This name, like *Catahoula, Chinchuba, Tchefuncta,* and not a few others of Indian origin, has lost its initial syllable in French, so that its Choctaw equivalent is naturally *hăkhobanosi,* "mallard roost," a compound of *hăkhoba,* "the wild ducks called mallards," and *anosi* or *anusi,* "to sleep there."

Michel Cantrelle, who designated his home by the Indian term for a stream, was actually a Frenchman by birth. After serving as commandant of the county of Acadia for twenty-eight years, Miguel Cantrella was reappointed to his office in 1804 by Governor Claiborne. Cantrelle, as the French knew him, was a wealthy planter, whose fine character and gracious manners endeared him to the inhabitants of his district. He was a member of the legislative council of 1804, and he represented his parish at the meeting of the convention that drafted the first constitution of the state of Louisiana in 1811.[5]

CHACTIMAHAN. North of Raceland, in Lafourche Parish, there is a bayou by the name of *Chactimahan,* a tributary of Bayou Folse, which empties in turn into Bayou Boeuf. *Bayou Chactimahan* is shown on Survey T. 14 S.-R. 18 E., West of the Mississippi.

Chactimahan seems to be a corruption either of Choctaw *Chahta tàmaha,* "Choctaw Town," or of Choctaw *Shakchi tàmaha,* "Crawfish Town," the latter analysis finding support in the fact that one of the Choctaw clans was called *Shakchukla,* "Crawfish People," and that *shakchi,* when forming the first element of a compound word, has actually been changed to *chac* or *chacti* by some French writers. Thus *Shakchi Humma,* Choctaw for "Red Crawfish," appears in Tonti's *Memoir* as *Chacoumas,*[6] the name of an Indian tribe, and in Thomas Jefferey's spelling as *Chactioumas.*[7] The fact, on the other hand, that a small settlement in the vicinity of the bayou is called *Chactas,* "Choctaws," makes the former analysis decidedly the more plausible.

---

[5] Cf. Alcée Fortier, *Louisiana,* I (1914), 254-255; James A. Robertson, *Louisiana Under the Rule of Spain, France, and the United States,* II, (1911), 301.

[6] B. F. French, *Hist. Coll.* I (1846), 72.

[7] *The Natural and Civil History of the French Dominions in North and South America,* I (1761), 163.

CHEGBY. *Chegby,* a name usually given to the upper part of Grand Bayou in Lafourche Parish, is pronounced by the French approximately like the English syllables *chock-bay* or *chog-bay,* with the stress on *bay.* English speakers call it *chack-báy.* The adjective *'Tit* (=*petit*) usually precedes the French designation. The name is recorded as *chegby* in McCarty and Henderson's field notes (1831) for Survey T 14 S—R 17 E, West of the Mississippi River. Chackbay ridge runs towards the southwest from Lake des Allemands, and the settlement of Chackbay is situated about six miles from Thibodaux.

If *Chegby* is of Indian origin, the second syllable is perhaps a derivative of Choctaw *àbi,* "killer," an element found in many personal names and words like *chulàbi,* "fox hunter," *nanàbi,* "fisherman," *hushàbi,* "fowler," *isàbi,* "hunter" (deer killer). The first syllable, on the other hand, will probably remain obscure so long as one cannot obtain any reliable historical clue to its meaning. Thus *cheg-* may have been corrupted from Choctaw *sheki,* "buzzard," whereas the French pronunciation *choque-* points rather to *shukha,* "hog," or to *shakchi,* "crawfish." If the bayou, however, was not named after an Indian, it may owe its designation to some trivial incident, such as the killing of a bird or an animal in its vicinity. The sight of a dead buzzard near the bayou may have led a Choctaw to call the stream *Bok sheki aiabi,* "the bayou where the buzzard was killed"; and *sheki aibi* may readily have been corrupted to *chegby.*

It has been suggested to me that the name results from a combination of La.-Fr. *choc* or *choque,* "blackbird," with *baie,* "bay." Though the local pronunciation may indeed rest on some form earlier than *Chegby,* the term *baie* is wholly inapplicable to this stream. Perhaps the analysis of the name as "blackbird bay" is a product of folk etymology. Finally, I am not at all sure that the name is of Indian origin.

Chegby and *Chackbay* (for *Chackby*) may represent the Old English personal name *Caecca* or *Ceacca* plus late Old English *bȳ,* "farm, hamlet, or town." Cf. the place-names *Checkley,* in Essex, and *Chackmore,* in Buckinghamshire.

CITAMON. Bayou Citamon breaks into two arms in the southern part of St. James Parish, forming Bayou

Chevreuil on the north and Grand Bayou on the south. The western end of Bayou Citamon joins Bayou Verrett in Assumption Parish.

Mr. Frank Waddill, of New Orleans, has kindly called my attention to the name that the Citamon bears on A. L. Mershon's survey of A. B. Roman's claim numbered 43 and approved by an act of Congress on July 17, 1854. This survey, which is marked T. 13 S.-R. 16 E., West of the Mississippi River, shows the stream as Bayou *Icetaman* or *Citamahan.* Either spelling is sufficient to establish Choctaw *isi tàmaha,* "deer village," as the source of the modern name of the bayou. The fact, too, that one arm of this stream is called *Chevreuil,* the French name for "deer," tends to corroborate this analysis of *Citamon. Citamon* is locally pronounced in French fashion; or sometimes, like a French word spelled *Citama-on.*

COLEWA. *Colewa,* the name of a bayou in the parish of West Carroll, is doubtless derived from the Choctaw form of *Koroa,* according to a friendly hint given me by Dr. John R. Swanton. Albert S. Gatschet remarks that the Choctaw called the Koroa *Kolwa* or *Kulua*;[8] and it is significant that Iberville uses the form *Coloa* or *Coloas* by the side of *Coroa.*[9] The Choctaws, it should be noted, generally substitute *l* for *r,* the latter sound being unknown in their dialect.

The history of the Koroa, an Indian tribe formerly inhabitating Louisiana, is included in Swanton's *Indian Tribes of the Lower Mississippi Valley* (Washington, 1911), pp. 327-332, *et passim*; but the source of the name *Koroa* has never been clearly established.[10]

The Indian names that have just been discussed are too few to reveal the extent of the Indian element in the geographical nomenclature of Louisiana. I will, therefore, comment briefly on some other Indian names, selecting from my former studies such as seem to be especially characteristic of Louisiana. Some of these are:

ABITA (Springs)—Choctaw *ibetàp,* "fountain, head of a stream."

[8] *A Migration Legend of the Creek Indians,* I (1884), 48.

[9] Margry, IV, 179, 180, 184.

[10] For further information about *Colewa,* see my paper in *The Louisiana Historical Quarterly* for July, 1928, page 454.

ATCHAFALAYA, "Long River,"—Choctaw *hàcha,* "river," and *falaia,* "long."

BAYOU GOULA, "Bayou or River People,"—Mobilian *bayuk ougoula.*

BOGALUSA, "Black Creek,"—Choctaw *bog,* "creek," and *lusa,* "black."

BOGUE CHITTO, "Big Creek or River,"—Choctaw *bog,* "creek," etc., and *chitto,* "big."

BOGUE FALAYA, "Long River,"—Choctaw *bog,* "creek," etc., and *falaia,* "long."

BONFOUCA—corrupted from Choctaw *bok fuka,* "bayou residence," a home situated on a bayou.

CALCASIEU, "Crying Eagle,"—Atakapa *katkōsh,* "eagle," and *yōk,* "to cry." This name was the war-title of an Indian chief.

CATAHOULA, "Beloved Lake,"—Choctaw *okhàta,* "lake," and *hullo,* "beloved."

CHAPPEPEELA, "Hurricane River."—Choctaw *ḥàcha* and *apeli,* "hurricane."

CHINCHUBA, "Alligator,"—Choctaw *Hachunchuba.*

COUSHATTA, "White Reed-Brake,"—Choctaw *kũsha,* "reed," and *hàta,* "white"

ISTROUMA, "Red Pole,"—Choctaw *iti,* "pole," and *humma,* "red." See the present writer's discussion of this name, in *The Louisiana Historical Quarterly,* XIV, No. 4 (October, 1931), pp. 503-515.

KEATCHIE, "panther,"—from Caddoan *kishi*: pronounced *kē′chī,* in Webster's transcription.

MANCHAC, "Rear Entrance,"—Choctaw *imashaka,* "rear."

NATALBANY, "Lone Bear,"—Choctaw *nita,* "bear," and perhaps *bano,* "only."

+NATCHITOCHES, "Pawpaws,"—Caddoan *Nashitosh.*

OKALOOSA, "Black Water,"—Choctaw *oka,* "water," and *lusa,* "black."

SHONGALOO, "Cypress Tree,"—Choctaw *shãkolo.*

TALISHEEK, "Gravel, Pebbles,"—Choctaw *Tàlushik.*

TCHEFUNCTA, "Chinquapin" (River)—Choctaw *hachofakti.*

TICKFAW, From Choctaw *poa,* "wild beasts," *a,* "there," and *tikafa,* "shed their hair."

TUNICA, "The People,"—Tunica *ta,* "the," *uni,* "people," and suffix *-ka.*

WHISKEY CHITTO, "Big Cane" (Creek)—Choctaw *uski*, "cane," and *chitto*, "big."

2. FRENCH PLACE-NAMES

AMULET. A bayou in the town of Natchitoches is recorded as *Bayou a Muller* on Survey T 9 W—R 7 W, Northwest Dist. of La., Feb. 25, 1850. A street in Natchitoches appears as *Amulet* on the same survey.

Two hundred years ago, says Professor J. E. Guardia, in his pamphlet on *Historic Natchitoches*, pp. 3, 7, Bayou Amulet served as a rendezvous for French and Spanish traders, who tied their mules along the banks of this stream.

The *Bayou a Muller*, on the survey of 1850, is evidently a corruption of Fr. *Bayou à Mulet*, "Mule Bayou." The original meaning of *à mulet* has been lost, and the local pronunciation of the name is the same as that of English *amulet*.

BARBUE. *Bayou Barbue*: Survey T 6 N—R 5 W., La. Mer., 1830. Bayou Barbue, "catfish bayou," empties into Cane River Lake, in the southeastern part of the parish of Natchitoches.

+BEAKLANCE. Bayou Beaklance is in the northeastern part of St. Landry Parish. In William Darby's field notes, dated August 2, 1809, and marked T. 3 S.—R. 5 E., the name of this stream is given as *Bayou Beakalance;* on Darby's map of 1816 it is *B. Beak au Lance;* on a survey of December 24, 1838, the spelling *Beaklance* appears. *Beaklance* is a corruption of *bec à lancette*.

The clue to the origin of this name is found in the following statement from N. Bossu's *Nouveaux Voyages aux Indes Occidentales*[2] . . . , 2d partie (1768), 178: "Il y a un autre oiseau nommé bec à lancette, qui a effectivement le bec fait de même." In J. R. Forster's translation of this passage *bec à lancette* is rendered by "lancet-bill."[11] The bayou was named because of the fact that it was the haunt of the lancet-bill, or American Snakebird (*Plotus Anhinga* L.), commonly known as the *Water Turkey*, but still called *bec à lancette* by the French of Louisiana. At the mouth of the Mississippi this bird goes by the name of the *Water Crow*.[12]

BEAUCOUP. Bayou Beaucoup takes its name from the size and extent of the stream. It is, of course, the French

[11] Bossu-Forster, I, 374-375.
[12] Audubon, *Birds*, VI (1859), 433.

beaucoup, "much," "a great deal." This bayou flows into Bayou Castor, in Caldwell Parish.[13]

The name *Beaucoup* is recorded on a survey of 1833—T 13—R 2 E, La. Meridian. A short distance to the south of Bayou Beaucoup there is another stream, which since about 1886 has borne the name *Bayou Buckoo*, but which was formerly designated as *Flat Creek* on some of the best maps of Louisiana. Bayou Buckoo, like Bayou Beaucoup, is a tributary of Bayou Castor. *Buckoo* is evidently a corruption of *Beaucoup.*

BEDICO. *Bedico* is the name of a creek that empties into the Tangipahoa River, in the southern part of Tangipahoa Parish. The earliest reference that I have found to the name occurs in Clinch Grey's survey of 1821, designated T 6 S—R IX E, Greensburg Land District, East of the Mississippi. On March 10, 1828, another survey marked T VII—R IX E, Greensburg Land Dist., East of the Miss., records the form *Beedico*, evidently in consequence of the surveyor's effort to accommodate the spelling of the name to the long "ee" sound of the first syllable. Another variation in the form of the name is found in *De Bow's Review*, XII (1852), 456, where the editor makes mention of the "Bayou Betico."

Bedico is undoubtedly a corruption of the French personal name *Béthencourt* or *Béthancourt*. As early as May 25, 1793, a certain Michael Bitancourt is declared to have been the original claimant of a tract of 270 acres situated in the district of Baton Rouge, his claim resting on a Spanish patent issued by Carondelet. Some other early references to the name I owe to my friend, Mr. Cecil Bird, of Baton Rouge. Thus the form *Betancourt* is recorded, under date of June 7, 1827, in *Book N, Parish Judges of East Baton Rouge*, p. 124; both *Bitancour* and *Betancour* are found in the same volume (1827), p. 157; and finally, *Bitancourt* is the spelling in *Book M, Parish Judges of East Baton Rouge* (1824), p. 35.

A glance at the variant spellings given me by Mr. Bird shows that the name has either "i" or "e"—the latter with or without the accent—in the first syllable, and either *cour* or *court* as the last syllable. The loss of the final *t* is naturally an echo of the pronunciation current among the French of Louisiana; whereas the lowering of the vowel of *court* to the long *o*-sound heard

[13] Cf. Kilpatrick, in *De Bow's Review*, XXII, 267.

in the last syllable of *Bedico* is a result partly of the spelling, and partly of the Southern tendency to change *ōō* to *ō* before a written *r*. Compare the Southern pronunciation of *poor,* which often rhymes with *"door"* and in careless or old-fashioned speech even with *low*. Again, the *r* of *Béthencourt* was first vocalized to the sound of "a" in *sofa,* and was then absorbed by the preceding lowered *ō*. Next the *t* in the first syllable was voiced to *d,* a change that seems to be characteristic especially of persons of French descent. Finally, the medial nasal vowel of *Béthencourt* was changed under the disturbing influence of weak stress in spoken English. The corruption of *Béthencourt* to *Bedico* is, therefore, decidedly more plausible than the spelling of the two names would lead an unwary observer to imagine.

In France Jean de Béthencourt, the chamberlain of Charles VI, is famous as the discoverer of the Canary Islands in 1402. In Louisiana the name still lives. Mr. Peter W. Béthancourt, of New Orleans, has kindly written me that four of his ancestors settled in different parts of Louisiana, but that he does not know whether any of these lived in the vicinity of Bedico Creek or not. He is aware, however, that his father Pierre Hildevert Béthancourt died in the parish of St. John in 1853. Nevertheless, the derivation of *Bedico* from *Béthancourt* is not rendered invalid merely because no evidence can be found of a Béthancourt's occupying land in Tangipahoa Parish. It is a well-known fact that a place may perpetuate the name of a transient settler, of whose very existence no record is ever preserved.

The etymology of *Béthencourt* is clear. The first element is derived from *Bettonis,* the genitive of *Betto,* an ancient Germanic pet-name for *Bertrand, Bertram* and similar formations, in which *Bert-* signifies "bright"; compare Old High German *breht,* "bright," which was Latinized as *Bertus,* the latter yielding French *Bert-, Ber-,* or *Bé-*.[14] Perhaps I should add that since Old High German *hraban,* "raven," appears in French as *-ran, -ram, -rand,* or *-rant,* it readily became confused with *ran(t)* from Germanic *-rand,* "shield," a confusion that had already made itself felt in German.[15] Hence French

[14] Cf. Auguste Longnon, *Les Noms de Lieu de la France,* p. 257: J. Jud, "Sprachgeographische Untersuchungen," *Archiv,* CXXIV (1910), 101.

[15] Cf. Werner Kalbow, *Die Germanischen Personennamen des Altfranzösischen Helden-Epos* (1913), p. 31; M. Schönfeld, *Wörterbuch der Altgermanischen Personen- und Völkernamen,* p. 51.

Bertrand may mean either "bright shield" or "bright raven."

The second element of the name is the French *court*, a derivative of low Latin *cortis* or *curtis;* cf. *cohortis*, the genitive of Latin *cohors*. The original genitive was employed as a nominative, and *cortis* or *curtis* at first signified the "court-yard of a farm"; subsequently the word assumed the meaning of "rural domain."[16]

BOEUF. Bayou Boeuf: Survey T 2 N—R I W, La. Mer., 1807. Bayou Boeuf leaves Bayou Rapides near Cypress Lake, in the northwestern part of Rapides Parish, and flowing in a southeasterly direction, joins Bayou Cocodrie several miles north of Washington, in St. Landry Parish.

Bayou Boeuf, according to an old tradition, owes its name to the fact that some cattle belonging to Mexicans were drowned in its waters. Bearing in mind how early the French explored the valley of Red River, where indeed they established plantations and *vacheries*, "stock farms," in the first quarter of the eighteenth century, I believe that the bayou was called *Boeuf* by reason of the large number of buffaloes which the early French settlers encountered in its vicinity.

It would be worse than fruitless to give here even an outline of the history of the bison, or American buffalo. A reference or two to its former existence in Louisiana must suffice. Thus Iberville, writing in February, 1699, remarks: "Le chef des Bayogoulas me vint trouver, me dire qu'il alloit à la chasse aux boeufs et aux coqs d'Inde, et qu'il seroit de retour dans quatre nuits."[17] Again, H. Bry, in an interesting study of the Ouachita region, comments as follows on the extermination of the buffalo in that part of Louisiana:

"The last buffalo seen in the neighborhood of Fort Miro was killed in 1803." "A herd of about one hundred and fifty," he continues, "remained near the Bayou Saline, in Arkansas, about 150 miles above Monroe, where, being surrounded with settlements, they were all destroyed in 1807 and 1808."[18]

Nevertheless, in the very year that Bry's article appeared, Parkman, in *The Oregon Trail,* described a buffalo hunt and noted the vast herds that still roamed over the prairies of the West.[19] That the buffalo was finally

[16] Longnon, *op. cit.*, p. 225.
[17] Margry, *Mémoires*, IV (1881), 156.
[18] *De Bow's Review*, III (1847), 226.

saved from extinction is due, as almost every one knows, to the efforts of Canada and the United States.

Boeuf is pronounced approximately, or by some speakers exactly, as in French.

The bayou just described is not unique in possessing the name *Boeuf*. One finds a *Lake Boeuf* in Lafourche Parish; a *Bayou Terre Aux Boeufs* in St. Bernard Parish; and a *Boeuf River* in the northeastern part of the State.

BOIS CONNIE. *Bois Connie,* a corruption of *Bois Connu, supra,* is the name of a bayou in Cameron Parish.

BOUILLON. Bayou Bouillon is in the Atchafalaya swamps, fifteen miles northeast of St. Martinville.

Bayou Bouillon signifies "bubbling or boiling water"; a better spelling would be *Bayou Bouillant.* The bubbling of the water in this bayou is said to have been observed as early as 1833.

BREAUX BRIDGE. Breaux Bridge is situated on Bayou Teche, in the parish of St. Martin. During the early history of Southwest Louisiana the inhabitants of the Breaux Bridge area crossed the bayou on a small toll ferry. Subsequently a settler by the name of Agricole Breaux built a toll-free bridge across the bayou, and the settlement became known as Breaux's Bridge, I am informed by Mr. R. J. Patin, postmaster at Breaux Bridge. Breaux Bridge was incorporated in 1850, and its present population is estimated at 1399.

The name *Breaux,* which is spelled more accurately *Braud* in the *American State Papers,* III (1816), 169, ed. Green, is a derivative of the Old High German personal name *Beroald,* "mighty bear," a compound of OHG *bero,* "bear," and the stem of OHG *waldan, waltan,* "to rule." Cf. Förstemann, *op. cit.,* pp. 265, 1497.

BURBIE. *Bayou Burbie:* Survey 2 T N—R 5 E, La. Mer., 1808.

Bayou Burbie is a tributary of Bayou Avoyelles.

Burbie is clearly a corruption of French *bourbeux,* "muddy." The local pronunciation, indeed, is said to be in accord with the form *bourbeux,* and a copy of Survey T 2 N—R 4 E, La. Mer., approved March 19, 1859, gives the name of the stream as "Muddy Bayou."

CARRON. Bayou Carron, in the parish of St. Landry, owes its name to Joseph Caron or Carron.[20]

[19] Cf. The New Orleans *Times-Picayune,* Friday, Dec. 26, 1930, p. 8.

[20] Cf. *American State Papers,* Public Lands, II, 826, 845, ed. Gales and Seaton.

The name *Caron* is the Picard form of French *Charron,* "wheelwright," which is a derivative of the Gallo-Roman stem *carro-,* "wagon." Cf. Henri Moisy, *Noms de Famille Normands* (1875), p. 70.

CHEF MENTEUR. The name *Chef Menteur* was first applied in 1763 to a tract of land lying at the confluence of Bayou Gentilly, or Sauvage, and Chef Menteur Pass in Orleans Parish. Here are situated the ruins of Fort Macomb, which was originally named *Chef Menteur.* Across from Fort Macomb on the other side of the pass, is Chef Menteur, a station on the Louisville and Nashville Railroad.[21]

Chas. Gayarré thus explains the origin of *Chef Menteur:*

"What the Choctaws were most conspicuous for was their hatred of falsehoods and their love of truth. Tradition relates that one of their chiefs became so addicted to the vice of lying that in disgust they drove him away from their territory. In the now Parish of Orleans, back of Gentilly, there is a tract of land, in the shape of an isthmus projecting itself into Lake Pontchartrain, not far from the Rigolets, and terminating in what is called *Pointe-aux-Herbes, or Herb Point.* It was there that the exiled Choctaw chief retired with his family and a few adherents near a bayou which discharges itself into the lake. From that circumstance the tract of land received and still retains the appellation of *Chef Menteur,* or 'Lying Chief.' "[22]

N. Bossu gives a different version of the story. "Though they [Choctaws] are barbarous and ferocious," he says, "it is necessary, in order to gain their confidence, to take great care to keep your promises to them, without which they treat you with the greatest contempt, proudly telling you that you are a liar, an epithet which the Indians have given to the present governor, whom they call *Oulabé Mingo,* i. e., 'the lying chief.' "[23]

As Bossu made the foregoing assertion at the fort of Tombigbee on September 30, 1759, the Choctaws must have been referring to Baron de Kerlerec, who was governor of Louisiana from 1753 to 1763. *Oulabé*

---

[21] See P. M. Milner, "Fort Macomb," in *Publications of the Louisiana Historical Society,* VII, (1913-1914), 143-152.

[22] *History of Louisiana,* IV, (1903), 351.

[23] N. Bossu, *Travels Through That Part of North America Formerly Called Louisiana.* Translated by J. R. Forster. Vol. I (1771), 306-307.

Mingo, which Bossu renders by *le Chef Menteur,* is intended for Choctaw *holabi mĩko,* "liar-chief." The Choctaw for "lying chief" is *mĩko holabi. Ialeské-Chata,* indeed, renders *Chef Menteur* by *Mingolabee.*[24]

Bossu's explanation of the origin of *Chef Menteur* is more convincing than Gayarré's. What connection, however, there was between Kerlerec's standing with the savages and any particular locality in Louisiana is far from being clear.

CHER AMI. Cher Ami is a small bayou situated in the southern part of Assumption Parish. In 1816 Darby has *B. Cher Amie.* There is, moreover, proof that land in the old parish of Lafourche Interior was surveyed as early as 1796 for one Joseph Cherami. Cf. *ASP,* II, 427, 430, 435, ed. G. and S.; and see La Tourrette's map of 1846 for the location of Cherami's claims.

The French family name *Cherami,* literally "Dear Friend," is still found in Louisiana, where it is now usually written *Cheramie.*

CHICOT. Bayou Chicot is a tributary of Bayou Cocodrie in Evangeline Parish. A village of the same name as the bayou had a population of 161 in 1930; it is recorded by La Tourrette in 1846 as *Bayou Chicot P. O.* The shores of the bayou also formed the site of a Choctaw village at the beginning of the nineteenth century; see Claiborne, in *Amer. State Papers, Indian Affairs,* I, 755. Besides the bayou and the village in Evangeline Parish there are at least two other places that attest the popularity of *Chicot*—first, a lake in the parish of St. Martin, and secondly, a point on an island off the shore of St. Bernard Parish. The former is given by Graham-Tanner in 1834 as *Chicot Bay;* the latter, by Tanner in 1820 as *Pt. Chico.*

Bayou Chicot signifies "*Stump Bayou.*" Sixteenth-century French *chicot,* "stump," is perhaps connected with *chiquet, chiquette,* "trifle," "bit"—cf. Vosges *chicot,* "trifle"—and is probably a hybrid of *chipot-er,* "to haggle," and the stem of *chiche,* "niggardly," "stingy." With *chiche,* the twelfth-century feminine of Old French *chic,* may be compared Provençal *chic,* "small," and the Latin *ciccu-m,* "a trifle" (Gamillscheg).

COCODRIE, *m. Cocodrie* is the La.-Fr. form of French *crocodile,* "crocodile." Already in late Latin the form *coco-*

[24] *Mandeville* (New Orleans, 1918), pp. 8, 10.

drillus shows metathesis of the *r* from *crocodilus*.[25] A similar change is manifest till late in seventeenth-century French. Thus Nicolas de La Salle says, "On fit festin avec le cocodrille, qui sembla fort bon";[26] and he remarks further that the water was "pleine de cocodrilles ou de caymans."[27]

In 1807 Robin uses both *cocodrile* and the plural *crocodiles*.[28]

In 1769 Nugent and Kelly refer to a bayou in Southwest Louisiana by employing the Spanish *cocodrilo*.[29] In 1846 the cartographer La Tourrette seems to have established *cocodrie* as the preferable form for most of his successors.

Cocodrie is sometimes applied to a full-blooded African. Some Acadians use the St.-Fr. form *crocodile*, as do most Creoles. At French Settlement the usual term is *cocodrie*.

The name *Cocodrie* designates several bodies of water in Concordia Parish—Lake Cocodrie, Bayou Cocodrie, and Cross Cocodrie Bayou. In the parish of Rapides there is also a Cocodrie Lake, the source of the Bayou Cocodrie that unites with Bayou Boeuf in the parish of St. Landry.

It is perhaps needless to add that the alligator, not the crocodile, is responsible for the name *Cocodrie*. Cf. *caïman, supra*.

Canadian-French has *cocodrile* by the side of *corcodrile*.

COQUILLE. Lake Coquille is in St. Bernard Parish. See Survey T 15 S—R 16 E, St. Helena Mer., 1843-45. The mollusk shells at the lake suggested the use of the name.

French *coquille*, "shell" of mollusks, is a derivative of Latin *conchylium*, but has been influenced in its evolution by French *coque*, "shell," of an egg, etc.

COULÉE DES GRUES. *Coulee des Grus:* Lockett's map of 1873; *B. Coulee des Grues:* Hardee's map of 1893; *Coulee des Grues:* War Department's map of Southern Louisiana, revised to 1925.

---

[25] F. Sommer, *Handbuch der Lateinischen Laut und Formenlehre*, p. 301.
[26] Margry, I (1682), 556.
[27] Margry, I (1682), 562.
[28] *Voyages*, III, 15, 292.
[29] Cf. *The Louisiana Historical Quarterly*, VII, No. 1 (January, 1924),

The Coulée des Grues is situated near Marksville. The name of this stream signifies the "Coolie of the Cranes."

Various species of heron are abundant in Louisiana, to some of which the term *crane* is inaccurately applied. The Acadians, however, usually refer to the yellow-crowned night-heron as a *gros-bec,* and give to the American bittern the name *garde soleil* because of its habit of gazing by the hour at the face of the sun. The whooping crane, now almost extinct, formerly migrated in vast numbers to Louisiana during the winter season.[30]

Coulée, a substantive from the feminine past participle of French *couler,* "to flow," is generally used in Louisiana of a small stream that may become dry in summer. *Coulée* is also written *coulee, -ie, coolie, -ey,* as an English word.

COULÉE MALAGAIE. The name of this stream, a tributary of Bayou Boeuf in the northern part of Lafourche Parish, appears on McCarty and Kennedy's survey of 1830, marked T 14 S—R 18 E, Southeastern District, La., West of the Mississippi River. The same name is recorded on the War Department's map of Southern Louisiana, 1925.

Malagaie is probably identical with *Malaguet,* the name given, in the Langue d'Oc region of France, to the wild cherry tree. Rabelais has the form *maguelet,* whence has been formed *malaguet* by metathesis of *g* and *l.* The ultimate source of this word is Arabic *mahlab,* Rabelais's *maguelet,* as used in the phrase *"l'huyle de maguelet,"* being a doublet of *mahaleb, the* name of the Perfumed Cherry Tree (*Cerasus mahaleb* Mill).[31]

The wild Black Cherry Tree (*Prunus virginiana* L.), is fairly common in Louisiana. Its wood, hard, strong, and reddish-brown, is used in the manufacture of cabinets; its fruit was formerly so well known as an ingredient in the making of cherry bounce that the tree acquired the name of *Whisky* or *Rum Cherry.*

COURTABLEAU. Bayou Courtableau is formed by the union of Bayous Cocodrie and Boeuf, in the parish of St. Landry.

Nugent and Kelly, in the diary of their voyage to "Atacapas, Opelusas, and Natchitoches," speak of trav-

[30] Cf. A. R. Kilpatrick, in *De Bow's Review,* XI, (1851), 55; Audubon, *The Birds of America,* VI (1859), 95.

[31] See Thomas, *Mélanges d'Étymologie Française,*[2] pp. 136-137.

eling eight leagues on December 15, 1769, in an effort to reach "Santiago Courtablau's house at Opelousas." "This," they add, "we could not have done had it not been for two Indians and several countrymen [*paysanos*] who came to our assistance attracted by the continuous gunshots which we fired in the woods." See *La. Hist. Quar.*, January, 1924, p. 29. Furthermore, a man by the name of *Santiago Courtableau* granted his general power of attorney, on July 9, 1770, in the Court of Governor Luis de Unzaga, "to Leonard Mazange, Public Attorney, for all his law suits and negotiations which he had or would have," etc. *La. Hist. Quar.*, April, 1925, p. 243. This Santiago Courtableau is no doubt the Mr. Courtableau who is said to have been the original proprietor of a tract of land situated on the right bank of the river Opelousas, "sometimes called the river or bayou Courtableau," a tract that he held under a patent of May 21, 1765. Cf. the *Amer. State Papers*, III, 97, ed. G. & S. And as *Santiago* is merely the Spanish for the French *Saint Jacques,* one need not hesitate to identify Santiago with Jacques Courtableau or Catableau, an owner of land on the bayou Teche, in the old county of Opelousas. Cf. the *Amer. State Papers,* I, 841, ed. Green; *ibid.*, II, 818, ed. G and S.

Without access to medieval spellings one can only guess at the etymology of *Courtableau.* The first element is no doubt Fr. *Court,* from Low Latin *cortis* or *curtis,* "farm, villa, rural domain"; the second element, *Ableau,* may be a derivative, with an intrusive *b*-glide, of the Old High German personal name *Amala* or *Amalo,* which Förstemann, *op. cit.*, p. 90, connects with Old Norse *aml,* "labor." Cf. the geographic name *Ablancourt* (Marne) and see Kaspers, *Etymologische Untersuchungen,* p. 301; Longnon, *op. cit.*, p. 252.

How deceptive the origin of a name like *Courtableau* may be is illustrated by that of *Fontainebleau,* which popular etymology associates with *belle eau,* "beautiful water"; whereas the real source is shown in the medieval Latin *Fontana Blidaldi,* "fountain or spring of Blidaldus." *Blidaldus* corresponds to the Old German name *Blidoald* a compound of *blīd-,* cognate with English *blithe,* and of *wald* as found in OHG *waldan* or *waltan,* "to rule." See Förstemann, *op. cit.*, pp. 316, 1497; Kalbow, *Die Germanischen Personennamen,* pp. 100, 134.

DEGRUY. Bayou Degruy enters Bayou des Allemands not far from the junction of the latter with Lake Salvador in St. Charles Parish.

Bayou Degruy bears the name of Jean Baptiste Degruy, who purchased from Francisco Bouligny, on May 8, 1792, a tract of land situated on Bayou Ouachas, according to the *American State Papers,* VI, 675, ed. Gales and Seaton. The name *Degruy* is also spelled *Degruis,* in the *American State Papers,* II, 340, 840, ed. Gales and Seaton.

The curious patronymic *Degruy* looks like a nickname for a miller; compare Old French *gruis,* "bran, gruel" (Sainte-Palaye, VI, 433). This name, however, may be connected with Fr. *grue,* "crane," dialectal *gruis* signifying a noise resembling that which is made by this bird (Larchey, *Dict. des Noms,* p. 209). Pachnio, in *Die Beinamen der Pariser Steuerrolle von 1292* p. 14, notes the nicknames *Jaques la Grue, Martin la Grue,* and *Vincent Gruel.* Here *Gruel* is the diminutive of *Grue.*

DE LESIARE. Bayou De Lesiare enters Chef Menteur north of Bayou Dupont, in Orleans Parish. Cf. Survey T II S —R 14 E, St. Hel. Mer., 1843, 1844.

De Lesiare looks as if it had been corrupted from the French family name *De Lessart,* "of the cleared land." Cf. the etymology of *Desir, infra.*

DES GLAISES. *Bayou de Glaize*: Survey T I N—R 6 E, La. Mer., 1808.

The name *Bayou des Glaises* is applied to a stream that unites with Bayou Rouge at the Junction, between Cottonport and Longbridge, and flowing so as to form a great bend, finally enters the Atchafalaya River at Simmesport.

The early French inhabitants of Louisiana applied the word *glaises* to spots to which animals resorted for the purpose of licking the salt or salt earth found there. The corresponding American term is *licks, buffalo-licks,* or *salt-licks.* These licks abound in the valleys of the Red River and Ouachita as well as in the prairies of Southwest Louisiana.

French *glaise,* "marl," found in the twelfth century as *glise* by the side of *gloise,* is derived from Gallic **glîsa,* **glêsa,* on the strength of the first element in Pliny's compound *glisomarga,* "a kind of marl." The source is Low Latin **glitia,* occurring in glosses as *glit-*

eus, which is cognate in turn with the Latin *glis*, "humus tenax," of obscure origin.[32]

DESIR. Bayou Desir, which formerly flowed between Lake Maurepas and Lake Ponchartrain, has been filled. That the name of this bayou is a corruption of *Desert* becomes clear from a glance at Cabell and Grant's (1836) survey of Township 10 S—R 8 E, Southeastern District of Louisiana, East of the Mississippi, where one finds the following names: *Bayou Desert, Old Desert's Field, Desert Station*, and *Jos. Desert*.

The personal name *Desert* is derived from French *de*, "of," "from," and the participial substantive *essart*, "cleared land," a compound which is not infrequent as a French family name in such forms as *Delessart, Dessart, Dessert*, etc. See Josef Kremers, *Beiträge zur Erforschung der Französischen Familien-namen* (1910), p. 93.

DE SOT. *Bayou des Sots*: *Survey* T I N—R 7 E, La. Mer., 1808—and also approved September 22, 1851. *Bayou de Sott:* Hardee, 1895.

Bayou de Sot connects Little Prairie Bayou with Bayou Natchitoches, in the eastern part of Avoyelles Parish.

I have another early reference to Bayou de Sot: A certain Charles Mulhollen testified that in 1795 or 1796 he crossed a tract of land situated on the Mississippi river and bounded on the lower side of Bayou Desot.[33]

About three miles below the mouth of Bayou De Sot there is a body of water called *Fool's Bay*, I am informed by Mr. Byron F. Lemoine, of Big Bend, Louisiana. The name of the bay at once suggests a literal interpretation of *Bayou De Sot* as the French for *Fool's Bayou*. On Hardee's map of 1895 the name of the bay is inaccurately printed as *Pool's Bay*.

Under the influence of the spelling the "t" of *De Sot* is now usually pronounced.

Jefferson Parish has a stream known as "John the Fool's Bayou," according to Survey T 19 S—R 23 E, La. Mer., 1840.

DUGDEMONA. Dugdemona River or Bayou flows through Winn Parish, and empties into Castor Bayou. A station named *Dugdemona*—it is recorded by La Tourrette in

[32] Gamillscheg, *Wb.*, under *glaise;* Meyer-Lübke, *REW* 3788. But see also the *New English Dictionary*, under *marl*.

[33] *American State Papers*, Public Lands, II, 780, ed. G. and S.

1846—is on the Chicago, Rock Island & Pacific Railroad, in the same parish.

In 1805 John Sibley remarks that the French give the name *Dogdimona* to a stream which falls into Acatahola [Catahoula] lake.[34] In 1817 William Darby mentions the Dugdomoni River as the western branch of the Ocataahoola.[35] In 1846 La Tourrette's map records the modern spelling of the name. During the nineteenth century other variations in the form of the name are found—for instance, *Dogdemene, Dogdamane, Dugdamoney,* and *Dugdimona,*† but it is apparent that none of these varies sufficiently to furnish a clue to the origin of *Dugdemona.* Nor does a spelling with initial *B,* such as *Bugdemon,*[36] cast any light on the etymology of this strange name. There is, however, an early small-scale map of Louisiana, drawn by H. S. Tanner, which seems to offer trustworthy information with respect to the source of *Dugdemona.* On this map the name of the stream is recorded as *Ducdumani Cr.*; and *Ducdumani* I take to be a corruption, possibly Spanish, of the French name *Duc du Maine.* A slight acquaintance with French phonetics will convince one that the final "c" in *Duc* has the value of *g* if the word is followed without pause by a voiced consonant. A similar change takes place in such phrases as "avec Jean," "un bec d'aigle." The voicing of the final *k*-sound in *Duc* is responsible for the forms with *g,* which are noted in Sibley's reference to the French name of the stream. Variants, finally, are to be expected in a name that must have been common on the lips of Indians, Frenchmen, Spaniards, and Americans. Nowadays yet another variant seems likely to establish itself—*Dugdemonia*—which is evidently due to an effort to harmonize the spelling with the local pronunciation.[37]

That a stream should have received the name of the Duc du Maine is not at all surprising. A son of Louis XIV and Madame de Montespan, the duke is mentioned as one of the sponsors of the famous Company of the West, formed in 1717 for the development of the resources of Louisiana. His name, indeed, was bestowed upon a vessel which played a conspicuous role in the

[34] *American State Papers,* Indian Affairs, I (1832), 727.

[35] *A Geographical Description of Louisiana,*[2] p. 342.

† See, respectively, Graham-Tanner's map of 1834, *De Bow's Review,* III (1847), p. 408; XI (1851), p. 88; XII (1852), p. 267.

[36] Cf., for example, Tanner's map of 1839.

[37] Cf. Milton Dunn, *History of Natchitoches,* p. 3 (reprint).

early history of this company. On the 6th of June, 1719, the *Grand Duc du Maine* and the *Aurora* are said to have arrived from the coast of Guinea with five hundred negroes; on the 23rd of March, 1721, the *Duc du Maine*, a vessel of thirty-six guns under the command of Monsieur Roscair, reached the coast of Louisiana with 394 negroes; and finally, on the 15th of April, 1721, the *Duc du Maine* was one among six of the company's ships that set sail for France.[38] The duke's name also survives in that of a New Orleans street, interesting now especially because it forms the background for several of Cable's Creole stories.[39]

It is fitting to note, in the last place, a few facts about the career of the man whose name may survive in the strange form *Dugdemona*. Born March 30, 1670, he was officially recognized by Louis XIV on December 29, 1673, and was rapidly promoted by the king to a number of important offices. At the early age of twelve the Duc du Maine was declared Prince of Dombes and Governor of Languedoc; in 1694 he was appointed Grand Master of Artillery, a post of which he proved himself worthy by serving with distinction on the battlefields of Flanders. He was the recipient of other honors at the hands of the king. In 1692 the duke married Anne- Louise-Bénédicte, the granddaughter of the Great Condé. The duke was highly praised by Madame de Staël, who ascribed to him a fine, cultivated mind, polished manners, and a noble character. He died May 14, 1736.

DULAC. Dulac, a bayou about four miles long, connects Lake Quitman with Bayou Grand Caillou, in Terrebonne Parish. See La Tourrette's map of 1846.

The hamlet of Dulac, which is situated on the bayou, has a population of 90. The hamlet takes its name from that of the bayou.

Another bayou by the name of *Dulac* is a tributary of Pearl Lake, in Avoyelles Parish. See Ludlow's map of 1818, and Survey T 1 N—R 3 E, La. Mer., 1807.

The meaning of *Dulac* is self-evident—literally "of the lake." As cited here *Dulac*, in other words, is not a personal name.

---

[38] See Bernard La Harpe, *Journal Historique de l'Establishment des Français à la Louisiane* (1831), pp. 148, 245, 250.

[39] Cf. The New Orleans *Times-Picayune* for Sunday, November 21, 1926, Magazine section, p. 5.

HÉRON or ROND-POMPON. The name of this stream is recorded as early as 1830 on Survey T 14 S—R 18 E, Southeastern District of Louisiana, West of the Mississippi River. Bayou Héron or Rond-Pompon empties into Bay Chevreuil, in the northern part of Lafourche Parish.

Héron is obviously the name of a species of water bird, and *Rond-Pompon* signifies, I believe, "round pumpkin." *Pompon* is common in sixteenth-century French as a designation of the pumpkin, the fruit of the vine *Cucurbita pepo* (De Candolle.). Ronsard, *Odes*, III, 21, has *pompon tourangeau* for *La citrouille de Touraine* (*Cucurbita pepo* Var.); Cotgrave (1650) uses the feminine *pomponne* for *la citrouille* (*cucurbita pepo*) and the masculine *pompon succrin* for *La Sucrine*, a variety of *Cucurbita pepo*.[40]

JEAN DE JEAN. *Bayou Jean de Jean*: Survey T 4 N—R 3 W, La. Mer., 1808.

Bayou Jean de Jean leaves Red River near Boyce, and forms a junction both with Bayou Cotile and with Bayou Rapides, not far northwest of Cypress Lake.

The early records of the parish of Rapides seem not to record the claim of the particular settler after whom the bayou must have been named. The name *Dejean* is, however, not unknown in Louisiana. A certain Jean Dejean, for example, claimed in 1817 a tract of land in the Eastern District of Louisiana;[41] and another settler, by the name of *Jean Baptiste Dejean*, claimed a tract of land in the county of Iberville, basing his claim on an old conveyance given by Peter Boré to Messrs. Debuys and Remy on December 1, 1798.[42]

The patronymic *Dejean*, the equivalent of *Jones*=*John's*(*son*), is characteristic especially of the department of Hérault, in Southern France. The direct agglutination of *de* with a personal name is found in a region extending from Bas-Langue d'Oc, on the southern coast of France, as far to the Northwest as Annecy; whereas the agglutination of the preposition *à* with a personal name, as in *Ajam* (=*Dejean*) or *Aujean*, has not penetrated into the area of the Langue d'Oc. The place of contact between the former and the latter method of expressing possession is said to be the city

---

[40] See Rolland, *Flore*, VI, 20, 27.
[41] *ASP*, IV, 232, ed. Green.
[42] *ASP*, II, 312, ed. G. and S.

of Lyon, where the immigrants from the northwest have the *a*- names; those from the south, the *de*-names.[43]

Jean is Old French *Jehan,* a derivative of Latin *Joannes* (later *Johannes*), which descends through Greek from Hebrew *Jehohanan,* "Jah (or Jahveh) is gracious."

LABADIEVILLE. The town of Labadieville was named after Jean Louis Labadie, who came to Assumption Parish about 1830 and who died on the Labadie plantation about 1853, I learn from Mr. J. A. Barthet, postmaster at Labadieville. The population of the town is estimated at 530. Cf. *Abadie, infra.*

LACASSINE. The name of a bayou and village, *supra.*

LACOMBE. The census of July 1, 1727, gives the name *La Combe* as that of two persons, the one a master and the other a negro, who lived on the northern shore of Lake Ponchartrain.[44] This name is doubtless perpetuated by that of Bayou Lacombe, in St. Tammany Parish, though the bayou was long in finding a place on modern maps. It is recognized, however, by Robin in 1802. The village of Lacombe must have taken its name from that of the stream. In 1930 the population of Lacombe was 630.

This name is composed of the French *la,* "the," and *combe,* "valley," the latter being a derivative of the Gallic *cumba,* "valley"; cf. Gaelic *cwm,* Irish *cum.* Thus a Frenchman by the name of *Henri,* if he lived in a valley, would come to be known as *Henri de la Combe.*

LARTO. *Larto* is the name of a lake and bayou situated in the southern end of Catahoula Parish. I at first thought that *Larto* might be an error for *Largo*; but I am now persuaded that *Larto* is a French personal name. The history of the lake begins with Charles Defrance's survey of November, 1814, his field notes, pp. 53-54, referring to the Larto Lake as well as to a large "bayau" called the *Larto.*

The French personal name is not unknown in Louisiana. Thus among those who were massacred by the Natchez Indians on November 28, 1729, there was a tailor by the name of *Lartault.* See *Miss. Prov. Archives,* I (1927), 124. Furthermore, a certain Barthelemy Gravemberg claimed on June 19, 1811, a tract of

[43] See A. Dauzat, *Les Noms de Personnes,* pp. 124-125.

[44] *Recensements* 1706—1741, p. 263, in the Library of the Louisiana Historical Society, New Orleans.

land, which is said to have been situated on Lartot Island in the old county of Atakapas. See the *American State Papers,* II, 827, ed. G. and S.

The name *Larto* may be analyzed in two ways. First, it may have come into French from the Germanic stems *hart,* "bold," and *Walt,* "rule." Cf. OHG *harti* and *Gi-walt,* and for the development of *Walt* in French, see Kremers, *Beit. zur Erförschung der französischen Familiennamen,* pp. 53-54 (1910). Secondly, it may have come from *Arto,* a Latinized form of the Gaelic *artos,* "bear" (ursus), which was also used as a man's name. Cf. D'Arbois, *Recherches,* pp. 597-598 (1890). In either case the initial letter of *Larto* is from the French definite article.

LAMOURIE. This bayou connects with Bayou Boeuf in Rapides Parish.

The changes that a name may undergo within less than half a century are aptly illustrated by *Lamourie.* Thus:

Bayu Lamoureux: Spanish Survey, *Book F*, p. 7. 7. 1802.
B. Le Mourir: Darby's map of 1816.
Bayou L'Amour: Graham-Tanner's map of 1834.
B. Lamourie: Tanner's map of Louisiana and Mississippi. 1839.

This stream, according to a local tradition, owes its name to the fact that a young man drowned himself in its waters because his sweetheart had proved unfaithful to him. Compare the form *Lamoureux,* "the lover." The name of the bayou, according to another view, was originally that of an Indian chief. It is true, indeed, that the Biloxi Indians have adopted the geographic name *Lamourie,* which they pronounce Lamo'ri. But the most plausible explanation, in the present writer's opinion, is that the name was conferred on the bayou because of the numerous mulberry trees which grow in its vicinity. *Lamourie* would be, then, a corruption of Fr. *le mûrier,* "the mulberry tree," rather than of Fr. *l'amoureux,* "the lover." Note here dialectal French *mouréi* and *amouri, f.,* as given by Behrens, *op. cit.,* p. 12.

A hamlet by the name of *Lamourie* is in Rapides Parish

+

L'OURS. French *L'Ours,* "the bear," survives in the names of several streams. Thus Bayou L'Ours, situated in the southern end of what is now Assumption Parish, is shown on the maps of Louisiana as early as 1816. There is, too, a bay of this name that unites with Little Lake in Jefferson Parish; in 1583 Bayley calls this bay a "Bayou." A third Bayou L'Ours is an affluent of Bayou Grand Caillou, in the southern part of Terrebonne Parish. Yet another Bayou L'Ours empties into the waters that lap the southern shore of Jefferson Parish. A *Bayou des Ours* (*e*) is in the northern part of the parish of St. Martin.

The form *L'Ourse,* which is used by some modern cartographers, is not to be taken in the sense of "the she-bear"; the final *e* is here due merely to English spelling habits. In Louisiana the name is as a rule pronounced like English *loose.*

Some other streams in Louisiana are called by the English name for the animal. But only one stream, strange to say, has preserved the Indian term for the bear—the *Natalbany,* which owes the first element of its name to the Choctaw *nita,* "bear." Cf. the author's *Louisiana Place-Names of Indian Origin,* pp. 40-41.

The bear is still hunted in Louisiana. How plentiful it was in the early days is too well known to require verification. Two brief items of long ago, however, may not be without interest here. The first informs us that on June 9, 1741, Nicolas Adam, alias Blondin, bought of one Le Clerc, alias Belhumeur, settler at Pointe Coupée, 600 jars of bear's grease at 25 sols a jug. See the *La. Hist. Quar.* for October, 1927, p. 585. The *sol* is an archaic form of French *sou.* The second item is equally significant: In 1813 G. W. Lovelace, of Catahoula Parish, is said to have shipped on a flatboat 243 bearskins. See *De Bow's Review,* XII (1852), 274. It may not be amiss to add Bossu's comment that bear's oil is very good to eat; that in Louisiana it is preferred to hog's lard, and is used for salads, for sauces, and for frying. See Bossu's *Travels,* I (1771), 208.

MALLET. Bayou Mallet, an affluent of Bayou des Cannes in Acadia Parish, bears the name of Pierre Mallet, who owned tracts of land on Bayous Teche and Courtableau at the beginning of the nineteenth century. Cf. *ASP,* II, 871, ed. G. and S.; *ibid.,* III, 162, 190, ed. Green

The name *Mallet* is apparently due to confusion of the diminutive suffix *-et* with the final syllable of Norman *Maillard,* a word that appears in Old French as *mallart,* and in the Anglo-French dialect as *mallard.* From Anglo-French *mallard* has come English "mallard."

Unfortunately, the old French *mallart* is of dubious origin, some authorities connecting it with Old High German *madal-hart,* "strong in the council," and others with Old French *maslart,* wild "drake," a derivative of OF *masle,* "male." Yet another origin is given by Moisy, *Noms de Famille Normands,* 302, where one finds *Mallet* traced to the Old French participle *maleit,* "accursed." With this name Moisy contrasts *Benoît,* "blessed." Weekley, *Surnames,* p. 169, also notes that *Mallet* may be a diminutive of *Mal,* that is, *Mary.*

A certain William Malet, it is interesting to note, was appointed guardian of William the Conqueror's castle in York.

MAMOU. *Mamou* is the name of a prairie lying between Bayou des Cannes and Bayou Nezpiqué, in the parishes of Acadia and Evangeline, and of a village, with a population of 800, situated in the southern part of Evangeline Parish. The form *Mamou* is clearly due to the omission of the final *t*-sound in French *mammouth,* "mammoth," an eighteenth-century loan from Russian *mamont* or *mamut,* which is derived in turn from the Finnish dialect of East Siberia. An early translation of the name—*Prairie Mammoth*—is given in Joshua Knowlton's survey of 1807, marked Southwestern District of Louisiana, T 3 S-R I E.; but Darby's well-known map of 1816 records the name in the spelling that has ultimately prevailed. Bones of the Mastodon have been found on Avery Island, in Iberia Parish.[45]

MARIE CROQUANT. The Bayou Marie Crocan is mentioned in an act of relinquishment to land signed by Courtableau in favor of Lasonde, and passed and approved by Commandant Pellerin, on March 6, 1767. The original document, which is in French, is preserved as No. 191, in Package 807, at the State Land Office in Baton Rouge. An abstract of the act is given in the *American State Papers,* Pub. Lands, III, 189, ed. G. and S. The modern spelling of the name is found on a survey of 1900. The bayou flows southward, east of Opelousas, into Bayou Teche, in the parish of St. Landry.

---

[45] *Geological Survey of Louisiana,* Preliminary Report (1899), pp. 245 ff.

The term *Croquants,* "vagabonds," "worthless countrymen," is said to have been applied to the peasants of Guyenne who in 1594 rose in revolt against Henry IV. Their rallying cry was "sus aux croquants!" —that is to say, "sus à ceux qui croquent (mangent) le peuple!" (*Dict. Gén.*) A literal translation is "at those who devour the people!"

As none of the early names of the bayou have the feminine form *croquante, Marie* is here apparently the well-known French family name, and not a girl's baptismal name. What particular Marie, however, conferred his name on the bayou, I have not been able to ascertain.

NA BONCHASS. The name of this bayou, which connects with an arm of Bayou Pierre Lake, in De Soto Parish, is interesting chiefly because of the corruptions it has undergone. Lockett's maps of 1873 and 1882 record a *Big Narbonne Chasse B.,* and a little farther north a *Lit. B. Narbonne Chasse.* The official surveys show such spellings as *Bayou Na Bonchass,* T 13 N—R 12 W, NW Dist. of La. (1892), and *Nabonchasse* T 14 N—R 12 W, SW Dist. of La. (1833). The clue to the source of the name is found in a reference to the waters of Bayou Labonne Chasse, in the *American State Papers,* Series of Public Lands, IV (1825), 101-102, ed. G. and S.; Cf. *La. Bonne Chasse, ibid.,* p. 144. The name signifies literally "the good hunting."

NEZ PIQUÉ. The designation "Tattooed Nose," which was bestowed by the French on an important bayou in Southwest Louisiana, simply emphasizes the fact that the Indians in its vicinity practised the art of tattooing. The custom of tattooing the body prevailed, indeed, among all the Indians of North America. A great Natchez chief went by the name of *Serpent Piqué,* "tatooed Serpent." Joutel, writing in March, 1687, thus describes the manner in which the Indians tattooed themselves:

"The Indians are generally handsome, but disfigure themselves by making scores or streaks on their faces, from the top of the forehead down the nose to the tip of the chin; which is done by pricking the skin with needles, or other sharp instruments, till it bleeds, whereon they strew fine powder of charcoal, and that sinks in and mixes with the blood within the skin. They also make, after the same manner, the figures of living creatures, of leaves and flowers on the shoulders, thighs, and other parts of their bodies, and paint themselves, as has been said before, with black or red, and sometimes both together."[46]

Du Pratz notes that the women of those nations who use an *r* were especially prone to tattoo their entire persons—even their breasts: these nations were the Yazoo and Koroa.[47]

PALOURDE. This is the name of a lake, recorded by Darby in 1816, in the parish of St. Mary.

Fr. *palourde,* a "mussel," from Low Latin *pelōrida,* "the giant mussel," is used in the dialects of Brittany and Poitou, according to Gamillscheg, *Wb.*, p. 663.

PELTO. Lake Pelto lies between the southern coast of Terrebonne Parish and the Isle Dernière. See Survey T 23 S—R 17 E, La. Mer., 1842.

A man by the name of Jacques *Pelleteau* was a claimant for land in the parish of Jefferson, according to the *American State Papers,* VI, 696, ed. G. and S. I cannot connect his name, however, with a settlement near the lake.

Pelto is intended for *Pelletot,* or, as it is also written, *Pelleteau,* a diminutive in *-ot* formed from the French *Pelletier,* "furrier."

PETRE. Bayou Petre is an affluent of *Bayou la Loutre* in the parish of St. Bernard. See Survey T 14 S—R 18 E, St. Hel. Mer., Dec. 4, 1847.

The French family name *Pêtre* descends from the Old French nominative *pestre,* "baker," a derivative of Latin *pistor.* A variant form is French *Pitre,* a name which has been conferred on an island off the northeastern coast of St. Bernard Parish. On some maps of Louisiana the *Isle au Pitre* is corrupted into the *Isle au Pied.*

French *Petre* may be equivalent in some cases to *Pierre* (Latin *Petrus*). Moreover, dialectal Fr. *petre,* from Low Latin *pedester,* "pedestrian," signifies "idle," "lazy" (*REW* 6346).

POINTE AU CHIEN. Bayou Pointe au Chien, which runs close along a part of the eastern boundary of Terrebonne Parish, is shown in 1831, on Survey T 18-R 19 E, La. Mer., as *Bayou Chin.* On a survey of 1856 the name is given as *Bayou Point*(*e*) *au Chien.*

[46] B. F. French, *Historical Collections of Louisiana,* I (1846), 149.

[47] *Histoire,* II, 195-196, 226; cf. also Charlevoix, *Journal,* III, 327-328; *Handbook of American Indians,* II (1910), 699-701.

Inasmuch as La Tourrette in 1846 prefers the reading *B. Chene* and is followed in 1873 by Lockett, I do not doubt that the original designation of the bayou was taken from French *chêne,* "oak," and that the early *Bayou Chin,* together with the present *Pointe au Chien,* "Dog Point" bayou, is due to the carelessness of the surveyors.

POINTE EN POINTE. Bayou Pointe en Pointe, a tributary of Lake Eloi in St. Bernard Parish, owes its name to two short arms that extend from the same side of the stream. These projecting "points" of water are clearly shown on Survey T 14 S—R 17 E, St. Helena Mer., 1843, 1844.

PRAIRIEON. *Prairieon* is the name of a bayou in Ouachita Parish. Jean Filhiol, who came to the Post of Ouachita as the Spanish commandant in 1783,[48] was the claimant for a tract of land situated in the Little Prairie of the Woods—or in the *Prairiellon de la Prairie des Bois,* as the name is given in the *American State Papers,* III (1823), 525, ed. Green. The earliest reference that I have found to the prairie is in the corrupted spelling *Priarillon,* recorded on a Spanish survey of 1797. Here it designates a small part of the immense tract of land that was claimed by the Marquis de Maison Rouge.[49]

In old surveys of 1813 and 1814 the name of the bayou is written *Prairion* and *Prairieon;* see T. 16 N.—R. 3 E., Dist. North of Red River, La. It signifies "Little Prairie," and is clearly a formation with the diminutive suffix *-on,* as in French *cabanon,* "little cabin." Originally indeed the name may have been formed, like that of the prairie, with the lengthened suffix *-illon,* as in French *postillon,* "postilion"; in this case the meaning would not be affected.

QUEUE DE TORTUE. Lacasine, an Attakapas chief, died about 1799, and was succeeded by Celestine le Tortue, who owned a good deal of land in Southwest Louisiana, one of his tracts being situated on Bayou Queue de Tortue. The nickname "Turtle's Tail" may have been conferred on this bayou by some one who remembered Celestine's family name. The name of the bayou is pronounced as if it were written *Queue Tortue.*

About six miles north of the bayou a railroad switch near Estherwood, on the Southern Pacific, is said to have been named *Tortue* after an Indian. At least two other

[48] *ASP,* III, 527, ed. Green.
[49] See the illustration, *infra.*

members of the Attakapas tribe were called *Le Tortue* —W. le Tortue and Jacob le Tortue, Jun.[50]

Does Bayou Tortue, a small stream near Breaux Bridge, also bear an Indian's name, or signify literally "turtle bayou?"

RIGOLET DE BON DIEU. The *Rigolet de Bon Dieu* is the name of an arm of Red River that extends from a point about two miles below Grande Écore to Colfax, where it again unites with the Red. The name signifies the little "strait of the good God," *Rigolet* being a diminutive formation from French *rigole*, "canal." (See Gamillscheg). The name is very old. Milton Dunn, in his *History of Natchitoches* (1920), p. 7, observes that in the office of the clerk of court at Natchitoches there is a receipt marked "Bon Dieu Falls" and dated 1712. In 1816 Darby's map records the name as *Rigolet de Bon Dieu.*

RIGOLETS, *m. pl. Rigolets* is the name of the strait that connects Lake Borgne with Lake Pontchartrain, in the parish of Orleans. A station on the Louisville and Nashville Railway is also called *Rigolets.*

An early instance of *rigolet* is found in La Harpe's reference to *le Rigolet du Diable,* which he reached on February 15, 1719, on his expedition up Red River.[51]

ROSEAUX. *La Rosean*: Lockett's map of 1873.

L. Roseaux: Hardee's map of 1895.

Lake Roseaux lies a few miles west of Big Bend, in Avoyelles parish.

The French plural *Roseaux,* "reeds," "reed-canes," is a diminutive formation from French *ros,* "weaver's reed," the latter being taken in turn from Gothic *raus,* "reed." The French trappers of South Louisiana apply the term *Roseau* to the Common Reed-Grass (*Phragmites phragmites* (L.) (Karst.) The name of the lake is pronounced as in French.

ROW GULLY. *Row Gully* is the local name of Bayou Rigolette, a stream that drains Iatt lake and empties into Red River about a mile above Pineville, La. Mr. G. W. McKnight, of Colfax, La., informs me that the name of the bayou was corrupted into *Row Gully* by Charles de France, who surveyed this part of the State between 1813 and 1815.[52]

---

[50] Cf. *American State Papers,* Public Lands, III, 93, 114, 239, ed. Gales and Seaton; *ibid.,* III, pp. 84, 91, 210, ed. Green.

[51] See Margry, VI, 251.

[52] Cf. the survey marked T 6 N—R 3 W, La. Meridian, as well as the *Amer. State Papers,* III, 204, 527, ed. Green.

SABINE. The Sabine River, which forms a part of the boundary between Louisiana and Texas, flows through Sabine Lake and Sabine Pass into the Gulf of Mexico. Sabine Parish was created on March 27, 1843, during the administration of Governor Mouton. The name of the river was also given to the cross-roads at Mansfield, La., where on April 8, 1864, the Confederates under Taylor defeated the Federals under Banks.

References to the *Rio Sabinas* by the Spanish explorers of the seventeenth century point unmistakably to the true source of the river name. In 1689, for example, Governor Alonso de Leon, with a force of over one hundred men, crossed the river Sabinas in search of the French settlement at Fort St. Louis, which he reached on April 22, of the same year.[53] Again, in 1691 Governor Domingo Teran of Coahuila, who had been instructed to make a thorough exploration of the country, joined a number of Franciscan friars on the Rio Sabinas;[54] and finally, in 1699 Friar Diego de Salazar, crossing the Rio Sabinas, founded the mission of San Juan Bautista, which he entrusted shortly afterwards to the care of Friar Francisco Hidalgo of Queretaro.[55] Virtually a hundred years after these events—to be explicit, on June 17, 1797—a certain Vicente Michelé received permission of Done José Guadiana, lieutenant governor for the king at Nacogdoches and its dependencies, to settle at a place called *Las Sabinas*, which was situated on the east side of the river Sabine, at the ferry where the old road from Natchitoches to Nacogdoches crossed the river. The land mentioned in this claim lay as a matter of fact within the Neutral Territory, which extended from the Rio Hondo westward as far as the Sabine, and the control of which was in dispute between Spain and the United States until the treaty of February 22, 1819.[56]

As Spanish *Rio Sabinas* signifies "river of cedar trees," the stream clearly acquired its name because of the cedars that were growing on its banks. In Cuba the red cedar (*Juniperus virginiana* L.) is called *Sabina Criola*.[57] About the beginning of the eighteenth century

[53] Cf. Hubert H. Bancroft, *North Mexican States and Texas*, I, 414; and see R. C. Clark, in the Texas *Quarterly*, V (1901-2), 178.

[54] Bancroft, *op. cit.*, I, p. 416.

[55] Bancroft, *op. cit.*, I, 379.

[56] See the *American State Papers, Public Lands*, IV, 510 ff., ed. G. and S.

[57] C. Suárez, *Vocabulario Cubano* (1921), p. 464; cf. A. Zayas, "Sabina," in *Lexicografía Antillana* (1914), p. 424.

the Spanish term for the river gradually gave way to the French Latinized form *Sabine,* which is in turn responsible for the appearance of the word in English. It is remarkable that most maps of the eighteenth century ignore the term *Sabinas,* popular as it was among the Spanish, and substitute the name "Mexicano"—as do, for instance, Bellin's in 1744 and Bowen's in 1752. Even the Robin-Poirson map of 1802-06 designates the stream as the "Mexicana ou Sabine."

In Lower Louisiana *Sabine* designates a person of mixed negro and Indian blood, doubtless because this kind of half-breed was first observed in the vicinity of the Sabine River. Here *Sabine* is used as an adjective or as a noun, masculine or feminine.

SALÉ. Bayou Salé in the parish of St. Mary takes its name from the French participial adjective *salé,* "salted," "salt." That *salé* is the origin of the name, and not the French *sale,* "foul," "dirty," is clearly proved by the earliest records. Thus William Bundick claimed on July 30, 1806, 677 superficial acres of land lying in the county of Atacapas on the Bayou Sallé. A copy of Bundick's claim is filed in package No. 901-1020, at the State Land Office in Baton Rouge. Again, Bayou Sallé is named in 1827 on Survey T 16 S—R 9 E, La. Meridian. The name is correctly given as *Bayou Salé* on the War Department's map, revised to March, 1925. Bayou Salé, on the Southern Pacific Railway, is recorded on Lockett's map of 1882.

Salé is usually pronounced like English *Sally,* the French pronunciation being rare except among those whose mother tongue is French.

SANCHO SANK. Lake Sancho Sanck: Survey T 6 N—R 5 W, La. Mer., 1809.

Sanco Sank L.: La Tourrette, 1856.

L. Sancho Sank: Hardee, 1895.

About four miles and a half north of the village of Gorum, in the southern part of Natchitoches Parish, there is a lake, now dry, which is designated in writing as *Sancho Sank,* but which is locally known as *Samp-Samp.*

In October, 1731, a band of two hundred Natchez Indians, under the leadership of the Flour Chief, marched against the Natchitoches, and succeeded in capturing the Natchitoches village. But St. Denis, the intrepid commandant of the French post at Natchitoches, assaulted the enemy's entrenchments with a small force of Frenchmen, Spaniards, and Indians, slew eighty-two warriors, among whom was the Flour Chief himself, and put the rest of the Natchez band to flight. Such is the gist of Charlevoix's account of this fight.[58]

Du Pratz, whose notice of this episode differs in some particulars from Charlevoix's, says that the Natchez first tried to gain admission to the French fort under the pretext of presenting to St. Denis the pipe of peace; but that, exasperated by their failure to deceive the commandant, they burned in plain view of the fort a French woman whom they had taken captive. Thereupon St. Denis, leaving a handful of men to hold the fort, made a sudden sally and inflicted on the enemy a severe defeat.[59] Some of the Natchez, according to an obscure tradition, were slain as far south as the present Lake Sancho Sank, which the French settlers very appropriately called *Sang pour Sang,* "Blood for Blood." The local pronunciation, *Samp-Samp,* is apparently a corruption of the French name.

The form *Sancho Sank* remains unexplained. An American surveyor, however may have mistaken the French *Sang* for *Sank,* and a Spanish settler who was ignorant of French may have substituted the familiar personal name *Sancho* for the first two elements of the name. I refrain from making any other guesses at the origin of this strange term. It is remarkable, finally, that Lockett's map of 1873 records the name of the lake as *St. Bassant.* This seems to be intended for *St. Baussant,* the French equivalent of Latin *Sanctus Balsamus.*[60]

SARA. In a charming sketch of West Feliciana Parish Miss Louise Butler says that Bayou Sara was named after an old woman who resided on the banks of this stream.†

I have not been able to find any historical evidence in support of Miss Butler's statement. Trudeau's reference, in a survey of 1787, to a "Bayu vulgarmente llamado Bayu Sara" indicates that the name of the stream was well known in the second half of the eighteenth century.[61] Whether the identity of the person

[58] Charlevoix, *Histoire,* II (1744), 498 ff.

[59] Du Pratz, *Histoire,* III, 272 ff.

[60] Cf. H. Cocheris, *Origine et Formation des Noms de Lieu* (1874), p. 142.

† *The Louisiana Historical Quarterly,* VII, No. I, 97.

[61] See *Liber* J, p. 158; and *Liber* E, p. 92, in the library of the Louisiana State University.

whose name was conferred on the bayou will ever be discovered is, in my opinion, highly doubtful. Here, however, is a clue from *De Bow's Magazine,* III, (1847), 122, footnote:

"The Bayou Sara has long been known by this name, but in a copy in my possession taken from an old map in the Bureau de la Marine, in Paris, this stream is called *La Rivière de la Pucelle Juive.*"

The old settlement of Bayou Sara has virtually been transplanted to the hills of the neighboring town of St. Francisville. In the middle of the nineteenth century, the village of Bayou Sara, situated at the confluence of the stream of the same name and the Mississippi, was an important business center and steamboat landing. Though the village is now deserted, its name will be remembered chiefly because John James Audubon landed there in 1821, and spent nine years in the study of the birds of the Bayou Sara region.[62]

SORREL. It is barely possible that Bayou Sorrel, in what is now called Iberville Parish, took its name from that of Jacques Sorrel, in whose favor an order of survey for a tract of land on Bayou Teche was signed on June 1, 1768, by Governor Antonio de Ulloa of Louisiana.[63] A certain Jacques Sorel is known to have been living in 1773 at the Post of Atakapas, a name conferred in 1756 on the site of the present town of St. Francisville.[64]

It is much more probable, however, that the bayou bears the name of Joseph Sorrel, an early settler who owned extensive tracts of land on the Bayou Teche and the Bayou Cypre-mort, in the old county of Attakapas. Another bayou of the same name is found in the southern end of the parish of St. Martin. Early maps show Sorrel's plantation to have been situated on Bayou Teche, about twenty miles southeast of New Iberia.[65] An earlier reference to Sorrel is that made in Trudeau's survey of December 23, 1799, which fixes the boundaries of Don Joseph Saurel's claim for a tract of land, situated in the "Puesto de Attacapas," twenty-seven miles

[62] See Annette Duchein, in the New Orleans *Times-Picayune,* Sunday, July 27, 1930, Section 3, pp. 1 ff.

[63] See *American State Papers,* Public Lands, III, p. 153, ed. Green.

[64] Cf. Laura L. Porteous, "Index to the Spanish Judicial Records of Louisiana," *The La. Hist. Quarterly,* Vol. IX, No. 2 (April, 1926), p. 339.

[65] Cf. *American State Papers,* Public Lands, II (1813), pp. 823, 825, ed. G. and S.; William Darby, *Emigrant's Guide* (1918), p. 58.

south of the parochial church.[66] Measured by the standards of his time, Sorrel was a man of vast wealth; but he was so frugal that he served nothing but water to travelers, says Robin.[67]

The Old French diminutive *sorel,* "reddish brown" or "bright chestnut," appears in English and French as a nickname with reference to the color of the hair. Old French *sor,* from which the diminutive is formed, is derived from Germanic **saur,* "dry," and is related to English *sear.* The term *sorrel* was also formerly applied by hunters to a three-year-old stag.[68]

SOULOUQUE. A hamlet six miles below Plaquemine, in Iberville Parish, was named *Soulouque* after a mulatto slave who was reared on Sosthene Allain's plantation near Baton Rouge.[69] After the slaves were set free, Soulouque was elected to the State Senate and became famous for his skill in debate. When he came to Baton Rouge to attend the sessions of the legislature, he was greeted with the following negro-French refrain by some of the Acadians:

> Souris, chien, chien enragé!
> Mo tendé trois coups canon;
> Mo mandé, "Qui ça ça y'est?"
> Li di moin, "Soulouque 'rivé."
> ("Smile, dog, mad dog!
> I heard three cannon shots;
> I asked, 'What's that?'
> He [one] said to me, 'Soulouque
> has arrived.' ")

Soulouque of Louisiana was named after Faustin Élie Soulouque (1785-1867), the negro general and politician who was elected to the presidency of Haiti on March 1, 1847, and who was proclaimed emperor as Faustin I on August 26, 1849. He was deposed December 22, 1858, and spent nearly all the rest of his life in exile.

ST. MALO. Bayou St. Malo is a tributary of Lake Borgne, in the parish of St. Bernard. See survey T 13 S—R 16 E, St. Helena Mer., 1843. B. St. Malo is also recorded by Lafon in 1806.

[66] See *Survey Book E,* p. 66, in the Library of the Louisiana State University.

[67] *Voyages,* III (1807), 25.

[68] Cf. Weekley, *The Romance of Names* (1914), pp. 215-216.

[69] Grace King, *Creole Families of New Orleans* (1921), p. 449.

Malo, a derivative of Latin *Maclovius,* is the name that is borne by a fortress and seaport in the department of Ille-et-Vilaine, France, 51 miles north-northwest of Rennes by railroad. The port of St. Malo was founded towards the end of the eleventh century by the inhabitants of the neighboring town of St. Servan, and was named after Maclovius, bishop of Alet, France, in the sixth century.[70]

TESSON. Bayou Tesson, at Opelousas, is believed to have been named after Theophile Tesson, who once resided on its bank. For this information, which is doubtless correct, I am indebted to Mr. G. L. Lasalle, of Opelousas. I have also learned, however, that a certain John Tessan was one of the early settlers in the old county of Opelousas. See *American State Papers,* Public Lands, II, 834, edition Gales and Seaton.

Tesson, found in Old French as *taisson,* may be derived from Germanic *taxo,* "badger," the name of the animal. It is the Italian *tasso,* which, like *badger* in English, is used as a proper name. But Italian *Tasso* may signify "oak tree," from Low Latin *taxus.*

It is perhaps more plausible to take *Tesson* for a diminutive of *Tessier,* "weaver," the latter having its source in Low Latin *texerius.*[71]

TIMBALIER. An island off the coast of Terrebonne Parish is said to bear the nickname of a famous soldier, Sylvain Filiosa, who beat a kettledrum on a pair of cymbals so vigorously that he caused a band of Indians to cease their attack and gaze in alarm at his unknown weapon. Presumably this feat was performed on November 28, 1729, when the French who were stationed at Fort Rosalie were massacred by the Natchez Indians. Hence Filiosa became known as *Le Sieur Timbalier,* "The Kettledrummer."[72]

A bay and a grand pass bear the same name as the island. There is also an East Timbalier Island.

VALENTINE. *B. Valentine*: Lockett's map of 1873.

Bayou Valentine, an affluent of Bayou Boeuf, bears the Christian name of Valentine Lassard, who was commandant of the post of Rapides and agent of Indian affairs under the Spanish régime at the close of the

[70] Cf. Longnon, *Les Noms de lieu de la France,* p. 428.

[71] See Kremers, *Beiträge,* p. 97, and Ritter, *Noms de Famille,* p. 33.

[72] See Grace King, *Creole Families of New Orleans,* pp. 350-352; Gaspar Cusachs, in *The Louisiana Historical Quarterly,* II, No. 3 (July, 1919), pp. 303-306.

eighteenth and the beginning of the nineteenth century. He succeeded his father Étienne in the office of commandant, and is said to have been thoroughly familiar with the dialects of the Indian tribes that resided in the district of Rapides. He was sometimes called "Valentine" or "Mr. Valentine." He continued in office after the transfer of Louisiana to the United States.[73]

3. SPANISH PLACE-NAMES

ANACOCO. Anacoco Bayou empties into the Sabine River, on the southern boundary of Vernon Parish. Gray's map of 1878 records *Anacoco* as the name of a village—population now 305—in the northwestern part of the same parish. *Anacoco* has lost an initial *L* in the local pronunciation, this letter being apprehended as the French definite article *L'*.

This name appears under many strange forms in the *American State Papers,* series of Public Lands. Here are some of these forms, collected at random from volumes II, III, and IV of this publication: *Anacucu, Yanacoco, Yanecoocoo, Yanakoka, De Koocoque, Kan Coque.* Most of these refer to the prairie Lanacoco; several, to the bayou of the same name. William Darby's spelling of the name is *Llana Coucou.*[74] Two earlier forms than Darby's are *Lianacucu* and *Leaunacucou,* which are found in deeds of July 31, 1797.[75]

The first element of *Anacoco* is clearly meant for Spanish *llano* or *llana,* "plain," "level field"; and the second element is perhaps either French *coucou* or Spanish *cucu.* The name, then, may be the equivalent of "Raincrow Prairie." The raincrow is fairly common in Louisiana. In Huntingdonshire, England, it is interesting to note, there is a place by the name of *Yaxley,* which is derived from Old English *geaces-leage* (dat.), "Cuckoo's Clearing."[76]

Nevertheless, this analysis of *Lanacoco* may be erroneous; for *coucou,* "cuckoo"—dialectal *cocu*—has long been common in Normandy as a family name,[77] and Spanish *cucos,* too, is said to be a nickname given in Castile to the stonecutters who come from Asturia

[73] *ASP,* II, 785 ff., ed. G. and S., *et passim.*
[74] Map of 1816; and *Louisiana,*[2] (1817), p. 151.
[75] *American State Papers,* III, 88, ed. G. and S.; IV, 69, ed. Green.
[76] A. Mawer and F. M. Stenton, *The Place Names of Bedfordshire and Huntingdonshire* (1926), p. 202.
[77] Moisy, *Noms de Famille Normands* (1875), pp. 92-93.

(Velázquez, *v. cuco*). The landlord in George W. Cable's *'Sieur George*, I now recall, was an old Creole by the name of Kookoo. It is just possible, in other words, that *Lanacoco* may be a compound of *llana* and a personal nickname, the latter being connected either with French *coucou* or with Spanish *cuco*.

The difficulty of interpreting *Lanacoco* is further complicated by the fact that St.-Fr. *coucou* also signifies the barren strawberry plant (genus *potentilla*). I have not met any Acadians, however, who use *coucou* in this sense. The word *coco*, on the contrary, is common enough in Louisiana-French as a designation of nut-grass (*Cyperus rotundus* L.), a highly troublesome weed in the South. The meaning, then, of *Anacoco* may be "nut-grass prairie." Unfortunately, little significance can be attached, in my opinion, even to the earliest spellings of this word, and hence an absolutely satisfactory interpretation of its second element will probably never be found.

ARROYO HONDO. The Arroyo Hondo, "deep rivulet," is an insignificant stream situated approximately midway between the town of Natchitoches and the site of the old Spanish post of Los Adaes near Robeline. This stream became famous when it was tentatively accepted in the eighteenth century as the boundary between French Louisiana and the Spanish province of Texas. Nevertheless, the King of Spain asserted as late as 1754 that the boundaries between the Spaniards and the French in that territory had never been made, and ought not then to be made, the subject of a formal treaty.[78]

BARATARIA. D'Anville's map, which was drawn in 1732 but not published until 1752, records an "Isle Barataria." Going southward nowadays from New Orleans, one comes upon the name at several different points. First, there is the hamlet of Barataria, about sixteen miles south of the city, together with Little Bayou Barataria. This hamlet had a population of 650 in 1930, and its name appears on Nicholson's map of 1880. Then follow in succession Big Bayou Barataria, Barataria Bay, and Barataria Lighthouse, the last-named being situated on Grand Terre Island.

During the first quarter of the nineteenth century the shores and islands of Barataria Bay formed the rendevous of a band of pirates and smugglers, who had

[78] Cf. H. E. Bolton and Thos. M. Marshall, *The Colonization of North America* (1929), p. 300.

established a stronghold within a group of shell mounds formerly used by the Indians as burial places, near the junction of two bayous now called, respectively, *Perot* and *Rigolettes*. Far to the southeast, on the island of Grande Terre, the pirates had built a second fort, which, like the first, is marked on Tanner's map of 1820. Brown, in his *Western Gazetteer* (1817), p. 141, says that "both ends of this island were fortified in 1811, by the pirates under M. La Fitte." The pirates were led by the famous Jean Lafitte.[79]

. The source of the name *Barataria* is thus correctly explained by Du Pratz: "Ce terrein peut avoir une lieue de long sur une demi-lieue de large; on a nommé cet endroit *Barataria*, parce qu'il est enfermé par ces lacs & par leurs issues, ce qui forme à peu-près une Isle en terre ferme, comme étoit celle dont Sancho-Pança fut fait Gouverneur."[80]

Barataria is a Romance word that signifies "deception." Cf. Provençal *barataria*, Portuguese *barataria*, Spanish *barataria* (obs.), Old French and nautical *Baraterie*. As to the etymology Gamillscheg suggests that OF and Dial. *Barat*, "deception," seems to be a blend of ON. *baratta*, "battle," "turmoil," and the Breton *barad*, "deception."

CAMINADA. *Caminada* is the name of a bay and a pass situated in the southern end of Jefferson Parish. West of the bay, in the coast marsh, is an island of live oaks called *Chênière Caminada*. These geographical terms probably perpetuate the memory of a certain Francisco Caminada, who, according to the Spanish Judicial Records of the eighteenth century, appears several times as a defendant in suits tried in the Court of Unzaga. Caminada owned land at the site of the old Chapitoulas Indian settlement above New Orleans, as well as a tract of land below the city. He was a merchant in New Orleans, and a member of the "Milice Bourgeoisie."[81]

---

[79] See Fortier, *Louisiana*, II, 24-25, 464-468; Cusachs, "Lafitte, The Louisiana Pirate and Patriot," *La. Hist. Quar.*, II, No. 4, (October, 1919), 418-438; Lyle Saxon, *Lafitte the Pirate* (1930), pp. 34-43.

[80] *Op cit.*, I (1758), 289; cf. *Don Quixote*, translated by John Ormsby, II, 307. New York: T. Y. Crowell & Co. [n. d.]

[81] See Meloncy C. Soniat, "The Tchoupitoulas Plantation," *La. Hist. Quar.*, VII, No. 2 (April, 1924), 313, 314; Laura L. Porteous, "Index to the Spanish Judicial Records of Louisiana," *La. Hist. Quar.*, VIII, No. 3 (July, 1925), 508; *ibid.*, *La. Hist. Quar.*, IX, No. 2 (April, 1926), 322; *ibid.*, *La. Hist. Quar.*, IX, No. 3 (July, 1926), 537.

Compare *American State Papers*, III, 231, ed. Green; *ibid.*, VI, 671, 674, ed. Gales and Seaton.

Caminada is a derivative of Low Latin *caminata*, "a room provided with a chimney or fireplace." In Southern France the name occurs as *Caminade*. Provençal *Caminada* is found in the same sense.[82] Evidently, the proper name *Caminada* was applied to the owner or the occupant of a *caminata*.

COLYELL. *Colyell*, the name of a bayou and bay in Livingston Parish, perpetuates the memory of a Spanish officer who was active in Galvez's campaign of 1779-1781 against the British forces in West Florida. In old Spanish surveys of land in Livingston Parish one reads of a *bayou* or *arroyo* commonly called "Go to Hell." This play upon the name *Colyell* is still known to the natives of the parish. For the term *Arrayo Collell* as well as the nickname, see Pintado's survey of May 8, 1809, in Survey Book Z, p. 128 ff.

Captain Francisco Collel—he subsequently attained the rank of colonel—was one of the commandants of Fort Plaquemine, in Iberville Parish, and was also stationed for some time as commandant at Galveztown, an extinct settlement which was situated on the right bank of the Amite River near its junction with Bayou Manchac. After the cession of Louisiana to the United States Colonel Collel reappeared as Commandant of the Post of Mobile.[83]

Collel seems to be a diminutive of Sp. *Nicolás*.

LENANN. Bayou Lenann empties into the Sabine River, not far north of the old road that ran from Nacogdoches to Natchitoches.[84] *Lenann* must not be confused with the first element of (*L*)*anacoco, supra*. The former is derived from Spanish *La nana*, "the mother," "the lady of the house" (Low Latin *nanna*). That this analysis of the name is correct becomes clear from a reference to a tract of land called "Nana (mother)," and situated about eight miles from the Sabine river, on the road from Nacogdoches to Natchitoches. It seems that on July 1, 1798, Joseph Cayetano de Sapeda, commandant of Nacogdoches, gave this tract to Edward Murphy and conferred on it the name of *St. Peter of the Bayou La*

---

[82] See L. Larchey, *Dictionnaire des Noms* (1880), p. 76; Meyer-Lübke, *REW*, p. 118.

[83] See C. Robert Churchill, *Spanish Records*, pp. 1, 4, 21, 75; Hill, *Papeles Procedentes de Cuba*, p. 515; *Official Letter Books of W. C. C. Claiborne*, VI, 293; V. M. Scramuzza, "Galveztown," *The Louisiana Historical Quarterly*, XIII, No. 4 (October, 1930), 553-609.

[84] See Darby's map of 1816.

Nana. The name of the stream was also written *La Nan.*[85]

Another source for *Lenann* is equally probable: Chilean-Spanish *ñaña,* commonly "mother," a derivative of Kechuan *ñaña,* "wife's sister."[86]

+MARRON. A bayou by the name of *Marron* empties into Bayou Cane in Evangeline Parish. The French *marron,* thought to be an adoption of Spanish *cimarron,* "wild," signifies not only a fugitive slave, but also a domestic animal that has run wild. In Louisiana the word even distinguishes wild plants or trees from those that are cultivated. Robin refines *Marronnes* as *"Troupes de vaches* without any known masters."[87] But *Bayou Marron* is probably the equivalent of "fugitive slave" bayou. On La Tourrette's map of 1846 the name *Marron* is corrupted into *Murrens.*

The word *marron* is found as the name of several other streams. Thus Bayou Nègre Marron, or "Fugitive Negro" Bayou, is a tributary of Bayou La Loutre, in the parish of St. Bernard. See Survey T 14—R 17 E, St. Helena Meridian, 1843, 1844. Farther to the north, in the same parish, Bayou Maron connects the Lakes of Bayou Marron with the Lakes of Bayou Boudreau, according to Survey T 1 S—18 E, St. Hel. Mer., 1843-45. The English substantive *maroon,* "fugitive slave," is taken from French *marron.*

NEGREET. *Negreet,* the name of a bayou and a hamlet in Sabine Parish, is a corruption of American Spanish *negrito,* here used in the sense of "black." This designation was bestowed on the stream because black-haw trees (*Viburnum rufidulum* Raf.) grew in its vicinity. Reputable cartographers, between 1816 and 1839, record the name as "Black Haw" creek; La Tourrette, in 1846, first gives the name as *B. Negret.*

PINTOU. Bayou Pintou is east of Grand Pass, on the northern coast of St. Bernard parish. See survey T 10 S—R 20 E, St. Hel. Mer., 1845.

Pintou is probably a corruption of the Spanish personal name *Pinto,* "painted." The word is derived from late Latin **pinctus,* for *pictus,* the past participle of *pingere,* "to paint." In the dialect of the Southwestern United States a *pinto* is a piebald horse or pony.

---

[85] See *American State Papers,* Public *Lands,* III, 85, ed. G. and S.; IV, 43, 60, ed. Green.

[86] Cf. Lenz, *Diccionario Etimolojico,* pp. 528-529.

[87] *Voyages dans l'Intérieur de la Louisiane . . . ,* III (1807), 65.

The noun *Pinto* designates, too, one who is slightly intoxicated; the adjective *pinto* is applied in Cuba to one who is clever and far-sighted, but untrustworthy.†

PONTON. Bayou Ponton is a tributary of the River aux Chênes, in St. Bernard Parish.

As Spanish *pontón* and French *ponton* both mean "pontoon," or "floating bridge," one can now hardly determine with certainty from which language the name of the bayou has been taken. The absence of the accent on the final syllable of the name as recorded on survey T 16 S—R 15 E, St. Hel. Mer., 1844-46, cannot be considered conclusive proof of French origin.

PUENTE. Though not found on any of the modern maps of Louisiana, this name is recorded in 1840 on the survey of Township 6 S—R 4 E, Southwest Dist. La. This township is in St. Landry parish.

Bayou del Puente is of course merely the Spanish for the bayou "of the bridge."

SAN MIGUEL. La Tourrette's map of 1846, as well as survey T 10 N—R 12 W, NW Dist. La., shows that the Bayou St. Michael, in Vernon Parish, was originally called *San Miguel.* Perhaps the bayou received its name from that of the old mission of San Miguel, which under orders from the Duke de Linares, viceroy of Mexico, was founded in 1716 among the Adai Indians.[88] La Harpe gives the date as January 29, 1717. That such is the source of the name is, however, extremely doubtful; for San Miguel is apparently not recorded on reputable maps of Louisiana until nearly the middle of the nineteenth century. The stream was in all probability named after Augustin T. San Miguel or Maria San Miguel, who had each settled upon land sixteen miles southwest of Natchitoches as early as February 22, 1819.[89] Indeed, Mr. E. C. Leone, of Zwolle, La., writes me that the name of the bayou perpetuates the memory of an early settler; and that the local pronunciation still follows the Spanish form of the name.

TORO. *Toro,* the name of a bayou in Sabine Parish, may have been derived either from Spanish *toro* or from French *taureau,* "bull." *Taureau* was a popular spelling of the name during the first part of the nineteenth century; *toreau* appears in 1846, followed much later by

† Suarez, *op. cit.*, pp. 419, 554.
[88] Cf. Bienville, in Margry, VI, 223; and La Harpe, *Journal*, p. 139.
[89] See *American State Papers,* Public Lands, IV, pp. 45, 51, ed. Green.

Toro. Nevertheless, the existence of other Spanish place-names in this region makes the Spanish source the more probable. The hamlet of *Toro* takes its name from that of the bayou.

VIDAL. *Bayou Vidal*: *Survey* T 15 N—R 13 E, 1835.

Bayou Vidal rises in Palmyra Lake, and flowing in a southwesterly direction, enters Mill Bayou, a tributary of the Tensas River.

Bayou Vidal perpetuates the memory of José Vidal, a commandant of the old Spanish post of Concordia.

In the local pronunciation *Vidal* has the stress on the second syllable; the "i" sounds like that in *sit*; the "a" approximately like that in *sat.*

The Spanish and Provençal name *Vidal,* a derivative of Latin *Vītālis,* "vital," owes its popularity to the fact that Vidal is the name of several saints.

A famous Provençal troubadour, Pierre Vidal of Toulouse, accompanied Richard the Lion-Hearted to Cyprus in 1190. At Cyprus Vidal married a Greek lady who declared that she was related to one of the families which had occupied the throne of Constantinople. Believing himself to be beloved of every woman and to be the bravest of knights, he became the Don Quixote of Provençal poetry.

VIDALIA. *Vidalia* is the name of a town situated in the parish of Concordia, across the Mississippi river from Natchez. In 1930 the population of Vidalia was estimated at 1,141.

On the outbreak of hostilities between Spain and England (May 8, 1779), Bernardo de Galvez, the fourth Spanish governor of the province of Louisiana, undertook the conquest of West Florida. He captured Fort Bute, at Bayou Manchac, on September 7, 1779, and he forced the surrender of Fort New Richmond, at Baton Rouge, on the 21st of the same month. The surrender of Fort Panmure was included in the terms of capitulation of the fort at Baton Rouge. Fort Panmure was the name bestowed by the English in 1764 on Fort Rosalie, which had been founded by Bienville on the present site of Natchez, and had been named by him in honor of the Duchess of Ponchartrain.[90] Spain held Fort Panmure until four o'clock on the morning of March 30, 1798; the Spanish garrison then left, and the

[90] See Pénicaut, in Margry's *Mémoires,* V, 526. Charlevoix, *Histoire,* II, 565, errs in ascribing the designation of the fort to Iberville.

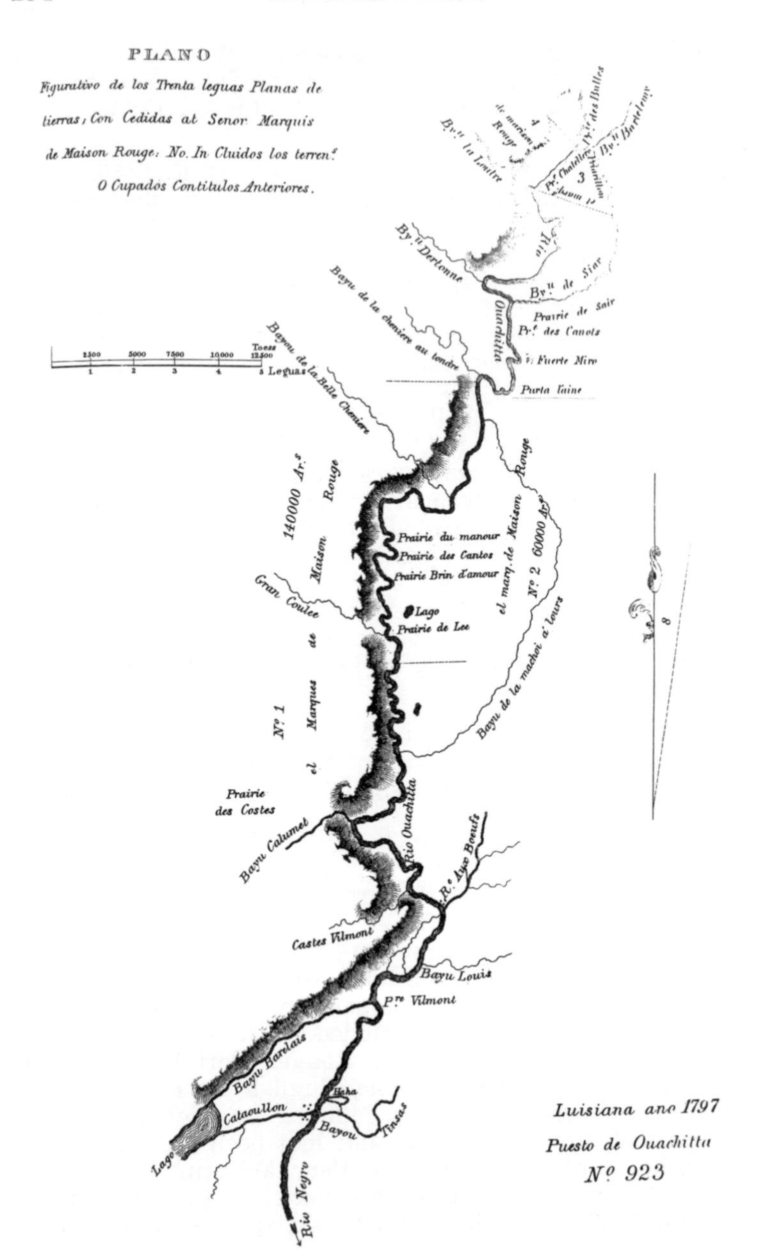

A Spanish Plan of the Ouachita Region in 1797. From *American State Papers,* Public Lands, II, facing page 774.

American troops, under the command of Captain Isaac Guion, immediately took possession of this post. The Spanish government next erected a new fort just across the Mississippi River from Natchez, and Don José Vidal, the Spanish commandant of this district, called the fort *Concordia* as a token of the amicable relations existing between Spain and the United States. The post of Concordia became in time a village, and the name of the latter was finally changed to *Vidalia,* in honor of José Vidal, who served as commandant of the district of Concordia from 1798 to the close of 1803. His successor was Ferdinand L. Claiborne.[91] *Vidalia* appears on Ludlow's map of 1818.

The old Spanish fort of Concordia must not be confused with the present hamlet of Concordia, situated near the town of Ferriday and first appearing on reputable maps about 1873.

Vidal's name was also conferred on a bayou situated in the northeastern part of Tensas Parish.

VILLAR. *Villar* is the name of a beautiful little lake in Ascension Parish, situated about twenty-five miles southeast of Baton Rouge. Mr. Joseph Villar, the owner of a part of the lake, thinks that it was named after his grandfather, Numa Villar. The latter's father, Jean Louis, probably came to Louisiana from Canada with the Acadians; but the name *Villar* may be Spanish or Catalonian as well as Provençal. Its source is Latin *villāris, -e*; compare French *Villiers,* "of or belonging to a villa or farm," from Latin *Villārius, a, um.*[92] It is often difficult to distinguish *Villar* from French *villa* in the Louisiana dialect; but careful speakers usually preserve the final *r*-sound of the former.

4. THE OUACHITA REGION IN 1797

The Spanish plan reproduced on the opposite page contains the following names:

BAYOU CALUMET. *Calumet,* the Norman-Picard form of Fr. *chalumet,* is the name bestowed by the French on the

[91] Cf. *American State Papers,* Public Lands, II, 763-764, ed. G. and S.; *ibid.,* II, 757, 767.

[92] See W. Kaspers, in *Zeitschrift für Ortsnamen-forschung,* I, 102; Kremers, *op. cit.,* p. 61, gives a second etymology—Germanic *Willo, n.,* "will," "striving."

tobacco-pipe that the American Indians used extensively as a symbol of peace and occasionally of war.[93]

BAYOU DE LA CHÊNIÈRE AU TONDRE. See *Tondre, infra.* The local pronunciation is like English *Shinny—Bayou Shinny*—rhyming with *finny.*

BAYOU LA LOUTRE. "Otter bayou." More than two thousand otters are captured annually in Louisiana, and their pelts bring from $15 to $25 apiece.[94] Modern surveys record this stream as *Bayou de Loutre.*

BAYOU TINSAS. The origin of *Tensas,* the name of a small Indian tribe, is unknown.[95]

BAYU BARELAIS. *Bayu* is a Spanish spelling of French *bayou.* The latter is derived directly from Choctaw or Mobilian *bayuk,* and is not related in any way to French *boyau,* "gut," with which the word has been connected by some etymologists. Cf. *bayou, supra.*

Barelais, perhaps an early settler's name, has fallen into disuse.

BAYU BARTÉLEMY. This bayou doubtless bears the name of an early immigrant. The French *Barthélemy* has been Anglicized to *Bartholomew* as the name of this stream.

BAYU DE LA BELLE CHÊNIÈRE. "The bayou of the beautiful oak grove" is now the *Bayou de la Pinière,* "the bayou of the pine forest." The local pronunciation disguises this name under the term *Bayou Peen,* in which *Peen* rhymes with English *seen.*

BAYU DE LA MÂCHOI À L'OURS. "Bayou of the bear's jaw." *Machoi* should be, and now is, *mâchoire*; and *lours, l'ours.* In the local pronunciation the final *s* of *l'ours* is sounded.

BAYU DE SIAR. This name and the *Prairie de Sair* are improper spellings of *De Siard,* the present name and the French equivalent of German *Sigihard,* "firm in victory." Already in Old High German one finds such forms as *Siiard, Seiard.*[96]

The identity of the *Siard* for whom the bayou and prairie are named is not known. *De Siard* is also the name of the main street in Monroe. In the local pronunciation *de* sounds approximately as in French; the first syllable of *Siard* is like English *see,* and the second is like *-ard* in *coward.* The stress falls on *si-*.

---

[93] See Hodge, *Handbook,* I, 191 ff.

[94] Arthur, *The Fur Animals of Louisiana,* p. 126.

[95] See my *Louisiana- Place-Names of Indian Origin,* p. 64. *Tinsas* is an inaccurate spelling of *Tensas.*

[96] Ernst Förstemann, *Altdeutsches, Namenbuch.*[2] p. 1326.

BAYU DERBONNE. This stream bears the name of some early settler. It is now written *D'Arbonne.*

BAYU LOUIS. It is difficult, if not impossible, to determine whether the name *Louis* is corrupted by folk etymology from Choctaw *lusa, "black,"*[97] or bears the name of an Indian chief. On January 11, 1804, Louis, chief of the Tensas Nation, sold for about $5,200, to Alexander Fulton and William Miller, lands belonging to the Tensas and Appalachian tribes. These lands, consisting of eleven thousand two hundred and thirty superficial arpents, were situated on both sides of Red River, and extended from the Pascagoula village down the river on both sides to the mouth of Bayou Jean de Jean, in the district of Rapides.[98]

BRIN D'AMOUR. In 1741 Bienville sent André Fabry de la Bruyère with a small body of men to discover a trade route to New Mexico by way of the Canadian River. On August 12, 1742, one of Fabry's party came upon the camp of a hunter named *Brin d'Amour,* who shortly afterwards joined Fabry's party in the capacity of guide.[99] Camden, Arkansas, was first named *Écore à Fabry,* "Fabry's Bluff."

The etymology of *Brin d'Amour* is interesting. Fr. *Brin,* "blade" (of grass), "bit," is taken from Modern Provençal *Brin,* "hemp-fibre," which has its source in Latin *prīmus,* "the first," the initial consonant of *brin* being due to the influence of *broyer* or *briser* "to break" (Gamillscheg). The second part of the name is syncopated from *de la more,* "of the swamp," so that *Brin d'Amour* designates one who occupies a bit of swampy ground. Compare OF *more,* "peat-bog," "swamp." I am not disposed to connect *Brin d'Amour* with the rare French personal name *Amour,* "love." The place-name *Brin d'Amour* is no longer known.

CASTES VILMONT. This is a poor spelling of *Carlos Villemont.* Carlos de Villemont is known to have been in the service of the Spanish government as commandant of the Arkansas Post in 1798. This post was established in 1686 by Henry de Tonti on the Arkansas river, 73 miles southeast of the present site of Little Rock. About

[97] Bayou *Funny Louis,* in La Salle Parish, is from Choctaw *fáni,* "squirrel," plus *lusa,* "black."

[98] See *ASP,* II, 796 ff., ed. G. and S.

[99] Margry, VI, 489.

thirty-five years later Bernard la Harpe repaired the stockade and placed a permanent garrison at the post. Arkansas Post was maintained as a trading station, and served as headquarters for the French and Spanish lieutenant-governors. In 1803 it passed into the possession of the United States with the purchase of the province of Louisiana.

It was undoubtedly Carlos de Villemont whose name appears twice on the Spanish plan.[100] That he was the owner of land situated on Black River is made clear by Dumont's testimony.[101]

The place-name *Castes Vilmont* has perished.

EL MARQUÉS DE MAISON ROGUE. In 1795 the Marquis de Maison Rouge, a French emigrant, received from Governor Carondelet a grant of four tracts of land on the Ouachita River, comprising all together about thirty superficial leagues, the equivalent of approximating 208,344 superficial arpents. An idea of the immensity of this grant may be gathered from the fact that Tract No. 1 began about five miles below Fort Miro (Monroe), and, following the bends in the river, extended down the stream for a distance of at least forty miles.

A copy of the contract between the Governor of Louisiana and Maison Rouge, details of Trudeau's survey of the tracts, and the reasons why the United States Government resisted the confirmation of the claim are given in the *American State Papers,* Public Lands, IV, 7, 8, 9, 306 ff (ed. Green).

The Marquis de Maison Rouge did not fulfill his part of the contract; and after his death the title to the property passed to Louis Bouligny of New Orleans.[102]

FUERTE MIRO. In 1783 Don Juan Filhiol made a permanent settlement at Prairie des Cânots, where he built a fort and named it *Miro* in honor of Estevan Miro, governor of Louisiana from 1785 to 1791. This name gave way to *Monroe* in 1819.

GRAN COULÉE. Large Coolie. This name is no longer used.

HAHA. *Haha,* an echoic formation in French, signifies an unexpected obstacle; hag; scarecrow.

---

[100] See Robin, *Voyage,* III, 156; J. W. Monette, "Public Lands Acquired by Treaty," in *De Bow's Review,* V (1848), 124-125.

[101] French, *Hist. Coll.* (1853), p. 22; cf. Pénicaut (1722), in Margry, V, 577.

[102] See Robin, *Voyage,* II, 340-341; *ASP,* II, 768, ed. G. and S.; and cf. Henry Chambers, *History of Louisiana,* I, 382, footnote 5.

"A league above the mouth of the Washita [Ouachita] the bayou Ha-ha comes in unexpectedly from the right," says John Sibley.[103]

LAGO CATAOULLOU, now *Lake Catahoula.* This is Spanish *lago,* "lake," plus *cataoullou,* a French spelling of Choctaw *okháta,* "lake," and *hullo,* "sacred." The adjective follows the noun in Choctaw.

PRAIRIE CHÂTELLERO. The identity of the person whose name was conferred on the prairie has been lost, and the name itself is no longer used. The castle of Chatellerault,—which is now a city of the same name in the Department of Vienne, France—was built by Airaud in the tenth century. *Airaud* is a Provençal name, for which the source is OHG. *Adrovald,* a compound of Germanic *athar,* "fine lineage,"—influenced probably by OHG. *atar,* "swift," "sharp,"—and of Germanic *wald*— as seen in OHG. *waltan* = Modern German *walten,* "to rule."[104]

PRAIRIE DE LEE. What particular Lee gave his name to this prairie, I do not know. *Lee* is the popular family name from Old English *leah,* dat. sg. *lēage,* to which in Medieval England Anglo-Norman *de* was often prefixed. In personal names *Lee* signifies a tract of open country. Darby writes *Du Lait* as the name of this prairie; but the present form is *De Lee.*[105]

PRAIRIE DES BUTTES. This name refers to the large number of Indian mounds that were discovered in this region. The name is virtually obsolete. Compare, however, the present *Bayou de Bute,* in Morehouse Parish, as recorded on Survey T 21 N—R 4 E, dist. North of Red River, June 1, 1855.

PRAIRIE DES CANOTS. "Prairie of the Canoes." During the last quarter of the eighteenth century the Prairie des Canots, where Monroe is now situated, served as a rendezvous for hunters and trappers, who descended in their canoes from this place to New Orleans. In the city they found a ready sale for their tallow, pelts, bear oil, and buffalo meat—this last being known as *viande de chasse.* "Bear oil," says John Sibley in 1805, "is much esteemed for its wholesomeness in cooking, being preferred to butter or hog's lard. It is found to keep longer

[103] *Annals of Congress,* 9th Congress, 2d session, p. 1110.

[104] See A. Dauzat, *Les Noms de Lieux,* p. 152; W. Kalbow, *Die Germanischen Personennamen,* p. 135; A. Longnon, *Les Noms de Lieux,* p. 455.

[105] *The Emigrant's Guide,* p. 46.

than any other animal oil without becoming rancid, and boiling it, from time to time, upon sweet bay leaves, restores its sweetness, or facilitates its conservation."[106] Sibley also says that the bears "usually yield from eight to twelve gallons of oil, each of which sells for less than a dollar a gallon, and the skin a dollar more; no great quantity of the meat is saved; what the hunters don't use when out, they generally give to their dogs.[107]

The name *Prairie des Cantos,* in which *cantos* is intended for *canots,* doubtless took its name from that of the first French settlement, higher up the river at Fort Miro. Neither name is now used.

PRAIRIE DES COSTES. William Darby gives this name more accurately as *Prairie du Côte,* "Prairie of the Shore." The latter is the present name.[108]

PRAIRIE DU MANOUR. This name is intended for the popular French personal name *Dumanoir,* "of the manor." A certain Jean Baptiste Faucon Dumanoir was for many years an agent of the Company of the Indies which held a charter to the Province of Louisiana from August, 1717, to July 1, 1731, operating at first under the name of the Company of the West[109]; but there is no evidence, so far as I know, that he received a concession of land on the Ouachita River. *Dumanoir* is the present name of the prairie.

PUESTO DE OUACHITTA. "Ouachita Post." The Commandant of the old Spanish Post of Ouachita claimed jurisdiction over Arkansas as far north as Hot Springs, and over that part of Louisiana which is now comprised within the parishes of Union, Morehouse, East and West Carroll, Ouachita, Franklin, and Jackson. He also exercised his authority over some of the area included in the present parishes of Madison, Tensas, Catahoula, and Claiborne.[110] The Post of Ouachita was built on the present site of East Monroe.

PURTA L'AÎNÉ. This is a misprint for *Punta L'Aînè,* "Pointe L'Aîné." As early as 1795 a settler by the name of *Madame L'Aîné* owned 203 acres, situated on the west bank of the Ouachita river, about a mile above Fort Miro

---

[106] *Annals of Congress,* Ninth Congress, Second Session, p. 1116.
[107] *Op. cit.,* p. 1086.
[108] *The Emigrant's Guide* (1818), p. 45.
[109] See Pierre Heinrich, *La Louisiane sous la compagnie des Indes, 1717-1731,* pp. 3, 4, 254.
[110] H. Bry, in *De Bow's Review,* III (1847), 226-227.

(= Monroe).[111] The name has not survived. French *L'Aîné* signifies "the elder," the eldest," or "senior."

R[e] AUX BOEUFS. "Buffalo river."

RIO NEGRE. Sp. *Rio,* "river," plus *negre,* an inaccurate spelling of Sp. *negro,* "black." That part of the Ouachita River which is below Tensas Bayou is called "Black River."

RIO OUACHITTA. The Ouachita river. The Ouachitas formed a small Indian clan. Every effort to solve the meaning of their name has proved futile.[112]

---

[111] *ASP,* III, 527, ed. Green.

[112] Cf. my *Louisiana Place-Names of Indian Origin,* pp. 47-48.

IV

SURNAMES FROM SOUTHERN FRANCE

A superficial observer might believe that a study of French surnames ought to cast a great deal of light on the sources of immigration to Louisiana. The form and meaning of a name may, indeed, furnish a clue to the home of its original bearer. A few examples will suffice to illustrate this point. Old High German *Walthari,* "commander-in-chief of an army," yields *Wautier* in the Walloon dialect, *Vautier* in the East, and *Gautier* in the Centre and the West of France. *Dumas,* "of the country-house," from Latin *Mansum,* "resting place," belongs to the South; *Dumez,* to the North of France; and *Delmas,* to Provence. *Dufeu,* "a dweller near a beech-tree," from Latin *fāgus,* is found in Picardy; *Delfau,* a name of the same origin and meaning, in Provence. Standard-French *Bouvier,* "herdsman," from Latin *bovārius,* gives way to *Boyer,* from Latin *Boārius,* in Provençal. *Duquesne,* "of the oak," that is, "a dweller near an oak,"—is typical of the far North of France—of Normandy and Picardy; *Duchêne,* of the Centre; and *Ducasse,* of the South. *Duchêne* is generally written *Duchein* in Louisiana.[1]

False inferences about French immigration to Louisiana may easily be drawn from the forms of such names as have just been cited. The drift of population from the country districts to the large cities, or from one part of the country to another, may well have carried these names to points quite remote from their original sources. French surnames have actually been scattered by immigration over the ends of the earth. Then, too, the steady encroachment of literary French on the dialects obviously tends to modify the forms of regional names.

[1] See A. Dauzat, *Les Nommes de Personnes,* p. 118, *et passim.*

Let us look, nevertheless, at some Louisiana surnames that must first have been used in the Pyrenees region of France or in the contiguous zones. Before making this survey, we should remember that local and occupative names may become personal in their application; that family names may be converted, with equal facility, into geographic names; that not a few surnames are known as patronymics, being derivatives of ancestral names; and that, finally, nicknames form an important class of surnames. Some French surnames, it should be noted in the next place, are used in the plural; others are preceded by a preposition —usually *de*—and the definite article; others still are combined with but one of these two words. Diminutive formations are likewise extremely common in French surnames.

The following list includes various types of surnames:

ABADIE. Low Latin *abbatia,* "abbey," "monastery," is represented by *Abadie* or *Abbadie* in the far south of France (the Pyrénées and Alpes-Maritimes), by *Abbie Abby* in the far north (Pas-de-Calais), by *Abbaye* in the central French zone, and by *Abadia* in Catalan, Provençal, and Spanish. Many of these geographic names are preceded by the definite article, as *Labadie, L'Abbaye,* and *L'Abby.* The personal name *Abadie,* signifying the occupant of an abbey or of land attached to an abbey, is popular both in France and in Louisiana. In the latter *Abadie* is found in New Orleans, Baton Rouge, and Rayne; *D'Abadie,* "of the abbey," in Houma; and the northern *Abby,* in Thibodaux. The town of *Labadieville,* in Assumption Parish, obviously contains the personal name *Labadie. Labadie* is also a New Orleans name.

BARRÈRE. Southern-French *Barrère,* a name found in New Orleans, corresponds to St.-Fr. *Barrière,* "barrier," "fence," "gate," "stile." Gascon *La barrère deu camp* signifies *La barrière* (*qui ferme l'entrèe*) *du champ.* As a personal name *Barrère* signifies the occupant of ground enclosed by a barrier or fence.

BÉGUÉ. *Bégué* varies with *Béguer* as a place-name in the Basses-Pyrénées. Raymond says that *Le Bégué* which is used as an alternative designation of the place-name *Pussacou,* in the Basses-Pyrénées, comes from Arnaud de Pussacou, who was the *béguer* (*viguier*) of the Viscount of Béarn in 1343-1344.[2] Old Béarn has *béguer* for *viguier.*[3]

Bégué signifies "governor of a province," "provost." It is the equivalent of Provençal *veguier,* a derivative in turn of Latin *vicārius.* Bégué's restaurant in New Orleans has long been famous throughout America for its unique and excellent cuisine.

Provençal *viguier,* a variant of *veguier,* shows perhaps the influence of latin *vīcus,* "quarter of a city." *Viguier* came into Standard French in the thirteenth century. From *viguier* has come *viguerie,* "function or jurisdiction of a governor," a word which appears as a family name in New Orleans and Houma, Louisiana.

BELLOCQ. *Bellocq,* which is found in New Orleans, has the same meaning as St.-Fr. *Beaulieu,* the occupant of a "beautiful place." Cf. Provençal *bel loc,* "beautiful place," from Latin *bellus locus.*

BESSE. Gallic **bettia,* "cluster of birch-trees," has yielded the place-name *Besse* or *La Besse* in the departments of Aveyron, Cantal, Charente, Dordogne, Isère, Maine-et-Loire, Puy-de-Dome, and Var. Compare Mod. Prov. *bes,* "birch-tree," from Gallo-Roman **bettium,* "birch-tree." The family name *Besse,* found in New Orleans and Rayne, Louisiana, signifies, therefore, a dweller near a group of birch-trees.[4]

BETBEZÉ. New Orleans *Betbeze* is a Gascon name, as the first element *Bet* for *Bel,* "beautiful" shows.[5] The second element is a southern French and Gascon (Vic-Bilh) form from Latin *vidére,* which is used as a noun in the sense of "view." Cf. Provençal *vezer,* "to see." In Southern France Latin intervocalic *d* is retained in the extreme west only (Béarn); elsewhere it appears as *z.* Latin initial *v* has become *b* in Gascony, as well as in Rouergue, Quercy, and a part of West Langue d'oc.[6]

BETPOUEY. *Betpouey,* a New Orleans name, signifies a dweller on a "beautiful mountain." In the Gascon dialect final *ll* appears as *t;* hence Gascon *Betpouey* is equivalent to *Bel(l)pouey.* *Béarn* (Gascon) *poey, poy,* and *pouy* signify "mountain," "hill," "knoll."

---

[2] V. Lespy et P. Raymond, *Dictionnaire Béarnais, Ancien et Moderne,* I, 95.

[3] *Op cit.,* 140; cf. 26.

[4] See A. Thomas, in *Rom.,* XXV, 382, 387; G. Dottin, *La Langue Gauloise,* p. 234; *Wartburg, Wb.,* pp. 345-346.

[5] Note the place-name *Betbezé, in Gers,* and cf. *Betpouey, infra.*

[6] E. Bourciez, *Eléments de Linguistique Romane,*[3] pp. 302-303; Lespy et Raymond, *Dict. Béarnais,* II, 246.

BLACHE. The New Orleans personal name *Blache* refers to the owner or occupant of an oak plantation. *Blache* is used in the western part of Southern France as the designation of a plantation of oaks, especially of the white variety. Cf. Prov. *blaca,* "coppice of oaks," Mod. Prov. *blacho,* "young white oak," as well as *blacas,* "white oak," old Dauphiné *blache,* "ground planted in oaks or chestnuts." Wartburg, who connects *blache* with Gothic **blakk-* "shining," observes that the word perhaps indicates the gleaming appearance of the oak leaves. The Gothic stem is identical with that of French *blanc,* "white."[7]

BORDENAVE. *Bordenave,* "new farm," is a geographic name in the Basses-Pyrénées and the department of Landes. As a personal name it signifies the occupant of a new farm.

Old French *borde,* "hut," a derivative of Frankish *bord,* "board," "plank," early acquired the sense of Fr. *métairie,* "a small farm let on shares." *Borde* and its derivatives are widely used in France as proper names, appearing in such forms as *Bordes, Laborde, les Bordes, La Bourdette, Les Bordages,* and many more.[8]

New Orleans has inherited from Southern France such names as *Bordenave* and *Labourdette* (dim.); both are common in the Pyrenees region.

CALVET; CHARVET; CHAUVET; CHAUVIN. These names are all diminutive formations in French from the stem of Low Latin *calvus,* "bald." *Calvet* is typical of Southern France, cf. Prov. *calv,* "bald"; *Charvet* belongs to the Dauphiné region; *Chauvet* and *Chauvin,* to the Langue d'Oïl.[9]

CAP. In the far south of France Latin *caput,* "head," appears as *cap,* "head," "end"; hence the original bearers of the New Orleans names *Capdeboscq* and *Capdepon* lived, the one on the edge of a wood and the other at the extremity of a bridge. Both of these names are found in the Basses-Pyrénées. Again, Jean Jacques Capdevielle, the founder of the Capdevielle family of Baton Rouge, came to Louisiana in 1868 from the village of Loucrup, near Tarbes in the Hautes-Pyrénées. His name points to residence at the end of a long village street.[10]

---

[7] *Wb.*, p. 393.
[8] Longnon, *Les Noms de Lieux*, pp. 587-590.
[9] Dauzat, *Les Noms de Personnes*, pp. 96, 118.
[10] Cf. A. Longnon, *Les Noms de Lieux*, p. 333.

Moreover, the spelling *-vielle* in this name is typical of Southwest France—of Gers, Landes, the Basses-Pyrénées, and the Hautes-Pyrénées. *Capdevielle* is also a New Orleans name.

It may be proper to note here that Latin *villa*, "country-house," which acquired the sense of "village," and finally of "city," in medieval times, has given to French the variants *ville, vialle, vielle,* and *velle*.[11] The last form, as in New Orleans *Develle* and *Lavelle*, is typical of the eastern zone of the ancient provinces of Champagne, Lorraine, and Franche-Comté.

Capdau and *Capdecomme* are two more New Orleans names that contain the word *cap*. The former is a Gascon variant of *capdal*, "chief," "leader," which is derived from the Low Latin adjective *capitālis*, "principal." Cf. also Provençal *capdal*, "chief."[12] The latter points to residence at the end of a valley or ravine. The element *comme* in this name is a variant of French *combe*, a derivative in turn of Gallic *cumba*, "valley," "ravine."

Perhaps I should mention here the New Orleans surname *Combel*, "a resident in a little valley," which I take to be identical with the geographic name *Combelle* in the departments of Aveyron and Gironde.

CAZE and Its Derivatives. Low Latin *cāsa*, "house," from Latin *casa*, "hut" is found in numerous family names in Louisiana. Mr. Romain *Cazedessus*, for example, the founder of a prominent Baton Rouge family, came to Louisiana in 1856 from Ganties, a village situated near St. Gaudens in the Pyrenees mountains. *Cazedessus* signifies the owner of a house built on the top, or perhaps on the slope, of a mountain.

Casa, "house," is represented by other Southern names in Louisiana, such as *Caze*, "house," *Lacaze*, "the house," *Cazes*, "houses," *Bonnecaze* or *Cazebonne*, "good house" (Basses-Pyrénées) *Cazenave* (Basses-Pyrénés), "new house," *Cazenavette*, "little new house," and *Cazentre*, "house between" (two others?). Some of these names are found in Baton Rouge; all in New Orleans.

Another New Orleans name is *Cas*(*s*)*adaban*, which signifies the occupant of a house situated either towards the east, or in the foreground, Gascon *dabant* being the equivalent of "east" as well as of "before" (Fr. *de-*

[11] See Dauzat, *Les Noms de Lieux*, p. 157; Longnon, *op. cit.*, p. 236.
[12] See Lespy and Raymond, *op. cit.*, I, 148.

vant).[13] *Cazadeban* is recorded as a place-name in the commune of d'Ogenne-Camptort, Basses-Pyrénées.[14]

As to New Orleans *Cassnau*, I should say that it is a variant of Southern French *Casnau*, "new house."

The name *Cazayoux*, found in New Orleans, Baton Rouge, and New Roads, must not be overlooked. The first element is *caze*, "house," and the second seems to be intended for Gascon *en jus* (*à jus?*), from Low Latin *jūsūm*, "down," "downwards." Cf. Prov. *casa*, "house," and Prov. *jos, jus, jotz*, "down," "below." *Cazayoux* is the "house situated below."

The name *Cazabatt* is probably similar in meaning to *Cazayoux*. The former, which I have found in Houma, Louisiana, is apparently intended for Gascon *caze en bat*, "house (situated) below."

CAZEAUX and Kindred Forms. Akin to Low Latin *casa* is Low Latin *casale*, "location suitable for a house," "house," sometimes "village." *Casale* has given to New Orleans such surnames as the plural *Cazeaux*, the diminutives *Cazalé*, *Cazalot*, and the compound *Cazaubon*.

Cazalé may be compared with Prov. *cazalet*, "cottage," or it may be identical with Gascon *Cazalée*, *cazaler*, "countryman," one who owns a *casau* or *cazal*.[16] *Cazaubon* is clearly composed of *cazau*, "house," and *bon*, "good." *Casaubon* and *Cazaubon* are geographic names in the Basses-Pyrénées.

Gascon *Casaubieilh*, which reproduces Low Latin *casale veclum*, "old house," is also an interesting New Orleans name. In the Gascon dialect *v* has the value of *b*, and *lh* is the Southern French symbol for *l-mouillée*. *Cazaurang*, another New Orleans name, owes its present spelling to popular etymology, the primitive form being *Casaufranc*, which is recorded in 1385 as a place-name in the Basses-Pyrénées.[17] As a personal name *Casaufranc* signifies the inhabitant of a free village, the adjective *franc*, from Frankish *franc*—that is, "free" from public taxes—referring to the franchise that had been obtained by this community. *Casaufranc* was misunderstood and corrupted into *Casaurang*, which indicates residence in a row of houses. In the department of Haute-Garonne a place-name of the same meaning as *Casaufranc* is called *Francazal*.

[13] Cf. Lespy et Raymond, *Dict. Béarnais*, I, 217.
[14] Raymond, *Dict. Top.*, p. 47.
[15] *REW* 2567
[16] Lespy et Raymond, *op. cit.*, I, 57.
[17] Raymond, *op. cit.*, p. 42.

Finally, New Orleans *Delcazal,* "of the house," is characteristic of Southern France. Cf., for example, Gascon (Béarn) and Provençal *del cazal.*

Gallo-Roman *CASSANUS. It is necessary to distinguish the French derivatives of Low Latin *cāsa* from those of Gallo-Roman **cassanus,* "oak." **Cassanus* has given *Casse* (Lot-et-Garonne) and the popular *Ducasse,* "of the oak," "dweller near the oak," both of which are well known in Louisiana. Again, the collective *Cassanea* or *Cassania,* "oak grove," is responsible for the New Orleans surname, *Cassagne,* "dweller near, or in, an oak grove." *Cassagne* is found as a place-name in the department of Haute-Garonne.[18]

Casso and *cassou* designate the oak-tree, in the province of Béarn.[19]

As a personal name New Orleans *Cassou* designates a dweller near an oak. But *Casso,* a family name in Donaldsonville, Gonzales, and New Orleans, is of Italian origin, as far as I have been able to ascertain.

The name *Cassegrain* does not belong here. It is a nickname for a miller—literally, "break-grain."

CASTET. *Castet,* "castle," from Low Latin *castellum,* (dim. of *castrum*), is a common place-name in the Basses-Pyrénées. The change of *-ll* to *t* is typical of the Gascon dialect. The New Orleans name *Castet* designates the occupant of a castle.

CIEUTAT. Low Latin *civitātem,* "city," "community," has yielded *cieutat* in the South (*Langue d'Oc*) ; *cité,* in the North (*Langue d'Oïl*). Both derivatives at first signified the old quarter of a town or its ancient site, but later they acquired the meaning of "city."

New Orleans *Cieutat,* "dweller in the city," is found as a geographic name in Gers and the Hautes-Pyrénées. Cf. Provençal *ciutat,* "city," Gascon (Béarn) *ciutat,* Old Bearn *cipdat* (Bay).[20]

DE BAT. The New Orleans name *De Bat* is of Gascon origin, being the equivalent of central French *De* (*la*) *val,* an inhabitant of the valley. The *v* of Low Latin *vallis, -em* appears as *b,* and the *ll* as *t* in Gascon. Cf. *Labat, infra.*

DOMECQ. From the thirteenth until far down into the eighteenth century *Domec* or *Domecq* is recorded as a popu-

---

[18] See A. Thomas, in *Romania,* XXV, 387.
[19] Lespy et Raymond, *op. cit.*, I, p. 159.
[20] Lespy et Raymond, *op. cit.,* I, 176.

lar geographic name in the old province of Béarn, situated in the extreme southwest of France.[21] There, too, *Domec* is a family name. *Domecq* is a New Orleans spelling.

The relation of Old Béarn *Domec*, "domain," to the derivatives of Latin *dominicus* (scil. *dies*), "day of the Lord," "Sunday," is obscure.[22] In the modern Béarn dialect *domec* signifies the castle and domain of a squire, a noble of the fourth degree. The owner or the occupant of a domain would naturally be called *Domec*. Provençal *domec* also signifies "domain."

DROUILHET; DRUILHET. The New Orleans names *Drouilhet* and *Druilhet* designate alike a dweller in a small oak grove. *Druilhet* is also a family name in Houma, Louisiana.

The source of these two names is Gallo-Roman **druillia*, which is presumably connected in turn with Gallic **d(a)rulla*, a species of oak. Both names came from Southern France, a fact clearly shown by the spelling with *lh* for *l-mouillée*.[23]

The final *-et* in these names is of course the diminutive ending.

DUTILH. New Orleans *Dutilh*, a dweller near a linden tree, is clearly a Southern French form. Place-names in the departments of Landes and the Basses-Pyrénées, as well as farther north in Charente, bear the name *Tilh*.[24] Gascon has *tilh*; Provençal, *telh, tel*, "linden tree." Low Latin *tilia* is the source of this name.

Here, too, should be mentioned New Orleans *Dutel*. Rolland, *Flore*, III, 119, gives *tél* as a place-name in the departments of Hérault, Aveyron, Cantal, Lot, Tarn, and Corrèze.

DUVIEILH. The New Orleans name *Duvieilh* is a southern correspondent of central French *De la Ville*, a dweller in the city.

ÉLICHALT. Longnon analyzes the place-name *Élissalt*, situated in the Basses-Pyrénées, as a Gascon derivative of Basque *Eliçaalt*, "near the Church."[25]

The family name *Élichalt*, found in New Orleans, must have signified originally a dweller near the church.

---

[21] Raymond, *op. cit.*, pp. 55-56.
[22] Wartburg, *Wb.*, *Lieferung* 13, p. 129.
[23] See Wartburg, *Wb.*, p. 326; Rolland, *Faune*, X, 175-176.
[24] Raymond, *op. cit.*, p. 167; Rolland, *Flore*, III, 119.
[25] *Les Noms de Lieux*, p. 334.

In the Basses-Pyrénées the Basque name *Élicetche,* "the house of the church," shows, like *Élichalt,* a variant spelling with *-ch*—that is, *Élichetche.*[26]

ESCUDIER. Escudier, "esquire," "squire"; "riding master"; "maker of shields"; the Southern correspondent of St.-Fr. *écuyer* (Latin *scūtārius, -um*). Cf. Provençal *escudier,* "squire"; "maker of shields." *Escudier* is a personal name in the city of Lafayette, La.

Here, too, belongs the Gascon name *Escudé,* found in New Orleans and equivalent to *Escudier.*

ESTÈVE. *Estève* is a Southern French and Provençal form, the equivalent of St.-Fr. *Étienne* (Latin *Stephanum*). *Estève* is found in Thibodaux; *Estèves,* with a parasitic *-s,* in New Orleans.

ETCHEGOYEN. *Etchegoyen* is the name of a fief created in 1435, in the commune of Méharin, Basses-Pyrénées. The same name is recorded for the commune of Camou-Cihigue.[27]

This Gascon name is of Basque origin: compare Basque *etche,* "house," and *oihan* or *oyan,* "forest," the latter term giving Gascon *goyen.*

New Orleans *Etchegoyen* signifies, then, the occupant of a house situated in a forest.

FABRE. Low Latin *faber,* "smith," has given rise to numerous different forms in French.[28] The New Orleans representatives of *faber* and their provenience are shown in the following list:

Fabre—Provence, Southern Langue d'Oc, Rouergue.

Faivre, *Lefebvre*, *Lefèvre* }—Langue d'Oïl.

Faure, *Faures* }—Provence; Southern Dauphiné.

Favret, *Favrot* }—diminutives of *Favre*—Franco-Provençal.

Haurie, "smithy"—Gascon; with initial *H* for *F* and the suffix *-ie*; but *Haurie* may be, in some cases, a French spelling of *Ory,*[29] *infra.*

[26] Raymond, *op. cit.,* p. 58.
[27] Raymond, *op. cit.,* p. 63.
[28] See Dauzat, *Les Noms de Personnes,* pp. 93, 118.
[29] Raymond, *Dict. Top.,* records *Haurie,* by the side of an earlier *Faurie* (1385), as a place-name in the Commune de Viellességure, Basses-Pyrénées.

The New Orleans name *Foret* is probably an inaccurate spelling of *Forêt*, "Forest." *Foret*, however, may be a variant form of *Fauret*, a diminutive of *Faure*.

The importance of the smith in France during the Middle Ages is shown by the popularity of the variant names that have sprung from Latin *faber* and *fabrica*, *infra*. That the occupation of the smith, who was a skilled workman in metals, was held in high esteem in other countries, accounts for the vast army of Smiths in English and Schmidts in German. In Spain, too, the work of the craftsmen in metals became so fine that even Locksley's mighty bow was bent three times in vain against the Spanish coat of mail worn by De Bracy at the siege of Torquilstone.

FAGET. Low Latin **fāgetum*, "beech grove," from Low Latin *fāgus*, "beech-tree," appears as the geographic name *Faget* or *le Faget* in Dordogne, Gers, Haute-Garonne, Lot, Lot-et-Garonne, Basses-Pyrénées, and Savoie. The New Orleans name *Faget* means "a dweller near a group of beech-trees."

FARGE; LAFARGUE; LAFORGUE. Low Latin *fabrica*, "smithy," appears in the New Orleans names *Farge*, *Lafargue*, and *Laforgue*. All three of these names are from Southern France. *Farge* is especially common in Auvergne and Limousin, whereas *Lafargue* and *Laforgue* belong to the far South, the former being typical of Ariège, Ande, Aveyron, Lot, and Tarn, the latter of the Hautes-Pyrénées.

HAURIE. The New Orleans name *Haurie* is from Gascon *Haurie*, "the owner of a forge or smithy."

Sometimes, however, the name *Haurie* is a Louisiana-French corruption of *Ory*. Nikolaus Ory, a German who came from Maryland in 1774, has left many descendants in Louisiana.[30] *Ory* is from OHG *Uodalric*, "home-rich."

HOURCADE. The New Orleans name *Hourcade*, which signifies a dweller where a road forks, is unmistakably of Gascon origin; for the Gascon dialect changes initial *f* to *h*. Equivalent New Orleans names are *Fourcade* and *Lafourcade*, with the definite article preceding the latter. These two names are also from Southern France. Cf. *Hourcade* and *La Hourcade*, *Fourcade* and *La Fourcade*, place-names in the Basses-Pyrénées.[31]

---

[30] Deiler, *op. cit.*, pp. 109, 104.

[31] Raymond, *op. cit.*, pp. 65, 79.

Another interpretation of *Hourcade* is possible. In the Gascon dialect it may have the same meaning as *Forcade*—namely, "oak grove."[32] Cf. also Provençal *Forcada,* which signifies either "cross roads," or "oak grove."

JAUFFRET. New Orleans *Jauffret* is a variant form of Southern *Jaufré,* or *Joffret,* which corresponds to St.-Fr. *Geoffroy* (Germanic *Gautfred, Gaudifrid,* etc.).[33]

Germanic *Gaut-,* "Goth," the first element of the Germanic source, became confused both with *gut-,* "good," and with *Gott,* "God." The second element signifies "peace," more especially "safety," "protection." Cf. modern German *Gottfried.*

LABAT. *Labat,* "the abbot," from Low Latin *abbātem,* is a well-known family name in the Basses-Pyrénées. The diminutive is *Labadot.*[34] *Labat* is found in New Orleans, Baton Rouge, and Houma; *Labadot,* in New Orleans.

In some cases *Labat,* if Gascon, may signify a dweller in "the valley." Cf. the comments on *De Bat, supra.*

Parisian French *Labbé,* "the abbot," is found in Lafayette and Houma.

LABESQUE; LEBESQUE. These two New Orleans names have the same meaning—"the bishop." They are derivatives, respectively, of modern Gascon *abesque* and *ebesque,* variant equivalents of St.-Fr. *évêque,* which springs from Low Latin *episcopus, -um.*

LAGARIGUE. In the Pyrenees region *Lagarrigue,* together with certain variants, is largely used as a family name and as the designation of an oak or oak grove. Its source is *garric,* "oak," presumably an Iberian word.[35] Cf. Mod. Prov. *garrigo,* "oak grove." Rolland gives *garrigue* as the name of the *Quercus coccifera* (L.).[36]

New Orleans *Lagarigue* designates a dweller near an oak or oak grove.

LALANNE; LANNE; LANNES. In Southwest France Gascon *Lalanne, Lanne,* and (*les*)*Lannes* are popular place-names. *Lanne* signifies "plain," "grassy plateau," in the Pyrenees region. *Lalanne,* a name found in the city of

---

[32] Cf. Lespy et Raymond, *op. cit.,* I, 313, 378.

[33] Cf. Förstmann, I,[2] 610, 615; A. Heintze, *Die Deutschen Familiennamen,*[4] p. 153; Kremers, *Beiträge,* p. 50.

[34] Cf. Lespy et Raymond, *op. cit.,* I, 4.

[35] Longnon, *Les Noms de Lieux,* p. 25; but see Meyer-Lübke, *Das Katalanische,* p. 113, footnote 2.

[36] *Flore,* X, 172.

Lafayette, La., designates a dweller on a grassy plateau. *Lanne* and *Lannes* are New Orleans names.

The place-name *Lannes,* in Haute-Marne, may be a derivative of *Latona,* the name of a goddess.[37]

LANUSSE. *Lanusse,* formed from *Lanne, supra,* with the aid of a diminutive suffix (= Latin *-ūcea, -ūcia*), is a common place-name in the Gascon area.[38] As a personal name *Lanusse,* found in New Orleans and Opelousas, designates the dweller on a small plain.

LAPEYRE; LAPEYROUSE; PEYREFITTE; PEYROUX. All four of these names are typical of Southern France, and all four are found in New Orleans. *Lapeyrouse* is also a Baton Rouge name.

A dweller near a rock was called *Lapeyre,* literally "the rock." If he lived on stony ground he became known as *Peyroux,* from Latin *petrōsus,* "stony," or as *Lapeyrouse,* "the stony" (ground), from Latin *petrōsa.*

Peyrefitte is the designation of any monolith that was erected as a boundary mark in ancient Gaul. The corresponding Latin term is *petra ficta,* "a stone set upright," *petra,* "stone," being the equivalent of *peyre* in Southern France—of *pierre* in the domain of Langue d'Oïl—and *ficta,* the source of *fitte,* being an archaic past participle of Latin *fīgo,* "to erect." As a personal name *Peyrefitte* was applied to one who resided near an ancient boundary stone.

LAPOUBLE. Gascon *pouble, pobla,* or *poble, f.,* signifies "construction," "house," "barn," sometimes "hamlet." New Orleans *Lapouble* refers, then, to the owner of a house or barn, or to a dweller in a hamlet.

The Gascon word is cognate with Provençal *pobla, f.,* "construction," "house."

LARTIGUE. *Lartigue,* a New Orleans and Baton Rouge surname, reproduces a popular name of Southern France. Authorities differ about the origin and meaning of the word. H. Gröhler derives the variant *Artige* (Vienne) from Gallic *are* (= Latin *ad*) plus Gallic *tegia,* "hut." *Lartigue,* then, would signify the occupant of a hut.[39] Schuchardt, however, traces the cognate Spanish *Artiga* to the Low Latin past participle **ex-sartum,* "land

---

[37] Longnon, *op. cit.,* p. 112.

[38] Raymond, *op. cit.,* p. 92.

[39] *Uber den Ursprung and die Bedeutung der Französischen Ortsnamen,* p. 161.

newly cleared," plus the suffix *-ic.*[40] Schuchardt's etymology is correct.

In the Gascon dialect *artigue* signifies "meadow"; *artigau,* "cleared land."[41]

LAUHLÉ; LAUILHÉ. These two New Orleans names signify "the shepherd," the source being Gascon *aulhé,* "shepherd." A variant Gascon form is *oulhè.*[42]

Lauhlé, with an early variant *Lauhler,* is recorded as a place-name in the commune of Simacourbe, Basses-Pyrénées.[43]

Gascon *aulhé,* like Provençal *ovelhier,* "shepherd," points to Low Latin *ovicula, -am,* "lamb," followed by the suffix *-ārius—*oviculārius.*

LOUSTALOT. *Loustalot* is properly "the little house," Southern French *oustal,* "house," from Low Latin *hospitāle,* "inn," being preceded by the definite article and followed by the diminutive suffix *-ot.* Cf. Prov. *ostal,* "house," and *ostalot,* "cottage." *Loustalot* is a place-name in the commune of Ney, Basses-Pyrénées. The family name *Loustalot,* "owner or occupant of the little house," is found in New Orleans and Franklin, Louisiana. Cf. the New Orleans name *Oustalet,* owner or occupant of a "little house." See also *Loustau* and *Loustaunau, infra.*

LOUSTAU; LOUSTAUNAU. *Loustau,* a New Orleans name, signifies the owner or occupant of "the house." Its source is the Gascon *oustau,* "house." As a geographic name *Loustau* appears in the Basses-Pyrénées.[44]

Loustaunau is the Gascon for "the new house," Gascon *nau* being the equivalent of St.-Fr. *neuf. Loustaunau* is found as a place-name in the department of Landes. New Orleans *Loustaunau* signifies the owner or the occupant of the new house.

MAZÈRES. *Mazères,* a geographic name in the Basses-Pyrénées, is a derivative of Low Latin *māceriae,* "walls," enclosing a garden or a village. As a personal name *mazères* was generally applied to a dweller near an ancient ruin. *Mazères* is a New Orleans name.[45]

OUBRE. The name *Oubre* is found in New Orleans, Baton Rouge, New Iberia, and Donaldsonville.

---

[40] *ZRPh.,* XXIII, 187 ff; cf. Rolland, *Flore,* X, 11.
[41] Lespy et Raymond, *op. cit.,* I, 60.
[42] Lespy et Raymond, *op. cit.,* I, 70.
[43] Raymond, *Dict. Top.,* p. 97.
[44] Raymond, *op. cit.,* p. 105.
[45] Longnon, *op. cit.,* p. 290.

In some cases the Louisiana name *Oubre* may be intended for *Oubré,* which is a derivative of Modern Gascon *oubré,* "workman," "artisan." Here Standard French has *ouvrier,* from Low Latin *operārius, -um.*

Most of the *Oubres,* however, in Louisiana are descendants of Jacob *Huber,* a German immigrant who in 1723 occupied a part of the land now extending from the present First Street of New Orleans to Napoleon Avenue. This land belonged to Bienville.[46] The name *Huber,* which was changed to *Oubre, Ouvre,* and *Hoover* in Louisiana, may be derived from Old High German *Hugubert,* "bright mind," "clear intelligence," or from Middle High German *hubaere,* "owner (tenant) of approximately thirty acres."[47]

OULLIBER. *Oulliber,* a New Orleans name, signifies a dweller near an olive tree. Cf. Modern Béarn *Oulibè,* Old Béarn *oliber,* "olive tree." Gascon *Oulibé* is the equivalent of St.-Fr. *Olivier,* a name found in New Orleans, Houma, Lafayette, New Iberia, St. Martinville, Franklin, and Opelousas.

Gascon *oulibè* is formed from Gascon *oulibe,* "olive," and the latter corresponds to Low Latin *olīva,* "olive."

OULLIÉ. New Orleans *Oullié* is a derivative of Modern Gascon *ouliè,* "manufacturer of oil," "dealer in oil." *Ouliè* is formed from Modern Gascon *oli,* "oil," which springs in turn from Low Latin *olium,* "oil." Cf. St.-Fr. *huile.*

PENOUILH. The name *Penouilh* is composed of Gallic *penno-,* "head," "summit," and the Gallic suffix *-oialos,* Latinized as *-oialus, -oialum.*[48]

Raymond records *Penouilh* as the name of an extinct place in the commune of Montardon, Basses-Pyrénées.[49]

New Orleans *Penouilh* designates a dweller on or near a mountain top.

POUEY and Allied Forms. Low Latin *podium,* "height," "balcony," has produced a variety of French place-names signifying "mountain," "hill," "height."

The following are some place-names in Southern France:

---

[46] J. Hanno Deiler, *The German Coast of Louisiana,* pp. 92, 93, 104.

[47] Cf. A. Heintze, *Die Deutschen Familiennamen,* pp. 183-184.

[48] Cf. Holder, *Altcelt. Sprachschatz,* II, 966; Dauzat, *Les Noms de Lieux,* pp. 95, 208; Longnon, *Noms,* pp. 26, 65 ff.

[49] *Dict. Top.,* p. 133.

Pech (Ariège, Lot-et-Garonne)
Pouey (Hautes-Pyrénées)
Poujol (Hérault)
Puch (Ariège, Gironde, etc.)
Puech (Gard, Aveyron, etc.)
Puig (Roussillon)
Puisségur (Haute-Garonne)
Pujade (Haute-Garonne, etc.)
Pujol (Haute-Garonne, Landes)
Pujols (Gironde)
Pujos (Gers)
Puy (Haute-Loire)

It is not surprising to find numerous representatives of Latin *podium* among New Orleans surnames. Here are some of them:

Delpit, "of the mountain peak."
Dupouey or *Dupouy*, "of the mountain, hill, or height."
Lapoutge, "the height."
Lapuyade, "the height."
Pechon, dim. in *-on*.
Pouey, cf. mod. Gascon *poey, pouy*, "hill," "height," "mountain."
Poujol, dim. in *-ol*.
Poujade, "height," *-ade* from Low Latin *ata*.
Puchot, dim. in *-ot*.
Puech, "mountain."
Puig, "mountain." *-g* = *tch*. Catalan of Roussillon.[50]
Puisségur, "podium securum."
Pujol, -dim. in *-ol*. Cf. Gascon *puj*, "height."
Pujos, -dim. plural.
Puyau.

In the foregoing list *delpit* has virtually the same signification as the Southern French *del puy*, "of the mountain." Compare Gascon *del pite*, "of the mountain peak."[51] But the spelling of the name *Delpit* may be due to confusion with *puits*, "well," "spring of water," from Low Latin *puteus*.

Lapoutge signifies a dweller on "the height." Raymond gives *"Le chemin de la Poudge,"* as the designation of a road that follows the heights, and records

[50] Dauzat, *Les Noms de Lieux*, p. 68, footnote 1.
[51] See Lespy et Raymond, *op. cit.*, II, 166.

Poutge, Poudge, Pouge, and *Potge* as representatives of Latin *podium.* Modern Gascon *poudge* signifies "height."[52]

Lapuyade and *Poujade* refer to residence on a height; compare Provençal *pojade, pu-,* "ascent," "elevation," and Gascon *puyade, pujade,* ascent by which one climbs a hill or mountain.

Puisségur, from Low Latin *podium secūrum,* "safe elevation," refers to the security enjoyed by a village, perhaps because of its impregnable location on a mountain, or because of its strong walls. *Puyau,* the last name in the list, is either graphic for the diminutive *Puyot,* or has sprung from Low Latin *podium altum,* "high elevation." A. Houzé translates *Pujaut* (Gard) by *la roche haute.*[53]

I might add here the name *Dupuy,* "of the mountain," which is popular in southern and central France, but for the fact that it was carried to England by French immigrants; consequently its form alone cannot show whether it traveled to Louisiana from France or by way of England.

ROQUEVERT. Low Latin *rocca,* "rock," "boulder"; "fortress," is the source of Fr. *roche* and *ro(c)que.* The former is encountered as a place-name both in the north and in the south of France, whereas the latter is confined chiefly to the south, Normandy, Picardy, and the Walloon region.

Low Latin **rocca* has many representatives among the family names in New Orleans; such are *Roche, Roque, Roques, Rocquet, Rocquin, Rouquette, Larroque,* and *Roquevert.* Some of these, however, may be due to the popularity of Saint Roch, whose name is pronounced both *rŏk* and *rŏsh.*[54]

Roquevert is not without its complications. It may, indeed, refer quite simply to the occupant of a green fortress or a house built on a green rock. Numerous places in France bear the parallel name *Château-vert,* "green castle." On the other hand, the adjective *vert,* in *Roquevert,* may have arisen through confusion with Old French and Provençal *vaire,* "variegated," from the Low Latin feminine adjective *varia.* The department

[52] *Op. cit.,* pp. 138, 149.
[53] *Étude sur la Signification des Noms de Lieux en France,* p. 33.
[54] Kremers, *Beiträge,* p. 60.

of Bouche-du-Rhône has a place-name *Roquevaire,* from Low Latin **Rocca varia.*[55]

No difficulty is presented by the apparent discrepancy between the gender of *Roque* and that of *vert*; for *vert* was once common as a feminine form.[56]

SABATIER. *Sabatier,* "cobbler," "shoemaker" (American English), is common especially in the Pyrénées-Orientales. This name, which is sometimes written *Sabathier,* is found in Crowley and New Orleans. In the Language d'Oïl region it occurs as *Savetier.*

SAHUC, SAHUQUE. New Orleans *Sahuc,* as well as its variant *Sahuque,* signifies a dweller near an elder-tree.[57] This name is the equivalent of Gascon *Sahuc* (Oloron), *sauc,* and of Catalan or Provençal *sauc,* which all spring from Low Latin *sabūcum,* "elder-tree."

Sahuc is found as a place-name in the department of Ariège. K. Salow records *saük* as the pronunciation of *Sahuc* in the dialect of St. Paul de Fenouillet, Pyrénées Orientales.[58]

SARRAILH. New Orleans *Sarrailh* is taken from Gascon *sarralh, m.,* "enclosure," "farm." The Gascon word is cognate with Provençal *serralh, m.,* "lock," "enclosure," from Low Latin *serrāculum,* "lock," "castle."

SARRAT. *Sarrat,* "enclosure," is a verbal substantive from the past participle of Gascon *sarra,* old Gascon *sarrar,* "to shut up," "to put in a safe place." New Orleans *Sarrat* signifies, then, the owner of some kind of enclosure. The source of Gascon *sarra(r)* is Low Latin *serrāre,* "to close," "to lock up."

Another source of the New Orleans name is Gascon *sarrat,* "mountain peak," which is connected with Low Latin *serre,* "a saw."

SARTRE. New Orleans *Sartre* has the same meaning as the English surname *Taylor*—namely, "tailor." The source is Low Latin *sartor. Sartre* is found in the Gascon dialect (Béarn) as well as in Provençal and Catalan.

The remarkable thing about these Louisiana surnames is the extent of the Gascon element, which is represented by such forms as *Bégué, Betbezé, Betpouey, Capdevielle, Cas(s)adaban, Cassou, Castet, Cazabatt,*

---

[55] Longnon, *Noms,* p. 465.
[56] Nyrop, *Grammaire,*[2] II, 283.
[57] Cf. Thurot, I, 193.
[58] *Katalanisch-Languedokisches Grenzgebiet,* p. 78.

Cazayoux, Cazedessus, Debat, Labat, Domecq, Etchegoyen (Basque-Gascon), *Haurie, Hourcade, Lalanne, Lanne*(*s*), and *Lanusse.* The Gascon patois are spoken in that part of France which is enclosed by the Garonne River, the Pyrénées, and the ocean.

Southern French names are found, too, in Canada, as N. E. Dionne has noted; but veritable Gascon forms, if they occur in his large volume of 611 pages, are almost entirely lacking. I have noted *Lalanne,* however. Dionne's *Legascon* is a St.-Fr. form, though it signifies of course a native of Gascony.[59]

Some Gascon names are met with in Louisiana outside New Orleans. Several have already been noted. A careful search would doubtless reveal others.

Considerations of space prevent me from making comments on any more Louisiana surnames from Southern France, or from extending the scope of this study so as to include names from other French dialects.

---

[59] *Les Canadiens-Français,* pp. 361, 384.

V

CONCLUSION

The cultivated Creoles of Louisiana speak good French. Their dialect is not the same as that of Paris; but it differs less in vocabulary, pronunciation, and syntax from Parisian French than American English differs from British. The speech of educated Creoles sounds, indeed, a little strange to a native of Paris, or Tours, or Grenoble, or Nancy, or Bordeaux; it does not, however, impress him as being corrupt in its syntax or especially novel in its vocabulary. It is recognized frankly as a type of standard French.

The speech of most Acadians, on the other hand, shows the unmistakable features of a genuine dialect. What some of these features are and from what French dialects they have come, I have already tried to point out. It is significant that of the four hundred and fifty or more words listed under *The Native Element* slightly more than a third were in all probability brought to Louisiana by the Acadians. The dialects of the north, the centre, and the west of France—chiefly these three—survive in Canadian-French and consequently also in the Acadian dialect of Louisiana.

But this is not all. Among the forty-odd Indian words that have been noted in this study approximately thirteen came from Canada, though some of them, it is true, preceded the great Acadian migration of the eighteenth century. These thirteen are *Acadien, babiche, batiscan, boucan* (originally Tupí) and its derivative, *Canadien, mataché, micoine, mitasses, ouaouaron, pichou, sacacoua, sassacoua,* and *sac(c)amité.*

Here the resemblance between the vocabulary of the Louisiana Acadians and their Canadian ancestors ceases to be conspicuous; for nine of the other Indian words in my list are derived from Choctaw, the language of a Southern tribe, and the rest have come from divers sources. The Choctaw words are *bachoucta, bayou, cantaque, chaoui, choupique, chouquechi, patássa, soco,* and *taïque.* Some Indian words, like *bayou, choupique, patássa, plaquemine, sacamité,* and *soco* are used both by the Creoles and by the Acadians. In speaking here of Indian words, I do not include geographical names of Indian origin.

The breach between Canadian-French and Louisiana-Acadian is still further widened by the relatively large Spanish element that appears in the latter dialect. Canadian-French, indeed, has inherited some old Spanish words, such as *acajou, ananas,* and *maïs*; but it knows nothing of *bajo, bosal, brème, cabresse, cachimbo, cachouque, lagniappe, pobon, soutadaire,* and other Spanish loans that are peculiar to Louisiana-French. Some Spanish words in Louisiana are the common property of Creole and Acadian—for instance, *brème, lagniappe,* and *pirogue.*

The African element, in the next place, is obviously found not in the speech of Canada but in that of Louisiana. Most of the African words that I have cited belong to the speech both of Creole and of Acadian. *Cala,* however, has fixed itself in the dialect of New Orleans, whereas *zinzin* just as certainly marks the language of the Acadian guides and hunters of Lower Louisiana. But *bamboula, calinda, Congo, couche-couche, gombo, gris-gris, jambalaya, voudou,* and *zombi* are not confined to any particular class or locality in Louisiana.

The English element, large as it is in Louisiana-French, may be dismissed with a single comment. Some of the English loans were probably brought from Canada; they were all undoubtedly borrowed, too, from the speech of the English settlers in Louisiana.

Only two points remain to be considered. First, among the surnames of Louisiana there are a goodly number that had their origin in Southern France. A few examples are *Bégué, Capdevielle, Cassou, Cazedessus, Haurie,* and *Pujol.*

Secondly, in the French language of Louisiana there are numerous descriptive terms that attest the quick wit and the ready imagination of Creole and Acadian. Some illustrations of these characteristics may be observed in the meanings assigned to *bête à chandelle, boscoyo, bougon, bourrelet, canard mulet, castor, chevalier de batture, chien, cochon, cornard, corneille fouetteur, couronne de chêne, dormir sur un rôti, du tasseau, estomac mulâtre, garde-soleil, graines à volée, grand écaille, Mexican, sauterelle cheval, tac tac, tourloulou,* and *vire-vire.*

BIBLIOGRAPHY

The following list contains the books, articles, and other publications that the writer has found helpful in the preparation of this study:

Acts of Congress. Washington, 1848.

Alemany, José. *Diccionario Enciclopédico Ilustrado de la Lengua Espagñola.* Barcelona, 1928.

American State Papers, Public Lands. Vols. I-VIII. Washington, 1832-1861; Indian Affairs, Vol. I. Washington, 1832.

Annals of the Congress of the United States. Ninth Congress, Second Session. Washington, 1852.

Arthur, Stanley C. "The Emblematic Bird of Louisiana," *The Louisiana Historical Quarterly,* II, No. 3 (July, 1919), 248-257.

——— *The Birds of Louisiana* (Department of Conservation, Bulletin 5). New Orleans, 1918.

——— *The Fur Animals of Louisiana* (*Department of Conservation,* Bulletin No. 18). New Orleans, November, 1928.

Audubon, J. J., and Bachman, John. *The Quadrupeds of North America.* Vols. I-III. New York, 1856.

Audubon, John James. *The Birds of North America.* Vols. I-VII. New York, 1859.

Bjork, David K. (editor). "Documents Relating to Alexandro O'Reilly," *The Louisiana Historical Quarterly,* VII, No. I (January, 1924), 20-39.

Bolton, H. E., and Marshall, Thos. M. *The Colonization of North America.* New York, 1929.

Bonnier, Charles. *Uber die Französischen Eigennamen in Alter und Neuer Zeit.* Dissertation. Halle, 1888.

Bossu, N. Nouveaux Voyages aux Indes Occidentales . . . Tomes I-II. Paris, 1768.

——— *Travels Through That Part of North America Formerly Called Louisiana.* Translated by J. R. Forster. Vols. I-II. London, 1771.

Bourciez, Édouard. *Éléments de Linguistique Romane.* Troisième édition révisée. Paris, 1930.

Breton, R. P. Raymond. *Dictionnaire Caraïbe-Français* . . . Réimprimé par Jules Platzmann. Leipzig, 1892.

Britton, N. L., and Brown, A. *Illustrated Flora of the Northern States and Canada.* Vols. I-III. Second edition, revised and enlarged. New York, 1913.

Brown, Samuel R. *The Western Gazetteer.* Auburn, N. Y., 1817.

Bushnell, David I., Jr. (editor). "Drawings by A. DeBatz in Louisiana (1732-1735), with Six Plates" (*Smithsonian Miscellaneous Collections,* Vol. 80, No. 5). Washinton, Dec. 1, 1927.

Butel-Dumont, Geo. M. *Mémoires Historiques sur la Louisiane* . . . Tomes I-II. Paris, 1753.

Butler, Louise. "West Feliciana—a Glimpse of Its History," *The Louisiana Historical Quarterly,* VII, No. I (January, 1924), 90-120.

Byington, Cyrus. *A Dictionary of the Choctaw Language.* Edited by John R. Swanton and Henry S. Halbert (*Bureau of American Ethnology,* Bulletin 46). Washington, 1915.

Cable, Geo. W. "The Dance in Place Congo," *The Century Magazine,* XXXI, (February, 1886), 517-532.

——— "Creole Slave Songs," *The Century Magazine,* XXXI (April, 1886), 807-828.

——— *The Grandissimes.* New York, 1908.

Carrighan, Judge. "The Parish of East Baton Rouge," *De Bow's Review,* XI, N. S. (1851), 252-268.

Century Dictionary and Cyclopedia, The. Ten volumes. New York, 1889.

Chahta-Ima (Father Adrien E. Rouquette). *La Nouvelle Atala.* Nouvelle Orléans, 1879.

Chalaron, Magda. "Louisiana Folklore and Language," *The Newcomb Arcade,* X, No. 2 (January, 1918), 75-80.

Chamberlain, A. F. "Indo-Canadian Words," *American Notes and Queries.* Vols. I, II, IV, *passim.* Philadelphia, 1888-1889.

Chambers, Henry E. *A History of Louisiana.* Vols. I-III. Chicago and New York, 1925.

Chapman, A. W. *Flora of the Southern United States.* Third edition. New York, Cincinnati, and Chicago, 1897.

Chapman, Frank M. *Handbook of Birds of Eastern North America.* Revised edition. New York and London, 1929.

Charlevoix, Pierre F. X. de. *Histoire et Description Générale de la Nouvelle France.* Tomes I-III. Paris, 1744.

Churchill, C. Robert. *S. A. R.: Spanish Records.* 1925. Howard Memorial Library, New Orleans.

Clapin, Sylvia. *Dictionnaire Canadien-Français.* Montreal and Boston, 1894.

——— *A New Dictionary of Americanisms.* New York, n. d.

Clark, Geo. H., et Fletcher, James. *Les Mauvaises Herbes du Canada.* Ottawa, 1909.

Clark, R. C. "The Beginnings of Texas," *The Quarterly of the Texas State Historical Association,* V, No. 3 (Jan., 1902), 171-205.

Cocheris, H. *Origine et Formation des Noms de Lieu.* Paris, 1874.

Colmeiro, D. Miguel. *Primeras Noticias acerca de la Vegetación Americana.* Madrid, 1892.

Commons, John R. *Races and Immigrants in America.* New York, 1907.

Cooper, James Fenimore. *The Deerslayer.* New York and London, 1912.

Cox, T. J. (editor). *The Journeys of René Robert Cavelier Sieur de la Salle.* New York, 1905.

Craven, Henry, and Barfield, John. *English-Congo and Congo-English Dictionary.* London, 1883.

Crescini, Vincenzo. *Manuale Per L'Avviamento Agli Studi Provenzali.* Terza edizione migliorata. Milano, 1926.

Cruzat, Heloise H. (translator). "Documents Concerning Sale of Chaouachas Plantation in Louisiana, 1737-38," *The Louisiana Historical Quarterly,* VIII, No. 4 (October, 1925), 594-646.

Cuervo, R. J. *Apuntaciones Criticas sobre El Lenguaje Bogotano.* Sexta edición. Paris, 1914.

Cuoq, J. A. *Lexique de la Langue Iroquoise.* Montreal, 1882.

——— *Lexique de la Langue Algonquine.* Montreal, 1886.

Cusachs, Gaspar. "Petition for Concession of Islands of Caillou and Timbalier," . . . *The Louisiana Historical Quarterly,* II, No. 3 (July, 1919), 303-306.

——— "Lafitte, the Louisiana Pirate and Patriot," *The Louisiana Historical Quarterly,* II, No. 4 (October, 1919), 418-438.

D'Arbois de Jubainville, H. *Recherches sur L'Origine de la Propriété Foncière et des Noms de Lieux Habités en France, Période Celtique et Période Romane.* Paris, 1890.

Darby, William. *A Geographical Description of the State of Louisiana* . . . Second edition. New York, 1817.

——— *The Emigrant's Guide to the Western and Southwestern States and Territories* . . . New York, 1818.

Darmesteter, A. *Traité de la Formation des Mots Composés dans la Langue Française Comparée aux Autres Langues Romanes et au Latin. Deuxième édition.* Paris, 1894.

Dart, Henry P. "A Great Louisiana Plantation of the French Colonial Period," *The Louisiana Historical Quarterly,* VIII, No. 4 (October, 1925), 589-593.

——— "The Slave Depot of the Company of the Indes at New Orleans," *The Louisiana Historical Quarterly,* IX, No. 2 (April, 1926), 286-287.

Dart, Henry P., and Sanders, Alfred G. (translator). "The First Cargo of African Slaves for Louisiana," *The Louisiana Historical Quarterly,* XIV, No. 2 (April, 1931), 163 ff.

Dauzat, Albert. *La Géographie Linguistique.* Paris, 1922.

——— *Les Noms de Lieux.* Paris, 1926.

——— *Les Noms de Personnes.* Paris, 1928.

——— *Les Patois.* Paris, 1927.

De Cubières, M. *Mémoire sur le Cyprès de la Louisiane.* Versailles, 1809.

Deiler, J. Hanno. *The Settlement of the German Coast of Louisiana* (*Americana Germanica,* N. S. No. 8). Philadelphia, 1909.

Delafosse, M. *Vocabulaires Comparatifs de Plus de 60 Langues ou Dialectes Parlés à la Côte D'Ivoire* . . . Paris, 1904.

De Sainte-Palaye, La Curne. *Dictionnaire Historique de l'Ancien François.* Vols. 1-10. Niort and Paris, 1875-1882.

De Tonti, Le Chevalier, *Nouvelle Relation de la Louisiane* . . . In *Relations de la Louisiane et du Fleuve Missisipi* (French spelling). Amsterdam, 1720.

Diccionario de la Lengua Castellana. Madrid, 1925.

Dickson, Harris. "Creole Gossip," *Good Housekeeping,* February 1931, p. 138. 1931.

Dictionnaire Français-Malinké et Malinké-Français. Par un Missionaire du Congrégation du Saint-Esprit. Conakry, 1906.

Didot Frères, Mm. Firmin. *Neuvelle Biographie Universelle.* Vols. I-XLVI. Paris, 1853-1866.

Diez, F. *Etymologisches Wörterbuch der Romanischen Sprachen.* Fünfte Ausgabe. Mit einem Anhang von A. Scheler. Bonn, 1887.

Dihigo, Juan M. *Léxico Cubano. Contribución al Estudio de las Voces que lo Forman.* Volumen I. Habana, 1928.

Dionne, N. E. *Le Parler Populaire des Canadiens-Français* . . . Québec, 1909.

——— *Les Canadiens-Français. Origine des Familles* . . . Québec and Montréal, 1914.

Ditmars, Raymond L. *The Reptile Book* (*Nature Library,* Vol. XIII). New York, 1908.

Dormon, Caroline. *Forest Trees of Louisiana and How to Know Them.* (*Department of Conservation,* Bulletin 15). New Orleans, n. d.

Dorsey, J. O., and Swanton, J. R. *A Dictionary of the Biloxi and Ofo Languages* (*Bureau of American Ethnology,* Bulletin 47). Washington, 1912.

Dottin, Georges. *Glossaire des Parlers du Bas-Maine.* Paris, 1899.

——— *La Langue Gauloise* (*Collection Pour L'Étude des Antiquités Nationales,* II). Paris, 1920.

Du Bois, W. E. B. *The Suppression of the African Slave-Trade to the United States of America* (*Harvard Historical Studies,* I). New impression. New York, 1904.

Du Cange, Carolo du Fresne Domino. *Glossarium Mediae et Infimae Latinitatis.* Vols. I-X. Niort, 1883-1887.

Duchein, Annette. "Father Mississippi Deserts Gay Towns He Nursed to Fame," The New Orleans *Times-Picayune,* Sunday, July 27, 1930, p. I ff.

Ducoeurjoly, S. J. *Manuel des Habitans de Saint-Domingue.* Vols. I-II. Paris, 1802.

Dunn, Milton. "History of Natchitoches," *The Louisiana Historical Quarterly,* III, No. I (February, 1920), 26-56, and Reprint.

Dutertre, Jean B. *Histoire Générale des Îles S. Christophe, de Guadeloupe, de la Martinique et Autres de L'Amérique.* Paris, 1654.

Egli, J. J. *Nomina Geographica.* Zweite, vermehrte und verbesserte Auflage. Leipzig, 1893.

Ellicott, Andrew. *The Journal of Andrew Ellicott* . . . Philadelphia, 1814.

Enciclopedia Universal Ilustrada, Europeo-Americana. Vols. I-LXX. Bilbao, Madrid, and Barcelona, 1930.

Essaie sur Quelques Usages et sur l'Idiome des Indiens de la Basse Louisiane (anonymous). Opelousas, La., September, 1862. A copy is in the Howard Memorial Library, New Orleans.

Eustis, Célestine. *Cooking in Old Creole Days; La Cuisine Créole à l'Usage des Petits Ménages.* With an introduction by S. Weir Mitchell. New York, 1928.

Éveillé, A. *Glossaire Saintongeais* . . . Bordeaux, 1888.

Favre, Leopold. *Glossaire du Poitou, de la Saintonge et de l'Aunis.* Paris, 1868.

Fleischer, F. "Studien sur Sprachgeographie der Gascogne," *Zeitschrift für Romanische Philologie, Beiheft,* XLIV (1913), 1-125.

Flint, Timothy. *History and Geography of the Mississippi Valley.* Second edition. Cincinnati, 1832.

Forster, J. R. (translator). See Bossu, N., *supra.*

Förstemann, Ernst. *Altdeutsches Namenbuch.* Zweite, völlig Umgearbeitete Auflage. Vol. I. Bonn, 1900; Vol. II, dritte Auflage . . . Herausgegeben von H. Jellinghaus. Bonn, 1911, 1916.

Fortier, *Alcée. Louisiana Studies.* New Orleans, 1894.

——— *A History of Louisiana.* Four volumes. Paris and New York, 1894.

——— "The Acadians of Louisiana and Their Dialect," *Publications of the Modern Language Association of America,* VI, No. 1 (1891), 1-33.

——— *Louisiana; Comprising Sketches of Counties, Towns, Events* . . . Biographical edition. Vols. I-III. Century *Historical Association,* 1914.

Frauca, D. J. C. Y. *Vocabulario Medieval Castellano.* Madrid, 1929.

French, B. F. *Historical Collections of Louisiana* . . . Parts I-V. New York, 1846-1853; *ibid.,* new series, New York, 1869; *ibid.,* second series, New York, 1875.

Fresh-Water Fish of Louisiana, The (*Department of Conservation,* Bulletin 4). New Orleans, November, 1917.

Friederici, Georg. *Hilfs-Wörterbuch für den Amerikanisten.* Halle, 1926.

——— (reviewer). "Lokotsch, Etymologisches Wörterbuch," *Göttingische Gelehrte Anzeigen,* Nr. 7-8 (1927), pp. 291-304.

——— "Vier Lehnwörter aus dem Tupi," *Zeitschrift für Französische Sprache und Literatur,* LIV (1930), 175-187.

Gafferel, Paul L. J. *Histoire de la Floride Française.* Paris, 1875.

Gagini, Carlos. *Diccionario de Costarriqueñismos.* San José de Costa Rica, 1919.

Gamillscheg, Ernst. *Etymologisches Wörterbuch der Französischen Sprache.* Heidelberg, 1926-1929.

Gatschet, Albert S. *A Migration Legend of the Creek Indians.* Vol. I (Brinton's *Library of Aboriginal American Literature,* No. 4), Philadelphia, 1884; Vol. II (*Trans. Acad. Sci. St. Louis,* Vol. V, Nos. 1 and 2), St. Louis, 1888.

Gayarré, Chas. *History of Louisiana.* Vols. I-IV. New Orleans, 1903.

Geddes, J., Jr. *Canadian-French.* Paris, 1902.

Geoffrion, L. P. *Zigzags autour de Nos Parlers.* Three series. Quebec, 1924, 1925, 1927.

Geological Survey of Louisiana, Preliminary Report, pp. 245 ff. State Experiment Station. Baton Rouge, 1899.

Gerard, W. R. "Term Tomahawk," *The American Anthropologist,* X, N. S., (April, 1908), 277-280.

Glossaire du Parler Français au Canada. Québec, 1930.

Godefroy, F. *Dictionnaire de l'Ancienne Langue Française.* Paris, 1880 ff.

Gonzales, Ambrose E. *The Black Border* . . . Columbia, S. C., 1922.

Grandgent, C. H. *An Outline of the Phonology and Morphology of Old Provençal.* Boston, 1905.

——— *An Introduction to Vulgar Latin.* Boston, 1907.

Griffin, Henry L. *The Attakapas Trail.* Lafayette, La., 1923.

Gröber, G. *Grundriss der Romanischen Philologie.* Zweite verbesserte und vermehrte Auflage. Strassburg, 1904-1906.

Gröhler, Hermann. *Über Ursprung und Bedeutung der Französischen Ortsnamen.* Heidelberg, 1913.

Grossman, Rudolf. *Das Ausländische Sprachgut im Spanischen des Rio de la Plata* (*Mitteilungen und Abhandlungen aus dem Gebiet der Rom. Philologie,* Band VIII). Hamburg, 1926.

Guardia, J. E. *Historic Natchitoches.* Natchitoches, n. d.

Hammond, Hilda Phelps. "Behind the Veil of Voodooism in New Orleans," *The Times-Picayune,* Sunday, October 5, 1930, Magazine section, p. 5.

Hatzfeld, Adolphe, et Thomas, Antoine. *Dictionnaire Général de la Langue Française . . .* Tomes I-II. Paris, 1892-1900.

Hearn, Lafcadio. *Gombo Zhèbes.* New York, 1885.

Heinrich, Pierre. *La Louisiane sous La Compagnie des Indes,* 1717-1731. Paris, n. d.

Henry, Victor. *Lexique Étymologigue des Termes les Plus Usuels du Breton Moderne.* Rennes, 1900.

Hill, Roscoe R. *Descriptive Catalogue of the Documents Relating to the History of the United States in the Papeles Procedentes de Cuba.* Carnegie Institution. Washington, 1916.

Hodge, Fred. W. *Handbook of American Indians* (*Bureau of American Ethnology,* Bulletin 30). Part 1, Washington, 1907; Part II, Washington, 1910.

Hoffman, W. J. *The Menomini Indians* (*Bureau of American Ethnology,* Rep. 14, Part I (1893), 1-328. Washington, 1896.

Holder, Alfred. *Altceltischer Sprachschatz.* Vols. I-III, *Leipzig,* 1896-1904; 1907-1908. *Nachträge* zu Bd. I (incomplete), Leipzig, 1908-1913.

Houck, Louis. *The Spanish Régime in Missouri.* Vols. I-II. Chicago, 1909.

Houzé, A. *Étude de la Signification Des Noms de Lieux en France.* Paris, 1864.

Ialeska-Chata. *Mandeville.* New Orleans, 1918.

Identification des Plantes d'Haiti par Leurs Noms Créoles (*Stations Expérimentales,* Port-au-Prince, Haïti, Avril, 1930, Bulletin XVIII, p. 17).

Irish, H. C. "A Revision of the Genus Capsicum with Especial Reference to Garden Varieties," *Missouri Botanical Garden,* pp. 53-110. St. Louis, 1898.

Jaberg, K. "Sprachgeographische Untersuchungen, II," *Archiv für das Studium der Neueren Sprachen und Literaturen,* CXX (1908), 96-98.

James, Edwin (compiler). *S. S. Long's Expedition,* 1819-1820, Part IV (R. G. Thwaites, *Early Western Travels,* XVII, 1-308). Cleveland, Ohio, 1905.

Jeffreys, Thomas. *The Natural and Civil History of the French Dominions in North and South America.* Parts I-II. London, 1761.

Johnston, Sir Harry H. *A Comparative Study of the Bantu and Semi-Bantu Languages.* Vol. I, Oxford, 1919; Vol. II, Oxford, 1922.

——— *The Negro in the New World.* London, 1910.

Jones, Howard M. *America and French Culture.* The University of North Carolina Press. Chapel Hill, 1927.

Jordan, David Starr, and Evermann, Barton Warren. *The Fishes of North and Middle America.* Four parts. Washington, 1898.

Jordan, David Starr. *Manual of the Vertebrate Animals of the Northeastern United States* . . . Thirteenth edition, completely revised and enlarged with illustrations. New York, 1929.

Jud, J. "Sprachgeographische Untersuchungen," *Archiv für das studium der neueren Sprachen und Literaturen,* CXXIV (1910), 83-108.

Kalbow, Werner. *Die Germanischen Personennamen der Altfranzösischen Heldenepos.* Halle, 1913.

Kaspers, W. *Etymologische Untersuchungen über die mit -Acum, -Anum, -Ascum, und -Uscum Gebildeten Nordfranzösichen Ortsnamen.* Halle, 1918.

——— "Die Weiler-Orte der Kölner Gegend," *Zeitschrift für Ortsnamenforschung,* I (1925), 100-121.

Kastner, L. E., and Marks, J. A. *Glossary of Colloquial and Popular French.* New York, London, and Toronto, 1929.

Kernion, George C. H. "Tragedy Marks Coming of Germans to Louisiana," The New Orleans *Item-Tribune,* Sunday, December 16, 1928, page 7.

Kilpatrick, A. R. "The Parish of Concordia," *De Bow's Review,* XI (July, 1851), 40-64.

——— "The Parish of Catahoula," *De Bow's Review,* XII (March, 1852), 256-273; (June, 1852), 631-646.

King, Grace. *Creole Families of New Orleans.* New York, 1921.

——— *New Orleans: The Place and the People.* New York, 1922.

Knox, Alexander. *Glossary of Geographical and Topographical Terms* . . . London, 1904.

Körting, G. *Lateinisch-Romanisches Wörterbuch.* Dritte Auflage. New York, 1923.

Krehbiel, H. E. Afro-American Folksongs. Fourth edition. New York, 1914.

Kremers, Josef. *Beiträge zur Erforschung der Französischen Familiennamen* . . . Dissertation. Bonn, 1910.

Labat, Jean Baptiste. *Nouveau Voyage aux îles de l'Amérique. Seconde édition* . . . Vols. I-VIII. Paris, 1722.

Lacombe, A. *Dictionnaire de la Langue des Cris.* Montreal, 1874.

La Harpe, Bernard. *Journal Historique de l'Establissement des Français à la Louisiane.* New Orleans, 1831.

Lahontan, Armand L. de D. *Voyages de Mr. le Baron Lahontan, dans lAmerique Septentrionale.*[2] Tomes I-III. Amsterdam, 1728.

Lapaire, Hugues. *Le Patois Berrichon.* Moulins, 1903.

Larchey, L. *Dictionnaire des Noms* . . . Paris, 1880.

Larousse Universel en Deux Volumes. Paris, 1922.

Larousse du XXe Siècle en Six Volumes. Vols. I-III. Paris, 1928-1930.

Laurent, L. F. "History of St. John the Baptist Parish," *The Louisiana Historical Quarterly,* VII, No. 2, April, 1924, pp. 316-331.

L'Héritier, L. F. *Le Champ d'Asile: Tableau Topographique et Histoire du Texas* . . . Paris, 1819.

Lenz, Rudolph. "Die Indianischen Elemente im Chilenischen Spanish," *Beiträge zur Romanischen und Englischen Philologie* (*Festgabe für Wendelin Foerster*). Halle, 1902.

———*Diccionario Etimolojico de las Voces Chilenas Derivadas de Lenguas Indijenas Americanas.* Vols. I-II. Santiago de Chile, 1910.

Le Page Du Pratz, Antoine S. *Histoire de la Louisiane.* Tomes I-III. Paris, 1758.

Lescarbot, Marc. *Histoire de la Nouvelle France.* Paris, 1612. Nouvelle édition, publiée par E. Tross. Vols. I-III. Paris, 1866.

Lespy, V., et Raymond, P. *Dictionnaire Béarnais, Ancien et Moderne.* Montpellier, 1887.

Levy, Émil. *Petit Dictionnaire Provençal-Français.* Heidelberg, 1909.

Lewis, Charleton T., and Short, Charles. *A New Latin Dictionary, revised. . . .* New York, Cincinnati, Chicago, 1907.

Lézermes, M. (translator). *Catalogue Alphabétique des Arbres et Arbrisseaux . . .* Paris, 1788.

Literary Digest, The. "Sarsaparilla," in the issue for July 25, 1931, p. 47.

Littman, E. *Morgenländische Wörter im Deutschen.* Zweite vermehrte und verbesserte Auflage nebst einem Anhang über die Amerikanischen Wörter. Tübingen, 1924.

Littré, E. *Dictionnaire de la Langue Française.* Vols. I-IV. Paris, 1875. *Supplement,* Paris, 1877.

Lommatsch, Erhard. *Tobler-Lommatsch Altfranzösisches Wörterbuch.* Lieferungen, I-XIV. Berlin, 1915-1931.

Longnon, Auguste. *Les Noms de Lieu de la France.* Paris, 1920-1929.

Lortie, Stanislas A. "De L'Origine des Canadiens-Français," *L'Origine et le Parler des Canadiens-Français,* pp. 1-12. Paris, 1903.

Louisiana Conservation Review, Vol. I, No. 6. New Orleans, March, 1931.

Luchaire, A. *Étude sur les Idiomes Pyrénéens de la Region Française.* Paris, 1879.

Lutz, Frank E. *Field Book of Insects.* Second edition, revised and enlarged. New York and London, 1921.

Maps of Louisiana.

Marbot, François A. *Les Bambous.* Seconde édition. Fort-de-France, Martinique, 1869.

Marchand, Sidney A. *The Story of Ascension Parish.* Donaldsonville, Louisiana, 1931.

Margry, Pierre. *Découvertes et Établissements des Francais dans l'Ouest et dans le Sud de l' Amérique Septentrionale* (1614-1754). *Mémoires et Documents Originaux,* Tomes I-VI. Paris, 1875-1886.

Martellière, Paul. *Glossaire du Vendômois.* Orleans, 1893.

Mawer, A., and Stenton, F. M. *The Place-Names of Bedfordshire and Huntingdonshire.* Cambridge University Press. 1926.

Meillet, A., et Cohen, Marcel. *Les Langues du Monde*. Paris, 1924.

Mencken, H. L. *The American Language*. Third edition, revised and enlarged. New York, 1923.

Mercier, Alfred. *Étude sur la Langue Créole en Louisiane,* no imprint.

Meyer-Lübke, W. *Einführung in das Studium der Romanischen Sprachwissenschaft*. Zweite neubearbeitete Auflage. Heidelberg, 1909.

——— *Historische Grammatik der Französischen Sprache.* Vol. I, Laut und Flexionslehre. Heidelberg, 1908.

——— *Romanisches Etymologisches Wörterbuch.* Heidelberg, 1911.

——— *Das Katalanische: Seine Stellung zum Spanischen und Provenzalischen.* Heidelberg, 1925.

Michaux. *Biographie Universelle, Ancienne et Moderne.* Vols. I-XLV. Paris et Leipzig, n. d.

Middendorf, E. W. *Wörterbuch des Runa Simi oder der Keshua Sprache.* Leipzig, 1890.

Milner, P. M. "Fort Macomb," *Publications of the Louisiana Historical Society,* VI (1913-1914), 143-152.

Moisy, Henri. *Dictionnaire de Patois Normand.* Caen, 1887.

——— *Noms de Famille Normands.* Paris, 1875.

Monette, J. W. "Public Lands Acquired by Treaty, etc.," *De Bow's Review,* V (1848), 111-127.

Montesson, Compte de Charles-Raoul. *Vocabulaire du Haut-Maine.* 3e édition, augmentée. Le Mans, 1899.

Montigny, L. de. *La Langue Française au Canada.* Ottawa, 1916.

Moody, V. A. "Slavery on Louisiana Sugar Plantations," *The Louisiana Historical Quarterly,* VII, No. 2 (April, 1924), 1-301.

Moore, R. C. (editor). *Geology of the Salt Dome Oil Fields.* Chicago, 1926.

Murray, James A. H. *A New English Dictionary* . . . Vols. I-X. Oxford, 1888-1928.

Newell, W. W. "Reports on Voodoo Worship in Hayti and Louisiana," *The Journal of American Folk-lore,* II, No. 4 (Jan.-March, 1889), 41-47.

——— "Waste Basket of Words," *The Journal of American Folk-lore,* IV, No. 12 (Jan-March, 1891), 70-71.

New Standard Dictionary of the English Language. New York and London, 1913.

Nicolson, P. *Essai sur l'Histoire Naturelle de Saint-Domingue.* Paris, 1776.

Nobiling, O. "Beziehungen zwischen Europäischen und Amerikanischen Sprachen," *Revue de Dialectologie Romane,* (1909), I, 425-428.

Nordenskiöld, Erland. *Comparative Ethnographical Studies,* No. 5. Göteborg, 1922.

Nott, G. William. "Marie Laveau," The New Orleans *Times-Picayune,* November 19, 1922, Magazine section, p. 2.

Nyrop, Kr. *Grammaire Historique de la Langue Française.* Tome I. Deuxième édition, revue et augmentée. Copenhague, Leipzig, New York, Paris, 1904.

Ormsby, John (translator). *Don Quixote.* Vols. I-II. New York, n. d.

Ortiz, Fernando. *Glosario de Afronegrismos.* Con un Prologo por Juan M. Dihigo. Habana, 1924.

Pachnio, Rudolf. *Die Beinamen der Pariser Steuerrolle von 1292.* Dissertation. Königsberg, 1909.

Palsgrave, Jean. *L'Éclaircissement de la Langue Française. Suivi de la Grammaire de Giles du Guez.* Publiés pour la première fois en France. Par F. Génin. Paris, 1852.

Pareja, Francisco. *Arte de la Lengua Timuquana Compuesta en 1614 (Bibliothèque Linguistique Américaine,* Tome XI). Paris, 1886.

Parish Judges of East Baton Rouge. Book M, July 23, 1824—Sept. 12, 1826; Book N, Sept. 15, 1826—Jan. 16, 1830. Baton Rouge, La.

Peñafiel, Antonio. *Nomenclatura Geográfica y Etimológica de México.* Vols. I-II. México, 1897.

Perez, L. M. "French Refugees to New Orleans in 1809," *Publications of the Southern History Association,* IX, No. 5 (Sept., 1905), 293-310.

Péroz, E. *Dictionnaire Français-Mandingue.* Paris, 1891.

Perrin, William H. *Southwest Louisiana.* New Orleans, 1891.

Perrin Du Lac, F. M. *Voyages dans les Deux Louisianes, et chez les Nations Sauvages du Missouri, par les États-Unis, en 1801-1803.* Paris and Lyon, 1805.

Petròcchi, P. *Nòvo Dizionàrio Universale della Lingua Italiana.* Vols. I-II. Milano, 1912.

Picayune Creole Cook Book, The. Sixth edition. New Orleans, 1922.

Pidal, R. Menendez. *Manual de Gramática Histórica Española.* Cuarta edición corregida y aumentada. Madrid, 1913.

Pierrehumbert, W. *Dictionnaire Historique du Parler Neuchâtelois et Suisse Romand.* Vol. I (*A-Alluré*). Neuchâtel, 1921.

Pitkin, Helen. *An Angel by Brevet.* Philadelphia and London, 1904.

Poirier, M. le Senateur Pascal. "Des Vocables Algonquins, Caraïbes, etc., qui sont Entrés dans la Langue," *Mémoires de la Société Royale du Canada,* X, Mars, 1917. Serie III, pp. 339-364.

Porteous, Laura L. "Index to the Spanish Judicial Records of Louisiana," *The Louisiana Historical Quarterly,* VIII, No. 3 (July, 1925), 508; *ibid.,* VIII, No. 4 (October, 1925), 707; *ibid.,* IX, No. 2 (April, 1926), 322; *ibid.,* IX, No. 3 (July, 1926), 537.

Puckett, N. N. *Folk Beliefs of the Southern Negro.* Chapel Hill: The University of North Carolina Press. Oxford, 1926.

Quicherat, J. *De la Formation Française des Anciens Noms de Lieu.* Paris, 1867.

Rafinesque, C. S. *Florula Ludoviciana*; or, *A Flora of the State of Louisiana . . .* New York, 1817.

Rand, The Rev. Silas T. *Dictionary of the Language of the Micmac Indians.* Halifax, N. S., 1888.

Raymond, P. *Dictionnaire Topographique du Département des Basses-Pyrénées.* Paris, 1863.

Read, William A. "Louisiana Place-Names of Indian Origin," *Louisiana State University Bulletin,* XIX, No. 2. Baton Rouge, La., 1927.

——— "Indian Place-Names in Louisiana," *The Louisiana Historical Quarterly,* XI, No. 3 (July, 1928), 445-462.

——— "Istrouma," *The Louisiana Historical Quarterly,* XIV, No. 4 (October, 1931), 503-515.

Recensements 1706-1741. Library of the Louisiana Historical Society. The Cabildo, New Orleans.

Reed, Chester A. *Bird Guide. Water Birds, Game Birds and Birds of Prey.* Revised edition. New York, 1926.

Relations de la Louisiane et du Fleuve Mississipi [French form]. Amsterdam, 1720.

Ridgway, Robert. *A Manual of North American Birds.* Fourth edition. Philadelphia, 1900.

Ritter, E. *Les Noms de Famille.* Paris, 1875.

Rivard, Adjutor. "Le Parler Franco-Canadien," *L'Origine et le Parler des Canadiens-Français,* pp. 13-30. Paris, 1903.

Robbins, W. W. *The Botany of Crop Plants.* Philadelphia, 1917.

Robertson, James A. *Louisiana Under the Rule of Spain, France, and the United States.* Vols. I-II. Cleveland, 1911.

Robin, C. C. *Voyages dans l'Intérieur de la Louisiane, etc.* Tomes I-III. Paris, 1807.

Rolland, Eugène. *Faune Populaire de la France.* Paris, 1877 ff.

——— *Flore Populaire ou Histoire Naturelle des Plantes.* Paris, 1896 ff.

Rouge, Jacques. *Le Parler Tourangeau. Paris,* 1912.

Rouillard, Eugène. *Noms Géographiques de la Province de Québec et des Provinces Maritimes.* Quebec, 1906.

Rowland, Dunbar (editor). *Official Letter Books of W. C. C. Claiborne, 1801-1816.* Vols. I-VI. Jackson, Miss., 1917.

Rowland, Dunbar, and Sanders, A. G. (editors and translators). *Mississippi Provincial Archives, 1729-1740.* Vol. I. Jackson, Mississippi, 1927.

Sagard Theodat, Gabriel. *Le Grand Voyage du Pays des Hurons Situé en l'Amérique . . .* Nouvelle édition. Tomes I-II. Paris, 1865.

Sainéan, L. "La Création Métaphorique en Francais et en Roman," *Zeitschrift für Romanische Philologie, Beiheft* I (1905), VI and 148; *ibid.,* X (1907), VI and 174.

——— *Les Sources de l'Argot Ancien.* Paris, 1912.

——— *Le Langage Parisien au XIXe Siècle.* Paris, 1920.

Salt-water Fish of Louisiana, The (*Department of Conservation,* Bulletin 3). New Orleans, June, 1917.

Saxon, Lyle. *Fabulous New Orleans.* New York and London, 1928.

——— *Lafitte the Pirate.* New York and London, 1930.

Schmidt, W. F. "Die Spanischen Elemente im Französischen Wortschatz," *Zeitschrift für Romanische Philologie*, Beiheft LIV (1914), IX and 210.

Schönfeld, M. *Wörterbuch der Altgermanischen Personen und Völkernamen.* Heidelberg, 1911.

Schuchardt, H. "Zum Iberischen," etc., *Zeitschrift für Romanische Philologie,* XXIII (1899), 174-200.

Schuchardt, H. "Zur Methodik der Wortgeschichte," *Zeitschrift für Romanische Philologie,* XXVII (1903), 609-615.

Schultz-Gora, O. *Altprovenzalisches Elementarbuch.* Zweite verbesserte Auflage. Heidelberg, 1911.

Scramuzza, V. M. "Galveztown," *The Louisiana Historical Quarterly,* XIII, No. 4 (October, 1930), 553-609.

Seidel, A. *Systematisches Wörterbuch der Suahilisprache.* Heidelberg, etc., 1902.

——— *Die Duala-Sprache in Kamerun.* Heidelberg, Paris, etc., 1904.

Seidel, A., et Struyf, I. *La Langue Congolaise.* Heidelberg, etc., 1910.

Skeat, W. W. *Notes on English Etymology.* Oxford, 1901.

——— *An Etymological Dictionary of the English Language.* Oxford, 1910.

Skok, Peter. "Die mit den Suffixen -Acum, -Anum, -Ascum und -Uscum Gebildeten Sudfranzösischen Ortsnamen," *Zeitschrift für Romanische Philologie, Beiheft,* II (1906), pp. viii and 265.

Socin, Adolf. *Mittelhochdeutsches Namenbuch.* Basel, 1903.

Solmsen, Felix. *Indogermanische Eigennamen als Spiegel der Kulturgeschichte.* Herausgegeben und bearbeitet von Ernst Fraenkel. Heidelberg, 1922.

Sommer, Ferdinand. *Handbuck der Lateinischen Laut- und Formenlehre.* Heidelberg, 1902.

Spanish Surveys of Louisiana, Book E; Book J. Hill Memorial Library, Louisiana State University, Baton Rouge (various dates).

Sperber, Alice. "Zur Bildung Romanischer Kindernamen," *Zeitschrift für Romanische Philologie, Beiheft,* XXVII (1911), 144-161.

Stiles, Henry R. *Joutel's Journal of La Salle's Last Voyage.* Albany, N. Y., 1906.

Soniat, Meloncy C. "The Tchoupitoulas Plantation." *The Louisiana Historical Quarterly,* VII, No. 2 (April, 1924), 313.

Stoddard, Amos. *Sketches, Historical and Descriptive, of Louisiana.* Philadelphia, 1812.

Suárez, Constantino. *Diccionario de Voces Cubanas.* Habana; Madrid, 1921.

Sulte, Benjamin. *Pierre Boucher et son Livre.* Ottawa, 1896.

——— *La Langue Française en Canada.* Levis, 1898.

Surveys of Louisiana. State Land Office, Baton Rouge.

Swanton, John R. "Indian Tribes of the Lower Mississippi Valley" (*Bureau of American Ethnology,* Bulletin 43). Washington, 1911.

——— "Early History of the Creek Indians and Their Neighbors" (*Bureau of American Ethnology,* Bulletin 73). Washington, 1922.

Telephone Directory, Southern Bell Telephone and Telegraph Company, Baton Rouge, Houma, Lafayette, New Orleans, etc., 1930.

Thomas, A. "La Dérivation en Français et en Provençal," *Romania,* XXV, 381-392.

———*Mélanges d'Étymologie Française.* Première série. Deuxième édition revue et annotée, Paris, 1927.

Thompson, H. C. *Sweet Potato Production and Handling.* New York and London, 1929.

Thurot, Charles. *De la Prononciation Française . . .* Tome I, Paris, 1881; Tome II, Paris, 1883.

Thwaites, R. G. (editor). *Jesuit Relations and Allied Documents.* Travels and Explorations of the Jesuit Missionaries in New France, 1610-1791. Vols. I-LXXIII. Cleveland, 1896-1901.

Tinker, Edward Larocque. *Toucoutou.* New York, 1928.

Tobler, A. "Zu Murets Ausgabe von Berouls Tristan," *Zeitschrift für Romanische Philologie,* XXX (1906), 743.

Turiault, J. *Étude sur la Langue Créole de la Martinique.* Brest, 1874.

Vandercook, John W. *Black Majesty.* New York, 1928.

Velázquez, M. *A New Pronouncing Dictionary of the Spanish and English Languages.* New York and London, 1900.

Verrier, A. J., et Onillon, R. *Glossaire Étymologique et Historique du Patois et des Parlers de l'Anjou* . . . Vols. I-II. Angers, 1908.

Walker, Norman. "The Geographical Nomenclature of Louisiana," *The Magazine of American History*, X, No. 3 (Sept., 1883), 211-222.

Ward, Herbert. *Five Years With the Congo Cannibals*. Second edition. London, 1890.

Wartburg, Walther von. *Französisches Etymologisches Wörterbuch*. Lieferungen I-XVI. Bonn, Leipzig, etc., 1922—; XVII—, Heidelberg, n. d.

Webster's New International Dictionary of the English Language. Springfield, Mass., 1927.

Weekley, Ernest. *The Romance of Names*. New York, 1914.

——— *An Etymological Dictionary of Modern English*. New York, 1921.

Wiener, Leo. *Africa and the Discovery of America*, Vol. I. Philadelphia, 1920; Vols. II and III. Philadelphia, 1922.

——— "Pseudo-Karaïbisches," *Zeitschrift für Romanische Philologie*, XXXIII (1909), 513-535.

Wilkinson, R. J. *An Abridged Malay-English Dictionary*. Third edition. Singapore, 1926.

Wilson, Harry D. *Louisiana Today*. Department of Agriculture and Immigration. Baton Rouge, 1924.

——— *Louisiana 1927-1928*. Department of Agriculture and Immigration. Baton Rouge, 1928.

——— *Louisiana's Message*. Department of Agriculture and Immigration. Baton Rouge, 1931.

Wissler, Clark. *The American Indian*. Second edition. Oxford, 1922.

Woodson, Carter G. *The Negro in Our History*. Fifth edition. Washington, D. C., 1928.

Zayas, A. *Lexicografía Antillana*. Habana, 1914.

Zéliqzon, Léon. *Dictionnaire des Patois Romans de la Moselle*. Strasbourg, 1922-24.

Zerolo, E. *Diccionario Enciclópedico de la Lengua Castellana*. Vols. I-II; Vol. III, *Suplemento*. Nueva edición. Paris, n. d.

APPENDIX

SUPPLEMENT TO TEXT

Most of the words listed in this supplement appear in the original text. Those that do not are followed by the gender, indicated by *f* or *m*. The index at the end of this volume covers the original text but not the supplement.

Page 3 BAIRE. From Norman-French *bers,* a curved framework over the body of a cart on which to spread a covering, such as a tarpaulin, to protect its contents. *Lettres Curieuses et Edificantes,* t. 4, p. 242 (Lyon, 1819), describes how the travelers along the Mississippi made a covering over their mattresses at night to keep away the mosquitoes. This covering was called a *baire.* See H. A. Major, "Étymologie de Quelques Termes Français-Louisianais" in *Athénée Louisianais,* March, 1960, p. 54; Wartburg, *Wörterbuch,* I, 337.

Page 3 BANQUETTE. See Albert Dauzat, *Dictionnaire Étymologique de la Langue Française* (Paris, 1912), 72b; Gamillscheg, *Wörterbuch,* 176; Wartburg, *Wörterbuch,* I, 237.

Page 8 BELLE-DAME, *f.* Paddlefish, Spoonbill Catfish. See *Spatule, supra.*

Page 9 BÊTASSE. This word is also used as an adjective meaning "foolish" or "stupid." It is a dialectal form of *bestia,* "animal."

Page 9 BÊTE ROUGE. P. Barrère in *Nouvelle Relation de la France Équinoxiale* (Paris, 1743), 67, notes: "Les poux d'Agouty, qu'on appelle à la Martinique et aux autres îles *bête rouge,* à cause de leur couleur, etc." See also Labat, *Nouveau Voyage,* I, 154; Thibault Chanvalon, *Voyage à la Martinique* (Paris, 1763), 112.

Page 12 BOIS CONNU. From Norman *bois cornu* (Norman pronunciation "connu"), because of the excrescences which grow on the trunk and large branches of the tree. They reminded early settlers of little horns. See Major, "Étymologie de Quelques Termes . . .," *loc. cit.,* 52.

Page 15 BOUGON. A small sack of rice. Buras Dial.

Page 17 CAILLE DES EPINIÈRES, *f*. Southern meadow lark.

Page 17 CAJEU, *m*. Raft. See Margry, *Mémoires,* III, 171.

Page 22 CASBURGOT. For etymology, see Dauzat, *Dictionnaire,* 120; Wartburg, *Wörterbuch,* III, 897. Dumont de Montigny notes: "Une espèce de raie et de beaux casseburgots," in "L'Établissement de la Province de la Louisiane," *Journal de la Société des Americanistes de Paris,* Vol. 23, n.s. (1931). Cf. Georges Musset, *Glossaire des Patois et des Parlers de l'Aunis et de la Saintonge* (La Rochelle, 1931), II, 54.

Page 24 CHAC, CHACALA, CHACALATA, *m*. Marsh hawk. Buras Dial.

Page 26 CHOROOK, CHEROOK, *m*. Pectoral and buff-breasted sandpiper. See Arthur, *Birds of Louisiana,* 273.

Page 37 ÉPERVIER. For the source of the second meaning, see *Bulletins of the Bureau of American Ethnology,* Bulletin 47, p. 322.

Page 37 ÉTOURNEAU, *m*. Cowbird. (*Molothrus ater ater* Bodd). Cf. William A. Read, "Some Louisiana-French Words" in *Zeitschrift für Französische Sprache und Literatur,* LXI (1937), 71.

Page 38 FAIS-DODO. Also said to be a corruption of *fête de dieu* or "Festival of God." See *Gumbo Ya-Ya,* 197.

Page 39 FRAPPE D'ABORD. See Ortiz, *Glosario,* 259; Wartburg, *Wörterbuch,* II, 763. LePage Du Pratz notes: "Les frappes-d'abord sont des mouches longues et jaunâtres que l'on nomme ainsi parce qu'elles piquent le même instant qu'elles se posent." *Histoire,* II, 146.

Page 40 GAMBIER. A more probable derivation is offered by Alfred Franklin in his *Dictionnaire Historique des Arts, Métiers et Professions* (Paris, 1906), 572: "La Maison Gambier, dont le nom est devenu populaire, fut fondé dit-on en 1780; elle fournit la plus grande partie des pipes débitées à Paris et aux environs. Je lis dans les rapports rédigés à l'occasion de l'exposition universelle de 1855 qu'à cette date, deux manufactures établies à Saint-Omer livraient au commerce environ 50 millions de pipes chaque année." With the spread of cigarette smoking, the house probably went into the manufacture of cigarette wrappers, hence the name *gambier*.

Page 40 GARDE-SOLEIL. A second definition, widely used, is "sunbonnet." Read, "Some Louisiana-French Words," *loc. cit.*, 72; Bloch-Wartburg, *Dictionnaire Étymologique de la Langue Française.*

Page 41 GOURDE. For another derivation, see "peso gordo" in *National Geographic Magazine*, October, 1934, Vol. 60, No. 4, p. 467; J. H. Craig, *Haitian Vignettes,* 435–36; Bloch-Wartburg, *Dictionnaire,* under "gourde."

Page 44 GROS-BEC, *m.* Night heron.

Page 47 LANGUE DE FEMME, *f.* Sycamore tree. So named because its leaves rustle in the slightest breeze. Buras Dial.

Page 51 MULLADER, *m.* Mulatto. Used even by educated persons in Buras.

Page 61 POISSON ROUGE. B. Romans in *A Concise Natural History of East and West Florida* (New York, 1775), I, 187, says: "The Red Drum, called in East Florida a 'bass,' and in West Florida a 'carp.' The French call it 'Poisson Rouge.' "

Page 63 PRALINE DE BENNÉS. "Bene" is the sesame plant. See L. D. Turner, *Africanisms in the Gullah Dialect* (Chicago, 1949) 62; Romans, *A Concise Natural History*, I, 130-31.

Page 66 RAVET. See Georg Friederici, *Americanistisches Wörterbuch* (Hamburg, 1947) ; Chanvalon, *Voyage,* 115.

Page 67 SACALAIT. This word is from the Choctaw *sakli,* "white fish" or "trout." See also William A. Read, "Some Fish Names of Indian Origin," in the *International Journal of Linguistics,* Vol. XI, No. 4, October, 1945, pp. 237 ff.

Page 71 SOURD, *m.* The horned snake *(Farancia Abacura).* In Buras, Pointe Coupée, and St. Martin: scorpion lizard (genus Eumeces).

Page 73 TASSEAU. This word is actually derived from Spanish *tasajo,* "jerked beef." See Joan Corominas, *Diccionario Crítico Etimológica de la Lengua Castellana* (Bern, 1954), IV, 396.

Page 73 TOMBOLA, *m.* A grab-bag. Buras Dial. This is a Haitian word.

Page 74 TOULOULOU. For an additional reference, see Friederici, *Wörterbuch.*

Page 75 VEILLÉE. Also a "wake." Buras Dial.

Page **87** CHAOUI. For further information on *chat sauvage,* see Claude Mélançon, *Nos Animaux Chez Eux* (Quebec, 1945), 30.

Page 90 GIRAUMON. For the source of the origin given, see Friederici, *Wörterbuch,* 260.

Page 90 GRIVE CHÉROKI. *Chéroki* is from Creek Indian *Chilokkita,* "to speak a different language . . ." BAE Bulletin 73, 1922.

Page 106 SOURQUE, *m.* A submerged log, a sinker. Buras Dial.

Page 110 TOPINAMBOUR. "Jerusalem" in this name is a corruption of *Helianthus girasole.* For further references, see Corominas, *Diccionario Crítico,* IV, 635; Poirier, "Des Vocables Algonquins Caraïbes . . ." *loc. cit.,* 362.

Page 112 TECHE. Derived from Tunica Indian *titihki,* "bayou". See Mary R. Haas, "Tunica," in *Handbook of American Indian Languages,* 23-25.

Page 118 CALA. From African *kala,* "rice", and *kolo,* "uncooked rice." See Turner, *Africanisms,* 196.

Page 122 COUCHE-COUCHE. See also Turner, *Africanisms,* 197.

Page 123 JAMBALAYA. From modern Provençal *jambalaia,* "ragout de riz avec une volaille." See Fréderic Mistral, *Lou Trésor dóu Félibrige, ou Dictionnaire Provençal Français* (Aix en Provence, 1879-87), II, 152; Read, "Some Louisiana-French Words," *loc. cit,* 76.

Page 133 CAÏMAN. Friederici, *Wörterbuch,* thinks *caïman* is probably of African origin, but see also Corominas, *Diccionario Crítico,* I, 576, who suggests a possible South American Indian source.

Page 136 CANOTTE, *f.* Lugger. Buras Dial.

Page 136 CAOUANE. According to Karl von Martius, *caouane* is from the Continental Carib *caouanne,* "a large turtle." *Wörtersammlung Brasilianischen Sprachen* (Leipzig, 1867), II, 369.

Page 137 CARANGUE. See Labat, *Nouveau Voyage,* 405–406.

Page 140 GALIMACHA, *m.* Mixture of all sorts of things, gibberish. From Spanish *galimatias,* "gibberish."

Page 140 GOFIO. This word is derived from the language of the Canary Islands. Ciro Bayo, *Vocabulario Criollo-*

espanol Sud-Americano (Madrid, 1910), 101, says: "Comida de los isleños de Canarias y también de otros países. Véase Esparto y La Lua." Augusto Malaret, *Diccionario de Americanismos* (3rd ed.; Buenos Aires, 1946), 436, comments, "El maíz tostado y molido en polvo y mezclado con azúcar, a estilo del de trigo en islas Canarias." See also Friederici, *Wörterbuch*, 262.

Page 140 GRÈGUE. For a more extensive discussion of the etymology of *grègue*, see Jules Faine, *Philologie Créole* (Port-au-Prince, 1934), p. 249; Major, "Étymologie de Quelques Termes . . ." *loc. cit.*, 55.

Page 142 MAÏS. The origin given is incorrect. Actually, *maïs* is from the Haitian *mahiz*. See Corominas, *Diccionario*, III, 195; Friederici, *Wörterbuch*, 368-69.

Page 143 MAQUECHOU. This word is possibly from Aymara *mokcchi, maíz mascado*. Ludovico Bertonio, *Vocabulario de la Lengua Aymara* (Peru, 1612), II, 224; Malaret, *Diccionario*, 252.

Page 149 YAMME. Possibly from Taino *niames, ames*, or Paria *inhame, inname*. See Martius, *Beiträge*, II, 240; Faine, *Philologie Créole*, 248.

Page 157 NATCHITOCHES. "Pawpaw people" is the correct definition of the Caddo Indian *Nashitosh*. BAE Bulletin 132, p. 26.

Page 158 BATON ROUGE. Capital city of Louisiana. Baton Rouge is the French equivalent of *Istrouma*, "red pole" or "red stick." cf. *Istrouma*, 157, *supra*. Baton Rouge does not appear in the original text.

Page 174 LECOMPTE. A town 16 miles south of Alexandria, originally called White's Settlement. The citizens renamed it Lecomte after the famous race horse which defeated Lexington for the Jockey Club Purse, April 8, 1854. Later, the spelling "Lecompte" was adopted by the post office and the railroads. Lecompte does not appear in the original text.

Page 191 MARRON. For more information, see Jay K. Ditchy, *Les Acadiens Louisianais et Leur Parler* (Paris, 1932), 145–46.

BIBLIOGRAPHY
OF WILLIAM A. READ

BOOKS AND PAMPHLETS

Keats and Spenser, Heidelberg, 1897.

The Southern R (Louisiana State University Bulletin, I, N.S., No. 2), Baton Rouge, La., 1910. (Reprinted from *Louisiana School Review*, XVII, 1910.)

Some Variant Pronunciations in the New South (Louisiana State University Bulletin, III, N.S., No. 5), Baton Rouge, La., 1912. (Reprinted from *Dialect Notes*, III, No. 7, 1911.)

A Vernerian Sound Change in English, a paper read at the meeting of the New Orleans Academy of Sciences on April 15, 1913; Leipzig, 1914. (Reprinted from *Englische Studien*, XLVII, 1913.)

Louisiana Place-Names of Indian Origin (Louisiana State University Bulletin, XIX, N.S., No. 2), Baton Rouge, La., 1927.

Indian Place-Names in Louisiana, n.p., 1928. (Reprinted from the *Louisiana Historical Quarterly*, XI, 1928.)

Louisiana-French (Louisiana State University Studies, No. 5), Baton Rouge, La.: Louisiana State University Press, 1931.

Florida Place-Names of Indian Origin and Seminole Personal Names (Louisiana State University Studies, No. 11), Baton Rouge, La.: Louisiana State University Press, 1934.

Indian Place-Names in Alabama (Louisiana State University Studies, No. 29), Baton Rouge, La.: Louisiana State University Press, 1937.

ARTICLES

"Modern English *ajar*," *Modern Language Notes*, XVI (1901), 127.

"Keats and Spenser," *Modern Language Notes*, XVIII (1903), 204–206.

"A Note on Nasalized Vowels," *Modern Language Notes,* XX (1905), 159–60.

"Notes on the University of Oxford," *The Alumnus,* V (1909), 23–27.

"The Vowel System of the Southern United States," *Englische Studien,* XLI (1910), 70–78.

"The Southern R," *Louisiana School Review,* XVII (1910), 235–45.

"Some Variant Pronunciations in the New South," *Dialect Notes,* III (1911), 497–536.

"A Vernerian Sound Change in English," *Englische Studien,* XLVII (1913), 167–84.

"On Chaucer's *Troilus and Criseyde* I, 228," *Journal of English and Germanic Philology,* XX (1921), 397–98.

"Some Phases of American Pronunciation," *Journal of English and Germanic Philology,* XXII (1923), 217–44.

"Some Remarks on American Pronunciations," *The Journal of the Louisiana Teachers' Association,* II (1925), 41–45.

"Creole and 'Cajan'," *American Speech,* I (1925–26), 483.

"Research in American Place-Names, c. 1920–1926: a Partial Review," *Zeitschrift für Ortsnamenforschung,* IV (1928), 185–91.

"More Indian Place-Names in Louisiana," *Louisiana Historical Quarterly,* XI (1928), 445–62.

"A Correction," *Englische Studien,* LXV (1930), 176.

"Istrouma," *Louisiana Historical Quarterly,* XIV (1931), 503–15.

"Research in American Place-Names since 1928," *Zeitschrift für Ortsnamenforschung,* X (1934), 222–42.

"Studies in Place Names," *The Southwest Review,* XIX (1934), 346–48.

"Henry Plauché Dart: In Memoriam," *Louisiana Historical Quarterly,* XVIII (1935), 250–51.

"Some Louisiana-French Words," *Zeitschrift für französische Sprache und Literatur,* LXI (1937), 62–84.

"Ten Alabama Place-Names," *American Speech,* XIII (1938), 79–80.

"The Hitchiti Name of Silver Springs, Florida," *Modern Language Notes,* LIII (1938), 513–14.

"A Score of Louisiana-French Words," *Zeitschrift für französische Sprache und Literatur,* LXIII (1939), 42–64.

"Notes on *A Dictionary of American English,* Parts I–VI," *American Speech,* XIV (1939), 255–60.

"Notes on an Opelousas Manuscript of 1862," *American Anthropologist,* XLII (1940), 546–48.

"*Caxambas,* a Florida Geographic Name," *Language,* XVI (1940), 210–13.

"*Botango,* an English Ghost-Word," *Modern Language Notes,* LVI (1941), 65–66.

"French Echoes from the Antilles and Tropical America," *Libro Jubilar de Homenaje al Dr. Juan M. Dihigo y Mestre en Sus Cincuenta Años de Professor de la Universidad de la Habana, 1890–1940* (Havana, 1941), pp. 373–93.

"Some Fish Names of Indian Origin," *International Journal of American Linguistics,* XI (1945) 234–38.

"Various Words from the Antilles and South America," *Philologica: The Malone Anniversary Studies,* edited by T. A. Kirby and H. B. Woolf (Baltimore, 1949), pp. 332–41.

"Indian Stream-Names in Georgia," *International Journal of American Linguistics,* XV (1949), 128–32.

"Indian Stream-Names in Georgia II," *International Journal of American Linguistics,* XVI (1950), 203–207.

"Panamá: Its Origin and Meaning," *American Speech,* XXV (1950), 307–309.

"Indian Terms in Vázquez' Compendio," *International Journal of American Linguistics,* XVIII (1952), 77–85.

"Some Words from French Louisiana," *Romance Philology,* VII (1953–54), 180–86.

"Four Indian-Brazilian Lexical Notes," *Romance Philology,* IX (1955–56), 30–31.

REVIEWS

Friedrich Kluge and Frederick Lutz, *English Etymology. Englische Studien,* XXVII (1900), 275–77.

Johannes Hoops (ed.), *Keats' "Hyperion." Modern Language Notes,* XV (1900), 121–23.

F. Holthausen (ed.), *Havelok. Journal of English and Germanic Philology,* III (1901), 510–11.

Gustav Cohen, *Thomson's "Castle of Indolence": eine Nachahmung von Spenser's "Faerie Queene." Englische Studien,* XXIX (1901), 133–34.

Eugene H. Babbitt, *College Words and Phrases. Englische Studien,* XXIX (1901), 275–77.

Mark H. Liddell (ed.), *Chaucer: The Prologue to the Canterbury Tales, the Knightes Tale, the Nonnes Prestes Tale. Modern Language Notes,* XVII (1902), 191–93.

Walter Rippmann, *The Sounds of Spoken English. Englische Studien,* XXXVIII (1907), 286–88.

Oliver F. Emerson (ed.), *A Middle English Reader. Literatur-Blatt für germanische und romanische Philologie,* XXVIII (1907), 152–53.

R. J. Lloyd, *Northern English: Phonetics, Grammar, Texts. Modern Language Notes,* XXV (1910), 230–31.

George P. Krapp, *Modern English: Its Growth and Present Use. Englische Studien,* XLIII (1911), 426–32.

John S. Kenyon, *American Pronunciation. Journal of English and Germanic Philology,* XXIV (1925), 270–73.

S. P. E. Tract No. 30 (H. Kurath, "American Pronunciation"; M. Barnes, "Words from the French—é, ée"; R. Bridges, "Pronunciation of 'Clothes,' &c."). *Englische Studien,* LXIII (1929), 408–14.

George P. Krapp, *A Comprehensive Guide to Good English. Englische Studien,* LXIV (1929), 75–77.

————, *The English Language in America. Englische Studien,* LXIV (1929), 77–80.

Jay K. Ditchy, *Les Acadiens louisianais et leur parler. Zeitschrift für französische Sprache und Literatur,* LVII (1933), 365–75.

Edward L. Tinker, *Louisiana's Earliest Poet: Julien Poydras & the Paeans to Galvez. The Southwest Review,* XIX (1934), 1–2 (books section).

Stanley Vestal, *New Sources of Indian History. The Southwest Review,* XX (1934), 7–8 (books section).

Edward L. Tinker, *Gombo: the Creole Dialect of Louisiana.* New York *Herald-Tribune,* "Books," XIII (1936), 29.

Arthur G. Kennedy, *Current English. Englische Studien,* LXXII (1938), 273–80.

Irène T. Whitfield, *Louisiana French Folk Songs. American Speech,* XV (1940), 87–88.

Mark Van Doren (ed.), *The Travels of William Bartram. American Speech,* XV (1940), 420–22.

Elijah H. Criswell, *Lewis and Clark: Linguistic Pioneers. American Speech,* XVI (1941), 124–27.

John F. McDermott, *A Glossary of Mississippi Valley French, 1673–1850. Language,* XIX (1943), 180–84.

Jacques Raimundo, *A Língua Portuguesa No Brasil. Language,* XX (1944), 260–64.

Georg Friederici, *Amerikanistisches Wörterbuch. Language,* XXIV (1948), 252–56.

Raymond R. MacCurdy, *The Spanish Dialect in St. Bernard Parish, Louisiana. Romance Philology,* V (1951–52), 231–32.

INDEX OF WORDS AND PHRASES